# Comprehensive Curriculum
## for Gifted Learners

*Related Titles of Interest*

**Restructuring Schooling for Individual Students**
William M. Bechtol and Juanita S. Sorenson
ISBN: 0-205-13929-9

**Making School Reform Happen**
Pamela Bullard and Barbara O. Taylor
ISBN: 0-205-14115-3

**101 Ways to Develop Student Self-Esteem and Responsibility, Volume I:**
**The Teacher as Coach**
Jack Canfield and Frank Siccone
ISBN: 0-205-13368-1 Paper   0-205-13370-3 Cloth

**101 Ways to Develop Student Self-Esteem and Responsibility, Volume II:**
**The Power to Succeed in School and Beyond**
Frank Siccone and Jack Canfield
ISBN: 0-205-14068-8 Paper   0-205-14067-X Cloth

**100 Ways to Enhance Self-Concept, Second Edition**
Jack Canfield and Harold C. Wells
ISBN: 0-205-15415-8

**Handbook of Gifted Education**
Nicholas Colangelo and Gary A. Davis (Editors)
ISBN: 0-205-12652-9

**Schools, Mathematics, and the World of Reality**
Robert B. Davis and Carolyn A. Maher
ISBN: 0-205-13445-9

**Physics Begins with an "M"**
John W. Jewett
ISBN: 0-205-15133-7

*Second Edition*

# Comprehensive Curriculum for Gifted Learners

**Joyce VanTassel-Baska**
*The College of William and Mary*

**Chapter Contributors**

**John F. Feldhusen**
**Dana T. Johnson**
**Kenneth Seeley**
**Linda Kreger Silverman**

**Allyn and Bacon**
*Boston • London • Toronto • Sydney • Tokyo • Singapore*

Copyright © 1994, 1988 by Allyn and Bacon
A Division of Simon & Schuster, Inc.
160 Gould Street
Needham Heights, Massachusetts 02194

**Library of Congress Cataloging-in-Publication Data**

Comprehensive curriculum for gifted learners / Joyce VanTassel-Baska
   [editor]. — 2nd ed.
     p.   cm.
   Includes bibliographical references and index.
   ISBN 0-205-15412-3
   1. Gifted children—Education—United States—Curricula.
  2. Curriculum planning—United States.  I. VanTassel-Baska, Joyce.
  LC3993.9.C66  1993
  371.95'3—dc20                    93-10740
                                   CIP

Printed in the United States of America

10 9 8 7 6 5 4 3 2 1  97  96  95  94  93

*To my family,*
*Lee and Ariel,*
*for their understanding and help*

# Contents

## PART III   Integrating Curriculum from Key Learning Realms

### 11   The Study of Humanities     262

### 12   Arts Curriculum for the Gifted     282

by Kenneth Seeley

# *Preface*

How can educators help a gifted student to excel? The answer to this question is a complicated one because much of the research on what impacts the lives of gifted individuals relates more to the role of parents (Feldman, 1985; Bloom, 1985), the role of internal factors and significant others (VanTassel-Baska & Olszewski-Kubilius, 1989), the role of crystallizing experiences (Gardner, 1985), or the role of chance (Tannenbaum, 1983). However, what happens to a child in school should have a significant positive effect on the processes of learning. The quality and character of a school's curriculum is a vital ingredient to the eventual realization of a child's capacity. Gifted and talented students, like all students, have the right to a continuity of educational experience that meets their present and future academic needs. When an organized, thoughtful curriculum plan is in place and when that curriculum is supported by an articulate, informed educational leadership, the probability of capturing the interest and energy of our ablest young thinkers is markedly enhanced. Certainly an organized curriculum is a key ingredient in this complex blending of circumstance so central to the transformation of a gifted learner's initial capacity for intellectual activity into a mature competence for academic and professional accomplishment.

Key beliefs and assumptions have guided the thinking of most recent curriculum theory in gifted education (Passow et al., 1982; Gallagher, 1985; Maker, 1982; VanTassel-Baska et al., 1988). These beliefs may be stated succinctly as follows:

1. All learners should be provided with curriculum opportunities that allow them to attain optimum levels of learning. Curriculum planned for gifted learners should be used with as many learners in our schools who can benefit from it.
2. Gifted learners have different learning needs compared with typical learners. Therefore, curricula must be adapted or designed to accommodate these needs.

3. The needs of gifted learners cut across cognitive, affective, social, and aesthetic areas of curriculum experiences.
4. Gifted learners are best served by a confluent approach that allows for accelerated and advanced learning, and enriched and extended experiences.
5. Curriculum experiences for gifted learners need to be carefully planned, written down, and implemented in order to maximize potential effect.
6. Curriculum development for gifted learners is an ongoing process that uses evaluation as a central tool for future planning and revision of curriculum documents.

The author acknowledges that there are at least three different curricula operative in schools: the "intended" curriculum that is written down, the "delivered" curriculum that is implemented, and the "received" curriculum that is evaluated at least partially through student performance. In order to ensure a reasonable relationship among these perceptual differences, ongoing monitoring and evaluation of both learner outcomes and curriculum content and process must occur. Although this issue is treated procedurally in Chapters 2 and 3, it needs to be considered here as a major premise of the book. Figure 1 presents the dynamic and multiple shifts that any written curriculum makes once it is enabled through the process of instruction to enter the arena of learning.

The author defines *curriculum* as a set of planned experiences for a targeted population. Thus, this book emphasizes the role of the intended curriculum over the other two types. Although classroom activities are highlighted throughout the topical chapters, the intent has been to focus on appropriate learning goals and objectives within key areas of learning.

## *The Integrated View*

An important perspective for developing appropriate curriculum for any learner in a comprehensive manner is to see it as an integrated set of experiences. The author has chosen to present this perspective through the metaphor of a house. Figures 2A, 2B, 2C, and 2D illustrate this framework. The house of comprehensive curriculum has four sides that are each characterized by fundamental realms or doors of learning: cognitive,

**Figure 1    The Operationalizing of the Curriculum**

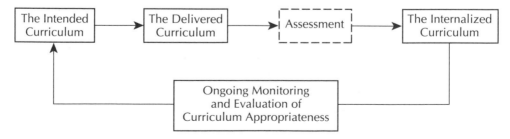

**Figure 2A   The House of Curriculum: Cognitive View**

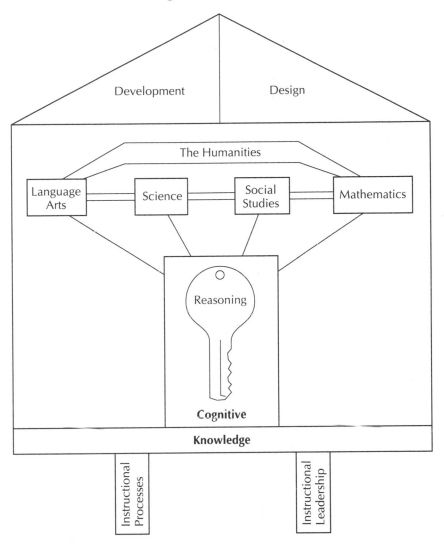

affective, social, and aesthetic.* Each door has a curriculum that unlocks a given realm of learning and allows access to more specific domains of study.

On each side of the house are windows that look in on rooms of individual study. The roof of the house is characterized as development and design—those organizational elements of curriculum work that both help define and protect the structure. The foundation of the curriculum house is knowledge, which is the basis for all sides of learning. The

*Psychomotoric learning with its domains of study are not treated formally within this book, although it is recognized by the author as an important realm of learning.

**Figure 2B    The House of Curriculum: Affective View**

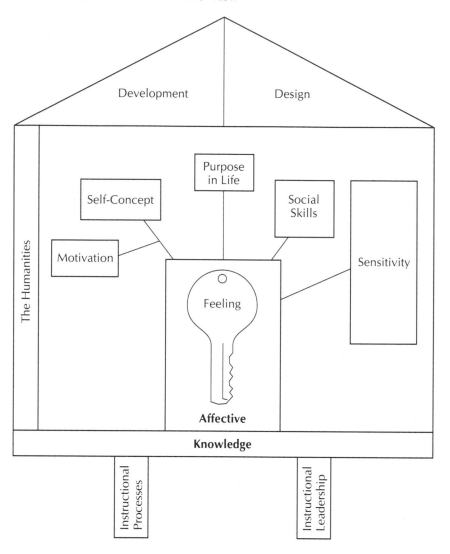

support structures of the curriculum house are twofold: instructional strategies and educational leadership. These structures serve as props to keep the total structure grounded in the operational day-to-day functions of schools. On the cognitive side, the humanities are viewed as the connective tissue among the knowledge domains, representing the major contributions of each knowledge area. Thus, they serve as the hallway between rooms and the corridor that connects all rooms. Language arts, science, social studies, and mathematics are the rooms of study unlocked through reasoning. On the affective side of learning, access to the rooms of self-concept, social skills, motivation, sensitivity, and purpose in life is acquired through the key of feeling. On the social learning side, the turnkey is behavior that unlocks the spaces of group dynamics,

**Figure 2C   The House of Curriculum: Social View**

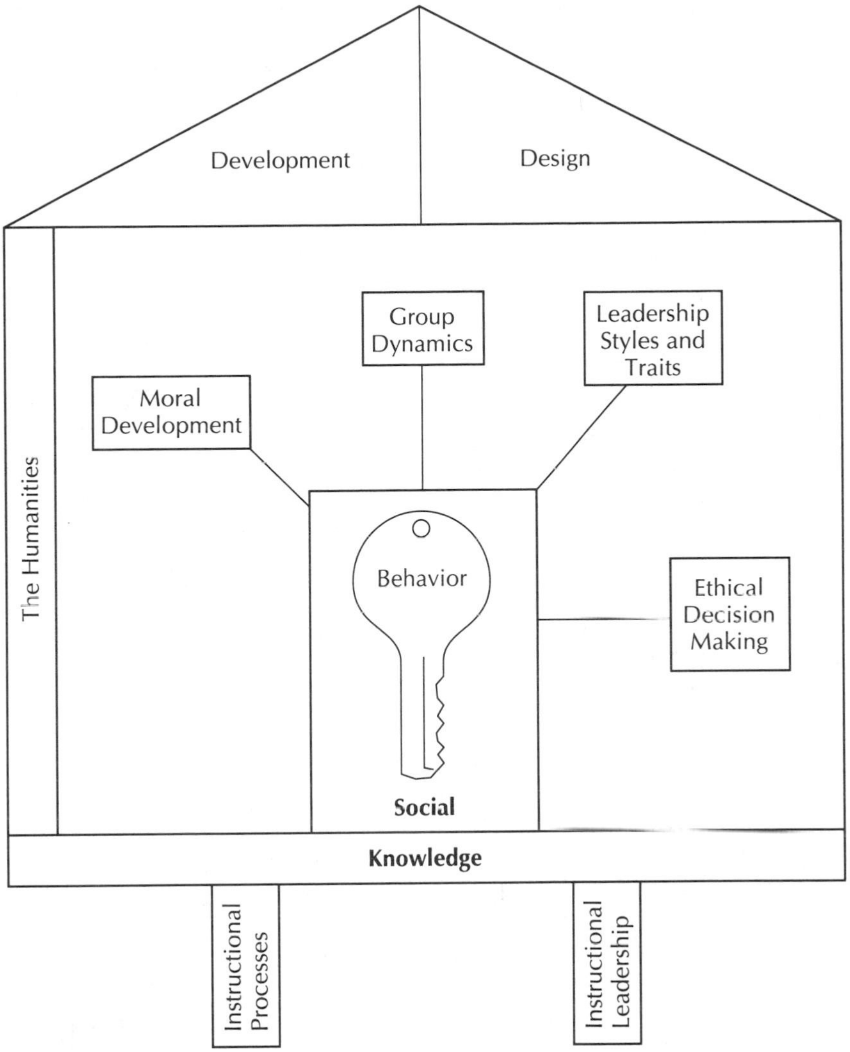

leadership and style traits, moral development, and ethical decision making. The final side of learning is aesthetic learning, accessed primarily through the expressive arts of music, graphic arts, drama, and dance, but with an interconnecting corridor to the fine arts areas.

Although all sides of the house are equally important in addressing the needs of learners, this book focuses more strongly on the cognitive, which represents the front side of most school curricula at the present time. In furnishing and decorating a house, one usually starts with the essential rooms so that daily functions can be performed easily. Thus, the author has chosen to focus on the domains of study viewed by schools as essential curriculum so that the majority of time gifted learners spend in school is not dysfunctional.

**Figure 2D    The House of Curriculum: Aesthetic View**

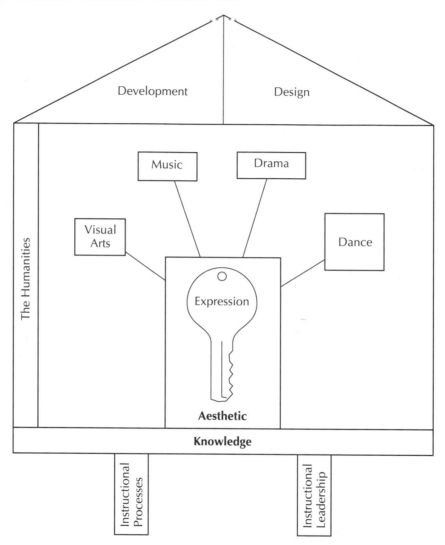

This house of curriculum reveals other relationships of importance. As one moves inside the house from any entrance point, it becomes clear that a perceptual shift has occurred. Now the sides of the house lose their meaning as one begins to explore the floor plan, room by room. Connections can be made across realms of learning as desired or needed, for each room has four walls that now can represent the four sides of learning, using a single domain of study as a focal point. For example, mathematics curriculum can be viewed as an aesthetic, social, and affective experience as well as a cognitive one, and ethical decision making can be treated in the cognitive realm of the social studies as well as a separate area of social learning. As the occupant of the house of curriculum, we hold four keys that serve to provide access to particular sets of rooms, yet they are intrinsically valuable as well. Reasoning, as translated through thinking skills curriculum, can be seen as a strand running through each traditional domain of study, and as a distinctive piece of curriculum in its own right. Leadership curriculum for the gifted can be woven through other curriculum areas or represent a singular focus in the curriculum—so too is the case with affective curriculum and the arts.

This metaphor of a house represents the superstructure of an ideal curriculum for learners that can be adapted to meet their needs at all stages of development. It also accounts for the multifaceted and adaptable aspects of any curriculum area and its shared interdependence with other areas. Furthermore, it envisions a comprehensive approach to curriculum making and doing in several realms. In practical terms, this perspective implies that schools can address the broad needs of students in cognitive, affective, social, and aesthetic realms through a program of study that includes all these realms of study from kindergarten through grade 12. The author strongly believes that this vision of curriculum must become a shared vision so that comprehensive curriculum becomes the norm and not the exception, as it currently is. You are invited to explore the house of comprehensive curriculum as it unfolds.

## References

Bloom, B. (1985). *Developing talent in young people.* New York: McGraw-Hill.

Feldman, D. (1985). *Nature's gambit.* New York: Basic Books.

Gallagher, J. (1985). *Teaching the gifted child.* Boston: Allyn and Bacon.

Gardner, H. (1985). The role of crystallizing experiences. In F. Horowitz and M. O'Brien (Eds.), *Developmental perspectives on the education of the gifted.* Washington, DC: APA.

Maker, J. (1982). *Curriculum development for the gifted.* Rockville, MD: Aspen.

Passow, A. H., et al. (1982). *Differentiated curricula for the gifted/talented.* Committee Report to the National/State Leadership Training Institute on the Gifted and Talented. Ventura County, CA: Office of the Superintendent of Schools.

Tannenbaum, A. (1983). *Gifted children.* New York: Macmillan.

VanTassel-Baska, J., et al. (1988). *Comprehensive curriculum for gifted learners.* Boston: Allyn and Bacon.

VanTassel-Baska, J., & Olszewski-Kubilius, P. (1989). *Patterns of influence: The home, the self, and the school.* New York: Teachers College Press.

## Acknowledgments

I would like to acknowledge the Keystone Consortium members, John Feldhusen, Linda Kreger Silverman, and Ken Seeley, who provided significant contributions to this edition and helpful support throughout the project. Thanks also to Dana Johnson for her chapter on mathematics for the gifted. I also feel a debt of gratitude to my administrative assistant, Cathy Prigge, without whose help this manuscript would lie unfinished. Finally, I would like to acknowledge A. Harry Passow for his continued wise counsel on curriculum issues.

# *Contributors*

**John F. Feldhusen** is a distinguished professor of education at Purdue University and the Director of the Gifted Education Resource Institute there. He has directed comprehensive teacher training programs with school district personnel both nationally and internationally. Listed in *Who's Who in America,* John is former editor of the *Gifted Child Quarterly* and past president of the National Association of Gifted Children. He has published widely in the field of education and in the area of gifted education.

**Dana T. Johnson** has extensive experience in teaching mathematics in grades 4 through 12 and in teacher preparation courses. She has conducted numerous workshops for teachers in mathematics education. Dana has participated in curriculum development and served as a principal member of the curriculum review team for the National Science Curriculum project.

**Kenneth Seeley** is a program director for the Piton Foundation in Denver, Colorado, and an adjunct professor at the University of Denver. His administrative work has been extensive in program development and evaluation for the fields of special education and gifted education. He has instituted successful teacher training programs and gifted programs at the University of Denver since 1976, and has written numerous articles and books in the field of gifted education.

**Linda Kreger Silverman** directs the Gifted Child Development Center in Denver, Colorado. A licensed psychologist, her center has offered assessment and counseling services for gifted children and their families since 1979. For nine years, she served on the faculty of the University of Denver in gifted education and counseling psychology. She has published widely on the education of the gifted and lectured throughout the country.

**Joyce VanTassel-Baska** is the Jody and Layton Smith Professor of Education at the College of William and Mary in Virginia where she has developed a graduate program and a research and development center in gifted education. Formerly, she initiated and directed the Center for Talent Development at Northwestern University. She has also served as the state director of gifted programs for Illinois, as a regional director of a gifted service center in the Chicago area, as coordinator of gifted programs for the Toledo, Ohio, public school system, and as a teacher of gifted high school students in English and Latin. She is past president of the Association for the Gifted of the Council for Exceptional Children. She has also been a member of the Board of Directors of the National Association of Gifted Children. Joyce has published widely, including six books and over 150 monographs, articles, and reports.

# *Comprehensive Curriculum for Gifted Learners*

# Curriculum for the Gifted: An Overview of Theory, Research, and Practice

*JOYCE VanTASSEL-BASKA*

> *In human affairs the logical future, determined by past and present conditions, is less important than the willed future, which is largely brought about by deliberate choices. —RENÉ DUBOS*

Over 20 years ago, national reports ushered in a new era for educational and curricular change, predominantly in science and mathematics. Today, educators again are faced with a barrage of reports that describe deficiencies in the current instruction in mathematics and science and in other content disciplines as well. *A Nation at Risk* (National Commission on Excellence in Education, 1983) reported on the abysmal failure of public education in exposing students to full secondary programs in science and mathematics. The Carnegie Report (1986) further documented the need for more advanced course taking in these subjects by larger numbers of the secondary school population. The College Board's *Project Equality* (*Academic Preparation for College,* 1983) outlined maximum competency skills in academic areas that require mastery in today's technologically advanced world. The most stringent recommendations on curriculum were reported by the National Science Commission (1983), which prescribed four full years of science and mathematics for the majority of students in U.S. schools.

In the early 1990s, the reform movement has moved to a global arena. All countries are focused on the importance of education. All nations see their future economic hopes

linked to an educated citizenry skilled in the world technologies. Moreover, the de
mographic makeup of many developed countries is pluralistic, thus globalizing the issues.
The reform issues as they are played out in the United States represent an important case
in point.

Some of the preeminent educational thinkers in the United States have published
treatises on the nature of ideal schooling. Adler's *Paedaeia Proposal* (1984) advocated a
basic liberal arts education for all, with a focus on traditional content and the objectives of
knowledge acquisition, thinking skill development, and aesthetic appreciation. This view
has been reinforced by Hirsch (1989) from an administrative perspective. Goodlad's *A
Place Called School* (1983) explored fundamental deficiencies in how schools are organized to carry out instructional tasks. Subsequent work further explicated our structural
problems, especially at secondary levels (Sizer, 1984; Boyer, 1983). The instructional
focus of Bloom's (1980) work on mastery learning provided a model for the systematic
and progressive development of skills in various domains of knowledge. Yet, newer work
in curriculum and instructional processes would favor deeper, more conceptual understanding over mere mastery of skills (Resnick, 1984). Moreover, studies of gifted
students support the need for differentiated strategies based on cognitive differences
(Rogers, 1986).

Based on the proliferation of reports on problems and remedies, it is clear that
education has and is experiencing significant pressure for reform and curricular change. In
particular, there is a strong interest in focusing efforts on raising the level of performance
for all learners and a belief that the successful approaches to the achievements of the gifted
can also enhance the educational enterprise for those who are less able.

Although many local school efforts have not been responsive to the perceived needs
of a modern technological society, curriculum for the gifted and talented provides a
starting point to upgrade these efforts, particularly in areas that reports have cited as most
deficient: mathematics, science, technology, and foreign language. Practitioners of
theoretical ideas about curriculum for the gifted must also be sensitive to the organizational structure of the schools, contemporary K–12 curriculum needs, and the recommendations for change being advocated by these major studies.

## The Forces That Drive Curriculum

Based on the calls for reform at steady rates over the last decade, one would expect a
commensurate interest in curriculum development projects—yet very few large-scale
curriculum projects have been funded since the splurge of the 1960s. However, curriculum development in math and science is now in the forefront of educational reform.
Examples include the Amoco Foundation's $50 million grant to the University of Chicago
to change the shape of U.S. mathematics education at the elementary and secondary
levels, new National Science Foundation projects in science and mathematics with a
heavy focus on technological application, and the American Association for the Advancement of Science projects that capitalize on new science concepts. Within gifted education,
two major curriculum development projects have been funded by the United States
Department of Education under the Javits Gifted and Talented Act. These projects presage
a renewed interest in serious curriculum work for gifted learners.

What has caused this resurgence of interest in curriculum? One of the social forces at work is our concern as a nation for meeting future workforce needs. Wirsup (1986) reported on the dismal status of U.S. students in math and science when compared to their Soviet, Japanese, and West German counterparts. Numerous reports over the last few years continue to document similar deficiencies in performance (Darling-Hammond, 1990; Stevenson & Stigler, 1992). At the national level, there has been a pronounced shift in focus from issues such as discipline and community involvement to hard questions about the content and sequence of curriculum. The egalitarian philosophy that dominated the last 20 years of educational policy altered curriculum standards, reduced requirements, and created an elective system that spawned low test scores and gaps in traditional knowledge. A concomitant focus on the education of students with disabilities sparked an examination of our educational priorities. The billions of dollars allocated to tailoring educational programs to the special needs of disabled children as a result of the passage of PL 94-142 raised consciousness about the cost of responding to individual needs of learners at appropriate levels. The current concerns about changing demographics, workforce, competency issues, and negative international education comparisons further exacerbate the need for reform.

Juxtaposed with these social, political, and economic forces within eduational systems is new research that affects thinking about the nature of curriculum change desired. Studies about intelligence (Gardner, 1983; Sternberg, 1985) and how children learn are available to shape the curriculum process.

While limited research has been conducted on curriculum for the gifted per se, current research in teaching and learning appears important to our conceptual framework for understanding appropriate curriculum for the gifted. For example, curriculum planners for the gifted have long advocated the optimal match between learner capacity and level of experiences provided. New evidence for this principle has emerged from studies of human development, where it was found that when both personal skill level and challenge level are correspondingly high, adolescents experience a state of "flow" that allows for optimal learning (Csikszentmihalyi, 1987).

Current learning research is also deeply rooted in the basic disciplines of reading, writing, mathematics, and science. Much ongoing research is attempting to explain how children master complex knowledge structures and procedures (Brown & Campione, 1986). In both reading and mathematics, current research has supported a meaning-based approach that provides appropriate drill and practice in key activities (Anderson, Herbert, Scott, & Wilkinson, 1985; Resnick, 1984).

Studies of thinking also contribute to understanding curriculum directions for the gifted. Expert-novice comparisons in various fields (Berliner, 1985; Sommers, 1980) have yielded differences favoring experts in metacognitive acts like planning and revising. A collection of research on expertise has revealed that the successful utilization of these skills may be content specific. Rabinowitz and Glaser (1985) found that expert performance entailed a large knowledge base of domain-specific patterns, rapid recognition of situations in which these patterns apply, and the use of forward reasoning based on pattern manipulation to reach solutions.

Further support for such domain-specific work comes out of studies that use general content-independent cognitive strategies and find no clear benefits outside the specific domains in which they are taught (Pressley, Snyder, & Carigha-Bull, 1987).

Thus, research on transfer suggests that "thinking at its most effective [level] depends on specific context-bound skills and units of knowledge that have little application to other domains" (Perkins & Saloman, 1989, p. 119).

Curriculum is also being affected by larger social and political contexts. Computer technology has found its way into the curriculum as a "basic" subject rather than as a peripheral. Global interdependence has become a major organizational theme of special programs in all content areas, not just social studies. On the other side of the ledger, moral majority advocates have brought about the dissolution of values education and other educational foci that encouraged free and open inquiry by students.

Goodlad (1979) posited that curriculum decision making is done at two levels, each in isolation from the other. School boards effect curriculum policy, and teachers implement classroom curriculum. Little curriculum leadership is provided at a middle level by building principals or central office staff. Consequently, curriculum implementation as a standardized process does not occur in most public school settings. Even skeptical parents are not likely to challenge teachers in an area heavily loaded with issues of expertise and academic freedom.

But curriculum is still mostly driven by the inertia of the status quo, a system of skill-based areas of inquiry that proceeds on a continuum from first grade to twelfth grade, buttressed by basal texts and little examination of the "why" of a curriculum offering at a particular point in the sequence. For example, algebra was not in the school curriculum 60 years ago; today, the debate rages as to its appropriateness at the ninth-grade level, where it was initiated and has tended to stay. Reading continues to follow a similar illogical path of development based on a curriculum model that ignores individual readiness issues.

Since curriculum is at a point of potential change, the opportunity for educators of the gifted to take a strong role in defining what it should be for the most able, the process by which it is formulated, and the diversity of products or outcomes to be anticipated is at hand. It is through appropriate curriculum design and delivery for the top 5 percent of the population that the whole of curriculum can be upgraded and enhanced. The curricular work for the gifted can spearhead higher standards and more rigorous methodologies in addressing the needs of the rest of the student body.

## A Curriculum Philosophy for the Gifted

Eisner and Vallance (1974) presented five conceptions of curriculum that have shaped the thinking of gifted educators. The roots of each of these conceptions can also be found in extant curriculum for the gifted, and represent strong philosophical orientations for what a view of curriculum for the gifted might be. A sixth orientation related to career preparation is also considered.

1. *Curriculum as the development of cognitive process.* This orientation in the education of the gifted has focused on process skill development and has led to the adoption of curriculum materials organized around higher-level thinkings skills. Having its roots in faculty psychology, it has fostered a content-independent model of curriculum that uses cognitive skills as the centerpiece of all learning activities. Implicit in this view is the assumption that learning cognitive skills will translate across, apply to, and enhance any

field of inquiry a student may encounter. Many pull-out programs for the gifted, which reflect this orientation, have emphasized critical thinking, creative thinking, and problem solving as the substance of their curricula, treating these process skills as content dimensions in their own right. Recent research would support this orientation if there are also ample opportunities for applying cognitive skills directly to content (Perkins & Saloman, 1989).

**2.** *Curriculum as technology.* This view of curriculum is also process oriented but focuses on the organization of curriculum into student inputs and outputs. This approach relies heavily on stated behavioral or performance objectives with measurable outcomes that can be tested in order to determine educational progress or achievement. Learner outcomes developed in individual states and by three national groups attest to the current centrality of this curriculum orientation. It assumes that curriculum standards must be explicit, taught to, and tested for. This view of curriculum sees curricular effectiveness and efficiency realizable if a learning system is adopted by schools rather than piecemeal changes (Spady & Marshall, 1991).

**3.** *Curriculum as personal relevance.* This orientation promotes a child-centered model that values curriculum experiences that are tailored to individual student needs. The interest of students in specific areas guides the curriculum. The goal of such curriculum is to be personally engaging and to offer consummatory experiences that will provide growth at each student's level of understanding. Several curriculum models in gifted education employ this orientation. Renzulli (1977), Feldhusen and Kolloff (1978), Betts (1991), and Treffinger (1986) favor this orientation because of its emphasis on self-directed learning. Gifted students become responsible for their own curriculum through contracts with a facilitator who assesses interest and ability. The interaction of student and facilitator in mutually agreed upon work form the central core of curriculum experiences.

**4.** *Curriculum as social reconstruction.* This view of curriculum holds that the purpose of educational institutions is to be an agent for social change and that the content of curriculum should be viewed within the larger social and cultural realm. Topics to be studied are chosen to promote community action programs needed in a student's immediate environment and to promote individual and collective social responsibility. Engaging students in social action such as drafting a piece of legislation, taking a poll of neighborhood opinions regarding nuclear energy, or organizing a school antipollution campaign typify the curricular experience as part of social reform. Work in the education of the gifted that best exemplifies this orientation is the curriculum for global futures and the theme of global interdependence developed at sites like the Center for Global Futures in Muncie, Indiana. Whole school districts also organize curriculum this way to serve high school gifted students, such as at Glenbrook Academy in Northbrook, Illinois, and Morgan Park High School in Chicago. Multicultural trends in curriculum also have their philosophic roots in this orientation (Hernandez, 1989).

**5.** *Curriculum as academic rationalism.* This curriculum orientation has its roots in the Western tradition of rational humanism. Specifically, it adheres to an ideal of education as a way of providing students with an understanding of great ideas and an ability to analyze and synthesize past achievements. It recognizes a core of work as central to our evolution as a culture (Hirsch, 1989). It further espouses a belief in the structure of knowledge as embodied in the organization of academic and artistic fields of inquiry, and seeks to instruct students within those content disciplines. Most of the "durable" curriculum that is used in gifted programs flows from this general orientation. The special National Science Foundation curriculum projects in mathematics, science, English, and social studies (MACOS) that were developed in the 1960s were all rooted in this orientation. Packaged curricula like *Junior Great Books* and *Philosophy for Children* also adhere to this view.

**6.** *Curriculum as a precursor to career/professional life.* This view of curriculum has its roots in both the professional school and vocational school models that have influenced curriculum offerings over the last 20 years. A strong focus on the practical and the utilitarian has been a preoccupation at secondary and postsecondary levels. In the field of the gifted, this orientation may best be seen through the career education models (see Hoyt & Hebeler, 1974) that have appeared to help students view curriculum as a preparation for their future. The work experience programs for the gifted, loosely termed *mentorships* and *internships,* also have a utilitarian "real-world" focus. In these programs, students relate to the practicing professional in his or her domain and come to understand and appreciate their own potential as future practitioners of a particular craft. New conceptions of curriculum also include a strong emphasis on developing the skills, attitudes, and traits of professionals (VanTassel-Baska, 1992).

Although educators are free to choose among these curriculum philosophies, the most effective curricula incorporate all of them to some extent. Whereas the academic rationalist's view most closely accommodates the current curricular organization of schools, and has guided most long-term curriculum efforts, it currently is being seriously challenged by the social reconstruction orientation. This view holds that curricular decisions reflect social and economic biases. Thus, any attempt to differentiate curriculum for the gifted may be seen, according to this orientation, as an elitism fostered by the educational forces that would oppress the poor and the minority members of our school community (Oakes, Gamoran, & Page, 1991). This viewpoint has led many school personnel to flee from issues of curriculum differentiation for the gifted to a more moderate position of higher curriculum standards for all learners that include the best features of curriculum for the gifted.

The other major challenge to the traditional view has come from those favoring individual student-centered approaches (e.g., Renzulli, 1977; Treffinger, 1986). In all fairness, this viewpoint has dominated gifted child education worldwide, especially at the elementary level. Thus, while a confluence of these orientations may be most desirable, clearly none exists at the present time.

## *Research on Curriculum for the Gifted*

Although the field of gifted education is not prolific with intervention studies, the body of literature on acceleration in curriculum areas places it in the category of an effective approach for many gifted learners. Perhaps more has been written about the efficacy of accelerative practices with the gifted than about any other single educational intervention with any population. Reviews of the literature on acceleration have appeared with some regularity over the last 25 years (Benbow, 1991; Daurio, 1979; Gallagher, 1969; Kulik & Kulik, 1984; Reynolds, Birch, & Tuseth, 1962; VanTassel-Baska, 1986). Each review has carefully noted the overall positive impact of acceleration on gifted individuals at various stages in the life span. Successful programs of acceleration, most notably offshoots of the basic talent search model developed by Stanley and others in the 1970s, have demonstrated significant positive impact on the learning of students (Benbow & Stanley, 1983; Kulik & Kulik, 1992; Swiatek & Benbow, 1991a, 1991b). Moreover, a broad-based research agenda has emerged in the field of gifted education, dedicated to understanding the long-term effects of educational acceleration of the gifted (Brody, Assouline, & Stanley, 1990; Brody & Benbow 1987; Brody & Stanley, 1991; Robinson & Janos, 1986; Swiatek & Benbow, 1991a, 1991b). These recent studies continue to show positive results in cognitive development from acceleration and no negative effects on social emotional development.

Much descriptive literature has been written about enrichment experiences that broaden a student's view of the world of knowledge (Gallagher, 1985; Kaplan, 1979; Renzulli, 1977; Feldhusen & Kolloff, 1978). In a review of research on enrichment, Treffinger, Callahan, and Vaughn (1991) found mixed results for programs that described themselves under the term. Counseling has also been mentioned as important to the emotional and social growth of the gifted learner, as well as an important underpinning to any devised academic program (Gowan, Demos, & Khatena, 1965; Colangelo & Zaffran, 1979; Picchowski, 1984). Although acceleration, enrichment, and counseling represent the major interventions used with the gifted over the last 80 years, it remains to be determined which approaches are most effective under what circumstances with which gifted learners.

Beyond these basic approaches, research into appropriate curriculum for the gifted child is rather meager. Until the *Sputnik* era of the late 1950s, which resulted in programs that addressed specific content areas, few ideas about differentiated curriculum for the gifted were systematically studied. Even though special classes had been in operation since 1919 in selected locations, usually large cities, the actual differences in instructional strategies, content, or materials were not examined. Grouping based on intelligence and achievement was the predominant strategy employed, although individual grade acceleration was practiced to some extent, and curriculum outlines and sometimes units were prepared for use with the identified gifted students (Hollingworth, 1926; Hall, 1956).

Over the past 20 years, however, educators in the field of the gifted have formulated some general principles about appropriate curriculum for gifted children. Ward (1961, 1981) developed a theory of differential education for the gifted that established specific principles about appropriate curriculum. Meeker (1969) used the Guilford Structure of Intellect (SOI) to arrive at student profiles that highlighted areas of strength and weakness so that curriculum planners could build a gifted program to improve weak areas. Curriculum workbooks were structured to address this need in the areas of memory, cognition, convergent thinking, divergent thinking, and evaluation. Renzulli (1977) focused on a model that moved the gifted child from enrichment exposure activities through training in thinking and research skills into a project-oriented program that dwelt on real problems to be solved. Gallagher (1985) stressed content modification in the core subject areas of language arts, social studies, mathematics, and science. Stanley, Keating, and Fox (1974) concentrated on a content acceleration approach to differentiate programs for the gifted. Feldhusen and Kolloff (1978), Kaplan (1979), and Maker (1982) have stressed a confluent approach to differentiation of curriculum for the gifted that includes both acceleration and enrichment strategies. Passow and colleagues (1982) formulated several cardinal curriculum principles that reflect content, process, product, behavioral, and evaluative considerations. VanTassel-Baska (1988, 1992) synthesized existing approaches to gifted education curriculum and translated them into each content area using a traditional curriculum design approach.

More current work in curriculum for the gifted has focused on a merger with the curriculum reform principles advocating world-class standards in all traditional curricular areas (VanTassel-Baska, 1992). The major shift in thinking regarding this orientation is from one that looks only at the optimal match between characteristics of the learner and the curriculum to a model based on professional competence in various domains, thereby letting the curriculum standard determine who may become proficient in an area rather than a predetermined test. Thus, differentiation for any population is grounded in differential standards of performance at a given period of time. Standards are constant; time is the variable. Such a model holds promise for gifted students in that the level and pace of curriculum can be adapted to their needs, and the stated standards imply the kind of focus that curriculum makers for gifted students have long advocated—higher-level thinking, interdisciplinary approaches, and an emphasis on student-centered learning.

The other current approach to curriculum for the gifted has been instituted as a result of newer conceptions of giftedness, notably Gardner's multiple intelligences (1983). This approach assumes that the majority of children have some talent area or intelligence that can be developed through focused curriculum attention. Similar in practice to the Talented Unlimited model developed in the 1970s by Calvin Taylor, the talent development model also eschews identification of children as gifted but rather favors the use of diagnostic information to determine strengths that can be used to develop an appropriate curriculum. Highly individualized, this approach has been implemented successfully in several school-based settings (Bolanos, 1991).

Some combination of both of these approaches is probably most productive. Gifted students need high but realizable expectations for learning at each stage of development. Other students can benefit also from working to attain such standards. By the same token, gifted students can also benefit from a more developmental perspective on fostering their abilities at a close-up level. Lingering questions over both approaches will remain until there is research evidence that supports gifted student growth in a context that has done away with formal identification.

## Theoretical Curriculum Models for the Gifted

Although research on curriculum for the gifted provides limited evidence regarding effectiveness, three relatively distinct theoretical curriculum models have proven successful with gifted populations at various stages of development and in various domain-specific areas. They are (1) the content mastery model, (2) the process/product research model, and (3) the epistemological concept model.

### The Content Model

The content model emphasizes the importance of learning skills and concepts within a predetermined domain of inquiry. Gifted students are encouraged to move as rapidly as possible through the content area; thus, content acceleration dominates the application of this model in practice. When a diagnostic-prescriptive instructional approach (D→P) is utilized, students are pretested and then given appropriate materials to master the subject area segments prescribed.

The D→P instructional approach has proved effective in controlled settings but has not been widely practiced in regular classrooms for the gifted. Several reasons appear to account for this. Like any individualized model, it requires a highly competent classroom manager to implement it. When used appropriately, each student may be working on a different problem, chapter, or book at the same time. Regardless of the rhetoric surrounding individualization, very little is actively practiced in basic curriculum areas. A second reason is that most pull-out programs do not focus on core content areas and therefore negate the possible employment of the model. Third, the approach has not been particularly valued by many educators of the gifted because of its insistence on utilizing the same curriculum and merely altering the rate. The lecture-discussion approach to the content model is more widely practiced at the secondary level, but its effectiveness is highly dependent on teachers being well versed in the structure as well as in the content of their discipline. Too frequently the content model disintegrates into learning the exact same skills and concepts as all learners are expected to do in the school context, only tediously doing more exercises and drills in a shorter period of time.

In the D→P approach, teachers and teaching assistants act as facilitators of instruction rather than as didactic lecturers, although many content-based programs for the gifted place a strong emphasis on lecture and discussion. The curriculum is organized by the intellectual content of the discipline and is highly sequential and cumulative in nature, making a proficiency-based model for measuring achievement very feasible.

The D→P approach to the content model has been utilized effectively by talent search programs across the world, particularly in mathematics (Keating, 1976; Benbow & Stanley, 1983). VanTassel-Baska (1982) has shown the effectiveness of the model in teaching Latin, and foreign language teachers have used the model for years to ensure English syntactic mastery in their students. Clearly, it represents the most individualized instructional approach to basic curriculum for the gifted, and it embodies a continuous progress philosophy that schools readily understand.

The more typical approach to content-based instruction, however, is one that presets an early mastery level for students, often requiring more advanced skills and concepts to be mastered one year earlier than normal. This advanced content model uses existing school curriculum and textbooks, so it is not costly to implement. Although it responds to the rate of needs of groups of students, allowing the able to advance a little more quickly through the traditional curriculum, it may still leave the highly gifted unchallenged.

In fairness to the content-based model, teachers who use it successfully have made important alterations in the organization of the subject matter being taught. For example, in the fast-paced Latin program, the concepts that are spread out incrementally over the first three chapters of the book are synthesized into a matrix study sheet, presenting students with all five Latin cases, three genders, and two numbers in their various combinations all at once. Homework is assigned only from the third unit, where all the interactions of gender, number, and case may be practiced. Thus, 30 hours of instructional time may be reduced to 4 or 5 at the most, so that gifted students can master the important concepts governing Latin syntax in an economical fashion.

What appears as a simple process of moving more quickly through the same basic material becomes more sophisticated in actual practice. The effective teacher reorganizes the content area under study according to high-level skills and concepts. The focus of student prescriptive work is in larger increments that carry with them a holistic picture of the topic under study.

The content mastery model for curriculum and instruction also has the capacity to cover the regular skill-based curriculum in reading and mathematics in approximately one-third the time currently expended. This condensation process occurs as a result of two curriculum modifications. Students move through skill areas at a rate commensurate with their capacity. By testing for proficiency, by assigning work based on documented increased levels of development, and by reorganizing basic skill areas into high-level skill clusters, mastery learning time is conserved, and more efficient and challenging learning experiences are promoted.

## *The Process/Product Model*

The process/product model places heavy emphasis on learning investigatory skills, both scientific and social, that allow students to develop a high-quality product. It is a highly collaborative model that involves teacher-practitioner-student as an interactive team in exploring specific topics. Consultation and independent work dominate the instructional pattern, culminating in student understanding of the scientific process as it is reflected in selective exploration of key topics.

Reported in the literature under the rubric of the enrichment triad and the Purdue model (Renzulli, 1977; Feldhusen & Kolloff, 1978), this approach to curriculum for the gifted has also enjoyed success. At the secondary level, special science programs for the gifted have used the model (VanTassel-Baska & Kulieke, 1987; VanTassel-Baska, Gallagher, Sher, & Bailey, 1992), and institutions like Walnut Hills High School in Cincinnati, Bronx High School of Science in New York, and the North Carolina School of Math and Science have practiced the model as a part of their high-powered science programs for years.

One manifestation of the model engages the student in problem finding and problem solving and puts the student in contact with adult practitioners. In the field of science, for example, scientists from National Science Laboratories work with academically talented junior high students during the summer to help them develop research proposals for project work during the following academic year. Students are actively involved in generating a research topic, conducting a literature search, selecting an experimental design, and describing their plan of work in a proposal. The proposal is then critiqued not only by the instructor but also the scientist. In this way, then, students focus on process skill development in scientific inquiry and strive to develop a high-quality product. Another manifestation of the model emphasizes problem-based learning—an approach that allows the student to generate learning tasks based on a paradigm of the known, the need to know, and the process by which needed knowledge can be acquired (Barrows, 1985).

The process/product model for gifted curriculum differs from the content-based model in that content is incidental. Student interest is the mainspring for what "content" will be studied. The nature of the evaluation effort is product based rather than proficiency oriented, and the focus is on studying selected topics in depth rather than moving through a given domain of inquiry in a fast-paced manner.

This curriculum and instructional model most closely parallels the recommendations of national curriculum groups in both science and mathematics who tend to favor a student-directed, hands-on, inquiry-based process of problem solving, where students are engaged in the act of constructing knowledge for themselves.

## *The Epistemological Model*

The epistemological concept model focuses on talented students' understanding and appreciating systems of knowledge rather than the individual elements of those systems. It reflects a concern for exposing students to key ideas, themes, and principles within and across domains of knowledge so that schemata are internalized and amplified by further examples. The role of the teacher in this model is as questioner, raising interpretive issues for discussion and debate. Students focus their energies on reading, reflecting, and writing. Aesthetic appreciation of powerful ideas in various representational forms is viewed as an important outcome.

This model has been used with gifted learners for several reasons. First, the intellectually gifted child has unusually keen powers to see and understand interrelationships. The whole structure of conceptual curriculum is based on constantly interrelating form and content. Conceptual curriculum is an enrichment tool in the highest sense, for it provides the gifted with an intellectual framework not available in studying only one content area, but exposes them to many ideas not provided for in traditional curricula. Furthermore, it provides a basis for students' understanding the creative as well as the intellectual process through critically analyzing creative products and being actively engaged in the creative process itself. It also provides a context for integrating cognitive and affective objectives into the curriculum. A discussion of ideas evokes feelings; a response to the arts involves aesthetic appreciation; and the study of literary archetypes creates a structure for self-identity.

Many writers in the field of gifted education have lauded the epistemological approach to curriculum (Ward, 1961, 1981; Hayes-Jacob, 1981; Maker, 1982; Tannenbaum, 1983). Some extant curriculum has been organized around the model at both elementary and secondary levels. The College Board Advanced Placement Program relies heavily on this curriculum approach in its history (both American and European) and literature and composition programs. The *Junior Great Books* program and *Philosophy for Children,* and *Man: A Course of Study* (MACOS) are elementary programs that promote the approach. Each of these programs stresses the use of Socratic questions to stimulate an intellectual discussion among students on an issue or theme. Creating analogies across a field of inquiry is encouraged, and interdisciplinary thinking is highly valued. Recent curriculum development efforts for the gifted have also attempted to utilize the epistemological framework (VanTassel-Baska & Feldhusen, 1981; Gallagher et al., 1984), and larger curriculum projects in the past—such as CEMREL's mathematics program at the secondary level and the Unified Mathematics program at the middle school level—have utilized a holistic approach to the organization of content.

The concept-based model for curriculum and instruction differs considerably from the nature of the previous two models described. (See Table 1–1 for an overview of key characteristics of each model.)

The concept-based model is organized by ideas and themes, not subject matter or process skills. It is highly interactive in its instructional context, which contrasts with the more independent modes of instruction used in the other two models. Concern for the nature and structure of knowledge itself is a major underlying tenet. The evaluation of students engaged in this model typically requires evidence of high-level aesthetic perceptions and insight rather than content proficiency. Culminating products tend to be well-crafted essays that show evidence of synthesizing forms and meaning across areas of study. Artistic products also demonstrate this synthesis of form and meaning (Eisner, 1990).

Effective curriculum and instruction for the gifted has reached a stage of evolution where existing theoretical and research-based models need to be systematically translated into practice at the local level. Competition among these models has dissipated the effect of building a strong differentiated program for the gifted that addresses all of their intellectual needs within the core curriculum as well as at all levels outside it. The synthesis of the content, process/product, and concept models has provided a clear direction for new curriculum work.

## *Conclusion*

Curriculum development for the gifted begins with a clear understanding of theoretical and research bases from which current practice derives its substance. It is important to understand the forces that contribute to the growth or demise of a particular curriculum trend and to be able to consider curriculum for the gifted in the larger context of curriculum for all students.

The field of gifted and talented education currently espouses two viewpoints regarding curriculum. One view places value in capturing curriculum on paper with appropriately delineated objectives, activities, and evaluation procedures; planning a child's curriculum in advance of the school year; and teaching toward predetermined program goals and outcomes. The second view places value in developing curriculum based on the perceived and stated interests of the child; planning situational contexts that contribute to student

**TABLE 1–1    Contrasting Curriculum/Instructional Models for the Gifted**

| A. Content | B. Process/Product | C. Concept |
|---|---|---|
| • Fast paced | • In-depth on selected topics | • Epistemological |
| • Proficiency based | • Product based | • Aesthetics based |
| • D→P approach | • Resource oriented | • Discussion approach |
| • Organized by intellectual content | • Organized around scientific or other process model | • Organized by themes and ideas |
| • Teacher as facilitator | • Collaborative | • Socratic method |

choice in objectives and activities for the school year; and teaching toward the emergent needs of the child in the context of the classroom.

Although each view has been incorporated into functional programs for the gifted, each carries with it a different perception of the role of curriculum in the overall education of the child. This book places credence in planned and well-described written learning experiences for the gifted, yet it does not seek to devalue the role of the learner or the teacher as each may uniquely interpret and activate those activities through the instructional process. The view of curriculum presented here is a synthesis of seemingly opposing views, an integration of perspectives that will best benefit schools and the gifted students they serve.

We need to take a broader and more circumspect look at what makes a curriculum effective for gifted learners and other learners as well. We must examine the relationship between what the curriculum currently provides and what the specific needs of the target population are, and to devlop new curriculum documents where discrepancies exist. We must examine the relationship of curriculum to instructional strategies to see that it is implemented effectively in classroom settings. We must attend to issues of world-class standards for curriculum for the gifted and the means by which those standards can be set and documented. We need to be clear about what should be included in a curriculum for the gifted, why it is appropriate, and how it might be implemented for more high-ability learners. We also need to be cognizant of our overall curriculum design and to give attention to areas such as scope and sequence and monitoring and evaluation. And lastly, we should carefully consider the type of school leadership necessary to undertake major curricular work. Clearly, the task of curriculum development is complex and arduous, but it is the most important area of work to be done in the field of gifted education.

## References

*Academic preparation for college.* (1983). *Project equality.* New York: The College Board.

Adler, M. (1984). *The Paedaeia proposal.* New York: Macmillan.

Anderson, R., Herbert, E., Scott, J., & Wilkinson, I. (1985). *Becoming a nation of readers.* The report of the commission on reading. Washington, DC: National Institute of Education.

Barrows, H. S. (1985). *The tutorial process.* Springfield, IL: Southern Illinois University of Medicine.

Benbow, C. P. (1991). Meeting the needs of gifted students through use of acceleration. In M. Wang, M. Reynolds, & H. Walberg (Eds.), *Handbook of special education: Research and practice* (pp. 23–36). New York: Pergamon Press.

Benbow, C., & Stanley, J. (1983). *Academic precoc-*

*ity: Aspects of its development.* Baltimore: Johns Hopkins University Press.

Berliner, D. (1985). Presidential address to the American Educational Research Association. San Francisco, CA.

Betts, G. (1991). The autonomous learner model for the gifted and talented. In N. Colangelo & G. A. Davis (Eds.), *Handbook of gifted education* (pp. 142–153). Boston: Allyn and Bacon.

Bloom, B. (1980). *All our children learning.* New York: McGraw-Hill.

Bloom, B. (1985). *Developing talent in young people.* New York: Ballantine.

Bolanos, P. (1991). *Curriculum for the key school.* Washington, DC: Presentation at National Javits Project Directors meeting.

Boyer, E. L. (1983). *High school: A report on education in America.* New York: Harper and Row.

Brody, L. E., Assouline, S., & Stanley, J. (1990). Five years of early entrants: Predicting successful achievement in college. *Gifted Child Quarterly, 34,* 138–142.

Brody, L. E., & Benbow, C. P. (1987). Accelerative strategies: How effective are they for the gifted? *Gifted Child Quarterly, 3* (3), 105–110.

Brody, L. E., & Stanley, J. C. (1991). Young college students: Assessing factors that contribute to success. In W. T. Southern & E. D. Jones (Eds.), *Academic acceleration of gifted children* (pp. 102–132). New York: Teachers College Press.

Brown, A., & Campione, J. (1986). Psychological theory and the study of learning disabilities. *American Psychologist, 14* (10), 1059–1068.

Carnegie Forum on Education and the Economy, Task Force on Teaching as a Profession. (1986). *A nation prepared: Teachers for the 21st century.* New York: Author.

Colangelo, W., & Zaffran, R. (1979). *New voices in counseling the gifted.* Dubuque, IA: Kendall-Hunt.

Csikszentmihalyi, M. (1987). *Intrinsic motivation.* Paper presented at the Northwestern University Phi Delta Kappa Research Symposium.

Darling-Hammond, L. (1990). Achieving our goals: Superficial or structural reforms. *Phi Delta Kappan, 72,* 286–295.

Daurio, S. (1979). Educational enrichment versus acceleration: A review of the literature. In W. C. George, S. Cohn, & J. Stanley (Eds.), *Educating the gifted: Acceleration and enrichment* (pp. 13–63). Baltimore: Johns Hopkins University Press.

Eisner, E. (1990). *The enlightened eye: Qualitative inquiry and the enhancement of educational practice.* New York: Macmillan.

Eisner, E. W., & Vallance, E. (Eds.). (1974). *Conflicting conceptions of curriculum.* Berkeley, CA: McCutchen.

Feldhusen, J., & Kolloff, M. (1978). A three stage model for gifted education. *Gifted Child Today, 1,* 53–58.

Gallagher, J. (1969). Gifted children. In R. L. Ebel (Ed.), *Encyclopedia of education research* (4th ed.) (pp. 537–544). New York: Macmillan.

Gallagher, J. (1985). *Teaching the gifted child.* Boston: Allyn and Bacon.

Gallagher, J., et al. (1984). *Leadership unit.* New York: Trillium Press.

Gardner, H. (1983). *Frames of mind.* New York: Basic Books.

Goodlad, J. I. (1979). *Curriculum inquiry: The study of curriculum practice.* New York: McGraw-Hill.

Goodlad, J. I. (1983). *A place called school.* New York: McGraw-Hill.

Gowan, J., Demos, J., & Khatena, J. (1965). *The guidance of exceptional children.* New York: David McKay.

Hall, T. (1956). *Gifted Children: The Cleveland story.* Cleveland: World Publishing.

Hayes-Jacob, H. (1981). *A model for curriculum and instruction: Discipline fields, interdisciplinary, and cognitive process.* Unpublished doctoral dissertation, Columbia University.

Hernandez, S. (1989). *Multicultural education.* Columbus, OH: Merrill.

Hirsch, E. D. (1989). *Cultural literacy.* Boston: Houghton Mifflin.

Hollingworth, L. (1926). *Gifted children.* New York: World Book.

Hoyt, K., & Hebeler, J. (1974). *Career education for gifted and talented students.* Salt Lake City, UT: Olympus.

Kaplan, S. (1979). Language arts and social studies curriculum in the elementary school. In H. Passow (Ed.), *NSSE yearbook: The gifted and the talented.* Chicago: University of Chicago Press.

Keating, D. (1976). *Intellectual talent.* Baltimore: Johns Hopkins University Press.

Kulik, J. A., & Kulik, C. C. (1984). Synthesis of research on effects of accelerated instruction. *Educational Leadership, 42* (2), 84–89.

Kulik, J. A., & Kulik, C. C. (1992). Meta-analytic findings on grouping programs. *Gifted Child Quarterly,* 72–76.

Maker, C. J. (1982). *Curriculum development for the gifted.* Rockville, MD: Aspen.

Meeker, M. (1969). *The structure of intellect: Its interpretations and uses.* Columbus, OH: Merrill.

National Commission on Excellence in Education. (1983). *A nation at risk.* Washington, DC: U.S. Department of Education.

National Science Board Commission on Precollege Education in Mathematics, Science, and Technology. (1983). *Educating Americans for the 21st century.* Washington, DC: National Science Foundation.

Oakes, J., Gamoran, A., & Page, R. N. (1991). Curriculum differentiation: Opportunities, outcomes, and meanings. In P. Jackson (Ed.), *Handbook of research and curriculum* (pp. 570–608). New York: Macmillan.

Passow, A. H., et al. (1982). *Differentiated curricula for the gifted/talented*. Committee Report to the National/State Leadership Training Institute on the Gifted and Talented. Ventura County, CA: Office of the Superintendent of Schools.

Perkins, D., & Saloman, G. (1989). Are cognitive skills context bound? *Educational Research, 18* (1), 16–25.

Piechowski, M. (1984). Two developmental concepts: Multilevelness and developmental potential. *Counseling and Values, 18,* 86–93.

Pressley, M., Snyder, B., & Carigha-Bull, T. (1987). How can good strategy use be taught to children? Evaluation of six alternative approaches. In S. M. Corner & J. D. Hagman (Eds.), *Transfer of learning* (pp. 81–120). New York: Academic Press.

Rabinowitz, M., & Glaser, R. (1985). Cognitive structure and processes on highly competent performance. In E. D. Horowitz & M. O'Brien (Eds.), *The gifted and talented: Developmental perspectives* (pp. 75–98). Washington, DC: American Psychological Association.

Renzulli, J. (1977). *The enrichment triad.* Wethersfield, CT: Creative Learning Press.

Resnick, R. (1984). Beyond error analysis: The role of understanding elementary school arithmetic. In H. N. Check (Ed.), *Diagnostic and prescriptive mathematics: Issues, ideas, and insight.* Kent, OH: Research Council for Diagnostic and Prescriptive Mathematics.

Reynolds, M., Birch, J., & Tuseth, A. (1962). Review of research on early admission. In M. Reynolds (Ed.), *Early school admission for mentally advanced children* (pp. 7–18). Reston, VA: Council for Exceptional Children.

Robinson, N., & Janos, P. (1986). Psychological adjustment in a college-level program of marked academic acceleration. *Journal of Youth and Adolescence, 15* (1), 51–60.

Rogers, K. (1986). Do the gifted think and learn differently? A review of recent research and its implications for instruction. *Journal for the Education of the Gifted, 10,* 17–39.

Sizer, J. (1984). *Horace's compromise: The dilemma of the American high school.* Boston: Houghton Mifflin.

Sommers, N. (1980). Revision strategies of student writers and experienced writers. *College Composition and Communications, 31,* 378–387.

Spady, W. J., & Marshall, K. J. (1991). Beyond traditional outcome-based education. *Educational Leadership, 49* (2), 67–72.

Stanley, J. Keating, D., & Fox, L. (1974). *Mathematical talent.* Baltimore: Johns Hopkins University Press.

Sternberg, R. (1985). *Beyond IQ.* New York: Basic Books.

Stevenson, H. W., & Stigler, J. W. (1992). *The learning gap: Why our schools are failing and what we can learn from Japanese and Chinese education.* New York: Summit Books.

Swiatek, M. A., & Benbow, C. P. (1991a). Effects of fast-paced mathematics courses on the development of mathematically precocious students. *Journal for Research in Mathematics Education, 22,* 139–150.

Swiatek, M. A., & Benbow, C. P. (1991b). Ten-year longitudinal follow-up of ability-matches accelerated and unaccelerated gifted students. *Journal of Educational Psychology, 83,* 528–538.

Tannenbaum, A. (1983). *Gifted children.* New York: Macmillan.

Treffinger, D. (1986). Fostering effective, independent learning through individualized programming. In J. S. Renzulli (Ed.), *Systems and models for developing programs for the gifted and talented* (pp. 429–468). Mansfield Center, CT: Creative Learning Press.

Treffinger, D. F., Callahan, C. M., & Vaughn, V. L. (1991). Research on enrichment efforts in gifted education. In M. C. Wang, N. C. Reynolds, & H. J. Walberg (Eds), *Handbook of special education, research and practice,* Vol. 4 (pp. 37–55). New York: Pergamon.

VanTassel-Baska, J. (1982). Results of a Latin-based experimental study of the verbally precocious. *Roeper Review, 4* (4), 35–37.

VanTassel-Baska, J. (1986). Acceleration. In J. Maker (Ed.), *Critical issues in gifted education* (pp. 179–186). Rockville, MD: Aspen.

VanTassel-Baska, J. (1988). Curriculum for the gifted: Theory, research, and practice. In J. VanTassel-Baska et al. (Eds.), *Comprehensive curriculum for gifted learners* (pp. 1–19). Boston: Allyn and Bacon.

VanTassel-Baska, J. (1992). *Planning effective curric-*

*ulum for gifted learners*. Denver, CO: Love Publishing.

VanTassel-Baska, J., & Feldhusen, J. (Eds.). (1981). *Concept curriculum for the gifted*. Matteson, IL: Matteson School District #162.

VanTassel-Baska, J., Gallagher, S., Sher, B., & Bailey, J. (1992). *Developing science curriculum for high ability learners K–8*. Final project report. Washington, DC: U.S. Department of Education.

VanTassel-Baska, J., & Kulieke, M. (1987). The role of community in developing scientific talent. *Gifted Child Quarterly, 31* (3), 111–115.

Ward, V. (1961). *An axiomatic approach to educating the gifted*. Columbus, OH: Merrill.

Ward, V. (1981). *Educating the gifted: An axiomatic approach*. Ventura County, CA: Leadership Training Institute on Gifted and Talented.

Wirsup, I. (1986). The current crises in mathematics and science education: A climate for change. In J. VanTassel-Baska (Ed.), *Proceedings from the 9th annual research symposium*. Evanston, IL: Phi Delta Kappa.

# Chapter 2

## Learning and Cognition of Talented Youth

*JOHN F. FELDHUSEN*

*Talents differ; all is well and wisely put;*
*If I cannot carry forests on my back,*
*Neither can you crack a nut.*
*—RALPH WALDO EMERSON*

Gifted and talented youth are characterized by their superior memory functions and large, well-organized knowledge bases. Their precocity is reflected in their ability to learn—to acquire new and complex information more rapidly than less able students. They process new information at a deeper and more complex level, and use their knowledge bases as tools in acquiring new knowledge. They develop schemata or networks of meaningful concepts in a more complex and comprehensive fashion than youth of average ability.

Learning is remembering declarative or procedural knowledge. Declarative knowledge is information in the general sense, such as facts, concepts, theories, and so on. It is well described in level one of the Bloom Taxonomy (1956), as shown in Figure 2–1. Procedural knowledge is represented by cognitive processing, or knowing how to carry out a sequence of ideationally controlled steps. Knowing how to solve a class of problems, how to analyze complex concepts, or how to synthesize a set of ideas are all illustrations of procedural knowledge. Gifted and talented learners are able to amass and effectively retrieve larger amounts of both types of knowledge because of their superior long-term memory and because they are able to organize knowledge into schemata and networks during the learning process. New information acquires meaningfulness and retrievability insofar as it is well placed in long-term memory. New information first enters short-term memory (STM), is transmitted to working or processing memory (WM),

**Figure 2–1    Knowledge**

| | |
|---|---|
| 1.11 | Knowledge of specifics |
| | Knowledge of terminology |
| | Knowledge of specific facts |
| 1.20 | Knowledge of ways and means of dealing with specifics |
| | Knowledge of conventions |
| | Knowledge of trends and sequences |
| | Knowledge of classifications and categories |
| | Knowledge of criteria |
| | Knowledge of methodology |
| 1.30 | Knowledge of the universals and abstractions in a field |
| | Knowledge of principles and generalizations |
| | Knowledge of theories and structures |

and the latter evokes retrieval of related information from the schemata in long-term memory (LTM). The material from LTM may be modified in relation to or by incorporating the newly arrived information and the residual goes back to LTM for possible future use. Gifted and talented youth have superior capacity to take information into STM, retrieve relevant material from LTM, process in WM, derive meaningfulness, and assign the new information to LTM.

Sternberg (1988) referred to this entire process as knowledge acquisition in his triarchic theory of intelligent functioning. There is first the cognitive process of selective encoding. This is sorting out relevant from irrelevant incoming information. It is learning to attend to important details. While Sternberg sets forth the process as applicable to all intelligent processing, we relate it to gifted youth who are more sensitive to details in the world around them than less able youth.

The second component in Sternberg's theory is selective combination. For gifted youth this is the special capacity to synthesize larger amounts of new information in working memory. There may be a variety of combinations that different individuals can create and some combinations of information that turn out to be more useful or more proceduarlly effective than others.

The third component of knowledge acquisition, according to Sternberg, is selective comparison. This is a process of relating newly encoded information to other information or schemata in long-term memory in the working memory register. It involves retrieval of material from LTM that can be related to the new information. All three processes are clearly aspects of human intelligence and function at higher levels in gifted and talented youth.

## *Intelligence and Human Abilities*

Carroll (1989) has been delineating the factors of human ability by reanalyzing all of the data sets available from previously reported factor analyses over several decades. He has presented a tentative taxonomy that includes the following factors:

1. Idea Production
2. Crystallized Intelligence
3. Fluid Intelligence
4. Visual Perception
5. Auditory Perception
6. Memory
7. Speed

Overriding this taxonomy is General Intelligence. Carroll (1989) reported this taxonomy as having been designed by Snow but as embracing representations he had already published.

The first factor, Idea Production, includes associational, expressional, figural, ideational, speech, and word fluency and originality—generally all the processes subsumed under the heading of creative abilities. The second factor, Crystallized Intelligence, includes all the school-related learning abilities such as verbal comprehension, vocabulary, phonetic coding, and grammar. The third factor, Fluid Intelligence, embraces the so-called thinking skills of inductive reasoning, deduction, logic, quantitative reasoning, and accuracy in information processing. The Visual Perception factor includes spatial relations, ability to visualize, and speed and flexibility of closure. Auditory Perception involves the sense of pitch, speech perception, and sense of rhythm. Memory, as an ability factor, includes episodic recall of information related to time and place, associational memory, memory span, and visual memory. Finally, Speed, as a factor of human intelligence, embraces perceptual functions, naming, and reaction speed.

These conceptions of the factors or components of human ability define the realms of differential ability within which learning takes place and instruction is carried out. Children differ not only in their general capacity to learn but also in specific factors such as those delineated in the Carroll-Snow model.

Two other major conceptions of human intelligence that are currently receiving widespread attention are those of Sternberg (1988) and Gardner (1983). The knowledge acquisition components of Sternberg's (1988) theory of intelligence were described earlier in this chapter. Two other major parts of the system of intelligence are metacomponents and performance components (Sternberg, 1988). Metacomponents are control processes used in monitoring, planning, and evaluating one's execution of cognitive tasks. Sternberg (1988) listed the following eight operations as the most important metacognitive functions:

1. *Recognizing that a problem exists*
2. *Determining the nature of the problem*
3. *Selecting lower-order nonexecutive components to perform a task*
4. *Selecting a strategy for task performance*
5. *Representing the information mentally*
6. *Allocating attentional resources*
7. *Monitoring task performance*
8. *Comprehending and using feedback about the success of task performance. (p. 269)*

Performance components include such activities as encoding a stimulus, inferring relationships between stimuli, and applying a known relationship in a new situation.

It is apparent that humans differ in their capacity to carry out all these cognitive functions described by Sternberg (1988), and that gifted and talented learners excel especially in the knowledge acquisition and metacomponential aspects of intelligent activity. Gifted and talented learners, nevertheless, need opportunities to develop their cognitive capacities to acquire knowledge and control thinking processes through exposure to much more complex and abstract conceptual material and problem situations. Intelligent behavior does not arise naturally; it grows through exercise and guidance. Nature may establish potential for high levels of intellectual functioning; parents, teachers, peers, and the community provide the conditions through which the intelligence of gifted and talented youth is brought to fruition.

Gardner's (1983) *Frames of Mind,* or seven intelligences, also provide an additional framework for our understanding of intellectual functioning and learning. Gardner reported that he reviewed evidence from studies of gifted individuals and prodigies as well as studies of idiot savants, experts in different professions, and normal people. He also reviewed carefully the work of Piaget (1959) and the final stages of cognitive development proposed by Piaget—formal operational thinking—the highest form of logical-rational thought achieved by mathematicians and scientists. Gardner (1983) noted, however, that Piaget offers insights only about the intellectual aspects of development. Other areas of mental development were also reviewed and incorporated in the seven intelligences:

1. Linguistic
2. Musical
3. Logical-mathematical
4. Spatial
5. Bodily-kinesthetic
6. Intrapersonal
7. Interpersonal

Linguistic intelligence is the ability to develop skill or expertise in the uses of language in audition, speaking, and writing. Musical intelligence or talent is capacity to develop competence or artistry as composer or performer. Logical-mathematical intelligence is the potential to reason—to see and solve problems. Spatial intelligence is the ability to visualize and to treat or process visual information. The ability is common in both the arts and sciences. Bodily-kinesthetic intelligence is a mental capacity reflecting mind-body interaction and control. It is the skill of the chimpanzee digging for termites with a probe and the physician carrying out a complex surgical procedure. Intrapersonal intelligence is the capacity to access one's feelings about life, as in the novelist, poet, or actor. Interpersonal intelligence is the capacity to understand and use data from observations of motivation, intentions, and moods in others. Our efforts to assess or identify capabilities in youth and to devise nurturing educational experiences call for recognition of these differing forms of human intelligence.

The Key School in Indianapolis, built on the Gardner (1983) conception of intelligence, is a good illustration of the applicability of the model to school curriculum and program development. In the Key School, strong efforts are made to assess a range of talents analogous to the seven intelligences. The program and curriculum seek to nurture development in students' areas of strength (Olson, 1988). Gardner and Hatch (1989) reported that three projects based on the multiple intelligences model were in progress and that one already showed that the intelligences are independent and different from abilities measured by standard intelligence tests.

The Key School program also incorporates other aspects of learning and cognition discussed so far. For example, in individual and small group project activities, children can exercise all of the metacognitive functions described by Sternberg and the ability factors of Carroll's Taxonomy. Growth in these abilities occurs when children have opportunities to engage in cognitive and learning activities at an appropriately challenging level.

The lesson to be derived for special curriculum designed to serve gifted and talented youth is that talent, giftedness, intelligence, or ability *is not* a unitary trait, measurable as one dichotomous variable—gifted or not gifted. School curricula and programs *should* recognize and seek to assess a variety of talents or special aptitudes and provide opportunities for nurturance of the diverse talents identified in different children. Our educational programs should be especially prepared to provide high-level educational activities to meet the needs and nurture the talents of youngsters who are precocious in one or more areas of ability. Precocity or advanced development is the *sine qua non* of talent and talent development.

## Research on Aptitude-Treatment Interactions and Talent Development

Ackerman, Sternberg, and Glaser (1989) edited a series of papers on *Learning and Individual Differences, Advances in Theory and Research.* These papers recognize and report research that acknowledges differences among learners and call for differential instructional practices to meet the differing needs. Snow (1989) reviewed the research on aptitude-treatment interactions (ATI) from the viewpoint that *aptitude* refers generally to individual differences and *treatment* refers to the variety of instructional conditions and activities we use in school to effect learning. Snow begins by observing that children differ profoundly in what they bring to learning situations and in their success in learning situations. He goes on to review both laboratory-based and classroom research on ATI as well as the experimental paradigms used in ATI research. He begins the deductive phase of the review with the assertion that "less able learners need help in developing effective strategies [for learning], and direct instruction can be designed to provide this help" (p. 38). Direct instruction is analogous to teacher presentation, didactic instruction, drill and practice, and so on.

In contrast, Snow (1989) concluded that structure and complete specification of the strategies to be used interferes with the learning of more able students. In problem-solving tasks, for example, he found that precise teaching of algorithm is good for anxious and less able students and bad for more able and less anxious students. He also noted that learners' entry intentions have a strong impact on learning. If a student actively seeks meaning in a learning situation, he or she will process deeply. If a student merely strives to reproduce information on a test, he or she will adapt a surface level of processing.

Snow concluded that "more able learners do better with less structure, and less able learners do better with more" (Snow & Lohman, 1984). *Structure* here refers to the level of prior cognitive organization by the teacher and the degree of explanation and description of concepts during the instructional process. In a sense, the teacher can predigest and present new material with didactic finality, or the teacher can do less predigesting and leave much of the structure and organization of new content to be organized by students. Gifted and talented youth thrive with the latter approach. Snow goes on to suggest that

> *more able learners benefit from most of the instructional tasks presented by indirect, unstructured methods because task difficulty and complexity in these situations is either just below their threshold or only enough above threshold to be challenging or motivating. But the task in these situations is far above the threshold for less able learners; without explicitly structured teaching, they are left helpless, anxious, or unmotivated. Direct and complete instruction provides the extensive scaffolding needed to raise the thresholds of less able learners. But it makes the task far enough below threshold for the able learner that it becomes boring, and imposing its particular algorithmic structure may even interfere with the able learner's own preferred processing style. (p. 49)*

These results from ATI research clearly indicate that children differ in characteristics that they bring to learning situations, particularly in ability and prior knowledge or skill related to the new learning. It also reveals that they differ with respect to the type and level of instruction that will be most productive for them. Talented youth need less structure, less didactic instruction, less drill and practice, and more opportunities to use their own heuristics—to guide themselves, to seek or use their own strategies and structures in learning. Above all, they need to be taught new material at a level and pace commensurate with their advanced achievement levels.

The all-school program at Holt, Michigan, illustrates basic concepts from ATI research in its efforts to meet the individual learning needs of children. Based on Treffinger's (1986) Individualized Program Planning Model (IPPM), the Holt program offers a wide variety of curricular and extracurricular learning opportunities and individualized assessments to bring about the best possible match between children's talents, aptitudes, learning styles, and interests on the one hand and learning opportunities on the other. There is special attention to the needs of gifted children for advanced, accelerated, and complex learning experiences, as well as the needs of less able and less precocious children for more basic and structured learning experiences. Kyllonen and Shute (1989) proposed the following taxonomy of learning-teaching strategies:

1. Rote learning or memorization
2. Learning by deduction
3. Learning by drill and practice
4. Inductive learning
   a. Observation
   b. Inquiry
   c. Examples
   d. Discovery
   e. Analogies

We would conclude that the fourth category is the appropriate strategy for talented or highly able youth. The program at Holt, Michigan, incorporates all of the activities of category 4.

Gallagher (1966) analyzed the conceptually oriented and complex curricula that emerged from the "new curriculum" development projects of the 1960s and 1970s such as SAPA, (Science A Process Approach), Chem Study, and MACOS (Man: A Course of Study). He noted that the new curricula emphasized the basic concepts, themes, issues, problems, and ideas of the respective fields developed. These curricula clearly called for more complex structuring from students and more of the inductive strategies, especially inquiry and discovery. Research on those curricula relating entry-ability level of students to achievement revealed the following:

> *The introduction of conceptually complex material in the various sciences and mathematics curricula and in some social studies curricula, has made almost academic the question of whether students should be grouped by ability. The introduction of conceptually complex material makes ability grouping almost mandatory, since so much of the current learning in those classes depends upon mastery of previous concepts. Virtually the only way a wide range of ability can be tolerated in the classroom is to teach conceptually simple materials. (p. 7)*

It seems clear that differential grouping and methods of instruction are needed to produce effective learning for talented and less able learners when the material is cognitively complex. Talented youth profit most from instruction in which they have opportunities to strive for or construct their own meanings and organization, and they can do this best in cooperation and interaction with other talented youth when they are grouped together in the classroom.

## Evidence from Studies of Experts

A body of research has examined the problem-solving skills of experts and novices in different professional fields (Schunk, 1991). A major finding is that experts have larger knowledge bases in their fields of expertise, and their knowledge bases are conceptually better organized to facilitate retrieval from long-term memory. Faced with a new problem, experts are able to identify key features of the problem and retrieve information related to the problem, whereas novices have to retrieve large amounts of information, much of which turns out to be irrelevant. Schunk (1991) also suggested that novices tend to respond to problems exactly as presented, whereas experts reinterpret problems and seek underlying structure. In summary, Schunk concluded that experts:

1. Have more declarative knowledge
2. Have better hierarchical organization of their knowledge bases
3. Recognize problem structure more easily
4. Monitor their own performance more carefully
5. Use strategies that are more effective

The lessons to be learned for the instruction of gifted and talented youth are easily derived from Schunk's (1991) summary. Curriculum for talented youth should stress the importance of developing large and well-organized knowledge bases gained from reading, lectures, and discussion, as well as direct observational experience in research and analysis. The teacher should encourage analyzing, conceptualizing, and synthesizing activities to facilitate the development of well-organized knowledge bases.

Additional lessons are derived from the emphasis on problem-solving experiences. One aspect of such experiences is deriving skill in analyzing and classifying problem situations, especially as in case study analysis, laboratory experiments, and inquiry-discovery encounters with complex and abstract phenomena. Further, there is a need to teach and stress the skills of self-monitoring in problem solving and the selection of strategies for solution appropriate to the problem. The teacher must be able to design problems or inquiry situations that evoke opportunities for the learning and use of monitoring and problem-solving strategies, and model the role of "expert" for talented students. Clearly, such high-level instructional activity also calls for a peer group in which the level of cognitive interaction is very high. The level and pace of instruction then fits the level of precocity of the students.

## Acceleration

Acceleration of instruction means that students are given a curriculum that is higher level than the normal curriculum, more complex information is presented, the material is denser or more information is covered, the material is presented more rapidly than in typical classroom instruction, and students are confronted by a greater challenge than is customary with regular on-grade level material. Elkind (1988) argued that the term *acceleration* may be an inappropriate choice of words with reference to gifted and talented students since the students are not pushed ahead of their developmental level; the school is simply bringing instruction up to an appropriate level for them.

In a series of studies on children's readiness for new learning in mathematics and problem solving (Feldhusen, Check, & Klausmeier, 1961; Feldhusen & Klausmeier, 1959; Klausmeier, Check, & Feldhusen, 1960; Klausmeier & Feldhusen, 1959) a wide range of achievement or readiness levels was revealed. The results showed that children learned, retained, and transferred new learnings effectively under circumstances of accelerative instruction.

Benbow (1990) reviewed the basic, underlying psychological supports for acceleration of instruction. She concluded that acceleration gives able youth the advanced knowledge base needed for creative work in a field or discipline. She also concluded that able students need to acquire knowledge of a field early to become cognizant of the problems or gaps in knowledge as a prelude to creative problem solving in the field. Moreover, Benbow argued that an established curriculum or instructional pattern is in place in schools and that teachers are most proficient in delivering the established curriculum, so able children can most easily have their needs met in an accelerative version of the existing system.

Kulik and Kulik (1991) reviewed all the available research on acceleration. They concluded that "talented youngsters who were accelerated into higher grades performed as well as the talented older pupils already in those grades" and that "talented accelerates showed almost a year's advancement over talented same-age nonaccelerates" (pp. 190–191). These results show clearly that from an instructional point of view there are some students, the highly able ones, who are ready for more advanced levels of instruction, and that given such instruction, they progress rapidly to higher levels of learning. From his study of mathematically precocious youth (SMPY), Stanley (1973) concluded that academic acceleration is the most fundamental need of talented youth. The long-range success and achievements of SMPY (Brody & Benbow, 1987) attest to the soundness of acceleration as a major instructional strategy for talented youth.

## *Motivation*

"Individuals' perceptions of their competence or ability play a central role in achievement behavior. . . . The development of the concept of ability is central to the development of achievement motivation" (Nicholls & Miller, 1984, p. 186). Nicholls and Miller go on to report that by age 12, children's self-ratings of ability correlate highly with teacher assessment of their ability. They also suggest that social comparison is necessary to the development of children's conceptions of their ability. To be smart, they say, means "to be smarter than others" (p. 201). Thus, there are both positive and negative consequences in the differentiation process. Children of high ability often come to see themselves as competent and thereby have greater achievement motivation, whereas less able children often perceive themselves as low in ability and low in competence, and suffer loss of achievement motivation (p. 210).

Good teachers can often minimize the ability comparisons that children experience in the classroom, but good grouping practices can also reduce negative effects for less able children and provide appropriately high normative comparisons for highly able or talented students. In their review of the effects of ability grouping, Snyderman and Rothman (1988) found no evidence of damage to self-esteem, even in low-ability groups.

Sosniak (1985) described the development of the sense of ability and competence among youth who had achieved world-class recognition before the age of 35 in music, sculpture, swimming, tennis, mathematics, and neurology. They all had early experiences in the talent domain and in general learning activities that showed them to be special, more able, and more competent, and they continued to have experiences that confirmed their superior ability. Experiences in the talent area became a part of their lives and evoked a continuing sense of competence, thus increasing motivation to achieve in the talent domain.

Dweck and Leggett (1988) have presented evidence that children differ in conceptions of their own ability. Some see their ability as a fixed entity and strive in learning situations to show that they have it. Other children have an incremental conception of their ability; that is, it is malleable and can grow. Students who view their abilities as incremental are much more likely to be mastery oriented, to seek challenges, and to use good strategies in solving problems. Entity-oriented students are more helpless in learning situations and seek to preserve their status.

From the research, we may conclude that motivation to achieve at a high level derives first from a sense of superior, malleable, and growing ability, as compared with age peers, and then from experiences in a talent domain, learning and performance experiences, which generate feedback and a sense of superior performance. Success then feeds upon success, and competence or achievement motivation is evoked and sustains efforts to learn and grow strong in the talent domain.

Talented youth need increasing opportunities to work with peers who are highly able and superior achievers to increase their achievement motivation, and they need learning-performance experiences in specific areas that provide the feedback communication from which a growing sense of competence is derived and motivation to strive onward and upward is evoked.

## The Teacher

Talented students need a series of teachers with differing characteristics. In the early stages of talent development, Bloom (1985) reported that teachers were often inspirational and firm, and made learning enjoyable. In the middle years, the teachers encouraged greater independence and self-direction and were more demanding. They expected students to be well prepared and often to perform or exhibit publicly. In the final stage of talent development, the student comes into contact with the expert or the true artist who is highly demanding and who agrees to work only with youth who have demonstrated superior talent. There are long hours of practice or study in isolation. There is a sense of striving for higher levels of achievement.

Silverman (1982) has also described the established teacher of gifted youth as one who relates to students at a personal level, who expects them to think for themselves and to inquire. Seeley and Hultgren (1982) described the competencies of teachers of the gifted as including (1) knowledge of the nature and needs of the gifted, and approaches to extending and enriching their curricula; (2) skill in promoting higher cognitive thinking abilities, questioning techniques, research and study skills, and individualization; and (3) ability to develop appropriate methods and materials for the gifted, such as creative problem solving.

Linking desirable characteristics of teachers of the gifted to learning needs of students (Feldhusen, 1985), teachers of talented students should:

1. Be knowledgeable and proficient in their discipline at a level appropriate to students' level of talent development.
2. Know and be able to teach problem-solving and metacognitive strategies appropriate to the discipline.
3. Be able to model some aspects of expert or artist behavior.
4. Know the fundamental conditions of human learning, cognition, achievement motivation, and intelligent performance as they relate to talent development.

## Conclusion

Gifted and talented youth are active, continuous learners who—by virtue of their superior ability, prior achievement, superior memory, and intense motivation to learn—acquire much more of the outcomes of learning than children of average or low ability. Their base of knowledge is usually much larger than that of other children; they may have a larger network of conceptual structures providing organization to the knowledge base; and they have superior capacity to retrieve, reorganize, or relate information in the knowledge base to solve problems or to make sense of newly encountered phenomena. The latter processes, solving problems and making sense of new phenomena, always result in new learning.

Memory functions operate at much higher levels among gifted youth than other children. Short-term memory, working memory, and long-term memory are storehouses of intelligent functioning. While powerful memory is the hallmark of talented youth, there is nevertheless a need to provide new learning experiences at a level, pace, and density of information to maintain and enhance the growth in cognitive functioning.

### *Key Points Summary*

- *Gifted students profit from curriculum that allows for flexible approaches to solutions rather than a tightly prescribed convergent teaching method (able learners do better with less structure).*
- *Acceleration is probably the best solution to matching the gifted students' cognitive ability to academic challenge.*
- *Finding intellectual peers for the gifted student is an important component in affirming ability, as well as providing a challenging milieu for the development of specific talent.*
- *Differential grouping is necessary for the gifted when the material is cognitively complex.*
- *Teachers need to provide differing supports during the development process, such as being inspirational, technically demanding, and offering a professional role model for behavior.*

## *References*

Ackerman, P. L., Sternberg, R. J., & Glaser, R. (Eds.). (1989). *Learning and individual differences*. New York: W. H. Freeman.

Benbow, C. P. (1990). Mathematically talented children: Can acceleration meet their educational needs? In N. Colangelo & G. A. Davis (Eds.), *Handbook of gifted education* (pp. 154–165). Boston: Allyn and Bacon.

Bloom, B. S. (1956). *Taxonomy of educational objectives. Cognitive domain*. Handbook I. New York: David McKay.

Bloom, B. S. (1985). Generalizations about talent development. In B. S. Bloom (Ed.), *Developing talent in young people* (pp. 507–549). New York: Ballantine.

Brody, L. E., & Benbow, C. P. (1987). Accelerative strategies: How effective are they for the gifted? *Gifted Child Quarterly, 31* (3), 105–110.

Carroll, J. B. (1989). Factor analysis since Spearman: Where do we stand? What do we know? In R. Kaufer, P. L. Ackerman, & R. Cudeck (Eds.), *Abilities, motivation, and methodology* (pp. 43–67). Hillsdale, NJ: Erlbaum.

Dweck, C. S., & Leggett, E. L. (1988). A social-cognitive approach to motivation and personality. *Psychological Review, 95*, 256–273.

Elkind, D. (1988). Acceleration. *Young Children, 43* (4), 2.

Feldhusen, J. F. (1985). The teacher of gifted students. *Gifted Education International, 3* (2), 87–93.

Feldhusen, J. F., Check, J., & Klausmeier, H. J. (1961). Achievement in subtraction. *The Elementary School Journal, 61,* 322–327.

Feldhusen, J. F., & Klausmeier, H. J. (1959). Achievement in counting and addition. *The Elementary School Journal, 59,* 388–393.

Gallagher, J. J. (1966). Research summary. Report to Illinois Superintendent of Public Instruction.

Gardner, H. (1983). *Frames of mind: The theory of multiple intelligences.* New York: Basic Books.

Gardner, H., & Hatch, T. (1989). Multiple intelligences go to school. *Educational Researcher, 18* (8), 4–10.

Klausmeier, H. J., Check, J. F., & Feldhusen, J. F. (1960). Relationships among physical, mental, achievement, and personality measures in children of low, average, and high intelligence at 125 months of age. *American Journal of Mental Deficiency, 65,* 69–78.

Klausmeier, H. J., & Feldhusen, J. F. (1959). Renrention in arithmetic among children of low, average and high intelligence at 117 months of age. *Journal of Educational Psychology, 50,* 88–92.

Kulik, J. A., & Kulik, C. C. (1991). Research on acceleration. In N. Colangelo & G. A. Davis (Eds.), *Handbook of Gifted Education* (pp. 190–191). Boston: Allyn and Bacon.

Kyllonen, P. C., & Shute, V. J. (1989). A taxonomy of learning skills. In P. L. Ackerman, R. J. Sternberg, & R. Glaser (Eds.), *Learning and individual differences* (pp. 117–163). New York: W. H. Freeman.

Nicholls, J. G., & Miller, A. T. (1984). Development and its discontents: The differentiation of the concept of ability. In J. G. Nicholls & M. L. Maehr (Eds.), *The development of achievement motivation* (pp. 185–218). Greenwich, CT: JAI Press.

Olson, L. (1988). Children "flourish" here. *Education Week, 7* (18), 1, 18–19.

Piaget, J. F. (1959). *Judgment and reasoning in the child.* Paterson, NJ: Littlefield, Adams & Co.

Schunk, D. H. (1991). *Learning theories: An educational perspective.* New York: Macmillan.

Seeley, K. R., & Hultgren, H. (1982). *Training teachers of the gifted* (Research monograph). Denver: University of Denver.

Silverman, L. K. (1982). The gifted and talented. In E. L. Meyen (Ed.), *Exceptional children and youth* (pp. 184–190). Denver: Love Publishing.

Snow, R. E. (1989). Aptitude treatment interaction as a framework for research on individual differences in learning. In P. L. Ackerman, R. J. Sternberg, & R. Glaser (Eds.), *Learning and individual differences* (pp. 13–59). New York: W. H. Freeman.

Snow, R. E., & Lohman, D. F. (1984). Toward a theory of cognitive aptitude for learning from instruction. *Journal of Educational Psychology, 76,* 347–376.

Snyderman, M., & Rothman, S. (1988). *The IQ controversy, the media, and public policy.* New Brunswick, NJ: Transaction Books.

Sosniak, L. A. (1985). A long-term commitment to learning. In B. S. Bloom (Ed.), *Developing talent in young people* (pp. 477–506). New York: Ballantine Books.

Stanley, J. C. (1973). Accelerating the educational progress of intellectually gifted youth. *Educational Psychologist, 10,* 133–146.

Sternberg, R. J. (1988). Intelligence. In R. J. Sternberg & E. E. Smith (Eds.), *The psychology of human thought* (pp. 267–308). New York: Cambridge University Press.

Treffinger, D. J. (1986). Fostering effective, independent learning through individualized programming. In J. S. Renzulli (Ed.), *Systems and models for developing programs for the gifted and talented* (pp. 429–460). Mansfield Center, CT: Creative Learning Press.

# Curriculum Planning and Development

JOYCE VanTASSEL-BASKA

*Between the idea*
*And the reality . . .*
*Falls the shadow.*
*—T. S. ELIOT*

The process of curriculum planning and development is complex, dynamic, and generative in nature, and our approach to the task should reflect that reality. A stage theory approach will guide the reader in examining the nature of the processes involved in the overall curriculum development scheme. Figure 3–1 details the overall process of school district curriculum planning and development for the gifted. A brief description of each stage follows as a preview to extended commentary.

Each local school district should address curriculum development for gifted learners. A sound approach to begin a curriculum development plan should address the following areas:

| | |
|---|---|
| *Stage I* Planning | At this stage, the program coordinator for the gifted and a local committee should examine the basic issues and key questions regarding curriculum for the gifted. A general focus and direction should be delineated, a statement of curriculum philosophy developed, and general goals and objectives conceptualized. This planning effort should show a clear relationship to curriculum reform initiatives for all students. |
| *Stage II* Needs Assessment | This assessment should indicate areas of need in regard to curriculum development within the district. Questions such as At what levels does appropriate curriculum for the gifted exist? and Where are the gaps? are ways of beginning to focus on priority areas of need. |

**FIGURE 3–1   Curriculum Development Model**

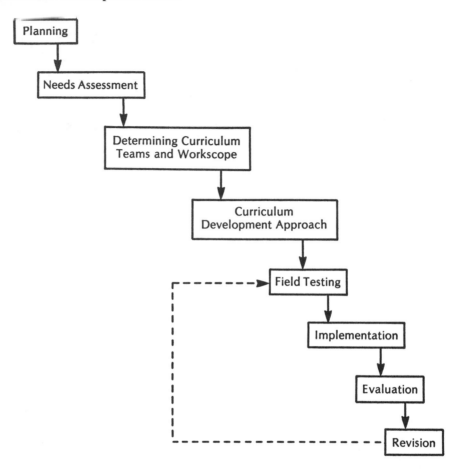

*Stage III*
Curriculum De-
velopment Teams
and Scope of Work

Based on the district curriculum needs assessment data, it is important to develop a work plan that sets parameters around the tasks to be undertaken. The district needs to decide who will be responsible for working on curriculum development for the gifted. A model approach would be to (1) select a district team comprised of a primary, intermediate, middle school, and high school teacher and a principal; (2) work with a content specialist who can provide expertise in the areas of the curriculum being developed; and (3) assign the writing tasks to one person with some written contributions from others on the team and agreement about the outline.

*Stage IV*
Curriculum De-
velopment: Adop-
tion, Modification,
and Development

Basically, districts have three general approaches to use in developing curriculum for gifted learners. They can: (1) adopt already existing curriculum for gifted learners available from other school districts, state departments, and commercial sources; (2) modify and revise the existing curriculum to make it more appropriate; or (3) develop new curriculum to supplement the current curriculum. More than one approach may be utilized and prove advantageous for school districts that are just beginning their work in curriculum development for the gifted.

*Stage V*
Field Testing or
Pilot Testing

A new curriculum developed for gifted learners should be field tested for a specified period of time in the gifted program. An assessment of its effectiveness should then be made so that the curriculum development team can make appropriate modifications and revisions.

*Stage VI*
Curriculum Implementation

The task of implementing a new curriculum needs to be perceived as gradual, with well-defined time specifications for each phase of the process. Consideration must be given to preparing the teaching staff for working with the curriculum, seeing that appropriate materials are available, and developing a plan for monitoring progress.

*Stage VII*
Evaluation

Evaluating a new curriculum is an important task but one that frequently is overlooked in the curriculum development process. Program problems are frequently related to an unchallenging, superficial, or insufficient curriculum for gifted learners. Thus, implementing an evaluation design and using results for curriculum revision is crucial to the success of any new curriculum venture.

## *General Assumptions Regarding Curriculum Development*

Why do we need to modify curriculum for gifted learners, particularly since curriculum is being upgraded for all learners? On what assumptions does such a development project rest? The underlying assumptions behind a school district's need to plan and develop a curriculum for gifted learners are fivefold:

Assumption #1: *The regular school district curriculum, as it is currently operationalized through basal texts, is insufficient and inappropriate for talented learners.*

We recognize that the needs of gifted learners are atypical in respect to several core areas: (Keating, 1976), capacity for in-depth learning (Renzulli, 1977), capacity to manipulate conceptual schemata (Sternberg, 1985), sophistication (Gallagher, 1985), and need for diversity and challenge in learning experiences (Passow et al., 1982). This recognition leads us to realize that most school curricula are organized around the needs of typical learners, where the spiral effect of incremental learning modules—coupled with heavy doses of reinforcement around a given skill or concept—constitutes the pattern for basic text materials and classroom instruction. Thus, one of the first issues to be addressed in assessing the curriculum for the gifted is how to modify or adapt the general curriculum within core areas to respond better to the atypical needs of the gifted. Clearly, accelerative, enriched, and conceptual reorganization must occur if the core curriculum is to be meaningful for the gifted during their K–12 experience.

Assumption #2: *General school curriculum needs to be modified for the gifted by reorganization rather than just adding or deleting.*

Our traditional approach to modifying curriculum for the gifted has been to speed it up, add to it, or subtract from it. Neither modification in isolation responds to learner needs, only to administrative efficiency. The fundamental problem lies in a lack of attention to reviewing the appropriateness of all aspects of the curriculum. An example from elementary mathematics may be useful to make this point. Most math texts organize fractions as a unit separate from decimals and percents rather than seeing these manipulations as different ways of expressing relationships and inequalities. For gifted learners, foregoing unnecessary practice with only one type of problem and reorganizing according to the concept of ratio and proportion in an applied problem-solving mode is a critical modification. Thus, approaches to curriculum development cannot ignore the proper adaptations needed to make the core curriculum, in whatever setting it may be delivered, more appropriate for gifted learners.

Assumption #3: *Curriculum development for the gifted has to be viewed as a long-term process that involves adaptation of the current curriculum, infusion of appropriate extant curricula for the gifted, and the development of new curriculum.*

Most curriculum work that has been done for the gifted has taken an isolationist perspective. It was conceptualized and written with the idea that it was to be "the" curriculum for the gifted. Consequently, committees of writers struggled with key models and concepts as they strove to create a "new" curriculum—one that was appropriate only for the gifted in some special setting. What that approach fosters, however, is a fragmentation of curriculum experiences for the gifted. Frequently such curriculum is organized on a faulty understanding of the models and concepts it purports to convey. Some of the best curricula that exist for the gifted were not written with their special needs in mind. The major curriculum projects of the 1960s in science, mathematics, English, and social studies have proven very successful with gifted populations, even though they were not so intended. The Junior Great Books program and Philosophy for Children, both widely used curricula in gifted programs, were not developed expressly for the gifted. Yet use of such tested curriculum material can save districts the time and expense of trying to reinvent what would clearly be an inferior wheel. More effort needs to be expended in bridging the district core curriculum to appropriate adaptations of it for gifted learners and other able learners who can benefit from it. To conceptualize curriculum development as a short-term activity is to misunderstand the nature and scope of the process that needs to be undertaken.

Assumption #4: *Curriculum for the gifted needs to be written down and communicated widely within a school district.*

A curriculum only has a recognizable shape or form when it is written. What goes on in a classroom between teacher and learner is instructional process, not curriculum. What written curriculum provides is a sense of purpose and direction in areas of educational value that both teacher and student explore. A curriculum for the gifted should provide educational personnel and the community with an understanding of what areas of investigation are valuable, how students will meet their learning objectives, and by what means they will be evaluated. A curriculum for the gifted places emphasis on purpose, means, and end somewhat equally and in a manner that the lay public can understand. The obligation to communicate what is distinctive about curriculum for the gifted is paramount and the strength of that distinction lies in effective curriculum planning.

> *Assumption #5:*  *Curriculum that is planned for the best learners in schools can benefit a wider spectrum of students as well.*

Recent national curriculum development projects have demonstrated that curriculum developed for the gifted can be used successfully with a broader group of learners (VanTassel-Baska, Gallagher, Bailey, & Sher, 1992). It remains for us to understand how wide the band of learners might be who could profit from more high-powered curriculum intervention. The movement toward setting world-class standards and adopting higher standards for all learners should provide us with a better sense of what percentage of learners can benefit from greater advancement and complexity in their curriculum diet.

## Stage I: Planning

Local district program planners need to be sensitive to several major issues in examining the area of planning curriculum for gifted learners. Clearly, curriculum philosophy is important (see Chapter 1), but other issues also affect the planning effort. One issue is the definition being used for curriculum. For purposes of this book, *curriculum* is defined as a set of organized experiences appropriate for gifted learners that are written down and adopted for use in a school district. In this sense, then, curriculum represents a formal codifying of the goals, objectives, and activities of a gifted program. The appropriateness of a district's *basic curriculum* for the gifted is a key consideration.

At the point that curriculum development work is undertaken, it is wise to examine the current curriculum and make appropriate modifications in the core content areas before developing a new curriculum.

A second issue relates to the curriculum *philosophy* adopted in the school district. What we believe about gifted learners will dictate strongly our values and attitudes about appropriate curriculum for them. As illustrated in Chapter 1, several philosophies of curriculum can prevail in a tailored curriculum for the gifted, but a school district must decide which philosophy or combination of perspectives will drive the development process.

A third issue focuses on the selection of *appropriate goals* to address in developing a curriculum for gifted learners. Objectives need to flow from the overall goals of the program. Model goals for gifted learners might be:

### Gifted Program Goals

1. To provide for the mastery of the basic skills of reading and mathematics at a pace and depth appropriate to the capacities of able learners. Students will participate in a diagnostic-prescriptive model of reading and mathematics instruction that would allow for individual rates of mastery, regardless of age or grade.
2. To promote critical thinking and reasoning abilities. Students will be instructed in the

areas of inference, deductive and inductive reasoning, analogies, and evaluation of arguments. These reasoning tools will be applied to all areas of the curriculum.

3. To provide an environment that encourages divergent thinking. Students will be encouraged in the development of originality, fluency, flexibility, and elaboration in their thought processes.

4. To foster inquiry and challenging attitudes towards learning. Students will be able to develop a commitment to learning as a lifelong process and to learn education, civic, social, and personal responsibilities.

5. To develop high-level oral and written skills. Students will become confident in expressing ideas through class discussions, panel discussions, debates, and oral reports; students will learn expository and creative writing skills and technical report writing.

6. To develop research skills and methods. Students will be able to understand the scientific method and its application to all areas of inquiry.

7. To develop an understanding for systems of knowledge, themes, issues, and problems that frame the external world. Students will be able to interrelate ideas within and across domains of study.

8. To develop self-understanding. Students will be able to understand their strengths and weaknesses in various contexts.

9. To facilitate opportunities for learning that are external to the school but provide an important match to the needs of learners. Students will be able to gain access to educational advantages provided by resources outside the environment of the school.

10. To enhance opportunities for future planning and development. Students will be able to develop goals and apply structure to the tasks of life planning for the future.

Such goals need to be translated into measurable objectives that become the focus of the curriculum delivery system. Specific objectives may be formulated for both teachers and learners since behavioral change is required for both in order to address stated goals.

A fourth issue of planning is that of *articulation*. Gifted students need to be exposed to increasingly complex and difficult material as they progress through school. Attention to the progressive development of skills and concepts is an essential component of curriculum development for this population. Articulation of skills and concepts in core curriculum areas is but part of the task; skills such as critical thinking, creative thinking, problem solving, and research all need to be structured hierarchically so that higher-level skills are taught through a developmental system. Product requirements also need to be articulated across content and grade-level dimensions.

Tyler (1961) posits four fundamental questions that have particular relevance for educators of the gifted in the curriculum planning process:

1. *What educational purposes should the school seek to attain?* This question is central to the development of curriculum for the gifted. The selection of educational objectives establishes initially the degree of differentiation the curriculum is apt to have. The following list of questions must be answered by curriculum developers regarding appropriate objectives for gifted learners:

    a. Do the educational objectives help gifted learners develop proficiency at a sufficient level of difficulty?

    b. Do the objectives help gifted learners become creatively productive?

    c. Do the objectives help gifted learners become self-directed learners?

    d. Do the objectives allow gifted learners to develop advanced skills, concepts, and knowledge about a field of inquiry?

    e. Do the objectives encourage cross-disciplinary applications?

Embedded in these questions are the major principles of differentiation of curriculum for the gifted: pacing, creative production, self-directed learning, challenge, and diversity.

    **2.** *How can learning experiences be selected that are likely to be useful in attaining these objectives?* Whereas the first question reflects on the scope of any given curriculum, this second basic question poses the problem of planning specific experiences for learning within a given curriculum area. Learning experiences can promote or inhibit retention, interest, satisfaction, and internalization of a given problem. In the education of the gifted, inquiry-based lessons, group problem-solving settings, independent investigations, and group discussion all characterize instructional techniques that contribute to good learning experiences. In the curriculum development process, those techniques that most effectively move students toward prescribed educational objectives should be selected and organized.

    **3.** *How can learning experiences be organized for effective instruction?* The sequencing and continuity of learning experiences for the gifted is a major issue in examining overall curricular experiences. The model chosen to deliver curriculum and instruction is critical. Pull-out models, unless they replace or introduce key areas of learning, lessen the concentrated amount of instructional time in such a way that the impact of given learning experiences is diminished. By the same token, daily contact in a given curriculum area may be equally inefficient for some learning areas. Nevertheless, curriculum planners need the flexibility of time to develop effective instructional models for the gifted learner. Criteria for effective organization must take into account vertical reiteration, progressive development of skills and concepts, and horizontal relationships of ideas and theories.

    **4.** *How can the effectiveness of learning experiences be evaluated?* This fourth question raises the issue of evaluating curriculum in some systematic way. At the present time, gifted education has not set about evaluating learning gains in an effective manner, let alone the experiences and processes by which those gains may have been reached. Nonetheless, the development of methodologies and instruments to assess the effectiveness of curriculum with gifted learners is integral to the task of responsible curriculum development. Criteria for initial consideration may include the following areas:

    a. Appropriateness for level of ability and age range

    b. Rich and complete treatment of topic

    c. Allowance of diversity in learning through the use of multiple sources and the presentation of varying perspectives

    d. Enhancement of opportunity for small group discussions

    e. Enhancement of opportunity for independent investigations

    f. Increase in interest and motivation for the topic under study

Recent work with authentic assessment approaches holds promise for better and more appropriate techniques.

These four questions are important to consider at the planning stage since they frame the overall structure of the curriculum development process.

## Stage II: Needs Assessment

One of the most practical aspects of the curriculum development process is a thorough needs assessment. This author has proposed the use of a needs assessment model that linked student needs to program components, and linked developmental concerns to the nature and extent of staff development that was necessary for effective program operation (VanTassel-Baska, 1979). Other perspectives on needs assessment more precisely focus on decision making in the area of curriculum.

### Perspectives on Needs Assessment

Both state and national needs assessments have been conducted in the field of gifted eduation in recent years. These surveys have highlighted areas that practitioners have identified as requiring more attention in the future. It is interesting to note that half of them directly bear on aspects of curriculum development.

1. Need for programs and services for special populations (VanTassel-Baska, Patton, & Prillaman, 1991)
2. Need for comprehensive programs that are articulated across grade levels (Illinois Office of Education, 1978; *Richardson Study,* 1985)
3. Need for in-service training for teachers (Gallagher et al., 1982)
4. Need for increased financial support bases (Gallagher et al., 1982; Illinois Office of Education, 1978)
5. Need for curriculum development (Gallagher et al., 1982; *Richardson Study,* 1985)
6. Need for valid instructional materials (Gallagher et al., 1982)
7. Need for more research on learning strategies (Robinson, 1990)
8. Need for demonstration programs (Gallagher, 1982; Richardson Study, 1985)
9. Need for consistency in identification procedures and standards (Gallagher et al., 1982; Richert, 1982)
10. Need for consistency in program delivery based on student needs rather than district resources (Illinois Office of Education, 1978)
11. Need for consistent and selective criteria for choosing teachers of the gifted (Seeley, 1985)
12. Need for philosophical and psychological support from professional colleagues (administrators and teachers) (Gallagher et al., 1982; *Richardson Study,* 1985)

However, needs assessment must also occur at the local level in order to determine what currently exists in the curriculum for gifted students and what needs to exist. This task can be accomplished through asking students, parents, administrators, teachers, and others to comment formally on this aspect of the district's educational plan. How can needs assessment be done? What are its most important components? It is useful to start with a list of questions that can guide the needs assessment process.

1. Based on the characteristics of gifted children in this district, what are the educational needs for which we are responsible?
2. What are the gaps in our current program that must be addressed in order to respond to the needs of gifted students?
3. What technical assistance will be needed in order to develop and implement new directions in curriculum?

## *Determination of Student Needs*

In order to plan effective curriculum for gifted learners, school districts must understand the special needs of the population involved. Gifted and talented students need:

*1. Activities that enable them to operate cognitively and affectively at complex levels of thought and feeling.*
*2. Opportunities for divergent production.*
*3. Challenging group and individual work which demonstrates process/product outcomes.*
*4. Discussions among intellectual peers.*
*5. A variety of experiences that promote understanding of human value systems.*
*6. The opportunity to see interrelationships in all bodies of knowledge.*
*7. Special courses in their area of strength and interest which accelerate the pace and depth of the content.*
*8. Greater exposure to new areas of learning within and outside the school structure.*
*9. Opportunities to apply their abilities to real problems in the world of production.*
*10. Emphasis on the skills of critical thinking, creative thinking, research, and problem solving. (VanTassel-Baska, 1979)*

This needs list can be used by districts in three major ways to document their student needs:

1. Districts can rank order this list of needs according to the percent of students demonstrating each of them, and according to the degree of each need (mild, moderate, severe) as ascertained by professional staff.
2. Districts can use the list as a student survey in current gifted programs to ascertain which needs gifted students feel are being met and which ones are not.
3. Districts can use the list to survey parents regarding their perceptions of the extent to which their children's needs were or are being met.

Figure 3–2 contains a form that can be used by school districts for any of the stated purposes to ascertain a current picture of curriculum needs of their gifted students.

Needs assessment, then, has two important components: the identification of needs and the prioritization of areas of need with which to begin curriculum development work. A needs assessment reveals what is considered most important by various constituency groups. If time, resources, and other constraints do not preclude it, proceeding to address these highest areas of identified needs should be viewed by program coordinators as very

## FIGURE 3–2   Needs of Gifted Students

Please rate the following according to the extent they are incorporated into our current program for gifted learners.

|  | To a great extent 5 | 4 | 3 | 2 | Not at all 1 | Cannot judge |
|---|---|---|---|---|---|---|
| 1. Basic cognitive skills: | | | | | | |
| a. Critical thinking | 5 | 4 | 3 | 2 | 1 | 0 |
| b. Creative thinking | 5 | 4 | 3 | 2 | 1 | 0 |
| c. Problem solving | 5 | 4 | 3 | 2 | 1 | 0 |
| d. Research | 5 | 4 | 3 | 2 | 1 | 0 |
| e. Decision making | 5 | 4 | 3 | 2 | 1 | 0 |
| 2. Basic affective skills: | | | | | | |
| a. Tolerance of self and others | 5 | 4 | 3 | 2 | 1 | 0 |
| b. Constructive use of humor | 5 | 4 | 3 | 2 | 1 | 0 |
| c. Coping with being different | 5 | 4 | 3 | 2 | 1 | 0 |
| d. Discriminating between the real and the ideal | 5 | 4 | 3 | 2 | 1 | 0 |
| e. Using their high-level sensitivity | 5 | 4 | 3 | 2 | 1 | 0 |
| 3. To be challenged by mastery level work in areas of strength and interest | 5 | 4 | 3 | 2 | 1 | 0 |
| 4. To be challenged by exposure to new areas | 5 | 4 | 3 | 2 | 1 | 0 |
| 5. To be challenged by the opportunity to see interrelationships | 5 | 4 | 3 | 2 | 1 | 0 |
| 6. To be challenged by experiences that promote understanding human value systems | 5 | 4 | 3 | 2 | 1 | 0 |
| 7. To be challenged through discussions with intellectual peers | 5 | 4 | 3 | 2 | 1 | 0 |
| 8. To be challenged by activities at complex levels of thought | 5 | 4 | 3 | 2 | 1 | 0 |
| 9. To be challenged through opportunities for divergent production | 5 | 4 | 3 | 2 | 1 | 0 |
| 10. To be challenged by the opportunity for real-world problem solving | 5 | 4 | 3 | 2 | 1 | 0 |

appropriate. The process by which the needs assessment data are obtained can also build support for and involvement in the overall curriculum development effort.

In addition to viewing curriculum needs from a student perspective, it may be helpful to gain a larger picture of district needs in curriculum for the gifted by assessing what is and has been done in the name of "curriculum for the gifted." How good is the current curriculum? Is there already written curriculum for gifted students at some levels? Questions such as these may be important to answer also as part of the needs assessment process. The form in Figure 3–3 may assist in capturing an understanding of current and future curriculum needs in the district. It may also help determine priorities for targeting resources for curriculum development work.

A third part of curriculum needs assessment concerns the nature of the curriculum documents that will be useful to develop.

One way to think about document needs is to conceptualize all of the relevant school groups who have a role to play in the curriculum development process, and then decide what written documents would best facilitate their role in curriculum. For example, administrators need documents that reflect the scope and sequence of curriculum at relevant developmental levels, whereas teachers prefer smaller units of curriculum such as lesson plans and topical units.

**FIGURE 3–3   Curriculum Needs Assessment**

1. Describe the current operating gifted programs in the district at each level:
   K–3:
   4–6:
   7–8:
   9–12:

2. Do you have a differentiated curriculum for the gifted at each level?
   ___ Yes ___ No Comment:

3. If yes, has gifted curriculum been evaluated for its effectiveness with gifted students?
   ___ Yes ___ No Comment:

4. Have gifted students assessed their curriculum?
   ___ Yes ___ No Comment:

5. Have teachers assessed the current curriculum for the gifted?
   ___ Yes ___ No Comment:

6. What are the perceived gaps in the current curriculum in general?
   K–3:
   4–6:
   7–8:
   9–12:

7. What are the gaps for gifted students?
   K–3:
   4–6:
   7–8:
   9–12:

8. Areas of need for curriculum development:
   K–3:
   4–6:
   7–8:
   9–12:

In summary, a needs assessment strategy must recognize (1) generic needs in the field of gifted education, (2) specific curriculum needs of gifted students, (3) discrepancies between what existing curriculum for the gifted currently provides and what it should provide, and (4) specific curriculum documents needed to codify and guide curriculum efforts. All of these elements are useful in ascertaining what appropriate curriculum for the gifted might be. As practitioners, we need to clarify better what we do with gifted learners and why we do it, and to develop a meaningful curriculum based on sound efforts of assessment.

## Stage III: Curriculum Development Teams and Scope of Work

As one examines the possibility of developing meaningful curriculum for the gifted, it becomes apparent that if the curriculum is content based or interdisciplinary in nature, curriculum developers must be well-acquainted with the content areas to be examined and have the ability to construct an organizational schema that focuses on the most important skills, concepts, and "cutting edge" ideas in that field.

An individual teacher may or may not have these insights. Consequently, it is useful to develop a team approach to curriculum development. Such a team approach to curriculum making allows the strength of each individual member to show. Good teachers know intuitively what is workable for the gifted in the classroom and can translate ideas at an appropriate level for gifted learners. Content experts, who may be university professors or practicing professionals, know their particular field of inquiry and are engaged in active research within it; thus, they can supply key ideas and concepts that can provide the curricular structure. The combined effort of teachers and scholars in this type of curriculum effort is most productive.

Another model to consider for curriculum team work is one that utilizes the key ideas of scholars but does not involve them integrally in the curriculum development process. Shane (1981) shared the work of scholar teams and their views on important content curriculum for the year 2000 in the key areas of the natural sciences, life sciences, chemistry, geology, and the social sciences. Rutherford and Algren (1989) organized core science concepts for various curriculum groups to use as a basis for development.

School districts might solicit outside experts in various fields to provide key ideas and concepts in a given field of inquiry. Then, within the school district, curriculum teams can shape those ideas to an advanced curriculum for the gifted. The outside expert might critique the work of the teams regarding the way the ideas were translated in respect to consistency and appropriateness.

Another approach is the more typical consultant model where the curriculum team is led by an educator within the school district, and outside consultants participate at particular stages of the process. This model may be preferable if the focus of the curriculum work is on planning rather than writing, and the mode of teamwork is discussion and deliberation.

Whichever model is preferred within a given school district, it is important to involve individuals with expertise outside the domain of a given district. There are several good reasons for this:

1. The consultant/scholar/expert can provide an objective assessment of any curriculum issue or problem; frequently school political issues tend to dominate curriculum deliberations.
2. He or she has an in-depth knowledge of the key area being considered. For example, in considering an appropriate sequence of mathematics courses for gifted students at the secondary level, a consultant in mathematics can share major approaches to organizing such courses, where exemplary programs based on those approaches may be operating, and the advantages and disadvantages of any given sequence from the viewpoint of higher education.
3. He or she can facilitate the discussion of a key topic. Curriculum teams need to read about the issues they are addressing and to discuss them in depth. Curriculum generalists in schools may have limited backgrounds in many specific areas of the curriculum and find it difficult to lead team deliberations in those areas of the process.

## *Organizing Structures for Curriculum Work*

The makeup of district curriculum teams should be determined by the scope of the curriculum effort. If the task is to be a comprehensive one—for example, restructuring a

K–12 curriculum for the gifted—then there will be a need for multiple teams that are guided by a central steering committee.

A clear distinction also needs to be drawn between data-gathering tasks, planning, and writing tasks when considering the composition of committees. Curriculum writers and data gatherers should be a subset of the committee, or, if warranted, a separate task force that works with the committee.

The number of people on a curriculum development committee is a crucial variable. This author can remember being the head of a curriculum council of over 100 people in a local school district. Clearly, curriculum issues were not handled by group discussion or even by ultimate consensus. Ideal sizes for curriculum planning committees range from 6 to 12 people, depending on the size of the district and the scope of the effort. A data-gathering and writing task force may be best conducted by one to four individuals.

Representation on the committee, of course, is another critical variable. The individual in a school district who is responsible for curriculum leadership for the gifted program should chair the committee, be able to communicate the work of the committee with clarity, and be able to move the agenda along a predetermined schedule to ensure that the committee work will be implemented. Involving building-level administrators in the committee work is vital. One principal can represent his or her counterparts on such curriculum committees. Teacher involvement is also critical but should be reserved for teachers who have knowledge and experience in working with gifted learners in a variety of classroom settings.

Representation by content disciplines rather than grade level only may be an important consideration for teacher selection since the education of the gifted as it is translated through school curriculum needs to be at an advanced level and have a clear emphasis on maximum rather than minimum competency issues. Selecting primary teachers based on their understanding of reading or mathematics rather than their teaching style is preferable. There are two reasons why curriculum work for the gifted should always be conducted across grade levels rather than only at one level. One is that gifted students' capabilities obscure the boundaries of typical grade-level designations so that primary program planning is more efficacious than kindergarten planning. A second reason is that the task of developing scope and sequence in the curriculum is simplified by structuring committees in this fashion. This procedure thereby reduces the potential number of assessment points to four—after third grade, after sixth grade, after eighth grade, and after twelfth grade.

## *Scope of Work*

It is important to consider several factors when deciding on the parameters of the curriculum development effort: time, resource allocation, and readiness for change.

### *Time*
The process model presented in this chapter for school district curriculum development is a generative one that builds toward continued improvement and refinement. Yet the reality of schools dictates that priorities change, study committees dissolve, and the world of education goes on. The curriculum leader must determine a realistic time schedule that can be balanced against the current need for curriculum work so that major writing, revisions, and recommendations can take place while the support mechanisms are in place

in the district. It is important, however, to stress that curriculum development in any form will take a minimum of three years' commitment on the part of the district and key personnel working on committees. A more realistic time frame for considering comprehensive curriculum development for the gifted would be five years.

### Resource Allocation

A second concern in determining the scope of work is the issue of resource allocation. What human and material resources are available to carry out curriculum development tasks over a three-year period? Has the district allocated the necessary budget to provide staff development seminars and consultant time at the planning, writing/adapting, and implementing stages of the project? Does the budget allow for released time for teachers to attend meetings or provide extra stipends for additional work time? Is there a product development allocation so that curriculum guides can be easily disseminated once they are developed? All of these questions are critical to the work since constraints around resources can adversely affect the overall process.

### Readiness for Change

Decisions about the scope of work should also consider in what areas of the curriculum there is a readiness for change on the part of staff. Sometimes at the secondary level, for example, a given department expresses real interest and enthusiasm for "tinkering" with the curriculum, whereas other departments show no such interest. If choices can be made, it may be wiser to capitalize on such organized enthusiasm rather than to effect widespread involvement in curriculum work at a particular time. No instructional leader can expect a staff to be thrilled with the idea of curriculum change. Thus, smaller, well-targeted efforts that prove successful may be superior to a comprehensive effort all at once that is blocked because a staff was not ready to be involved.

## Stage IV: The Curriculum Development Approach: Data Gathering, Adapting, and/or Writing

School district practitioners should look askance at any suggestion that appropriate curriculum for the gifted must be developed completely from scratch. Too much time, energy, and resources have already been used by school districts on an individual basis to create their own unique curriculum for the gifted or to allow individual teachers freedom to "do their own thing" with the gifted curriculum. That is not to say that some development may not need to be done as the process goes on, but creating new units of study, for example, is clearly not a first step.

### Data Gathering

Gathering extant curriculum that may be appropriate for gifted learners, even though it is not marketed by publishing companies as materials for the gifted, is the first step. Procedurally, this involves the following:

1. Contact appropriate commercial publishers regarding texts in areas under study. Obtain materials they feel are appropriate for "high-ability learners." Review and critique.

2. Contact curriculum libraries on university campuses to compile a list of their materials that are geared to gifted learners. Some of these materials may not be found through any other services and therefore constitute "fugitive" literature.
3. Contact state consultants for the gifted who should be able to provide lists of curriculum developed in their state for the gifted through special projects or state and local efforts.
4. Procure sample materials developed for gifted learners from companies specializing in curriculum for this population. Trillium Press is one example (see Appendix B for others).
5. Review curriculum guides from such prepackaged programs as Junior Great Books, Philosophy for Children, Man: A Course of Study, and College Board's Advanced Placement Program.
6. Contact at least five established gifted programs across the country and gather ideas on effective curricula.
7. Establish a set of criteria for judging curriculum materials for their appropriateness for gifted. (Figure 3–5, near the end of this chapter, might be adapted for this purpose.)
8. Determine what may be usable from all of these sources for your program and the degree to which it may need to be adapted or supplemented.

## *Adapting Existing Curriculum*

Another task that a curriculum development team must consider is modifying the core curriculum to make it more appropriate for gifted learners. After completing the data-gathering process, it will become clear that most published curricula designed solely for gifted learners are not sufficient in breadth or depth to carry a program for a school year. There is no way to avoid the difficult task of reorganizing and restructuring the school's basic curriculum in order to make it more appropriate for able learners. The following model suggests a procedural way to accomplish this task:

### *Content Modification Model for Gifted Learners*

**Step 1** Examine the general curriculum guide for required knowledge and skills in given content areas, at various stages of development.

**Step 2** Compress scope and sequence of skill mastery by 30 to 50 percent through reorganization according to higher-level skills.

**Step 3** Develop additional knowledge and skill areas appropriate for the gifted at various levels.

**Step 4** Integrate process skill development and independent work for the gifted into each level.

**Step 5** Identify key issues, problems, and themes that might be worked with at various levels.

**Step 6** Add needed curriculum materials or develop through a unit approach.

This content modification approach is particularly useful as an alternative to total curriculum change for several reasons. (1) The content modification approach starts with the state-of-the-art district curriculum; it is familiar, accepted, and usually board approved, and, in that sense, vested with curriculum policy implications. District curriculum guides are an important point of departure for developing gifted curriculum from both a political and a logical perspective. (2) Content modification allows the curriculum developer to challenge all underlying assumptions currently operating in the school district regarding a segment of curriculum. This challenging of assumptions and restructuring to accommodate specific learner needs is a key exercise in the overall process. (3) This approach keeps the curriculum focus on the content dimensions by which schools are organized and with which staff are somewhat comfortable, yet moves beyond basal text materials and forces schools to alter curriculum scope and sequence in the face of individual learner needs. No special jargon is necessary to talk about the curriculum for the gifted learner. We are all talking about the same curriculum areas: reading, mathematics, foreign language, social studies, science, language arts/English, and so on. (4) The content modification approach allows us to infuse the teaching of such process skills as critical thinking, creative thinking, and research into individual fields of inquiry rather than teach them in isolation. In this way, these skills can adapt to the idiosyncratic nature of individual disciplines rather than be viewed as applicable in all respects to every discipline. Problem solving in mathematics, for example, is quite different from problem solving in political science. The scientific method may not be applicable to the teaching of the American Revolution but it has great significance for the teaching of science content. (5) This approach allows for project development that is meaningful in the context of a student's total program, not just an invention pulled out of a laundry list of activity ideas. Thus, reading, discussion, and problem solving in a given content area can be merged with the application of high-level process skills and culminate in a high-quality product. (6) Individual units can always be developed or sought out as needed to fill in important gaps in a given knowledge area or its applied fields. Thus, in science, a unit of study on computer modeling might be developed to give students a sense of the technologically advanced uses for the computer by scientists.

Model curriculum projects in science and language arts for high-ability learners were developed around this content modification model (Center for Gifted Education, 1992). Each project has a set of relevant concept papers, a scope and sequence, and individual teaching units that have been field tested in a variety of school settings. Evaluation of existing curriculum materials was also conducted, resulting in assessment guides and consumer guides to exemplary materials. Project materials then provide a template for individual school efforts in content modification.

Through the use of such a content modification model, coupled with appropriate delivery methods, curriculum for gifted learners can maximize its opportunity for being integrated at a policy level in a given school district. Furthermore, appropriate treatment of the students in all of the basic curriculum areas is achieved, thus eliminating fragmentation, gaps, and general lack of curriculum coordination.

## Curriculum Writing: Unit Development

Because the task of writing curriculum units is in itself a complex one, Chapter 7 of this book is devoted to that process. However, the following outline focuses on salient aspects of unit development from a content, process/product, and concept perspective. Decisions regarding the topics of the units to be developed should flow out of the earlier phases of data gathering and adaptation. As school districts begin to consider the infusion of process/product curriculum and concept curriculum, frequently the need for teaching units emerges. As new topics are added to the core content areas, the need for new units may surface as well. Thus, careful planning for unit development needs to be undertaken.

### *Sample Outline for Curriculum Units*

| *Unit Element* | *Question It Answers* |
|---|---|
| 1. General instructions on the use of the unit (including grade levels, prerequisite skills, type of learner) | Who is the unit for? |
| 2. Unit rationale and goals | What is the purpose of the unit? |
| 3. Unit objectives | What will students learn from the unit? |
| 4. Specific learner activities (including sample questions for discussion, sample exercises, and study sheets) | What will students do? What questions will teachers/students ask? |
| 5. Dominant teaching strategies | How will teachers carry out instruction? |
| 6. Key materials and other resources | What tools will teachers need to implement this unit in the classroom? |
| 7. Appropriate tests and other evaluative tools such as inventories, checklists, etc. | How will teachers assess student learning? |
| 8. Student self-study material | What aspects of this unit can students explore on their own? |
| 9. Student and teacher references | What books, films, etc., increase understanding about this topic? |
| 10. Relationship of the unit to other aspects of the curriculum | How does this unit fit into the larger curriculum schemata? |

## Stage V: Field Testing or Pilot Testing the Curriculum

Whether one is adopting a prepackaged curriculum, adapting a currently existing curriculum, or creating new units of instruction, the stage of piloting or field testing is critical. There is often a "leap of faith" that occurs with the development of a curriculum piece. It is assumed that teachers can use it effectively in the dynamic context of the classroom. Frequently the gulf between intended curriculum and delivered curriculum is great. The field-testing stage thus allows individual teachers as well as outside process observers to monitor the use of a new curriculum in a systematic way. Tracking curriculum efficacy at this stage of development also allows the opportunity for important feedback to curriculum writers who may alter and revise learning segments based on teacher or observer responses.

**FIGURE 3–4  Field-Test Evaluation Form: Criterial Checklist for Curriculum Units for the Gifted**

Check one:          Check one;          Code:

K–3 _____    Social Studies _____    Objective(s) _____
4–6 _____    Math _____        Activities _____
7–8 _____    Science _____
9–12 _____    Lang. Arts _____
                    Other _____

Please circle the appropriate response for each.

| | To a great extent | | Not at all | | Does not apply |
|---|---|---|---|---|---|

1. The activities were age appropriate for gifted children.      5   4   3   2   1   0
   Comment:

2. The activities were appropriate in terms of level of difficulty and/or complexity for gifted children.      5   4   3   2   1   0
   Comment:

3. The activities were of interest to students.      5   4   3   2   1   0
   Comment:

4. The activities helped accomplish the specific objective(s).      5   4   3   2   1   0
   Comment:

5. The activities were differentiated from the regular school program in a specific content area(s).      5   4   3   2   1   0
   Comment:

6. The activities were easy to adapt and/or implement.      5   4   3   2   1   0
   Comment:

7. The teacher directions were sufficient.      5   4   3   2   1   0
   Comment:

8. The background information and materials/references were sufficient.      5   4   3   2   1   0
   Comment:

9. The activities were suitable to teaching the topic chosen.      5   4   3   2   1   0
   Comment:

10. The activities encouraged creative production in students.      5   4   3   2   1   0
    Comment:

11. The evaluation techniques or procedures were appropriate.      5   4   3   2   1   0
    Comment:

12. The unit encouraged teachers to develop additional activities.      5   4   3   2   1   0
    Comment:

13. The format facilitated understanding of unit purpose and direction.      5   4   3   2   1   0
    Comment:

14. The format facilitated recognition of the interrelationship of component parts.      5   4   3   2   1   0
    Comment:

Length of time to complete unit segments: _____

Suggestions for overall unit on change: _____

_____

Other comments: _____

_____
_____
_____

Figure 3–4 has been found useful in field-testing specific units developed by teachers of the gifted. Typically a meeting should be scheduled to review the field-test data and to make recommendations on how best to utilize such data for revision purposes.

## Stage VI: Curriculum Implementation

Field testing, disseminating, and institutionalizing curriculum within the political context of schools is a major phase in the curriculum process. The problems that change agents (like curriculum developers for the gifted) incur along the road of implementation are myriad. An effective strategy of curriculum change must therefore proceed on a double agenda, working simultaneously to change ideas about curricula and to change human dynamics. Taba (1962) delineated key issues in the implementation process:

1. Curriculum change requires a systematic sequence of work which deals with all aspects of the curriculum ranging from goals to means.
2. A strategy for curriculum change involves creating conditions for productive work.
3. Effecting curriculum change involves a large amount of training.
4. Change always involves human and emotional factors.
5. Since curriculum development is extremely complex, it requires many kinds of competencies in different combinations at different points of work.
6. Managing curriculum change requires skilled leadership.

Curriculum implementation should be viewed as the most complex stage of curriculum development, for it involves the translation of ideas from written form into classroom action, the transforming of individuals' thoughts and behaviors to new paradigms, and the accomplishment of this evolution in a reasonable period of time.

One of the first issues of curriculum implementation that confronts educational personnel is deciding on the scope of the implementation effort. Successful implementation of curriculum takes a cooperative and total effort by all staff to ensure a smooth and successful transition. Consequently, it may be useful to limit by grade levels, content disciplines, or schools the unit of analysis to be included at the first stage of implementation.

A second issue in curriculum implementation involves a thorough understanding of the change process on the part of the administrator responsible for instituting it. At a very fundamental level, this recognition involves understanding the school climate into which the curriculum innovation will be placed and having a clear idea about how key actors will respond to the demands placed on them in implementing new curriculum.

A third issue revolves around the selection of staff for the first stage of implementation. Even though the total staff may eventually become involved with several aspects of the gifted curriculum, the number of staff involved with implementation should be limited initially. Criteria for considering staff selection should include willingness and enthusiasm for the new direction, capacity to adapt curriculum appropriately in the classroom, and an interest in training fellow teachers in the use of the new curriculum. It is also important to select schools on the basis of the interest and follow-through involvement that may be anticipated at the principal level.

Staff development work at this stage of the curriculum development process is another issue vital to the success of the effort. Creating a curriculum that sits on shelves or is thrown away is a waste of everyone's resources. Yet frequently there is a void in the process of curriculum development in sensitizing and training personnel to use a new curriculum, laying out expectations regarding its implementation, and disseminating the work of the curriculum teams. These tasks need to be accomplished as part of the implementation stage.

Staff development on new curriculum should occur in segments. Initially, the implementation plan should be presented, followed by the curriculum teams who field-tested the materials serving as presenters or discussants regarding its use. The use of outside consultants may be useful if they were involved in the earlier development stages of the project. A two-day period of time should be set aside for this orientation session. Follow-up sessions at three-month intervals should focus on strengths and weaknesses in the curriculum as it is being tried out. Classroom monitoring observations should also be conducted. If possible, teachers implementing the curriculum should be videotaped and those tapes used as a part of the curriculum critique. In this way classroom dynamics become the focus for judging curriculum efficacy.

It is rare that curriculum implementation can occur without some problems. One common problem is the lack of supplementary materials to carry out the implementation tasks at the most effective level. How do we go about accessing appropriate materials at this stage of the curriculum development process? We can maximize the potential for obtaining such materials by taking several steps prior to this stage of the process: establishing lists of types of material needed by teachers and students in the course of using the curriculum, setting criteria for selection of the materials, and budgeting carefully to ensure purchasing power.

Another key issue to consider at the implementation stage is a work plan that charts the progress of this stage of the process. This work plan should chart the implementation schedule according to key turning points in the process, such as when teachers have demonstrated a full understanding of what the purposes are of the new curriculum and the specifics of how to implement it in the context of the classroom. The work plan should also be revised as the process goes along, with notes recorded on problems or issues encountered along the way.

Also, it is important to consider the monitoring process that needs to occur to ensure that classroom implementation is indeed going on. Are new materials being used? Are teachers applying appropriate strategies in teaching the new curriculum? Do students respond to what is being implemented? All of these questions are important checks on the actual degree of implementation that may be occurring in a given school. It is the responsibility of the administrator of a school and the coordinator of the gifted program to monitor the implementation process according to a predetermined agreement.

A final consideration to be made at the implementation stage is to have a process in place that will allow adjustments and adaptations in the curriculum to occur on the spot rather than waiting for the next formal phase of the process. If something is not working, then make the necessary changes and document what was done. Consequently, fine tuning of the curriculum can occur during implementation rather than being seen as an outcome of evaluation.

## Stage VII: Evaluation

Since there has been little systematic focus on curriculum work in the field of the education of the gifted, there has been less concern for evaluating the effectiveness of it. Many school districts will choose to assume a defect in their identification protocol rather than examine carefully the nature of their curriculum and its instructional delivery system. Consequently, the quest for the right test goes on and no effort is expended on behalf of a questionable educational treatment. It is as if a doctor constantly questioned his or her diagnosis and test results rather than altering the treatment of a patient who was not responding to one remedy. Such a doctor would not have patients long, yet educators persist with comparable approaches despite neglect of vital educational "treatment."

Evaluating the effectiveness of a curriculum for the gifted is an essential task that should be well planned and executed. Too frequently, curriculum developers discard what fails without examining the particularities of the situation; likewise, teachers will favor a curriculum unit or segment or a course merely because students like it. The key questions about what makes curriculum effective with a group of atypical learners never get asked.

One excellent way of ascertaining curriculum effectiveness is to pilot test segments of it and then respond to a series of questions like the following:

1. What should be deleted from the unit?
2. What should be added to the unit?
3. What should be changed in the unit?
4. Were the learning experiences appropriately challenging to gifted students?
5. Did gifted students find the unit of high interest?
6. What evidence exists that gifted students gain proficiency at a higher level in a new area?
7. Were the instructional strategies that were employed to teach the unit effective?
8. Were the materials used in teaching the unit appropriate?
9. What are the strengths of the unit?
10. What are weaknesses of the unit?
11. Will the teacher continue to use the unit with gifted students?

The answers to such questions should lead one to revise, modify, or delete the piloted segments from future curriculum.

Another approach to evaluation of curriculum is to establish the content validity of it through experts in the field of inquiry being taught who are also cognizant of the special characteristics and needs of the gifted. Such questions as the following might be posed:

1. Is the knowledge presented in the curriculum materials fundamental to the discipline under study?
2. Are the materials useful and applicable to the educational environments in which gifted students are found?
3. Do the materials provide for progressive skill development?
4. How well do the units articulate to the next level of curriculum?
5. Are the objectives and activities appropriate for academically talented students?

6. Do the materials contain appropriate scope and sequence models for the specified use?
7. Is there internal, logical consistency within and across the units?
8. Are the objectives of the unit clear and attainable for students, given the activities and readings suggested?
9. Are the units appropriately rich in suggested resources, activities, and readings?

Another use of such a list by curriculum developers and teachers is as a set of criteria for deciding what content topics should be stressed, which process skills should be emphasized, and what product outcomes are most suitable. Still another approach is to set up an evaluation research design that tests the effectiveness of alternate curricula or instructional strategies. In larger school districts the possibility of this approach is feasible and should provide helpful information regarding curriculum decision making over time in respect to gifted education.

Figure 3–5 illustrates a set of curriculum principles that may be used to assess the appropriateness of any given set of curriculum experiences for gifted learners. Therefore, the coordinator of gifted programs or the principal may use the checklist to judge the effectiveness of what has been developed.

## Conclusion

This chapter has presented a seven-stage model for developing curriculum for gifted learners in a school district setting. Issues and questions have been raised related to each stage of the development process, and useful forms, checklists, and other types of guidelines that may be used by the practitioner have been provided. It is important to note that the curriculum development process has relevance to any area of the curriculum in need of work. In that sense, it is a generic model that can be used by administrators to enhance curriculum renewal efforts in general education as well as in gifted education.

### Key Points Summary

- *Curriculum development is an ongoing process that involves the several stages of planning, needs assessment, determining the scope of work, adapting or writing curriculum, field testing, implementation, and evaluation.*
- *Curriculum development efforts require sustained commitment on the part of school personnel and budgetary support for key stages of the process.*
- *The actual writing of special curriculum for the gifted occurs when available materials are judged insufficient or inappropriate for use.*
- *The planning phase of the curriculum development process is the most critical one because it sets the focus and direction for the work that will follow, and it codifies the philosophy of the school district regarding appropriate curriculum experiences for gifted learners.*
- *Adherence to a curriculum development system ensures that a curriculum is dynamic and responsive to the needs of students and sensitive to the realities of the classroom.*
- *Evaluating curriculum at reasonable time intervals allows for feedback to the revision stage of the process.*

**FIGURE 3–5   Checklist of Curriculum Principles for Use in Developing Gifted/Talented Programs**

_____ 1.   *Continuity*   A well-defined set of learning activities that reinforce the specified curriculum objective

_____ 2.   *Appropriateness for gifted learners*   Definition of the curriculum based on assessment of abilities, interests, needs, and learning styles of gifted learners

_____ 3.   *Diversity*   Provisions for alternative means to attain determined ends within a specified curricular framework

_____ 4.   *Integration*   Integrative use of all abilities that include cognition, emotion, and intuition to the curriculum

_____ 5.   *Openness*   Elimination of preset expectations that limit the learnings within the curricular framework

_____ 6.   *Independence*   Provisions for some type(s) of self-directed learnings

_____ 7.   *Substantive learning*   Inclusion of significant subject matter, skills, products, and awareness that are of consequence or of importance to the learner and the discipline

_____ 8.   *Complexity*   Provision for exposure to systems of knowledge, underlying principles and concepts, and key theories about what students study

_____ 9.   *Interdisciplinary learning*   Provisions for transfer of learning to other domains of knowledge, new situations, etc.

_____10.   *Decision making*   Provisions for students to make some appropriate/relevant decisions regarding what is to be learned and how it can be learned

_____11.   *Consistent with good teaching/learning methodologies*   Inclusion of varied teaching practices that allow for motivation, practice, transfer of training, and feedback

_____12.   *Creation/recreation*   Provisions to apply the creative process to improve, modify, etc., one's creations; to challenge prevailing thought and offer more appropriate solutions

_____13.   *Interaction with peers and a variety of significant others*   Provisions to learn about and meet with individuals who share same and different gifts/talents

_____14.   *Value system*   Inclusion of consistent opportunities to develop and examine personal and societal values and to establish a personal value system

_____15.   *Communication skills*   Development of verbal and nonverbal systems and skills to dialogue, share, and exchange ideas

_____16.   *Timing*   Apportionment of time span for learning activities that is consistent with characteristics of gifted learners for shorter/longer allotments

_____17.   *Multiple resources*   Provision for utilization of a variety of material and human resources in the learning process

_____18.   *Accelerated/advanced pacing of content*   Provision of quickness and aptness of gifted students to master new material

_____19.   *Economy*   Compressed and streamlined organization of teaching material to match learning capacity of gifted students

_____20.   *Challenge*   Provision for a sophisticated level of learning experiences that requires learners to stretch for understanding

# *References*

Center for Gifted Education. (1992). *Developing science and language arts for high ability learners: Project materials.* Williamsburg, VA: Author.

Gallagher, J. (1985). *Teaching the gifted child.* Boston: Allyn and Bacon.

Gallagher, J., Weiss, P., Ogleby, K., & Thomas, T. (1982). *Report on the education of the gifted: Survey of education of gifted students.* Chapel Hill: Frank Porter Graham Child Development Center, University of North Carolina at Chapel Hill.

Illinois Office of Education. (1978). *Survey of provisions for gifted children in Illinois.* Springfield, IL: Author.

Keating, D. (1976). *Intellectual talent.* Baltimore, MD: Johns Hopkins University Press.

Passow, H., et al. (1982). *Differentiated curricula for the gifted/talented.* Committee Report to the National/State Leadership Training Institute on the Gifted and Talented. Ventura County, CA: Office of the Superintendent of Schools.

Renzulli, J. (1977). *The enrichment triad.* Wethersfield, CT: Creative Learning Press.

*Richardson study of gifted and talented education.* (1985). Fort Worth, TX: Richardson Foundation.

Richert, S. (1982). *National report on identification, assessment and recommendations for comprehending identification of gifted and talented*

*youth.* Sewell, NJ: Educational Improvement Center-South.

Robinson, A. (1990). Cooperation or exploitation? The argument against cooperative learning for talented students. *Journal for the Education of the Gifted, 14* (1), 9–27.

Rutherford, F., & Ahlgren, A. (1989). *Science for all Americans.* New York: Oxford University Press.

Seeley, K. (1989). Facilitators for gifted learners. In J. Feldhusen, J. VanTassel-Baska, & K. Seeley (Eds.), *Excellence in educating the gifted.* Denver: Love Publishing.

Shane, H. (1981). *Content curriculum for the future.* Paper developed for College Board, New York.

Sternberg, R. J. (1985). *Beyond I.Q.: A triarchic theory of intelligence.* New York: Cambridge University Press.

Taba, H. (1962). *Curriculum development, theory and practice.* New York: Harcourt, Brace, and World.

Tyler, R. (1961). *Principles of curriculum and instruction.* Chicago: University of Chicago Press.

VanTassel-Baska, J. (1979). A needs assessment model for gifted education. *Journal for the Education of the Gifted, 2* (3), 141–148.

VanTassel-Baska, J., Gallagher, S., Bailey, J., & Sher, B. (1992). *Final project report: Developing science curriculum for high-ability learners.* Williamsburg, VA: Center for Gifted Education.

# Curriculum Design Issues in Developing a Curriculum for the Gifted

*JOYCE VanTASSEL-BASKA*

*The proper study of mankind has been said to be man. But . . . in large part the proper study of mankind is the science of design. —HERBERT SIMON*

The last chapter examined the stages of curriculum development through the perspective of necessary administrative actions to be undertaken in moving the curriculum process along in the context of schools. Another perspective is required to implement effective curriculum. To be sure, the design issue is an integral part of the curriculum planning process described in the last chapter as Stage I. Yet it needs to be highlighted separately so that practitioners can understand (1) the total design process and how the pieces of it interrelate; (2) the application of the confluent approach of content, process/product, and concept models to curriculum making; and (3) the development of a comprehensive curriculum for gifted learners.

A curriculum and instructional design model that is useful for these purposes is adapted from Kemp's work (1977), which displays the circular nature of the basic design process (see Figure 4–1). Most practitioners will have encountered this type of design model or one similar to it in an introductory course in curriculum and instruction. It frequently serves as the type of model from which teachers learn how to do lesson plans. VanTassel-Baska (1992) used the model to develop an instructional guide to planning curriculum for the gifted.

**FIGURE 4–1    A Curriculum/Instructional Design Model for Constructing Curriculum for Gifted Learners**

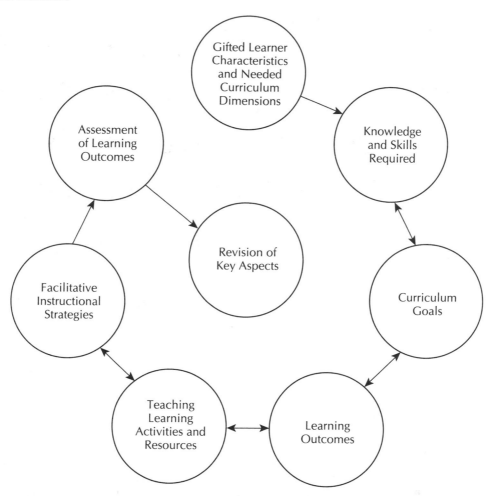

## *Gifted Learner Characteristics: A Prelude to Differentiated Curriculum Dimensions*

The basis for all differentiation in the curriculum for gifted students should emerge from the differences in their characteristics and needs as reflected in formal test data and careful observation of performance behaviors. Fundamentally, the view of differentiation taken in this book is one that emanates from an examination and synthesis of typical characteristics of these learners. Three fundamental differences emerge from the research that distinguish the gifted from more typical learners:

1. The capacity to learn at faster rates (Keating, 1976)
2. The capacity to find, solve, and act on problems more readily (Sternberg, 1985)

**3.** The capacity to manipulate abstract ideas and make connections more readily (Gallagher, 1985)

Thus, a differentiated curriculum should be based on these differences, and simultaneously address all three of them in the learner population if it is to meet their most important albeit diverse needs. The curriculum models presented in Chapter 1 are educational applications of these chracteristics in school settings.

Although individual gifted students may vary considerably in their capacities within these three areas, it is the role of the teacher to intensify or slacken the curriculum experience that has been planned in order to accommodate these individual differences. In the diagnostic-prescriptive approach to instruction, for example, there is clearly a methodology to promote an understanding of these differences and to act on them in instructional planning. In problem-solving contexts, the teacher can manipulate the complexity of the problem set and the instructional grouping pattern to accommodate such differences. And in the conceptual realm, the teacher can modify the extent and nature of the concept to be studied and into what areas it will be explored by all gifted students, thus setting the stage for further work on an individual basis. The important issue to be understood here is: *Not all gifted students are alike in respect to their characteristics or needs. Curriculum planning that proceeds from general behaviors of a gifted population needs to be modified appropriately for specific students at each stage of development.* VanTassel-Baska (1981, 1992) has used assessment profiles of a gifted population as a basis for a differential approach to the provision of program experiences. The more gifted the learner, the more intensive and extensive should be the experiences, both in respect to contact time and required curriculum resources. The needs of special populations like the disadvantaged, underachievers, and the learning disabled will also affect the nature and extent of the curriculum intervention. Thus, individual adaptations need to be considered at this stage of the design process.

## Content, Process/Product, and Concept Dimensions

The dimensions within which we design a curriculum for the gifted are based on the characteristics of these learners. In educational practice, they become the basic models discussed in Chapter 1. However, there is a major question to be addressed at this phase of the design process: How does one decide what are the appropriate content topics, process skills/products, and concepts to be studied by gifted learners at any given stage of development? This question needs to be explored according to a set of guided questions for each of the dimensions that practitioners may focus on in their work.

### Content

The content dimension determines the particular domain of inquiry to be explored and the aspects of that domain to be addressed. It may delineate the breadth and depth of the curriculum experience. For example, the narrower a content topic, the more likely the student will be able to study it intensively, given a reasonable period of time, as opposed to a broader topic that would require extensive study. Content topics need to be selected according to the following criteria:

**1.** *Is the content topic important and worthy of the time to be expended on it?* For example, spending six weeks studying designer jeans or the history of teddy bears (two topics actually explored in gifted programs) would be judged less important than topics such as consumer economics or political opportunities in the nineteenth century.

**2.** *Is the content topic conceptually complex enough to render it meaningful for gifted students?* Gifted students enjoy exploring a topical area, examining it from various perspectives. The topic choice has to be conceptually interesting and complex enough to hold up under intense investigation. Thus, the study of magnetism could offer more to the gifted than the study of horseshoes.

**3.** *Is the content topic relevant to how the world works?* The study of law or a language, it could be argued, is more appropriate for the gifted to study than movie stars of the 1940s since the more general areas of study could provide the gifted with insights into societal systems rather than transitory cultural fads.

**4.** *Is the content topic likely to be of interest to students?* Although student interest can be gauged formally before curriculum is constructed, it also frequently can be assessed more informally as topics are being considered. What is "likely to be of interest" may be more important than demonstrated interest since interest tends to follow exposure to particular types of experiences. Content topics to be chosen should not deliberately narrow a student's vision of knowledge areas available to be explored.

**5.** *Is the content topic one that could be taught effectively by the designated instructor?* This constitutes a key question in considering choices of content topics. A teacher must feel comfortable with what is being taught and be well trained in it. Teachers who do not know a content topic have a great deal of difficulty being creative with that topic. Thus, gifted students lose out at the instructional level if the content topic(s) chosen is not well matched to instructor background. Teachers are unable to answer student questions in any depth or lead them to higher levels of understanding when their own understanding is superficial. Too often students of high ability know more about content areas than their teachers, and are in the awkward position of correcting misinformation the teacher has given the class.

## Process Skills

Fundamental to our conceptualization of appropriate curriculum for the gifted is the focus on higher-level thinking skills that allow such students to learn to think independently of textbooks, materials, and other resources. We also want them to transfer these skills readily from one curriculum area to another and from one dimension (such as academic) to another dimension (such as their personal lives). Thus, the curriculum for the gifted needs to be infused and suffused with these lifelong skills. Ideally, those skills that include critical and creative thinking, problem finding and problem solving, and evaluation should be addressed across the K–12 years of schooling. This need, of course, raises the issue of how to organize these skills to ensure maximum internalization and transfer effect. Transfer is more likely to occur if the process skills are:

**1.** Well defined
**2.** Consistently addressed over time
**3.** Taught both within basic content domains as well as intensively as a separate instructional set

4. Organized by scope and sequence from K–12
5. Modeled by the teacher in the classroom
6. Employed as questioning techniques by the teacher

These higher-level thinking skills also can be taught better if they are viewed as abilities that aid in reasoning—the overall process of thinking.

## Product Alternatives

Both as a tool for evaluation of student synthesis capacities and as a core activity in the curriculum, the selection of projects for students to undertake individually and collectively is important. There is a key set of questions that should be considered when making educational decisions regarding the role of products in a curriculum for the gifted:

1. How and when should independent investigations be undertaken?
2. Should a group of gifted learners create the same type of product under certain circumstances (e.g., an essay written on the same topic)?
3. How should the selection of projects occur? Should teachers generate a list of alternatives for students to choose from or should students work on any project of interest to them?
4. What generative learning processes are important to teach through the product development process?
5. What new knowledge and at what level is it important for students to gain as a result of the work on a given project?
6. How can time allocations both in school and out of school be best utilized for optimal project work?

Thus the product dimension of curriculum deserves serious consideration as it interacts with process and content.

## Issues, Themes, and Concepts

Central to any vision of comprehensive curriculum for the gifted is the focus on the ideas that have guided the development of civilization as we know it. These large concepts, issues, and themes are those that dominate all areas of knowledge exploration, yet may have specific connotations within a given discipline of thought. So, the task of educators of the gifted is to seek out those ideas that can be best utilized with gifted learners at various stages of development both within and across traditional fields of inquiry. There are at least two ways that this might be accomplished:

### Procedure A

1. Decide initially on a set of important ideas to explore, such as "change," "war," "justice," "honor," "rights," "freedom," and so on.
2. Delineate generalizations that provide the central propositions around those ideas that students should learn.
3. Choose resources and materials that will facilitate the teaching and learning of these propositions.

**EXAMPLE:   Concept: Justice**

*Central Propositions*

1. Law is the codified form of justice used by civilized societies.
2. In order for justice to thrive, laws must be interpreted by humans who understand situations and the human condition.
3. One person's justice is another person's punishment.
4. Human behavior has tended to vacillate between practice of the Golden Rule and aggressive territoriality.
5. Justice begins with basic respect for the rights of all persons.

*Resources and Materials*

Film: *Twelve Angry Men*
History of case law
William Golding's *Lord of the Flies*
Harper Lee's *To Kill a Mockingbird*
Visit to local courtroom
Lawyer or judge as a guest speaker

### Procedure B

1. Take existing content topics and generate a list of ideas found within them.
2. Decide what aspects of the ideas should be explored.
3. Choose supplementary materials to explore the concept more fully.

**EXAMPLE:   Content Topic: Glaciers (Seventh-Grade Science Textbook)**

*Glaciers*

1. Move backward or forward over the span of time
2. Leave their imprint on the earth's landscape
3. Form in snow fields above the snow line in mountains and move because of gravity

*Generic Ideas To Be Studied Further*

1. Changes in the earth's surface over time
2. How climate affects the environment
3. How the study of natural conditions today can solve mysteries of the past
4. Provide evidence of past Ice Age activity and presage such future activity

*Types of Materials*

1. Books on geology, archaeology, ages of man
2. Books on "change" as a concept
3. Films that depict life under different climatic conditions

Both of these procedures are useful in deciding on important concepts to include in a curriculum for the gifted. It may be helpful to illustrate the transformation of these curriculum dimensions of content, process/product, and concept into a curriculum whole that integrates these four aspects for a differentiated curriculum (see Figure 4–2).

As we examine these curriculum dimensions, we can see the way in which each dimension fits with another to achieve curriculum balance. It is important to note that in this view of the curriculum dimensions, there is equal weighting of each. Big ideas are not valued more than content topics nor are projects a dominating force over the process skills they hope to instill. Rather, there is a comfortable blend of these major components within a curriculum for the gifted.

## Knowledge and Skills

How do we go about determining what gifted students should know and be able to do at a given stage of development? We have determined rather imprecisely what typical learners should know at key levels of development. In what skill areas should gifted students show proficiency as the result of schooling? At what level of proficiency? These questions are basic to our understanding of how the fundamental process of curriculum design works. In order for teachers to plan classroom experiences effectively, they must have a guide to help them formulate appropriate knowledge areas and skills to be acquired in the context of a gifted program. This means that they must be able to answer the following questions:

1. What are the knowledge and skill requirements for typical learners in my school district at each stage of development?
2. What are the desired knowledge and skill areas for the gifted that are different from these at each stage of development?
3. What is the relationship between the district requirements and the needs of the gifted?

**FIGURE 4–2   Curriculum Dimensions**

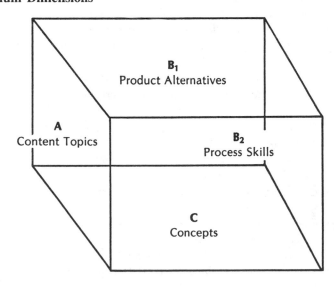

Since what constitutes local school district curriculum can be categorized as knowledge or skills, it may be useful to take an example from a state assessment model to illustrate this issue. By the end of third grade, students in Illinois are expected to possess the following knowledge skills in the area of mathematical methods:

1. Ability to read, write, and name numbers in several different ways
2. Ability to perform operations with numbers with and without a calculator
3. Application of computational and problem-solving skills to common life situations with or without calculators
4. Measurement in various contexts using appropriate units
5. Estimation of measurements
6. Simple geometric figures and patterns of relationships in two and three dimensions

From the vantage point of gifted learners, these knowledge-skill areas should be addressed at the K–3 level:

1. Counting, calculator, and estimation skills
2. Knowledge of simple probability
3. Knowledge of transformational geometry
4. Basic reasoning and inference skills
5. Knowledge of spatial dimensions
6. Algebraic manipulation skills
7. Basic problem-solving skills
8. Knowledge of modeling techniques

The relationship between the two sets of lists can be described in the following way:

- *The state list is more precise, concrete, and specific.*
- *The state list is simpler for gifted students to master.*
- *The state list is limited to work in general arithmetic.*
- *The state list requires less time to master.*
- *By itself, the state list is inappropriate for gifted learners in mathematics.*

However, these two sets of required knowledge-skill areas in mathematics at the primary level can be fused to create a powerful knowledge-skill set for the gifted learner:

- *Counting, calculation, and estimation skills*
- *Ability to perform basic computations*
- *Application of basic problem-solving skills to real life*
- *Knowledge of simple probability*
- *Knowledge of transformational geometry: three-dimensional patterns and figures in space*
- *Basic reasoning and inference skills*
- *Algebraic manipulation skills*
- *Knowledge of modeling techniques*
- *Ability to use the computer as a tool in problem solving*

This technique of curriculum alignment is essential to apply as one works out this aspect of the curriculum design so that the regular school curriculum is not abandoned nor viewed as totally inappropriate. Such alignment also forces the practitioner to be very precise about what is needed for each type of learner at a given stage of development, as well as what the curriculum overlaps are for both types of learners (see Figure 4–3).

## Goals and Objectives: Formulating Student Outcomes

These cells of the curriculum design determine the overall purpose for specific activities undertaken with gifted learners. The outcomes also represent an important specification for purposes of assessment at the student level. They usually answer the question: What do you want gifted students to have gained from their curriculum experiences? This question needs to be posed against the backdrop of what the regular school curriculum is not providing. As one views this aspect of the design, it is important to keep in mind the cell of learner characteristics and curriculum dimensions so that the formulation of student outcomes is appropriate for gifted learners. It is also useful to understand the shifts in specificity from generating a curriculum goal to a general objective to a student outcome that can be measured. The example provided in Table 4–1 illustrates this relationship.

The development of goals and objectives appropriate for gifted learners is a critical feature in curriculum design. It is at this stage of the conceptualization process that practitioners are forced to choose what will be emphasized in the curriculum and the reasonable performance level for gifted students in that area. Obviously, goals and objectives need to be generated for all aspects of the program and for all curriculum areas where gifted students will be served.

## Activities and Resources

The fourth cell in the curriculum design model focuses on the curriculum experiences that are provided at the classroom level. What activities and materials are selected by the

**FIGURE 4–3  Curriculum Alignment Model**

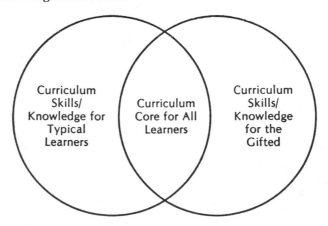

Curriculum Skills/ Knowledge for Typical Learners

Curriculum Core for All Learners

Curriculum Skills/ Knowledge for the Gifted

**TABLE 4–1   Goals and Corresponding Objectives**

| Examples: Curriculum Goal | Desired Student Outcomes: General Objectives | Student Outcome Translation | |
|---|---|---|---|
| *Model A* | To attain mastery in all areas of learning at a readiness stage of development and at a rate commensurate with capacity | To attain mastery of algebra at a readiness stage of development and at a rate commensurate with capacity | Based on a diagnostic test for placement, gifted students will achieve 90% mastery of algebra topics as assessed by the Cooperative Algebra Test in half the time allotted to average learners |
| *Model B* | To develop the higher-level thinking skills | To develop high-level inquiry skills (i.e., accurate observation, analysis, and interpretation of data, problem-finding strategies and defining capacities, etc.) | Gifted students will perform at an average of 4.0 on a 5.0-point teacher checklist designed to measure the application of inquiry skills |
| *Model C* | To develop the ability to integrate ideas across domains of inquiry | To synthesize ideas about "time" from multiple sources | Gifted students will create a product (i.e., an essay, a slide tape, a musical composition, a painting) that is judged excellent to superior by a panel of "experts" |

teacher to carry out the stated learning outcomes? What criteria might be applied to enhance appropriate choices? A good balance of types of activities should be used with gifted learners: independent, interactive whole group, and interactive small group. Other important criteria for activities and materials include:

1. Activities should be rich and complex enough to serve more than one instructional purpose.
2. Activities should be organized in clusters to build toward the fulfillment of a learning objective.
3. Whole-class activities should be motivational to encourage small group and independent learning.
4. Activities should not be textbook bound.
5. Multiple resources should be available.
6. Print, nonprint, and human resources should be effectively used.
7. Materials resources should be chosen for their congruence with gifted learner objectives.

## *Analysis of an Activity*

For many teachers, the approach to curriculum design that works best is an inductive model beginning with an activity and building from it to the more abstract issues of content, process, product, concept, strategy, objective, and purpose. Therefore, the following example has been included to show how this approach can work in thinking through the curriculum design process.

**EXAMPLE: Activity: The Holmes Case***

Holmes was a seaman on the *William Brown,* which set sail from Liverpool to Philadelphia in 1841. The ship struck an iceberg some 250 miles from Newfoundland and soon began to sink. Two boats were lowered. The captain, various members of the crew, and a passenger got into one of them and, after six days on the open sea, were picked up and brought to land. The other boat was called the "long-boat"; it was leaky and might easily be swamped. Into it Holmes jumped along with the first mate, seven other seaman, and thirty-two passengers, about twice as many as the boat could hold under the most favorable conditions of wind and weather. Just as the long-boat was about to pull away from the wreck, Holmes, hearing the agonized cries of a mother for her little daughter who had been left behind in the panic, dashed back at the risk of instant death, found the girl and carried her under his arm into the long-boat. The sailors rowed and the passengers bailed, but the over-weighted long-boat, drifting between blocks of floating ice, sank lower and lower as a steady rain fell on the sea. The wind began to freshen, the sea grew heavy, and waves splashed over the bow. Then, after the first mate had twice given the order, Holmes and the rest of the crew began to throw the male passengers overboard. Two married men and a little boy were spared, but the fourteen remaining male passengers were cast over, and two women—devoted sisters of one of the victims—voluntarily leaped to join their brother in his death. The long-boat sailed afloat. The next morning Holmes spied a sail in the distance, exerted himself heroically to attract notice of the passing vessel, and eventually brought about the rescue of everyone left in the boat.

When the survivors arrived in Philadelphia, the mate and most of the seamen, hearing talk of prosecution, disappeared. Holmes was put on trial for manslaughter.

In his charge to the jury as to the law, the judge stated that passengers must be saved in preference to all seamen except those who are indispensable to operating the boat. If no seaman can possibly be dispensed with, then the victims must be chosen from among the passengers by casting lots, provided—as in this case—there is time enough to do so.

**Question:** If you were to use this case in your teaching of the gifted, what *content topics* might you wish to explore?

*Sample response*

- *Maritime law (comparable disaster cases)*
- *Development of law in a society (case law)*
- *Navy—ships, navigation, historical background*
- *English society*
- *Comparative legal systems (moral dilemmas)*
- *Travel routes (geography, oceanography)*
- *Law vs. lawless*

*This activity is included in the social science chapter as an appropriate activity for gifted learners in grades 4–6. Source of case is unknown.

**Question:**   If you were to use this case in your teaching of the gifted, what *process skills would you focus on?*

*Sample response*

- *Decision-making skills*
- *Analysis skills*
- *Evaluation skills*
- *Generalization skills*

**Question:**   If you were to use this case in your teaching of the gifted, what *issues, themes, or concepts* would you explore?

*Sample response*

- *Justice (right vs. wrong)*
- *Spirit of law vs. letter of law*
- *Comparative perspectives on law*
- *Conflict and change*
- *The issue of the individual vs. society*
- *Value of human life*
- *Authority*
- *Moral integrity*
- *Probability and chance*

**Question:**   If you used this activity, what product *alternatives* would you suggest for students?

*Sample response*

- *Debates*
- *Mock trials*
- *Theme papers*
- *Creative writing pieces (poetry, drama, etc.)*
- *Reenactment (videotape)*
- *Role-playing simulation*

**Question:**   If you used this activity, what *instructional purposes* would it serve?

*Sample response*

- *To recognize multiple points of view on a given issue*
- *To promote the development of decision-making skills*
- *To establish the relevance of the past to the present and the future*
- *To explore moral and ethical issues at a personal level*
- *To demonstrate the relevance of law to the individual*
- *To gain an understanding of legal procedures*
- *To promote multiple thinking skills (analysis, synthesis, evaluation)*
- *To understand the historical context for individual cases*

**Question:** If you were to use this activity, what *instructional strategies* would you employ to teach it?

*Sample response*
- *Inquiry-based discussion*
- *Speakers/field trips*
- *Media*
- *Simulations*
- *Directed teaching (lecture)*
- *Small-group problem solving*
- *Individual/independent learning*

At this stage, teachers could generate other activities and resources that would contribute to the curriculum dimensions already conceptualized. Inductively, they have already developed the framework for a unit of study in law.

## Facilitative Instructional Approaches

One can build great curriculum designs and structure meaningful clusters of activities that have relevant content, process, and concept outcomes specified that will still be totally ineffective with gifted learners. Why? Because the piece of the puzzle that is still missing is the instructional glue—the processes and strategies employed by a good teacher to make the curriculum come alive and work in the classroom setting. What are these approaches that work? Research has demonstrated that many strategies are successful with gifted students, so the issue is not *which* strategy but rather what combination of strategies can be employed and under what circumstances for maximum effectiveness? Nevertheless, the following list of instructional processes has been adapted from the Martinson-Weiner Scale of Teacher Behaviors (1974) to provide a universe of successful approaches to facilitating curriculum experiences for gifted learners:

1. Conduct group discussions.
2. Select questions that stimulate higher-level thinking.
3. Use varied teaching strategies effectively.
4. Utilize critical thinking skills in appropriate contexts.
5. Encourage independent thinking and open inquiry.
6. Understand and encourage student ideas and student-directed work.
7. Demonstrate understanding of the educational implications of giftedness.
8. Utilize creative thinking techniques.
9. Utilize problem-solving techniques.
10. Synthesize student assessment data and curriculum content effectively.

In regular classroom settings where all students are served heterogeneously, special attention must be given to:

> • *Providing opportunities for access to advanced work and resources*
> • *Assessing Instructional levels of learning and teaching to a level of challenge*
> • *Pacing instruction at a rate that accommodates able learners*
> • *Teaching to varying learning styles and modalities*

## Assessment: Measuring Student Outcomes

This aspect of the curriculum design wheel is concerned with what happened to the learner as a result of a planned set of curriculum experiences. Did the learner grow in the dimensions anticipated? Did the learner grow to the extent hoped for? Did the learner grow in unanticipated ways? All of these questions are important ones to answer through the assessment process. Equally important from a curriculum perspective, however, are the questions related to curriculum implementation. Was the intended curriculum implemented as it was planned? To what extent were the instructional processes used by the teacher facilitative of student learning?

In the design process, it is anticipated that describing the assessment to be employed will be difficult. And with gifted learners, the task is even more problematic because standardized achievement measures cannot be readily used with that population, and appropriate criterion levels have to be approximated based on good judgment rather than on the typical standard of "nine month's growth in the area based on nine months in school."

Reasonable approaches to assessing the growth of gifted students who have been engaged in a specialized curriculum can be found, however. Kulieke (1986a) has conceptualized a model of alternative evaluation approaches to consider in deciding on student assessment techniques (see Table 4–2).

Generally, there are some important questions to ask in deciding on an assessment model:

**1.** *How often should students be assessed?* Clearly, growth in some dimensions takes longer than it does in others. Therefore, timing of the assessment is critical to showing learning gains. Some assessment of objectives could occur four times a year; other assessments might occur only once in a three-year period. The nature of the learning task should determine the timing of the assessments. The more complex the task, the longer the period prior to assessment.

**2.** *On what dimensions of learning should students be assessed?* Many times content-based learning becomes the only dimension to be measured among gifted students. Although it may be easier to show positive change in learning in these areas, it is important to assess what learning is occurring at other levels and in other dimensions.

**3.** *Who should be involved in the assessment?* The teacher in the classroom is in the best position to handle the details of assessment, but sometimes it is advantageous to use outside experts in a given field. Students should also have input into the assessment process through self-evaluation inventories and some form of "peer review" in certain areas of the curriculum. Whereas the teacher may develop some aspects of student assessment, it is useful to rely on a mix of measures that include standardized tests, inventories, and observational checklists that can be utilized by process observers at different points in time, and product assessment.

**TABLE 4–2  A Critique of Evaluation Approaches and Level of Experimental Designs***

| | Level 1 "Pre-experimental": One Group Examined at One Point in Time | Level 2 "Time Series": One Group Examined at Two or More Points in Time | Level 3 "Quasiexperimental": Two Nonequivalent Groups Examined at One Point in Time | Level 4 "Quasiexperimental Time Series": Two Nonequivalent Groups Examined at Two Points in Time | Level 5 "Experimental": Two Equivalent Groups Examined at One or More Points in Time |
|---|---|---|---|---|---|
| *Proficiency Based* Example: 90% of students have achieved 90% competency of a final test. | | | | | |
| How well can you attribute proficiency to the program? | Poorly | Somewhat poorly | Somewhat poorly | Somewhat well | Well |
| How well have you assessed program effects? | Poorly | Somewhat poorly | Somewhat poorly | Somewhat well | Well |
| *Product Based* Example: 100% of students have completed a final report with a grade of B or above. | | | | | |
| How well can you attribute the final report to the program? | Well | Well | Well | Well | Well |
| How well have you assessed program effects? | Somewhat poorly | Somewhat well | Somewhat well | Well | Well |

*(continued)*

**TABLE 4-2** (continued)

| | Level 1 "Pre-experimental": One Group Examined at One Point in Time | Level 2 "Time Series": One Group Examined at Two or More Points in Time | Level 3 "Quasiexperimental": Two Nonequivalent Groups Examined at One Point in Time | Level 4 "Quasiexperimental Time Series": Two Nonequivalent Groups Examined at Two Points in Time | Level 5 "Experimental": Two Equivalent Groups Examined at One or More Points in Time |
|---|---|---|---|---|---|
| *Attitudinal Based* Example: Students have a greater interest in the subject matter being taught. | | | | | |
| How well can you attribute the final report to the program? | Poorly | Somewhat poorly | Somewhat poorly | Somewhat well | Well |
| How well have you assessed program effects? | Poorly | Somewhat poorly | Somewhat poorly | Somewhat well | Well |

*From M. Kulieke, *An Evaluation Handbook for Evaluating Gifted Program Impacts* (Evanston, Ill.: Northwestern University, Center for Talent Development, 1986). Reprinted with permission.

**4.** *What are reasonable student growth expectations in a gifted curriculum?* Obviously, this answer depends heavily on the specific objectives of a given program. But it may be useful to delineate a standard for gifted programs compared to regular education programs. For example, consider the following:

| *If You Would Expect Regular Learners to Attain:* | *You Would Expect Gifted Learners to Attain:* |
|---|---|
| • Nine months' growth in nine months | • Fourteen months' growth in nine months |
| • Achieve 3 out of 5 on a product assessment scale | • Achieve 4 out of 5 on a product assessment scale |
| • Produce written essays at an acceptable level | • Produce written essays at a superior level |
| • Demonstrate minimum levels of leadership skills | • Demonstrate maximum levels of leadership skills |
| • Read 5 outside books a year | • Read 10 outside books a year |
| • Master language usage at a 70 percent level | • Demonstrate knowledge of grammar and usage through writing at a proficient level mechanically |

The issue is to decide on *what is appropriate* based on norms for average learners. Should the gifted be expected to do more as well as do it better? Or should they be judged according to an entirely different standard—one that gives them credit for being high achievers in a general context, and therefore does not shift its stringency pattern based on the population? For example, the general criterion for passing a course of study is 70 percent correct on a given test measure. Let's say that a special course is available to the gifted in statistics, and the teacher tells the gifted class that the expectation for success will be achieving 70 percent or above on a specially designed test in statistics. Is this an inappropriate evaluation standard for gifted students? In a sense, what we are faced with is a value question. Are there educational experiences, such as learning advanced content, where "passing" would be considered an appropriately high standard for the gifted? Conversely, are some standards too high, such as requiring 95 percent proficiency before moving on to new material? These issues are crucial to consider in determining criterion levels for success in gifted curriculum.

## Grading as a Manifestation of Student Assessment

Many teachers of the gifted agonize over the issues of grading gifted students on their work in special programs. In fact, individual assessment is done infrequently in elementary pull-out programs. It is difficult to argue against grading gifted students on their work as well as work habits. They benefit from clearly knowing their strengths and weaknesses. To deny them this opportunity seems to be a mistake. By the same token, the program administrator needs to know how groups of learners have performed in order to assess the effectiveness of the curriculum plan. Thus, grading serves an individual and a systems function in an educational setting.

Should grades be weighted for the gifted? This too is a value question related to the earlier one—should 70 percent be considered a grade of A? A clear set of expectations for gifted learners should pervade the curriculum design constructed by practitioners. This set of expectations can then be converted to whatever form of measurement is desired in a given setting. Using the student outcomes from earlier in this chapter, Table 4–3 provides an example of assessment expectations.

In each of these cases, traditional student grading was done that was tied directly to the assessment measures used. Yet different interpretations or values were placed on differing attainment levels for each outcome. In algebra, students were encouraged to drop the course if success was not at an 80 percent tested level; in inquiry skills training, a low rating resulted in remedial action in the skill area; and in the conceptual product assessment, a low grade resulted in the student being required to redo the product. Not only is it difficult to identify clear standards for success but it is equally difficult to define and address the problem of failure in gifted classrooms.

A set of guidelines may be helpful to consider at the assessment stage:

1.  Recognize the importance of evaluating student performance in gifted programs.
2.  Identify acceptable approaches to assessment based on the curriculum model being used.
3.  Set criterion levels for success that consider alternatives to normal distribution scales and yet are sensitive to standards in similar contexts for typical learners.
4.  Establish clear standards for performance at the beginning of a curriculum unit. Be as specific as possible.
5.  Use weighted grades or a restricted grading range to provide incentives for gifted learners to elect advanced curriculum at the secondary level.
6.  Consider placement out of curriculum experiences on an individual basis based on meeting performance expectations at a given time.

**TABLE 4–3   Measurement of Expectations**

| Outcome | Assessment Expectations |
|---|---|
| #1 (related to taking algebra) | To receive an A in algebra, gifted students will achieve a 90% score on the Coop Algebra Test by January of the year they take it. To receive a B, gifted students will achieve an 80% score on the Coop Test by May of the year they take it. Any expectation on the part of the teacher that a gifted student would perform below these levels would lead to another educational placement. |
| #2 (related to gaining inquiry skills) | The grading range for this aspect of the program is as follows: 4–5 rating = A, 3 rating = B, 2–1 rating = remedial action. |
| #3 (related to synthesizing ideas in a project) | Excellent/superior ratings = A<br>Good ratings = B<br>Fair ratings = C<br>Poor Ratings = Project or paper to be redone for credit |

## Monitoring as an Assessment Strategy

It is as important to focus on the degree of appropriate implementation that has occurred with a given curriculum unit or course of study as it is to focus only on the student's learning level. Certainly, there are times that learning is impeded because instructional time has not been adequately used or the emphasis of instruction was faulty or the processes of instruction were ineffectual. Gauging the extent of the implementation of a curriculum can best be done by a building principal, using assessment tools in the observation of classrooms on a regular schedule. One tool is a simple chart that records what was observed, its purpose, and the relationship of it to the overall curriculum objectives. The other assessment tool has been adapted by Kulieke (1986b) from the Martinson-Weiner Scale for Rating Teacher Behaviors. It provides a way to monitor the extent to which varied instructional processes are used and how effectively teachers are interacting with gifted learners (see Figure 4–4).

# Conclusion

This chapter has explored the key elements of curriculum design, including learner characteristics and curriculum dimensions, knowledge/skills areas, outcomes, activities, and resources; facilitative instructional strategies; and assessment. It has provided approaches to differentiate each aspect appropriately for gifted learners. The chapter has also included sample instruments, curriculum, and various models that may aid the practitioner in implementing the curriculum design process.

### Key Points Summary

- *Curriculum design elements include learner characteristics and curriculum dimensions, knowledge/skills areas, goals, outcomes, activities, and resources; instructional delivery; and assessment.*
- *Curriculum design elements that need particular attention in gifted programs are (1) goals and student outcomes because they establish the direction for the curriculum emphasis and (2) assessment because it allows us to ascertain effects of special curriculum intervention.*
- *Developing a comprehensive curriculum means having an articulated curriculum design in all major domains of study at all stages of the development of the learner.*
- *The steps in constructing a curriculum can be carried out from the level of outcomes to the most specific level of activities, or it can be constructed in the reverse, from the specific activities to the outcomes.*
- *The integration of the basic curriculum models/dimensions can be achieved at the goal, outcomes, and activity levels of the curriculum.*
- *Curriculum alignment at the knowledge and skills level of the curriculum is an important process in integrating the general school curriculum into one appropriate for gifted learners.*
- *Assessment of student growth and progress in a special curriculum is essential to the individual student and to the program.*
- *Monitoring the implementation of curriculum and instruction for the gifted is vital to any learning plan.*

## FIGURE 4–4    Observation Form for Use with Teachers of the Gifted*

Directions:

Taking into account the content of this class, how proficient do you feel the teacher is at using each of the following teaching strategies? It is recommended that teachers be observed for *two* 30-minute periods before and after relevant in-service work, using this form as guide.

| | Excellent | Good | Fair | Poor | Very Poor |
|---|---|---|---|---|---|
| **Conducts Group Discussions** | | | | | |
| Teacher withholds own ideas and conclusions. | 5 | 4 | 3 | 2 | 1 |
| Teacher encourages participation of students in discussions. | 5 | 4 | 3 | 2 | 1 |
| Teacher poses interpretive questions for students. | 5 | 4 | 3 | 2 | 1 |
| **Selects Questions That Stimulate Higher-Level Thinking** | | | | | |
| Students evaluate situations, problems, issues. | 5 | 4 | 3 | 2 | 1 |
| Students ask analytic questions. | 5 | 4 | 3 | 2 | 1 |
| Students generalize from concrete to abstract at advanced levels. | 5 | 4 | 3 | 2 | 1 |
| **Uses Varied Teaching Strategies Effectively** | | | | | |
| Teacher is sensitive to students' responses. | 5 | 4 | 3 | 2 | 1 |
| Teacher maintains a balance between active and passive activities. | 5 | 4 | 3 | 2 | 1 |
| Teacher deliberately shifts teaching strategies with students. | 5 | 4 | 3 | 2 | 1 |
| **Utilizes Critical Thinking Skills in Appropriate Contexts** | | | | | |
| Teacher utilizes inductive and deductive reasoning and is able to apply techniques in classroom. | 5 | 4 | 3 | 2 | 1 |
| Teacher encourages student development of inference and evaluation of argument skills. | 5 | 4 | 3 | 2 | 1 |
| Teacher encourages analogical thinking. | 5 | 4 | 3 | 2 | 1 |
| **Encourages Independent Thinking and Open Inquiry** | | | | | |
| Students compare and contrast different issues, using objective evidence. | 5 | 4 | 3 | 2 | 1 |
| Students engage in lively debate of controversial issues. | 5 | 4 | 3 | 2 | 1 |
| Students and teacher reflect an open/challenging attitude toward knowledge. | 5 | 4 | 3 | 2 | 1 |
| **Understands and Encourages Student Ideas and Student-Directed work** | | | | | |
| Teacher encourages students to try new approaches. | 5 | 4 | 3 | 2 | 1 |
| Teacher is tolerant to students' attempts to find solutions to problems. | 5 | 4 | 3 | 2 | 1 |
| Teacher encourages "guesses" by students and facilitates evaluation of guesses by students. | 5 | 4 | 3 | 2 | 1 |
| Teacher helps students to realize that research involves trial and error. | 5 | 4 | 3 | 2 | 1 |

**Demonstrates Understanding of the Educational Implications of Giftedness**

| | | | | | |
|---|---|---|---|---|---|
| Teacher uses implications of characteristics in the classroom operation, selection of materials, schedules, and questions. | 5 | 4 | 3 | 2 | 1 |
| Teacher uses management procedures that maximize individual differences of students in the learning process. | 5 | 4 | 3 | 2 | 1 |
| Teacher uses advanced organizers for instruction and organizes curriculum around the highest level skill, concept, or idea that a group of gifted learners can master. | 5 | 4 | 3 | 2 | 1 |

*Adapted from *Martinson-Weiner Rating Scale of Behaviors in Teachers of the Gifted* (Martinson, 1976).

## *References*

Gallagher, J. J. (1985). *Teaching the gifted child.* Boston: Allyn and Bacon.

Keating, D. (1987). *Intellectual talent.* Baltimore, MD: Johns Hopkins University Press.

Kemp, J. E. (1977). *Instructional design.* Belmont, CA: Fearson, Pitnam.

Kulieke, M. (1986a). *An evaluation handbook for evaluating gifted program impacts.* Evanston, IL: Northwestern University, Center for Talent Development.

Kulieke, M. (1986b). The role of evaluation in in-service and staff development for educators of the gifted. *Gifted Child Quarterly, 30,* (3), 140–144.

Martinson, R. (1974). Martinson-Weiner Rating Scale of Behaviors in Teachers of the Gifted in *A guide toward better teaching for the gifted.* Ventura, CA: Ventura County Superintendent of Schools Office.

Sternberg, R. (1985). *Beyond IQ.* Cambridge: Cambridge University Press.

VanTassel-Baska, J. (1981). *An administrator's handbook on developing programs for the gifted and talented.* Washington, DC: National Association of State Boards of Education.

VanTassel-Baska, J. (1992). *Effective curriculum planning for gifted learners.* Denver: Love Publishing.

# Developing Scope and Sequence

## JOYCE VanTASSEL-BASKA

*He builded better than he knew:*
*The conscious store to beauty grew.*
*—RALPH WALDO EMERSON*

Prior chapters have set the stage for both curriculum development and curriculum design work to begin. In this chapter, ideas about organizing the "macro" or big picture of curriculum will be shared. This aspect of curriculum development is crucial to ensuring coherence across the curriculum as well as within it. Thus, meaningful articulation of curriculum experiences in K–12 need to be captured at this stage of curriculum development. What should be the organizational pattern of experiences for high-ability learners across the span of years they are in school? How can we concisely describe the nature of these experiences? The answers to these questions are found in the curriculum planning effort of developing scope and sequence.

The organization of a curriculum for high-ability learners across the grades is an essential aspect of the work of curriculum development, yet few guidelines exist in the literature surrounding such work. Taba (1962) spoke to the importance of organizing the dimension of learning experiences as well as content topics in delineating a sequence of curriculum for all learners. Smith, Stanley, and Shore (1957) treated the issue as one of essentially grade placement with little attention to ideas about learner needs. Tyler (1949) viewed scope and sequence as two of the most vital questions one might ask about the curriculum experience: how broadly we define a set of learning experiences and how we order them. Bloom (1958) saw the framing of the curriculum according to key principles and concepts to be an important exercise but was less concerned with the ordering process, believing that the learner reorganizes experiences according to a personal schema. Recent emphasis on curriculum frameworks and standards of learning has tended to displace the language terms of "scope and sequence" while still retaining the central meaning. Within gifted education, only Maker (1982, 1986) and VanTassel-Baska (1988, 1992a, 1992b) have expressed the importance of considering issues of scope and sequence in a curriculum for gifted learners as integral to the curriculum development process. This chapter addresses important issues and approaches to both thinking about and creating a scope and sequence of learning for high-ability students, particularly within the core domains of learning.

*Scope* usually refers to how expansive a curriculum can be at a given level. Modification needs to occur when curriculum for high-ability learners is being conceptualized because these students can absorb a larger amount of material and ideas than can typical learners in the same period of time and stage of development. Thus, what would constitute scope for average learners for a two-year period in a given content dimension could easily be modified for gifted learners into a one-year continuum. For example:

|  | *7th Grade* | *8th Grade* |
|---|---|---|
| Typical learners | Pre-Algebra | Algebra I |
| Gifted learners | Pre-Algebra | Algebra II |
|  | Algebra I | College Algebra (III) |

*Sequence* generally refers to the order in which content topics, concepts, and skills are placed in the curriculum over a span of years. Implicit in most sequential work in school is the notion of a spiraling curriculum based on reinforcement and skill building from year to year and at subsequent levels.

In practice, however, the notion of sequence often deteriorates into simple repetition of large segments of a curriculum area. This situation creates an acute problem for gifted students who retain information over time, and who do (or have the capability to) master subject matter completely on first exposure. Thus, establishing sequential curriculum appropriate for the gifted learner implies attention to the following:

**1.** *Limited review of prior material learned.* In most curriculum situations, gifted learners do not need more than two weeks of review at the beginning of a given year. The nature of the review itself is also critical. Key ideas and concepts should be the organizing principle for review work with the gifted, not the small incremental approach so favored by traditional textbooks.

**2.** *Progressive development in skill acquisition.* Once gifted students have learned the fundamentals in any field of inquiry, it is important that they be allowed to progress at their own rate of mastery rather than be held back by other students or preconceived teacher plans for the rate of "conveying the material." Reading and mathematics curricula are frequently problems in this respect. Students are artifically kept at grade level rather than being allowed to progress more rapidly through the curriculum. There is much higher-order skill development work that could be done with these students but it is rarely attempted. For example, the gifted need work in reading comprehension, analysis and interpretation, inference, and evaluation, all higher-order skills that could appropriately be addressed once fundamental reading ability is demonstrated.

**3.** *Logical ordering of courses based on the underlying organization of the discipline of study* Part of the difficulty in curricular sequencing occurs because little attention has been paid to the relationship of one year's curriculum to the next, both within and across content dimensions. It is because of this situation that gifted students learn the same facts about English grammar from fourth to twelfth grades. No one in the school takes the responsibility for logical sequencing of curriculum offerings. Schools also are reluctant to go beyond prevailing curriculum norms at any given level. Intelligent sequencing of a program of study for the gifted must involve school staff across levels. Preschool teachers should plan with primary teachers, intermediate with junior high, and high school with universities. Otherwise, these students will continue to be shortchanged.

**4.** *Concern for progressive development of concepts.* Although the progressive development of skills is important to a curriculum, there also exists as strong a need for appropriately sequenced concepts and ideas. "The change of seasons" is a concept found in much of literature, art, and music. Discussing the concept at a more complex level would require the student to examine the symbolic or metaphoric aspects of "change of seasons," be able to see change in all aspects of nature, and relate to the concept at an intellectual, emotional, and personal level. In this way, then, carefully crafted ideas can be developed at more complex levels of meaning, and continue to challenge the gifted learner.

**5.** *Increasing complexity in product demands rather than increasing quantity.* Doing a research paper at every grade level may constitute practice in the medium without new challenges. Just as skills and concepts need to be organized progressively, so do special projects and product expectations. Rather than modifying the curriculum for the gifted by *adding* product requirements, closer attention to the nature of the product demand would lead educators to a sequential structuring of product expectations that would require a more complex response on the part of the learner. For example, an assignment to do a written report in seventh-grade English on the structural components of a short story might progress to an assignment to do a written critique of a piece of fiction read outside of class in eighth grade.

**6.** *Flexibility regarding entry and exit points based on age/grade-level designations.* A certain blurring of age/grade distinctions must be done if curricula are to be flexible enough to accommodate the diverse learning rates and styles of gifted learners. Preconceived notions about a given body of knowledge being reserved for a certain grade level and inaccessible any sooner is the type of curricular rigidity that impedes and even retards the development of the gifted. Language study is perhaps a good example. The typical age for starting foreign language study in this country is age 14, or ninth grade. Gifted students historically could master a foreign language as early as age 9, or fourth grade. An example of a two-year sequence in Latin typifies many of these issues:

|  | *Grade 9* | *Grade 10* |
|---|---|---|
| Typical sequence | Latin I<br>Project: Do library research and a report on a famous Roman. | Latin II (6-week review)<br>Project: Do research and a report on a favorite myth. |

Gifted sequence      Grade 7, 8, and 9

Latin I/II

Project: Trace the development of modern romance languages from the classical. What factors led to these changes? Choose a medium to report your findings: research paper, oral presentation, or slide/visual display.

Grade 8, 9, or 10

Latin II/III (2-week review)

Project: What is language and what causes it to change? Respond to this question by examining the following languages: English, computer, and sign.

Typically, Latin is considered a high school subject where the second-year curriculum would begin with a six-week review period of Latin I. Project work would stress library data collecting and the preparation of a written report on a very general topic loosely related to the course of study. For gifted learners, Latin might be studied formally as early as seventh grade (completing two years by eighth grade) or begun at whatever level deemed appropriate. Review work in Latin II could be limited to two weeks and mastery into the next level anticipated in both years. Thus, some students might complete three years of Latin in two, due to progressive development in mastering the fundamentals of the content area. Project work would be carried out at a more sophisticated level that required analytical and evaluative skills. Project demands in eighth grade are more complex but do not necessarily require more time to perform.

## Special Issues in Developing Scope and Sequence for the Gifted

There is a set of special issues related to developing a scope and sequence of curriculum for gifted learners that may be useful to discuss. First of all, there is the issue of how to code the curriculum work. The term *coding* used in this context refers to the elements to be included in a written scope and sequence and how they will be organized. This chapter presents varying approaches to that task, but a fundamental consideration of curriculum developers must be to make decisions on the most useful approach in their context. Within reason, using the regular curriculum as an indicator of form might be a place to start, but problems abound from being slavish to a given format.

A second more critical issue is the need to start scope and sequence work from a firm grounding in the philosophy, goals, and overall objectives of the gifted program. These general indicators must be stated and be capable of translation during the process of scope and sequence work. It is also necessary to start with a conceptualization of what embodies the core direction and focus of the gifted curriculum within each area of study, linked to an overall philosophy and set of outcomes. This level of planning is essential to the ongoing work of scope and sequence development at more discrete levels.

A third issue is related to the level of specificity with which the scope and sequence work is coded. Many general curriculum efforts in this area tend to be extremely precise and prescriptive in what is taught at any given stage of development. Whereas this may be a useful tool for the general classroom where expectations for a preset amount of student learning within a given school year need to be well defined, in working on the same task for gifted learners, greater flexibility and expansiveness is required since expectations are greater but also more elastic. In addition, the chunks of learning that the gifted are capable of handling are much greater than what would be the case for more typical learners; thus, the coding of scope and sequence work needs to reflect such a disparity in the level of attainment anticipated.

A fourth issue relates to the infusion of higher-level thinking skill deveopment into the curriculum for gifted learners. Virtually all gifted programs have at least one goal that addresses this issue in the curriculum. How to handle the infusion process for scope and sequence purposes needs to be addressed appropriately since process skill development in gifted programs tends to parallel basic skill development in general education programs. Teachers need to know which higher-level skills might be taught at what stages of the curriculum. They also need to know how they can be linked together to enhance the capacity of gifted students to utilize them effectively. A product like this can be useful to school districts in defining the specific skills they are teaching the gifted learner and at what levels. It can serve as a communication device to regular classroom teachers as well as parents on the overall direction of this aspect of the learning experience.

A final issue to consider in developing scope and sequence for a gifted curriculum is the relative sophistication of the task compared to what is needed in a general curriculum. There are no basal texts for the gifted. Text materials do not drive the curriculum experiences. Consequently, there are limited directions to follow in beginning the task. The multiple materials issue is compounded by the multiple objectives within a gifted program that are frequently being worked on simultaneously. Infusing higher-level thinking skills and higher-level products and key issues, themes, and problems, in addition to capturing the core curriculum within each subject area, is a formidable task. Thus, it is important to consider key stages in the process.

### Key Stages in the Process of Developing a Scope and Sequence

**1.** Select a small group of people to work on scope and sequence issues. These individuals need to be familiar with the regular curriculum and how it is organized across grade levels, understand the salient features of a sound curriculum for gifted learners, and be able to translate skills, concept, and themes across curriculum areas.

**2.** Start with establishing a framework for the process to evolve. What are the proficiency requirements of the core curriculum at primary, intermediate, junior high, and high school within each subject matter area? What is the current emphasis of the gifted program at each grade level? What are the guiding goals, outcomes, and key content strands to be considered in the curriculum for the gifted? What are the key process, product, and conceptual strands to be nurtured at each level of the curriculum?

**3.** Pilot test a coding structure that the group can reach consensus on. Use this coding approach to detail scope and sequence for the gifted at one grade level (or across two or three) and across content, process, and product dimensions. Share the product results with various school groups to ascertain its capacity to (a) communicate key features effectively, (b) capture the nature of the curriculum experience sufficiently, and (c) clearly demonstrate the relationship of the curriculum for gifted learners to that provided to more typical learners in the school district.

**4.** Develop drafts of all curricular areas of the gifted program from kindergarten through grade 12. Even though the pilot effort was in a narrow band of grade-level designations, work should proceed at the next stage in such a way that the total sweep of the K–12 curriculum is considered. Too frequently school districts run into problems with not extending the scope and sequence effort far enough in both directions in order to continue making appropriate curriculum inferences for the gifted. Attention to prerequisites and postrequisites in planned curriculum experiences is also an important consideration at this stage of the process.

**5.** Test the draft document against the reality of what is currently operative for gifted learners in the school district. Although it is important that the scope and sequence document be a planning tool for future efforts and implementation of program pieces, it still must be grounded in what is actually happening to students, particularly at levels where the program has been operative for a while. If there is little resemblance between the document and the curriculum being delivered, then key decisions need to be made regarding where and how revisions in both document and program will occur.

**6.** Refine the scope and sequence document as new insights emerge about the nature of curriculum experiences for gifted learners in the district. Since curriculum is presented as constantly evolving and changing in light of classroom instruction and the nature of the learner needs and expectations. Scope and sequence models must also be viewed as tentative and evolving in nature if they are to represent a synthesis of the actual and the ideal for gifted learners throughout the K–12 span of years in school.

**7.** Continue to monitor the implementation of a planned scope and sequence. There is no substitute for carefully observing the degree of consonance between what a scope and sequence document says is going on and what actually is going on. Little progress can be made toward K–12 articulation without someone assuming this oversight responsibility. Ideally, the gifted coordinator in cooperation with the curriculum director could undertake this effort. Staff development opportunities can best be developed through this stage of the process also as discrepancies in practice are observed.

## Approaches to Developing Scope and Sequence

There are several approaches to scope and sequence development that practitioners in gifted programs may wish to consider. Examples of each approach are included at the conclusion of this chapter.

One way to approach scope and sequence work is to limit the grade levels for examination but encompass all core content and process dimensions of the curriculum that are desired. In this approach one would:

**1.** Begin with the articulation of program goals.
   a. Identify content strands for considerations.
   b. Identify process strands for considerations.
**2.** Define content emphases and student outcomes desired within each content areas of the curriculum.

3. Collaborate across grade levels to determine meaningful sequence patterns based on developmental levels of students.
4. Check to ensure that the resulting written document adequately treats each program goal.

This model of scope and sequence work provides a matrix overview of the curriculum for high-ability learners. One useful feature is to point out gaps in curriculum materials and the need for curriculum units that have a particular topical focus. Example 5.A illustrates this approach for a gifted middle school program in language arts. This work sample was developed by a team of seventh- and eighth-grade teachers from Wilson Middle School, Rockford, Illinois.

The presentation of this curriculum example contains three sections:

1. *Specified program goals provide the superstructure for the content area matrices and the process skill paradigms*. Each aspect of the scope and sequence chart should be able to reflect back to these basic statements.

2. *Content area schemata, organized in matrix form*. Each curriculum matrix reflects global student outcomes intersecting with content topics to be presented. Topics are presented sequentially from left to right with an expectation of increasing levels of difficulty. The Xs reflect the major intersection of content topic and a particular desired student behavior. All content matrices also are keyed to the process skill paradigms that were developed collectively by the team. Organizational approaches varied by content dimensions. (The English matrix is provided as an example.)

3. *Process skill paradigms were developed for the areas of critical thinking, creative problem solving, and research*. All teachers agreed to the definition of these skills, as indicated in the paradigm, and team planning was utilized to promote a common understanding of how each discipline at each level was addressing specific parts of the paradigm. Parameters of project work were delineated on the research paradigm.

One example of incorporating higher-level process skills into content is the reading section of the Georgia Department of Education resource guide for secondary English teachers (VanTassel-Baska, 1992a). Each of the major learner outcomes, designated as quality core curriculum for all learners, is represented in the left-hand column, whereas the adaptations for gifted learners may be seen in the right-hand column. These adaptations illustrate the embedding of higher-level process skills into a content dimension, thus rendering the outcomes more appropriate for gifted learners.

| *Quality Core Curriculum* | *Gifted Adaptation* |
|---|---|
| *Reading* | |
| • Uses literal comprehension skills (e.g., sequencing, explicitly stated main idea) | • Demonstrates proficiency in working with inference, inductive and deductive reasoning, analogies, assumptions, and evaluation of arguments in literature |
| • Uses inferential comprehension skills (e.g., predictions, comparisons conclusions, implicitly stated main idea, propoganda techniques) | |

- Identifies and comprehends the main and subordinate ideas in a written work and summarizes ideas in own words

- Recognizes different purposes and methods of writing; identifies a writer's point of view and tone
- Interprets a writer's meaning inferentially as well as literally
- Identifies personal opinions and assumptions in a writer

- Comprehends a variety of written materials

- Uses the features of print materials appropriately (e.g., table of contents, preface, introduction, titles and subtitles, index, glossary, appendix, bibliography)

- Defines unfamiliar words by using appropriate word recognition skills

- Analyzes literary themes as they are developed within and across authors

- Discusses and synthesizes ideas about an author's form and content
- Develops an essay that compares key purposes and methods of writing used by one author to another

- Evaluates a given reading selection according to a set of standards

- Creates a written product that incorporates all major features of print materials and that is one of the following: a novel, biography, autobiography, poetry, short stories, book of essays

- Masters advanced adult vocabulary, using a variety of content-bound materials and selected word lists.

A second approach to developing scope and sequence is to organize the task thematically, according to ideas, and to translate those ideas across grade-level formats. Example 5.B taken from a local school district curriculum effort, presents a K–12 scope and sequence model that has been developed through a thematic approach, using the theme "Humanity Adapts and Develops."

Another type of scope and sequence development undertaken by school districts may relate to the affective domain of their program for gifted students. Just as learner outcomes are relevant to core areas of learning in the cognitive domain, so too are they important in providing a substantive base to affective skill development. Example 5.C from the Grand Rapids, Michigan, School District Spectrum program provides one illustration of the delineation of learner outcomes in the affective domain. It emphasizes two major goals of their affective curriculum: understanding self and understanding others. It also treats an area of the curriculum called dealing with special concerns as a way of focusing on key problems encountered with some gifted children at particular times during the six-year program. The organizational structure of the learner outcomes is based on a teaming model employed by the program to serve primary-age and intermediate-age gifted students one day a week in a separate school. A record of student progress on each of these outcome areas is shared with parents during each program year at quarterly intervals. Thus, the scope and sequence model is effectively linked to the assessment model used in the program.

All of these approaches to scope and sequence may be useful for different situations at different stages of the curriculum development process. Often it is useful to key a gifted scope and sequence chart to one for typical learners in a school district to illustrate the nature and extent of differentiation. Other times it may be useful only to reflect a scope and sequence model for the gifted since the linkage to regular curriculum may not exist, as in the case of foreign language at the primary level. A school district needs to decide what scope and sequence model is most useful and then proceed to develop it, remembering the importance of working teams that are horizontal as well as vertical in dimension (e.g., teachers working across grade levels but also across content areas to ensure understanding and communication). Under such circumstances, gifted learners become the beneficiaries of well-structured ongoing learning experiences.

## *Conclusion*

This chapter has presented several different ways of creating scope and sequence in a curriculum for gifted learners. It has provided samples of school district work in several key areas of curriculum. It has demonstrated a scope and sequence organizational approach based on each of the three dimensions of curriculum making described in Chapter 1. It has also demonstrated an approach to stressing affective skill development as a legitimate part of the curriculum emphasis. In this way, school districts may begin to move toward a broad curriculum planning endeavor that will provide the impetus for systems change on behalf of gifted learners.

The steps in developing a scope and sequence in curriculum can be summarized as follows:

1. Develop overall curriculum goals and learner outcomes relevant to each goal.
2. Determine major content, process, and concept strands to be stressed.
3. Examine the school district or state curriculum guide for learner outcomes in core content areas.
4. Adapt the existing curriculm guide in core curriculum learning areas for gifted learners.
5. Cross-reference adapted guides to overall curriculum goals and outcomes.
6. Develop additional strands of curriculum as needed to address the curriculum goal structure.

### *Key Points Summary*

- *Developing scope and sequence in curriculum for the gifted provides a way of ensuring vertical and horizontal articulation of learning experiences across the grades.*
- *Important considerations in building scope and sequence in gifted curriculum include the following: limited review of learned material, progressive development in skill and knowledge acquisition, attention to the structure of the discipline, and flexibility in age/grade designations.*

- *Curriculum goals and outcomes for gifted learners should provide the framework for scope and sequence considerations at each relevant grade level or grade level cluster.*
- *Scope and sequence work should be undertaken for all major dimensions of the program—cognitive, affective, aesthetic, and social.*

## References

Bloom, B. (1958). Ideas, problems, and methods of inquiry. In NSSE *Integration of educational experiences*. Chicago: University of Chicago Press.

Cox, J., Daniels, N., & Boston, B. (1986). *Educating able learners*. Austin: University of Texas Press.

Feldhusen, J., VanTassel-Baska, J., & Seeley, K. (1989). *Excellence in educating the gifted*. Denver: Love Publishing.

Gary Community School Corporation. (1991). *Language arts scope and sequence guide*. Gary, IN: Author.

Maker, J. (1982). *Curriculum development for the gifted*. Rockville, MD: Aspen.

Maker, J. (1986). Developing scope and sequence for the gifted. *Gifted Child Quarterly, 4,* 151–158.

Muskingham County Board of Education. (1990). *Muskingham county course of study for the gifted*. Zanesville, OH: Author.

Ornstein, A. C., & Hunkins, F. P. (1988). *Curriculum: Foundations, principles, and issues*. Englewood Cliffs, NJ: Prentice Hall.

Smith, B., Stanley, W., & Shore, H. (1957). *Fundamentals of curriculum development*. New York: World Book.

Taba, H. (1962). *Curriculum development*. New York: Harcourt Brace World.

Tyler, R. (1949). *Basic principles of curriculum and instruction*. Chicago: University of Chicago Press.

VanTassel-Baska, J. (1988, September–October). Developing a comprehensive approach to scope and sequence: Curriculum alignment. *GCT*, 42–45.

VanTassel-Baska, J. (1992a). *Georgia State Department of Education resource guide for secondary teachers of the gifted*. Atlanta: Georgia State Department of Education.

VanTassel-Baska, J. (1992b). *Effective curriculum planning for gifted learners*. Denver: Love Publishing.

**EXAMPLE 5.A   A Scope and Sequence of Middle School Curriculum for the Gifted by Goal, Content, Topics, Student and Process Skill Paradigms Outcomes**

### *Gifted Program Goals (Middle School)*

1. To provide for the mastery of basic skills while providing for greater depth and breadth of understanding within and across areas of study: Student instruction will differ from the normal course of studies by a pace and level of complexity that are more suited to students of exceptional abilities.
2. To promote critical thinking and reasoning abilities: Students will be instructed in the areas of inference, deductive and inductive reasoning, analogies, and evaluation of arguments. These reasoning tools will be applied to all areas of the curriculum.
3. To provide an environment that encourages divergent thinking: Students will be encouraged in the development of originality, fluency, flexibility, and elaboration in their thought processes.
4. To foster inquiry and challenging attitudes towards learning: Students will be able to develop a commitment to learning as a lifelong process and to learn their educational, civic, social, and personal responsibilities.
5. To develop oral and written skills: Students will become confident in expressing ideas through conversations, panel discussions, debates, and oral and written reports; students will learn expository, creative writing skills and technical report writing.
6. To develop research skills and methods: Students will be able to understand the scientific method and its application to all areas of inquiry.

## ENGLISH LITERATURE, GRADES 7–8

| Student Outcomes | Mythology/ Folk Tales | Short Story | Biography | Novel | Poetry |
|---|---|---|---|---|---|
| Acquiring an understanding of the elements or components of a literary form (i.e., plot, character, theme, setting, sequence) | | X | | X | |
| Acquiring an understanding of literary genres and types of literature | | | X | X | |
| Developing critical reading skills (analysis and interpretation) | | X | | X | X |
| Observing and investigating human motivation | X | X | X | X | X |
| Developing a sense of identity through reading about character prototypes | | | X | X | |
| Developing a literary appreciation of writing styles | X | X | X | X | X |

## ENGLISH ORAL COMMUNICATIONS, GRADES 7–8: CONTENT CATEGORIES

| Student Outcomes | Speech | Oral Presentations (Individual and Panel) | Oral Interpretation | Oral Debate |
|---|---|---|---|---|
| Developing poise and self-confidence in front of a group | X | X | X | X |
| Acquiring skills of speech (e.g., voice projection, inflection) | X | X | X | X |
| Developing critical thinking skills (i.e., inference, deductive reasoning, evaluation of arguments) | | X | | X |
| Developing the skills of persuasion and argument | | | | X |
| Acquiring proficiency in synthesizing thoughts, written ideas, and speech | | X | X | X |

## ENGLISH WRITING/COMPOSITION, GRADES 7–8: CONTENT CATEGORIES

| Student Outcomes | Paragraph Development | Theme Development | Creative Writing | Technical Report Writing |
|---|---|---|---|---|
| Understanding the structure of writing | X | X | X | X |
| Acquiring the skills of expository writing | X | X | | |
| Developing the skills of critical review | X | X | X | X |
| Acquiring the skills of creative writing | X | X | X | |
| Acquiring the skills of reporting data accurately and completely | | | | X |

## PROCESS SKILL EMPHASES ACROSS CURRICULUM AREAS

| Research Skills | Creative Problem-Solving Skills* | Critical Thinking Skills |
|---|---|---|
| 1. Defining a problem | Fact finding (brainstorming) | 1. Inference |
| 2. Gathering data (library research) | Problem finding and defining | 2. Deductive reasoning |
| 3. Developing a hypothesis | Idea generation and alternative solution finding | 3. Inductive reasoning |
| 4. Observing/experimenting and recording data | Evaluating among solutions | 4. Analogies |
| 5. Generating conclusions | Developing a plan of action (acceptance finding) | 5. Evaluation of arguments |

*Based on the Parnes and Osborne model.

**EXAMPLE 5.B Fayette County School Corporation (Connersville, Indiana) Social Studies/ Language Arts Content Scope and Sequence for GT Program—Overarching Theme: Humanity Adapts and Develops***

|  | Level K | Level 1 | Level 2 |
|---|---|---|---|
| Overarching Concepts | "Understanding Me. A Changing Individual" | "All Kinds of Families" | "From City to Farm" |
| A<br>Change is continual. | Individuals change. | The family unit changes. | Communities change. |
| B<br>Communication through language is a necessary element for the functioning of society. | Individuals communicate through language. | Families communicate with their members and society through language. | Communication aids in understanding likes and differences within and among communities. |
| C<br>Political frameworks are instituted to resolve conflicts and facilitate interaction. | Individuals are expected to follow rules. | Families establish rules. | Communities make and enforce laws. |
| D<br>Cultures adapt in response to the dynamics of social and physical environment. | Individuals adjust to their surroundings. | Family lifestyles are determined by interaction with the environment. | Communities differ because of their location and their citizenry. |
| E<br>Economic systems evolve from the management and utilization of scarce resources and the distribution of goods and services. | Individuals learn to use money. | Families use resources to satisfy needs and wants. | Community members depend on each other to provide for their needs and wants through specialization. |

| Level 3 | Level 4 | Level 5 | Level 6 |
|---|---|---|---|
| "Tracing Our Community" | "Indiana: Yesterday and Today" | "America, The Melting Pot" | "The Shrinking World" |
| The local community has changed since its founding. | As the Indiana population grows, economic, political and social structures adapt. | The people immigrating to America contribute to the development of American culture and history. | Interaction of world cultures produces conflict and/or change. |
| Communication is essential for the development of communities. | As Indiana grew and developed, people devised different methods of communication. | As the U.S. population grew, American literature reflected the impact of cultures and changes in the society. | As world population grew, greater communication among world cultures developed. |
| City and county governments solve community problems. | The government of Indiana developed social controls with influence from local and national levels. | National government cooperates with state and local administrators to stipulate social controls. | The federal government participates in a system to promote international cooperation. |
| A community's characteristics are the result of interaction between individuals in a specific environment. | In Indiana, Native-American and pioneer cultures adapted in response to interaction between the groups. | American society is a product of the interaction among many cultures. | World cultures are modified by their interactions. |
| A community determines the use of resources through the market system. | Indiana has developed into an agricultural and industrial state through management and utilization of its resources. | The United States has developed into a leading agricultural and industrial power. | The economic systems rely on the cultural values which determine resources, allocations and output distribution. |

| | Level 7 | Level 0 | World History | American History |
|---|---|---|---|---|
| Overarching Concepts | "World Cultures and Their Interdependence" | "America: The First Century" | "Learning From The Past" | "America: The Plentiful" |
| A Change is continual. | All societies experience conflict and change. | The development of our heritage is a timeless process in which the past blends into the present and helps shape the future. | World cultures change through the interaction of the values, mores and cultural heritage of many societies. | Out institutions and cultural mores are not static but rather are products of the past, present and future. |
| B Communication through language is a necessary element for the functioning of society. | Relationships between people require communication. | American hertiage and culture is expressed and preserved through written and oral communication. | Language is influenced through contact with and study of other cultures. | Written and oral communication, provides the record of our past and the means to report our present and future. |
| C Political frameworks are instituted to resolve conflicts and facilitate interaction. | The diverse political systems of the world are the result of the interaction of complex forces. | A democracy depends on participation of a responsible and knowledgeable citizenry. | Formal and informal structures are required to resolve conflicts among countries. | The American political system has evolved as a unique entity. |
| D Cultures adapt in response to the dynamics of social and physical environment. | Differing environments affect a variety of cultural mores and social institutions. | Our American culture is being determined by the interaction of ethnic background and geographic features. | Through interaction, whether victor or vanquished, civilizations adapt and adopt from others. | |
| E Economic systems evolve from the management and utilization of scarce resources and the distribution of goods and services. | Developments in one part of the world may influence the economics of other areas of the world. | One of the economic goals of America is economic stability without severe inflation and deflation. | The rise and fall of civilizations rest in part on mismanagement of resources. | The availability of both human and property resources and their use help to explain the development of the American economy. |

| Sociology | U.S. Government | Economics | Psychology |
|---|---|---|---|
| "Understanding Society" | "U.S. Government: Freedom and Responsibility" | "Buy American?!" | "Psychology at Work" |
| Relationships among groups are fluid and responsive to past practice, current concerns, and new issues. | Participation by citizens in our political system produces constant changes. | Economic "theories" may be interpreted in different ways according to current trends. | Individuals change as they mature. |
| Language defines social role and group identification. | Precision and ambiguity of language are elements which determine the effectiveness of language. | Language manipulation is a powerful tool. | Communication plays a role in determining human behavior and attitudes. |
| Interest groups have played a key role in influencing political decision making. | Our political system enables citizens to control their destinies and preserve their liberties. | Government intervention or lack thereof may alter functions of economic systems. | Resolving conflicts requires the reconciliation of individual differences in attitude, emotions, frustrations and aggression. |
| Group dynamics affect every phase of our lives and identities. | Our governmental structure has evolved as a result of social dynamics and environment. | Cultural conventions as well as physical environment affect economics. | An Individual's perceptions, relationships, and behaviors create cultural change. |
| Households, business, and governments influence economic activities. | Our market system encourages free enterprise which is regulated by the public sector. | Economic growth, that is, a rising standard of living propels use to develop new technologies and resources. | Psychological elements determine economic choices in a market economy. |

*Source:* Fayette County School Corporation personnel who developed the scope and sequence: Arlene Bliven, Louise Whitaker, Suellen Reed, Alvanell Elkin, Julie Slaubaugh, Sherry Anderson, Susan Shull, Penny Keller, Margie Yeager, Bob Julian, and Karen Armstrong

## Example 5.C Grand Rapids Public Schools Spectrum Program Scope and Sequence in Affective Skills

## AFFECTIVE SKILLS

| DESCRIPTION OF DESIRED BEHAVIORS | LEARNER OUTCOMES | |
|---|---|---|
| | *Early Elementary* | *Later Elementary* |
| **Understanding Self**<br>• Gifted children need to understand their giftedness and the myths that surround them as exceptional people. | • Identify some general characteristics of giftedness.<br>• Study biographies of eminent people. | • Identify myths of giftedness.<br>• Use a variety of talented community resources. |
| • Gifted children need to understand how to deal with appropriate and inappropriate expectations of self and others. | • Identify situations where talents can be utilized.<br>• Choose activities that are complementary to one's talent area. | • Set appropriate expectations for all self-selected activities.<br>• Accept responsibility for utilizing talents. |
| • Gifted children need to understand how to recognize, label, and appropriately express their genuine feelings. | • Identify feelings being exhibited in various situations.<br>• Identify appropriate expressions of feelings.<br>• Understand verbal and nonverbal behavior as ways to express feelings. | • Identify personal feelings through written and verbal expression.<br>• Share feelings appropriately. |
| • Gifted children need to understand and respect their own identities and personal strengths and weaknesses. | • Identify own areas of strengths and weaknesses.<br>• Identify own areas of interest. | • Identify own areas of strengths and weaknesses.<br>• Develop an appreciation of one's own style.<br>• Develop intrinsic motivation. |
| **Understanding Others**<br>• Gifted children need to understand and accept the differences in others and exhibit a tolerance for varying ability levels. | • Demonstrate cooperation in group activities.<br>• Identify differing abilities among individuals. | • Demonstrate cooperation in group study.<br>• Identify and integrate strengths of others into the group process. |
| • Gifted children need to understand the interrelatedness and value of people from all backgrounds and cultures within the world community. | • Develop techniques for group and cooperative learning.<br>• Identify individual role in the world community. | • Demonstrate an appreciation for similarities and differences among all persons.<br>• Demonstrate an appreciation for cultural differences.<br>• Evaluate group study process.<br>• Identify individual contributions to world issues or problems. |
| • Gifted children need to establish trusting relationships and explore ways to share their inner selves with other people. | • Share feelings with one another.<br>• Demonstrate respect if listening to others share personal information and feelings. | • Demonstrate a willingness to share personal information and feelings.<br>• Develop personalized techniques for sharing information in product/ presentation. |
| **Dealing with Specific Concerns**<br>• Gifted children need to be aware of how to use various methods to increase their positive self-images, to relax, and to reduce tension. | • Explore feelings, causes, and positive ways of dealing with stress, anxiety, and depression.<br>• Utilize preparation and practice to reduce anxiety involved in performance.<br>• Differentiate between positive and negative self-talk. | • Recognize that stress can be a normal and necessary part of growth and performance.<br>• Utilize preparation and practice to reduce anxiety involved in performance.<br>• Differentiate between positive and negative self-talk. |
| • Gifted children need to realize that feeling and being different is acceptable. | • Identify original thinking as creativity.<br>• Demonstrate respect and tolerance for creative ideas of others.<br>• Exhibit risk-taking behavior in verbal and written work. | • Generate divergent ideas.<br>• Utilize creative ideas in all activities.<br>• Display self-confidence in expressing one's own ideas. |
| • Gifted children need to recognize that their perfectionistic behaviors and fears of failure are normal tendencies. | • Identify factors and situations that contribute to frustration.<br>• Recognize that mistakes are part of the editing process. | • Adjust established goals/expectations for self and others to accommodate reality.<br>• Show acceptance of mistakes made by self and others.<br>• Demonstrate a willingness to take risks in verbal and written work. |

Chapter *6*

# Developing Units
# of Instruction

*JOHN F. FELDHUSEN*

*Make no small plans.* —DANIEL BURNHAM

Curriculum development is a planning process. It is best carried out by teams of individuals who know the subject matter or discipline well, who are skilled in the processes of curriculum, and who know and understand the characteristics and needs of gifted and talented youth. Curriculum development needs time and support resources to implement. The process ordinarily culminates in documents or narrative statements of plans.

One aspect of the curriculum development process in the education of gifted learners is the organization of specific units of instruction for use by a teacher with a specified group. The unit is an elaborated element of the broader scope and sequence plan described in the last chapter. The unit is micro, whereas the scope and sequence plan is macro. The unit gives much greater detail about the instructional plan and resource materials.

The unit of instruction is a teaching plan that typically begins with a title that broadly defines a domain of instruction such as "Solar Energy," "Lumbering," "Magnetism," "Probability," "Change in Western Society," or "Beauty as a Poetic Concept." Early in the planning of a unit, broad goals and specific instructional objectives may be formulated along with a topical or content outline. As a written statement, the unit may also have a narrative exposition that specifies the intended audience (e.g., gifted learners in math at the seventh-grade level), the prospective time frame, suggested teaching methods, and a rationale for how the unit is differentiated to serve the needs and characteristics of the gifted. All of this introductory material sets the stage for the presentation of the unit of instruction.

The unit may be developed for self-instructional use by students, for implementation in a learning center, for didactic presentation by the teacher, for out-of-school use, as a teaching-learning contract, or as a combination of these approaches with other variants. Regardless of the mode or nature of organization, there are apt to be common ingredients and common adherence to a set of unit development principles. Maker (1986) has presented one such set of principles:

1. *It must be flexible, to permit both students and teachers to pursue their individual interests.*
2. *It should focus on abstract principles and concepts rather than specific facts.*
3. *It should include process skills such as higher levels of thinking and problem-solving as a separate scope and sequence that is integrated with the development of content understanding.*
4. *It should include an emphasis on development of types of sophisticated products integrated with the content and process.*
5. *It must not restrict the students' opportunities to pursue accelerated content, processes, or products.*
6. *It must include input from scholars and researchers in academic areas regarding the importance of principles, concepts, skills, and values.*
7. *It should provide opportunities for exposure to a variety of content areas, skills, values, and types of content.*
8. *It should focus on concepts that are important in several academic areas, with the goal of integrating rather than separating what is learned.*
9. *It must build upon and extend the regular curriculum for efficiency and articulation in learning, but must not duplicate the regular curriculum.*
10. *It must include the input of a variety of professionals experienced in curriculum development and those experienced in education of the gifted. (p. 152)*

It seems likely that items 6 and 10 are idealistic. Local school districts developing units of instruction can scarcely be expected to have scholars, researchers, and professionals available to assist in curriculum development. Teachers may have to use their own resources as well as print sources to serve as guides for curriculum development.

We have developed and used the following simplified guidelines for the development of unit planning for the gifted learner.

1. Focus on *major ideas,* issues, themes, problems, concepts, and principles.
2. Emphasize the need for a large knowledge base.
3. When possible, use an *interdisciplinary* approach.
4. Emphasize in-depth *research* and *independent study* with original and high-level products or presentations.
5. Teach *research skills and thinking skills* as metacognitive processes.
6. *Incorporate higher-level thinking skills in content study*—in discussions, independent study, research, and writing.
7. *Increase the level, complexity, and pace* of the curriculum to fit the precocity of the students.
8. Teach methods for *independence, self-direction, and self-evaluation* in learning.

The new conceptions of constructivism in education also offer guidance for the development of units of instruction for gifted learners (Bishop, 1985; Sigel, 1984; von Glasersfeld & Cobb, 1983; Wittrock, 1974). Proponents of this new approach to instruction build on concepts originally promulgated by Bruner (1960), Piaget and Inheldler (1969), Taba (1962), and others. All of the approaches stress a more active, dynamic involvement of learners in instruction, focus on conceptual learning, advocate inductive strategies to achieve deeper understanding, and seek integration of learning into broader schematic frameworks. Constructivism stresses that learning outcomes are unique to each individual student and that each student builds or constructs his or her own conceptual framework. In practice, constructivism leads to much time for students to explore, investigate, solve problems, analyze, examine, evaluate, and hypothesize as vehicles to developing understanding. The approach of constructivism is uniquely appropriate for gifted learners whose curiosity, intrinsic motivation, and investigative abilities, as well as basic skills, are at advanced levels and whose capacity for abstract conceptualization makes the method seem tailored to meet their needs. The lesson for developers of units of instruction for the gifted is that these students need much opportunity to explore the world of subject matter for the concepts and generalizations that define knowledge, but also to develop their own unique constructions of those concepts and generalizations.

## The Resource Unit

One approach to the development of units of instruction is simply a compilation of the resources needed for teaching a unit on a given topic. The resources might include the objectives, suggested activities, print material and media, and suggested evaluation procedures. Example 6.A at the end of the chapter presents one simplified form of an instructional unit for gifted students on "Encounters with the Eminent," which we call a *resource unit*. The compilation of this unit includes all of the resources and information needed, but it does not present any guidelines for teaching the unit. We are simply given an introduction; a statement of the context and how it is differentiated for the gifted; the content or information to be covered; the objectives, discussion topics, and group activities; creative activities for students; the independent studies; suggestions for the use of mentors; teacher resources; media resources; and the text materials that may be used. This compilation of resources tells the teacher little about the teaching sequence, nor does it discuss methods of instruction except that the lists of objectives, content information, and discussion topics might indeed imply a sequence. Furthermore, in suggesting discussions, creative activities, independent study, field trips, mentors, and speakers, some aspects of teaching methodology are being advocated.

It would be easy to adapt the unit "Encounters with the Eminent" by including still one more ogranizational topic—namely, a list of materials and resources to be assembled for a learning center. Such a list might be as follows:

1. Pictures of eminent people
2. Sound recordings of their voices
3. Filmstrips on their lives

4. Products that some of them have created
5. Busts and statues of the eminent

The learning center serves several instructional purposes. First, it is an organizer that draws all the resources to one location (usually a table). Second, it is a motivator for gifted students in that the teacher tries to make it stimulating and enticing. Third, it is a technique for making the instruction and its resources readily available for student use. And finally, learning centers, particularly if there are several in a classroom, give gifted students an opportunity to learn how to do independent, small group, and self-directed study.

## Multicultural Education and Unit Development

With the growing tide of new immigrants of diverse racial and ethnic backgrounds entering the United States and the presence for several centuries of people with differing religions and value systems, there is great interest in finding ways to assure appreciation of our diversity and to avoid conflicts. We have lost faith in the "melting pot" concept in which all aspired to and yielded to Americanization, and instead we now encourage maintenance of the cultural heritage and life-styles of the diverse American subpopulations. This diversity is fraught with potential for conflict and strife; thus, we call for the schools to provide multicultural education so that all youth can learn about the ways and values of the various cultures with which they interact and develop both tolerance and enthusiasm for other cultures.

As a part of the social studies, units of instruction can be focused on each of the subpopulations in a community. Such units should have both cognitive and affective objectives. A cognitive objective might be stated as follows:

Analyze similarities and differences between Japanese and American schools.

An affective objective might be stated as follows:

Appreciate the differences between Japanese and American schools in their differing emphasis on art and music in the curriculum.

Activities in the area of multicultural studies provide excellent opportunities to challenge gifted students by introducing them to language, political and ideological contrasts, cultural values, religious beliefs, professional activity, and the trade and commerce of other countries. The United States is rapidly becoming a part of the world community in which multicultural knowledge and understanding will be crucial to our future leadership roles. Our gifted and talented youth will be those future leaders, and they must have the multicultural education to ready them for those new challenges of the twenty-first century.

## Content-Oriented Units

Treffinger, Hohn, and Feldhusen (1989) proposed a content-matrix approach to the development of instructional units that has been widely used in the development of units for gifted learners. Their approach begins with the development of a content outline, which becomes one of the two dimensions of a matrix. The following example shows such a content outline for a social studies unit on the American colonies:

    **I.** Identifying the Colonies
    **II.** History, Government, and Politics
    **III.** Food, Clothing, and Housing
    **IV.** Home Life
    **V.** Economics
    **VI.** Schools
    **VII.** Sports, Recreation, and Social Life
    **VIII.** Religion, Values, and Beliefs
    **IX.** Transportation and Communication

Whereas the outline is brief, the elaboration will take place in the later development of objectives and instructional activities for the unit. We call this a *content unit* of instruction because it often focuses on content or discipline-based material.

The second dimension of the content matrix is the type or level of objectives to be written for the unit. Treffinger, Hohn, and Feldhusen recommended a union of the Bloom (1956) *Taxonomy of Educational Objectives, Cognitive Domain* and the creativity concepts of fluency, flexibility, orginality, and elaboration. If appropriate, they also advocated using concepts from the *Taxonomy of Educational Objectives, Affective Domain* (Krathwohl, Bloom, & Masia, 1964) and *A Taxonomy of the Psychomotor Domain* (Harrow, 1972). Of course, other dimensions of critical or logical thinking (Ennis, 1985) could also be included. Since a majority of instructional units for the gifted are developed for use in academic subjects such as mathematics, science, English, and social studies, the concepts of creativity, cognitive operations, and the Bloom cognitive levels are most often used as organizational guides. The Bloom cognitive levels of application, analysis, synthesis, and evaluation are stressed as most appropriate for teaching the gifted, but a necessary underpinning role of knowledge (content information) and comprehension is recognized as prerequisite and essential learning before gifted students can operate and learn at the higher levels. Figure 6–1 shows a matrix that incorporates the content outline and the dimension for classifying objectives.

The matrix serves as a guide and reminder for the writing of objectives, instructional activities, and evaluation procedures. After several years of experience with groups of teachers developing units of study for gifted learners, we have found that a sound and workable procedure is to have teachers create the matrix framework on large sheets of poster board or newsprint so that there is a large space for each matrix intersect of a level of objectives with a content topic. The matrix then serves as a guide for the writing of objectives in that it graphically shows the union of each topic with each potential level or type of objective that might be written. It is important to note, however, that a teacher who is developing a unit should not feel that there must be objectives at each intersect. Rather, it is the teacher or the development group's task at each intersect to decide which, if any, objectives are needed and, if so, to proceed to write them. We should also note that there may be a need for one or several objectives at an intersect, depending on how complex the topic item is.

Typically a teacher works across the matrix horizontally, staying with a topic and

**FIGURE 6–1    A Matrix of Content by Levels of the Taxonomy**

| | Knowledge | Comprehension | Creative Thinking | Application | Analysis | Synthesis | Evaluation |
|---|---|---|---|---|---|---|---|
| I. Identifying the Colonies | | | | | | | |
| II. History, Government, and Politics | | | | | | | |
| III. Food, Clothing, and Housing | | | | | | | |
| IV. Home Life | | | | | | | |
| V. Economics | | | | | | | |
| VI. Schools | | | | | | | |
| VII. Sports, Recreation, and Social Life | | | | | | | |
| VIII. Religion, Values, and Beliefs | | | | | | | |
| IX. Transportation and Communication | | | | | | | |

considering all the possible levels of objectives that might be written for that content topic. Many teachers prefer to design the instructional activity and to specify the evaluation procedure as or while they are writing objectives. Whereas it is usually the case that instructional activities must be specified for every objective, evaluation procedures might be specified only periodically, for example, at the end of a content line, as shown in Table 6–1, where it is called a *checkpoint*.

The design of instructional activities for each objective is facilitated by the immediate presence of the behavioral objective Mager (1975) urged that the properly stated objective include a transitive verb that specifies the action a student should be able to carry out after learning has occurred and the objective has been achieved. He also suggested that a well-stated objective must specify the conditions under which the student must be able to demonstrate learning and the level or quality of performance expected. Thus a completed objective might be stated as follows:

> Able to point out 90 percent of the errors in word usage, spelling, punctuation, or grammar in a specially prepared short essay.

However, many objectives do not lend themselves well to such precision in the specification of the condition of performance or the level of efficiency. For example:

**TABLE 6–1 Objectives and Activities by Content Topic and Evaluation Checkpoint**

| | Knowledge Comprehension | Application | Analysis | Synthesis | Evaluation | Creativity |
|---|---|---|---|---|---|---|
| IV. Home Life | *Objective:* Be able to describe major features of colonial house life.<br><br>*Activity:* Read one of the following: Jones: Colonial House Life<br>Arrow: The Colonial Family<br>Hansen: Life in Early America | | *Objective:* Be able to delineate the relationships among colonial children, parents, and other extended family members.<br><br>*Activity:* Write a short story depicting colonial family life, and particularly portraying relationships between family members. | *Objective:* Write a fictional account of a colonial family life.<br><br>*Activity:* Write a short story depicting colonial family life, and particularly portraying relationships between family members. | *Objective:* Compare and evaluate the quality of family life in colonial and western America.<br><br>*Activity:* Write an essay comparing the quality of life in colonial and modern America as depicted in your earlier assignment.<br><br>*Checkpoint:* Present your short story and essay to several students for critiquing. Revise and critique it yourself. Submit it for teacher evaluation. | *Objective:* (Already covered in synthesis objective) |

Able to write a short scenario describing health conditions in the future.

This objective could be rewritten to conform to Mager's three criteria as follows:

Able to write, as a homework assignment, a short scenario describing health conditions in the future, with no more than five errors in grammar, usage, punctuation, and spelling.

Many teachers find such elaboration tedious and unnecessary as a guide to teaching.

The design of instructional activities for each objective is also facilitated by the teacher-developer's knowledge and flexibility in relation to optional and alternative techniques in teaching, as well as by knowledge of alternative resource materials. Some teachers also choose to offer alternative instructional activities to the student for each objective, thereby accommodating different learning styles and preferences. For example:

*Objective*

Able to design a survey of energy problems in the community.

*Instructional Activities*

Design a survey instrument to use in conducting an energy survey and specify the data gathering design.

or

Use an existing energy survey questionnaire, plan a small survey sample, conduct the interviews, analyze results, write a report.

or

Enroll for a mentoring experience in which you work with the staff of a survey research company.

An alternative to writing the objectives, instructional activities, and checkpoints in the boxes on the big newsprint is to use 5 × 8 cards to represent each intersect box, writing the three components on cards. Later, when using the unit with a class, many teachers will also choose to present the unit to students as a card pack, with the intent that students themselves take the pack in hand and do the cards, one at a time, as method of working through the unit. The cards and the activities can be coordinated with a learning center or resource file that the student can use to access resources for the learning activities and evaluation procedures.

As an opener for all such teaching units, there should be a statement directed to the student that tells him or her how to use the unit, that stimulates interest, and that gives an organizational statement of how the unit fits into or relates to other learnings and a broader framework. At the close of a unit, there should be a similar summary statement regarding what has been learned and its relationship to other learnings.

Some teachers develop units with the intent to share them with other teachers. In such cases there should be an opening statement from the teacher-developer, specifying the targeted grade level of the unit and how the unit is adjusted to the needs of gifted learners. There should also be some guidelines offered on how to teach the unit, how to secure the resources, and how to handle student assessment.

A complete unit following the model presented in *Reach Each You Teach* (Treffinger, Hohn, & Feldhusen, 1989) is presented in Example 6.B. The topic is fairy tales; its target grade levels are 2–5. Note that the assessment of student progress or achievement of objectives is called *assessment checkpoint*. Some teachers who used the term *evaluation* in units found that it created confusion with the sixth level of the Bloom Taxonomy, which is also called *evaluation*. Thus, we suggest the terms *checkpoint* or *assessment* as alternatives. Treffinger, Hohn, and Feldhusen described a variety of procedures for evaluating student progress and for keeping records of student progress and achievement.

This author has had extensive experience in helping teachers develop units of the type described here and then later seeing teachers use the units in teaching gifted learners. The settings have included full-time, self-contained classes for the gifted at the elementary level, resource room/pull-out programs, regular classrooms with a gifted cluster, honors classes and seminars at the secondary level, and Saturday/summer extra-school enrichment programs. The units, often combined with learning centers, seem to work well, but an occasional complaint from supervisors is that the unit activities arc not high enough in cognitive level nor fast enough in pace to provide the necessary challenge for the gifted. Special efforts are often needed to get teachers to upgrade the level of expectations and the pace at which students should work. Ordinarily, homework should also be expected with these units.

## Conceptually Oriented Units

An ideal program for gifted and talented youth involves them in ideational challenges and activity as a vehicle to learn subject matter and as a stimulus for their cognitive development. Wittrock (1974) has described the ideal mode of learning as "generative." He suggested that in generative learning situations the student is interacting cognitively with the subject matter through problem solving, experimentation, and inquiry. Through such interaction the student constructs his or her own knowledge basc, which involves much deeper understanding and fluency in using the knowledge. Wheatley (1984) argued that much time is spent in classrooms drilling students on basic skills, teaching rules, and showing students how to use specific algorithms in solving problems. He argued that these basic skills can be taught to gifted students more effectively in the context of exploring concepts, solving problems, discovering new relationships, or conducting an experiment.

Kaplan and colleagues (1979) presented a set of principles of a differentiated curriculum for gifted learners that enunciates several of the points made so far for conceptually oriented curriculum:

1. *Present content that is related to broad-based issues, themes, or problems.*
2. *Integrate multiple disciplines into the area of study.*
3. *Present comprehensive, related, and mutually reinforcing experiences within an area of study.*

4. *Allow for the in-depth learning of a self-selected topic within the area of study.*
5. *Develop independent or self-directed study skills.*
6. *Develop productive, complex, abstract, and/or higher level thinking skills.*
7. *Focus on open-ended tasks.*
8. *Develop research skills and methods.*
9. *Integrate basic skills and higher level thinking skills into the curriculum.*
10. *Encourage the development of products that challenge existing ideas and produce "new" ideas.*
11. *Encourage the development of products that use new techniques, materials, and forms.*
12. *Encourage the development of self-understanding, i.e., recognizing and using one's abilities, becoming self-directed, appreciating likenesses and differences between oneself and others.*
13. *Evaluate student outcomes by using appropriate and specific criteria through self-appraisal, criterion referenced and/or standardized instruments. (p. 5)*

A number of these principles are relevant guides in designing a conceptually oriented curriculum unit for gifted learners, notably items 1, 6, 8, and 9. That is, such units should focus on broad themes or concepts, involve students in using higher-level thinking skills, develop research skills for experimentation and scientific inquiry, and teach basic skills along with higher-level thinking activities.

A concept unit, then, begins with the selection of a concept or theme around which the unit will be developed. For the teacher at the elementary or secondary level, some effort might be exerted to find broad themes or concepts that are particularly relevant or intrinsic to the teacher's discipline or major subject matter area. Thus, a unit on "Beauty" may be particulary relevant in language arts, art, or even social studies, whereas a unit on "Reasoning" might seem to be particularly relevant for a unit in mathematics or science. However, it should be noted in the preceding list of principles from Kaplan and colleagues (1979) that item 2 advocates integration of multiple disciplines into the area of study. Thus, either of these themes might form the base for an interdisciplinary unit of study for a group of gifted and talented youth. VanTassel-Baska and Feldhusen (1981) developed a set of units for the gifted in grades K–8 on the themes of problem solving, change, reasoning, and signs and symbols. Three of these themes were selected from Adler's (1952) *The Great Ideas: A Syntopicon of Great Books of the Western World.* The *Syntopicon* presents essays on 102 of the great ideas from Western world literature. A sample of the concepts is presented in Figure 6–2. These themes present an excellent conceptual framework for developing units of instruction and complete curricula for the gifted.

In his classic work, *Differential Education of the Gifted,* Ward (1961, 1981) argued that curriculum for the gifted should explore concepts extending over broad expanses of the chief branches of knowledge. He also pointed to the *Syntopicon* as an excellent resource for identifying themes or concepts to be taught. In a highly elaborate set of principles, Ward delineated the nature of a differentiated and appropriate curriculum for the gifted. Such a curriculum, he argued, deals with theory and abstractions and involves gifted learners in the challenges of intellectual activity.

We present in Example 6.C a conceptually oriented unit of instruction for middle

**FIGURE 6–2  Concepts found in the *Syntopicon***

| | | |
|---|---|---|
| Aristocracy | Honor | Progress |
| Astronomy | Immortality | Reasoning |
| Beauty | Infinity | Religion |
| Being | Judgment | Revolution |
| Cause | Justice | Rhetoric |
| Chance | Knowledge | Science |
| Change | Labor | Sense |
| Citizen | Language | Signs and Symbols |
| Courage | Law | Sin |
| Custom and Convention | Liberty | Soul |
| Democracy | Life and Death | Space |
| Desire | Logic | State |
| Dialectic | Love | Temperance |
| Duty | Matter | Theology |
| Emotion | Metaphysics | Time |
| Eternity | Mind | Truth |
| Evolution | Monarchy | Tyranny |
| Family | Nature | Virtue and Vice |
| Fate | Necessity and Contingency | Wealth |
| Form | Oligarchy | Will |
| Good and Evil | One and Many | Wisdom |
| Happiness | Pleasure and Pain | World |

school gifted students. The unit focuses on the concept of "inverse" in mathematics. The teacher-developer began by identifying the theme as a part of a larger curricular sequence of experiences in a high school mathematics class. He then proceeded to identify associated subconcepts, ideas, and resources that might become a part of the ideational framework of the unit. That analysis and elaboration took the form of a conceptual network analysis. Out of this analysis, there emerged the more articulate framework for the unit.

In the next stage of developing the concept unit, the teacher-developer gathered resource materials, wrote the objectives for each topic (often using a matrix approach like that described earlier), planned the specific instructional activities and/or alternatives that might be used, and established the assessment or evaluation procedures. In all forms of instructional units for gifted learners, the assessment procedure ought to involve students in learning how to evaluate their own work and experiencing self-assessment prior to teacher evaluation. Gifted learners can develop their own criteria or standards for evaluation of their productions or performances. This can often best be done in small groups. The criteria can then be used by individuals. We have observed a procedure in some gifted classes where children use a checklist of criteria for evaluation of their independent study projects. In other classrooms we have observed groups of children formulating criteria to evaluate student oral presentations. We have also seen gifted classes in which students are doing their own report cards before the teacher does them. In all these situations gifted students are learning to be self-evaluators, free from dependence on teachers and other adults for evaluation of their work.

The unit presented in Example 6.C has been used in a variety of settings with gifted middle school students. Evaluations of student achievement indicate that the unit is effective in helping students master the objectives. Teachers find the unit very teachable, and students are highly motivated by the learning activities.

## *Steps in Developing a Unit of Instruction*

The steps in developing a unit of instruction can be summarized as follows:

1. Selecting content or concepts
2. Developing outline and sequence
3. Gathering ideational resources
4. Developing an overall design
5. Establishing goals
6. Planning and writing objectives
7. Planning and writing activities
8. Specifying evaluation
9. Assembling resources
10. Assembling units

Teachers who are developing units for gifted students may vary the sequence somewhat to suit their own creative styles. For example, some teachers prefer to begin with activities and work backward to objectives and forward to evaluation, but whatever the order, the essential elements of a unit are contained in this model for unit development.

## *Conclusion*

We have described three types of instructional units that can be developed by individual teachers of gifted students or by teams of teachers in a curriculum development project. The procedures set forth in this chapter provide for the development of teaching units—that is, the specific guidelines and materials for classroom interaction with a group of gifted learners. These units can form part of the larger, articulated curriculum plan with grade level, subject matter, scope, and time sequence specifications. Thus, the larger plan might specify that the unit on language be used in fifth-grade gifted resource room in November, to be followed by the solar energy unit in December. Ordinarily, an articulated curriculum plan would cover several years of instruction.

The resource-type unit that was presented first provides a format for organizing all of the components of an instructional unit, but it says little directly about how to teach it. The content-oriented unit, on the other hand, specifies more directly the procedures and sequence of activities for teaching and evaluating achievement of gifted students. The content-oriented unit and the resource unit are both adaptable in respect to focus. However, the concept-oriented unit specifically demands that the substance of the unit be conceptual or thematic in nature while permitting alternative structural approaches.

The design of units presented in this chapter is an element of Stage IV of curriculum planning set forth in Chapter 2. An outline was presented there for steps and considerations in creating units of instruction. Item 10 in the Sample Outline for Curriculum Units called for relating the unit to other or broader aspects of the macrocurriculum plan. The first two units illustrated at the end of this chapter, "Encounters with the Eminent" and "Fairy Tales" are parts of their schools' language arts curriculum, whereas "Mathematical Inverses" is multidisciplinary and hence related to several areas, notably mathematics, economics, and the arts. Ultimately, units of instruction should provide accelerated and enriched learning experiences that challenge and motivate gifted students to strive for excellence and commit themselves to the highest and most creative levels of achievement.

### Key Points Summary

- *A unit of instruction is a teaching plan that defines objectives, activities, evaluation procedures, and resources.*
- *Macrocurriculum plans in the form of scope and sequence statements need to be translated into specific teaching units.*
- *One form of unit is the resource unit,* a compilation and statement of all the information and media resources needed for a unit of instruction.
- *Another form of unit is called the content unit.* It provides a more specific sequential teaching plan but focuses mainly on traditional content.
- *Conceptually oriented units focus mainly on broad, subsuming concepts. These units are similar to content-oriented units in that they provide a sequential teaching plan.*
- *Units of instruction are adaptable to all types of programs, levels of instruction, and educational settings.*
- *Units are particularly effective in learning center environments.*

## References

Adler, M. J. (1952). *The great ideas: A syntopicon of great books of the Western world*. Chicago: Encyclopedia Britannica.

Bishop, A. (1985). The social construction of meaning—A significant development for mathematics education. *For The Learning of Mathematics, 51*. 24–28.

Bloom, B. S. (1956). *Taxonomy of educational objectives, handbook I, cognitive domain*. New York: Longman.

Bruner, J. (1960). *The process of education*. Cambridge, MA: Harvard University Press.

Ennis, R. H. (1985). A logical basis for measuring critical thinking skills. *Educational Leadership, 43* (2), 44–48.

Harrow, A. J. (1972). *A taxonomy of the psychomotor domain*. New York: David McKay.

Kaplan, S. N., et al. (1979). *Inservice training manual: Activities for developing curriculum for the gifted/talented*. Los Angeles: National/State Leadership Training Institute on The Gifted and Talented.

Krathwohl, D. R., Bloom, B. S., & Masia, B. B. (1964). *Taxonomy of educational objectives, handbook II, affective domain*. New York: David McKay.

Mager, R. F. (1975). *Preparing instructional objectives*. Belmont, CA: Fearon-Pittman.

Maker, C. J. (1986). Developing scope and sequence in curriculum. *Gifted Child Quarterly, 30* (4), 151–158.

Piaget, J, & Inhelder, B. (1969). *The psychology of the child*. New York: Basic Books.

Sigel, B. (1984). A constructivist perspective for

teaching thinking. *Educational Leadership, 42* (3), 18–21.

Taba, H. (1962). *Curriculum development: Theory and practice.* New York: Harcourt, Brace and World.

Treffinger, D. J., Hohn, R. L., & Feldhusen, J. F. (1989). *Reach each you teach II.* Buffalo, NY: DOK Publishers.

VanTassel-Baska, J., & Feldhusen, J. F. (1981). *Concept curriculum for the gifted.* Matteson, IL: Matteson School District #162.

von Glasersfeld, E., & Cobb, P. (1983). Knowledge as environmental fit. *Man-environment Systems, 3* (5), 2 (6–224).

Ward, V. S. (1961). *Differential education for the gifted.* Columbus, OH: Charles E. Merrill.

Wheatley, G. H. (1984). Instruction for the gifted: Philosophies and approaches. In J. F. Feldhusen (Ed.), *Toward excellence in gifted education.* Denver: Love Publishing.

Wittrock, M. (1974). Learning as a generative process. *Educational Psychologist, 11,* 87–95.

---

**EXAMPLE 6.A    Encounters with the Eminent**

### A Resource Unit for Primary and Intermediate Grades

#### Debbi Ruckman
#### Gifted Education Resource Institute

The primary purpose of this unit, designed for third through sixth-graders, is to acquaint gifted students with a series of famous people. Through this study, the students will be able to draw conclusions and parallels that will affect the conduct of their own lives and potential careers.

*Encounters with the Eminent* by its very nature employs a wide variety of content areas through the diverse complex of people who may be studied. In the resource section, major attempts are made to include references about well-known people in many fields, both dreamers and doers, from many differing life-styles and eras, with a great divergence of characteristics. What they all have in common is success in career achievements, success in setting goals and attaining them, success in knowing who they are, and success in gaining the confidence needed to excel. Thus, the major theme to impart to the students as they use these persons as role models is SUCCESS.

## Context

*Encounters with the Eminent* is designed for use with academically talented students in a pull-out and/or Saturday setting, with time alloted outside of classroom meetings for investigation and readings. The unit was piloted with a group of third-through fifth-graders. This unit serves as a resource to plan for any type of classroom use, but is particularly suggested for use with the combination of group discussion and activities, learning center (creativity) activities, and independent study.

## Differentiation

This unit attempts to differentiate curriculum in one or more ways. Much of the content focuses more on higher levels of abstractness and complexity than the regular curriculum. A most substantial content modification is in the choice of topic itself: the study of people.

There is opportunity within the unit for many open-ended questions and activities. Students are asked to back up their lines of reasoning with proof. This is a great opportunity for group interaction with peers in the Saturday or resource room setting, and the interdisciplinary nature of the people studied provides great variety in both content and process.

Students will discover how the real problems of real people relate to their own real problems and will be encouraged to evaluate their own products as they use them in some real way with an appropriate audience.

Finally, environmental modifications will depend in part on the setting and the individual teacher leading the unit. The unit is designed to be student centered, with discussions and research taking place in an open and accepting atmosphere.

*Content Outline*

    I. Characteristics and Achievement
        A. Personal attributes
            1. relationship to personal achievement
            2. relative importance
        B. Intelligence
        C. Creativity characteristics

   II. Interests/Mentors
        A. Favorite books of the eminent
        B. Hobbies of the eminent
        C. Mentors of famous people

  III. Educational Backgrounds
        A. Importance of education
        B. Evaluation of educational needs for professions

  IV. Cultural/Racial and Religious Influences
        A. Cultural/Racial studies
            1. African American
            2. American Indian
            3. Non-American
        B. Religion

    V. Historical Influences
        A. Political implications
        B. Social implications
        C. Wars and their implications
        D. Inventions and their implications
        E. Present and future implications

  VI. Effect of Sex Roles
        A. Past

B. Present
C. Future

VII. Problems Encountered by the Eminent
   A. Troubled homes
   B. Dislike of school and teachers
   C. Domineering mothers/fathers
   D. Social difficulties/nonacceptance
   E. Disabilities

## *Objectives (Content and Process)*

The following list of stated objectives is coded by levels of the Bloom Taxonomy using these abbreviations:

   K  = Knowledge
   C  = Comprehension
   AP = Application
   An = Analysis
   S  = Synthesis
   E  = Evaluation

Following participation in group discussions, group activites, creativity activities, and independent study, students will be able to:

| | |
|---|---|
| E | 1. Recognize and evaluate the relative importance of personal attributes in achievement. |
| C | 2. Cite examples of famous people who exemplify these personal attributes. |
| Ap | 3. Recognize these attributes in themselves. |
| An | 4. Realize the importance of education in eminent individuals' lives. |
| E | 5. Evaluate educational needs for a given profession. |
| An | 6. Compare and contrast educational backgrounds of famous people with their own. |
| An | 7. Analyze the effect political viewpoints and conflicts of an era had on the lives of famous people. |
| An | 8. Recognize how social and moral values are reflected in life histories of famous people. |
| C | 9. Understand how wars have influenced the upbringing of many of the eminent. |
| An | 10. Relate lives of inventors to their inventions. |
| An | 11. Predict how the present and future will become influences on the eminent of tomorrow. |
| An | 12. Perceive how ethnic and religious convictions affect the lives of famous people. |
| An | 13. Assess how male-female roles of past, present, and future relate to the lives of eminent people. |

C        14. Recount personal struggles experienced by famous people in home life, school life, and society in general.
E        15. Evalute the means by which people overcame these problems.
S        16. Develop a plan for overcoming one's own personal hardships or disabilities.
An       17. Relate reading preferences and hobbies to the achievements of eminent people.
E        18. Evaluate the importance of mentors in the lives of eminent people.
E        19. Determine an appropriate mentor for themselves.
Ap       20. Develop a greater ability to produce ideas fluently, flexibly, originally, and elaboratively.
S        21. Use the creative problem-solving process effectively in the context of solving their own career problems.
An       22. Conduct an independent in-depth study of one or more eminent individuals using a comparison-contrast format.

*Group Activities and Class Discussion Topics*

1. Using these characteristics—optimism, health, patience, self-confidence, courage, perseverance, willingness to take risks, peer/family support, money, and ability to delay gratification—rank them from 1 to 10 in order of importance to a person's success or achievement. Compare your rankings with those of others in the class.
2. List ways to cope with failure.
3. List ways to cope with success.
4. Play "Who's Who in Black History?"—a card matching game.
5. Play the *People Magazine* Trivia Game.
6. Chart the steps you would follow in aiming at a particular famous individual's career.
7. If Thomas Edison would visit Disneyworld, what would he say? Discuss.
8. Describe an experience when you were reluctant to try a new task, sport, or skill. Who encouraged you to do so? How did they do so?
9. Discuss the changing role of women in sports.
10. Play excerpts from Bill Cosby comedy records. Discuss his humor and how it is derived from his life experiences.
11. Rank the following 10 people in relative importance as to their contributions to society: Jesus Christ, Thomas Edison, Ben Franklin, Abraham Lincoln, Christopher Columbus, Albert Einstein, Karl Marx, Sigmund Freud, Mark Twain, and Charles Darwin. Defend your decisions.
12. Listen to excerpts from *Cradles of Eminence* by Goertzel and Goertzel. How do the upbringings of famous individuals relate to each other and to you?
13. Discuss: How do today's headlines influence the eminent people of tomorrow?
14. Discuss: What famous women of the past could have used some "women's lib" influence in their lives? How?
15. What famous person of the past would you choose to have as your mentor? What would you have them do? Discuss how your life would be different as a result.

16. Choose a problem encountered in the life of a famous person. In a small group, use the creative problem-solving approach to elicit a solution different from the one the person may have actually employed.
17. Brainstorm characteristics other than those named in Activity #1 that are important in achieving success.

*Creative Activities*

1. Draw a caricature of a famous person; then do one of yourself. Any similarities?
2. Write a letter of advice to a famous person, counseling him or her on a personal problem.
3. Do a creative talent illustration—what kind of animal, bird, fish, weather, food, plant, flower are you like? Illustrate.
4. Design a birthday card to send to a famous person.
5. Collect quotations of famous Americans and compile a book of them.
6. Make bookmarks or greeting cards for friends using quotations from famous people.
7. Create a recipe of characteristics that make up an eminently successful person.
8. Imagine you are going to interview _____. What would you ask him or her?
9. Create a trivia game involving a related group of famous people.
10. Design a collection of posters showing people remembered in history in some related way.
11. Complete a time line relating the sequence of events in several famous person's lives.
12. There is room for one more: Draw your own face between those of Teddy Roosevelt and Abraham Lincoln on Mt. Rushmore.
13. Create a legend about yourself. Include what you want to accomplish.
14. Do humorous or serious artistic interpretations of quotations from famous people.
15. Create a work in the style that a famous person you admire uses, either in prose, poetry, song, or the arts.
16. Select a year of the past. Then consider famous persons working during that year (artists, actors, musicians, authors). Design an award given by an actual group of that period. Tell what the award is given for and the criteria by which the persons were judged.
17. A famous person from the past has called and left you a message. What was the message?
18. Make a chronological chart of an eminent person's life.
19. Make a time line of world leaders from Queen Victoria to John F. Kennedy. Show the issues involved in their times. Rank the leaders' influence.
20. Write an epitaph for a famous person. Suggestions: Mark Twain, Jesse James, Harry Truman.

## Independent Study

Independent research will be conducted on one or more creative, well-known people using one of the following optional themes.

1. An in-depth study of one famous person, relating that person to yourself in some way.
2. A comparison-contrast study of two or more people of the same era who worked in different fields.
3. A comparison-contrast study of two or more people in the same field of endeavor but who lived in different times.
4. A comparison-contrast study of a female and a male famous in the same field.
5. A comparison-contrast study of three people in the arts who lived in the same era (e.g., Pablo Picasso, Clark Gable, and Louis Armstrong).
6. A comparison-contrast study of two or more people with another well-defined relationship as seen by the student (e.g., father-daughter study of Henry and Jane Fonda).
7. Work through an entire unit from *Creative Encounters with Creative People* by Janice Gudeman. This will include readings, creative encounters, and independent projects.

## Mentors

A mentorship relationship can be developed with people in the community who are successful, eminent people like those studied in the unit. Possible choices could come from the following:

Political—mayor, legislator, judge, attorney
Media—newscaster, sportscaster, actor, comedian
Athletic—player, coach
Arts—musician, painter, sculptor, designer, architect, writer
Military—leader, pilot
Science—researcher, physician, psychologist, professor

## Teacher Resources

Bogojavlensky, A., & Grossman, D. (1977). *The great learning book.* Menlo Park, CA: Addison-Wesley.

DeBono, E. (1976). *The greatest thinkers.* New York: G. P. Putnam's Sons.

Feldhusen, J. F. (1984). *The Purdue creative thinking program.* Lafayette, IN: Gifted Education Resource Institute.

Forte, I., & MacKenzie, J. (1976). *Kid's stuff social studies.* Nashville: TN: Incentive Publications.

Goertzel, V., & Goertzel, M. (1962). *Cradles of Eminence.* Boston: Little, Brown.

Gudeman, J. (1984). *Creative encounters with creative people.* Carthage, IL: Good Apple.

Holmes, D, & Christie, T. (1978). *Thumbs up.* Carthage, IL: Good Apple.

Yapp, M., Killingray, M., & O'Connor, E. (1980). *Greenhaven world history program: History makers.* St. Paul, MN: Greenhaven Press.

## Media Resources

The following biographical sketches in filmstrip format can be obtained from the local media center.

| | | |
|---|---|---|
| George Rogers Clark | Story of James Oglethorpe | Francis Scott Key |
| Ethan Allen | William Penn | Dolley Madison |
| Susan B. Anthony | Paul Revere | Peter Stuyvesant |
| Johnny Appleseed | Captain John Smith | Booker T. Washington |
| John James Audubon | Robert Louis Stevenson | Story of George Washington |
| Johann Sebastian Bach | Buffalo Bill | Roger Williams |
| Ludwig von Beethoven | Columbus | Eli Whitney |
| Daniel Boone | Story of Hernando deSoto | Joan of Arc |
| Story of Admiral Byrd | Leif Ericson | Story of Dr. Lister |
| Andrew Carnegie | Benjamin Franklin | Wright Brothers |
| Story of Lewis and Clark | John C. Fremont | Sam Houston |
| Story of Abraham Lincoln | Lee and Grant | Martin Luther King |
| Horace Mann | Nathan Hale | Ponce de Leon in the New |
| Marco Polo | Patrick Henry | World |
| Story of Father Marquette | John Paul Jones | Betsy Ross |

## Text Materials

American Heritage. (1960). *Men of science and invention.* New York: Golden Press.

Asimov, I. (1972). *Asimov's biographical encyclopedia of science and technology.* Garden City, NY: Doubleday.

Baldwin, G. C. (1973). *Inventors and inventions of the ancient world.* New York: Four Winds.

Batten, M. (1968). *Discovery by chance: Science and the unexpected.* New York: Funk and Wagnalls.

Bell, E. T. (1937). *Men of mathematics.* New York: Simon and Schuster.

Berger, M. (1968). *Famous men of modern biology.* New York: Crowell.

Block, E. B. (1967). *Famous detectives.* Garden City, NY: Doubleday.

Bolton, S. (1961). *Famous men of science.* New York: Crowell.

Bolton, S. (1962). *Lives of poor boys who became famous.* New York: Thomas Y. Crowell and Sons.

Cane, P., & Nisenson (1959). *Giants of science.* New York: Gosset and Dunlap.

Chandler, M. H. (1964). *Man the inventor.* Chicago: Rand-McNally.

Chase, A. (1964). *Famous artists of the past.* Platt.

Clark, P. (1979). *Famous names in science.* Wayland.

Cooper, M. (1965). *The inventions of Leonardo da Vinci.* New York: Macmillan.

Cottler, J., & Joffe, H. (1969). *Heroes of civilization.* Boston: Little, Brown.

Cournos, J., & Norton, S. (1954). *Famous modern American novelists.* New York: Dodd, Mead.

Cox, D. W. (1974). *Pioneers of ecology.* Maplewood, NJ: Hammond.

Eberle, I. (1945). *Famous inventors for young people.* New York: Dodd, Mead.

Evans, I. O. (1962). *Inventors of the World.* London: Frederick Warne.

Gies, J., & Gies, F. (1976). *The ingenious Yankees.* New York: Crowell.

Haber, L. (1970). *Black pioneers of science and invention.* New York: Harcourt, Brace and World.

Hayden, R. C. (1970). *Seven black American scientists.* Reading, MA: Addison-Wesley.

Halacy, D. S. (1967). *They gave their name to science.* New York: Putnam.

Heath, M. (1956). *Great American inventors and scientists.* Menlo Park, CA: Pacific Coast Publishers.

Heyn, E. V. (1976). *Fire of genius: Inventors of the past century.* Garden City, NY: Doubleday.

Hoff, R., & de Terra, H. (1968). *They explored!* New York: McGraw-Hill.

Hollander, Z. D. (1966). *Great American athletes of the twentieth century.* New York: Random House.

Hughes, L. (1954). *Famous American negroes.* New York: Dodd, Mead.

Hughes, L. (1955). *Famous Negro music makers.* New York: Dodd, Mead.

Hylander, C. J. (1934). *American inventors.* New York: Macmillan.

Jacobs, H. D. (1975). *Famous modern American women athletes.* New York: Dodd, Mead.

Johnston, C. H. L. (1909). *Famous Indian chiefs.* Boston: L. C. Page.

Klein, A. E. (1971). *The hidden contributors: Black scientists and inventors in America.* Garden City, NY: Doubleday.

Kundsin, R. B. (1974). *Women and success.* New York: W. Morrow.

Land, B. (1968). *The telescope makers: From Galileo to the Space Age.* New York: Crowell.

Lavine, S. A. (1965). *Famous merchants.* New York: Dodd, Mead.

Leahy, W. (1975). *Stars of the Olympics.* New York: Hawthorne.

Leipold, L. E. (1971). *Famous American architects.* Minneapolis, MN: T. S. Denison.

Lovejoy, E. P. (1957). *Women doctors of the world.* New York: Macmillan.

McKinney, R. J. (1955). *Famous American painters.* New York: Dodd, Mead.

Marinacci, B. (1961). *Leading ladies.* New York: Dodd, Mead.

Milne, L. J. (1952). *Famous naturalists.* New York: Dodd, Mead.

Morrison, E. E. (1966). *Men, machines and modern times.* Cambridge, MA: MIT Press.

Norman, B. (1976). *The inventing of America.* New York: Taplinger.

Osen, L. M. (1975). *Women in mathematics.* Cambridge, MA: MIT Press.

Overmyer, G. (1944). *Famous American composers.* New York: Crowell.

Pickering, J. S. (1968). *Famous astronomers.* New York: Dodd, Mead.

Ploski, H. A., & Marr, W. (1976). *The Negro almanac: A reference work on the Afro-American.* New York: Bellwether.

Poole, L., & Poole, G. (1960). *Scientists who changed the world.* New York: Dodd, Mead.

Poole, L., & Poole, G. (1969). *Men who pioneered inventions.* New York: Dodd, Mead.

Pratt, F. (1955). *All about famous inventors and their inventions.* New York: Random House.

Rogers, J. A. (1972). *World's great men of color.* New York: Macmillan. Vol. I, Ancients; Vol. II, Modern.

Silverberg, R. (1965). *Scientists and scoundrels: A book of hoaxes.* New York: Crowell.

Stoddard, H. (1970). *Famous American women.* New York: Crowell.

Truman, M. (1976). *Women of courage.* New York: W. Morrow and Sons.

Walker, G. (1975). *Women today: Ten profiles.* New York: Hawthorn.

Western Electric Co. (undated). *Legacy for all: A record of achievements by Black American scientists.*

Williams, G. (1959). *Virus hunters.* New York: Knopf.

Wilson, M. A. (1972). *Passion to know: The world's scientists.* Garden City, NY: Doubleday.

Yost, E. (1962). *Modern Americans in science and technology.* New York: Dodd, Mead.

Yost, E. (1959). *Women of modern science.* New York: Dodd, Mead.

**EXAMPLE 6.B   Fairy Tales**

### *A Content-Oriented Unit for Gifted Students in Grades 2–5*

*Marcy Chudnov*
*Indianapolis, Indiana*

## *Rationale*

Fairy tales are a part of many children's cultural background, and hopefully most children have read or have had read to them folk and/or fairy tales. This unit teaches not only the components of fairy tales but also compares different versions of fairy tales and illustrates the effect of cultural influences on folk literature. The unit also introduces the concept of sterotypes and encourages the child to transfer knowledge from fairy tales to contemporary life.

## Differentiation

This unit is differentiated for gifted students in several ways. First, it assumes that the children will be reading two or three years above their grade level. Second, it engages them in a great deal of higher-level thinking activity. Third, it tries to integrate the teaching of basic skills with higher-level thinking activity. Fourth, it involves the youngsters in much creative project and production activity. Fifth, the students are expected to engage in self- and peer assessment of their work. And sixth, the students are allowed to become self-directing and independent as they go about the activities. At all times the teacher should encourage the children to strive for superior performance and products.

## To the Teacher

This unit is intended to be used as one semester's work for middle elementary high-ability students in the reading area. It is assumed that the students will be reading at two or more years above grade level. It is also assumed that the students have a background in folk and fairy tale literature. If you find that some of your students lack a working knowledge of folk and fairy tale literature, it is suggested that you teach to that deficit area before proceeding with the unit.

In order to accomplish the objectives in this unit, many activities have been listed. Hopefully, the children will be able to achieve their objectives using only some of the listed activities. Certainly, the ambitious student is welcome to try all listed activities.

This unit has been designed to proceed from one level of the stated taxonomy to the next in order to encourage higher-level thinking processes. Therefore, it is recommended that the teacher use the unit according to this design and not jump from one objective to another. It is also recommended that, if possible, the children view the unit as a gestalt and have the opportunity to learn the system of this particular taxonomy.

## To the Student

This unit has been designed in hopes that as you progress through its various phases you will increase your knowledge of the origin and purpose of fairy and folk literature and the many elements that combine to make good fairy tale reading.

Many activities are offered to help you understand and master the objectives listed. You are encouraged to be original and creative in your methods of working these activities. Try the unusual! Good luck!

## I. Topic: Identification of Fairy Tales—Origin and Purpose

*Objectives and Corresponding Activities*

### Objectives

1. Define the term *fairy tale.*

2. Identify several fairy tales.

1. *Knowledge Level*

### Activities

a. Work with some other children in locating some other tales you have not read yet.
b. Read the new fairy tales you have found.

---

### Objectives

Explain the cultural influences on style of a fairy tale that appears in several versions.

2. *Comprehension Level*

### Activities

a. Read several different versions of the same fairy story.
b. Listen to the "Cinderella" tape that discusses different versions of this tale.
c. Share what you have learned about cultural effects on tales with the class.

---

### Objectives

1. List as many different reasons for the need of fairy tales as possible.
2. List the different attributes of fairy tales.

3. *Creative Thinking Level*

### Activities

a. Listen to the teachers lecture on atttributes and attribute listing. Take good notes.
b. Brainstorm with a small group of classmates and list all the reasons you can think of for writing fairy tales.
c. Divide the list into categories to see if you can compose a new list of attributes common to most fairy tales.

---

### Objectives

1. Report your findings on the common attributes of fairy tales.

4. *Application Level*

*Activities*

a. Construct a chart listing attributes of fairy tales.
b. Interview other students to find how their lists differ or are similar to yours.

---

*Objectives*

1. Choose various characters from some of your favorite fairy tales to study in-depth as to character analysis.    6. *Synthesis Level*

*Activities*

a. Role-play these characters and explain their actions to the class.
b. Listen to the teacher-made tape on "Character Analysis" at the learning center.
c. Infer from the list of character attributes the reasons for the actions of the characters you have chosen.
d. Read Chapter 7 in our English book—"Character Analysis."

---

*Assessment Checkpoint*

This topic will be assessed in the following way:

1. Teacher assessment will be based on: ability to define a fairy tale, understanding of cultural influences on tales, ability to understand and explain society's need for tales, and ability to list and identify common attributes of fairy tales.

---

### II. Topic: Plot Structure-Theme-Story Line

*Objectives*

1. Develop an understanding of plot structure in fairy tales.
2. Read a variety of fairy tales.

*Activities*

a. Take good notes when you listen to the teacher lecture on theme and plot structure.    1. *Knowledge Level*
b. Read *Blue Beard, Diamonds and Toads,* and *Ricky with a Tuft* for enjoyment.
c. Discuss with teacher and class: plot development.
d. Match: who, when, and where elements in two or more tales.
e. Match: first, second, and third events in two or more tales.

*Objective*

1. Identify common elements in some fairy tales that you have read for the first time.

2. *Comprehension Level*

*Activities*

a. Make a tape to share your findings.
b. Make a diorama of a tale you have read.
c. Prepare a radio play of a favorite tale with other students.

*Objective*

1. Predict several different endings to the "Hansel and Gretel" story.

3. *Creative Thinking*

*Activities*

a. Write or create a chart that allows you to switch elements within this fairy tale.
b. Create a poster that would tell this story with a different ending.

*Objective*

1. Write a new beginning and ending to a fairy tale.

4. *Application Level*

*Activities*

a. Write a new beginning and ending to the "Hansel and Gretel" story.
b. Experiment with other possibilities in the story line.
c. Record an updated version of this tale and add it to the learning center.

*Objectives*

1. Compare stories/tales with similar plot structures.
2. Identify themes in several fairy tales that you have read.

5. *Analysis Level*

*Activities*

a. Write a report in which you compare and contrast stories/ tales with different themes.
b. Prepare a commercial that will entice the class to read one tale over another.

*Objective*

1. Relate how the style for a particular fairy tale matches its context.

6. *Synthesis Level*

### Activities

a. Create your own original dialogue to portray a specific character in a tale (for example; Puss in "Puss and Boots").
b. Infer and demonstrate dialogue to that story that would be relevant to today's contemporary life.

### Objective

1. Decide if fairy tales of the past have relevance in our society of today.

*7. Evaluation Level*

### Activities

a. Participate in a panel discussion that debates the above issue.
b. Prepare a news item that supports or does not support fairy tales as being relevant to today's contemporary life.

### Assessment Checkpoint

This topic will be assessed in the following ways:
1. Class assessment of reports, dialogues, and commercials (a total group score would be used).
2. Self-assessment by students of their own creative efforts in making original tapes, radio plays, posters, and diagrams.
3. Teacher assessment for this topic will be based on: students' understanding of plot structure, knowledge of common elements in fairy tales, and ability to identify themes within tales.

## III. Topic: Setting-Locale-Elements

### Objectives

1. Identify elements in a story that lead to fantasy.
2. Understand the concept of symbolism and how and why it is used.

*1. and 2. Knowledge and Comprehensive Level*

### Activities

a. Match similar elements in "The Three Bears" and "The Three Pigs."
b. Listen to the tape "Rapunzel" at the learning center. This tape will omit certain key elements in the story.
c. Locate and identify the missing elements.
d. Listen and take good notes on the teachers' lecture on symbolism.

e. Work with a small group of classmates and ask each other what symbols are present in "Sleeping Beauty" and "Dick Whittington."

### Objective

1. Invent your own brand of "fairly tale symbolism."

3. *Creative Think-ing*

### Activities

a. Write a fairy tale of your own using as many different kinds of symbolism as possible.
b. Compose a jingle that would go along with your fairy tale.

### Objective

1. Construct an artistic endeavor that records different types of symbolism.

4. *Application Level*

### Activities

a. Sketch or paint an illustration depicting the various types of symbolism in "The Emperor's New Clothes."
b. Prepare a diorama that shows the major symbolic event in "Snow White and The Seven Dwarfs."
c. Construct a puzzle that takes one "Down the Symbolic Road."

### Objective

1. Categorize the many elements you have found in fairy tales.

5. *Analysis Level*

### Activities

a. Prepare a graph showing which elements are used more than others.
b. Make a chart that separates elements that are used more often from those that are used less often.

### Objective

1. Combine more of the less-used elements with a few elements that are often used in fairy tales.

6. *Synthesis Level*

### Activities

a. Create a cartoon depicting the "Jack and the Beanstalk" fairy tale using the above combination.

b. Produce a puppet show for kindergarten students using this new combination of elements.

---

## Assessment Checkpoint

This topic will be assessed in the following ways:
1. Class assessment of graphs, charts, and fairy tales prepared by various students (using a total group score).
2. Self-assessment by students of their own creative efforts in making original cartoons, puppet shows, and jingles.
3. Teacher assessment for this topic will be based on: understanding of plot structure, knowledge of common elements in fairy tales, and ability to identify themes within tales.

---

### IV. Topic: Characters

*Objective*

1. Observe characters who remain the same in fairy tales and those who show growth and change.

1. *Knowldege Level*

*Activities*

a. Read "Jack and the Beanstalk" to learn how Jack changes as a person.
b. Identify other characters that grow and change in other tales.
c. Listen to the teacher's lecture on character development and take notes.
d. Watch the film *Character Development in Stories.*

---

*Objectives*

1. Explain why some changes are necessary in characters.
2. Ask others what their feelings are about various characters they have read about.

2. *Comprehension Level*

*Activities*

a. Read several different fairy tales to see if there are characters in each that show growth and change.
b. Watch the filmstrip on *Characters in Fairy Tales.*
c. Ask and observe other children felt about "the wolf eating grandmother." How did you feel about this? Share your feelings.

---

*Objectives*

1. Develop a storyboard for a roll movie.

4. *Application Level*

2. Dramatize a scene from a story.

### Activities

a. Illustrate each segment of your storyboard.
b. Share your storyboard with the class.
c. Dramatize the scene from the fairy tale "The Princess and The Pea" when the Princess could not sleep.

---

### Objectives

1. Compare one character with another as to likenesses and differences.
2. Compare the treatment of animals as characters in fairy tales.

5. *Analysis Level*

### Activities

a. Compare and contrast the likenesses and differences between Hansel and Jack.
b. Compare and contrast the initial treatment of Wilbur the Pig to Charlotte the Spider.

---

### Objective

1. Given different teacher suggested situations, predict how you think a character would act.

6. *Synthesis Level*

### Activities

a. Estimate how Jack would have acted if he knew there was a mean giant at the top of the stalk *before* he climbed it!
b. Predict what Snow White would have done if she knew:
    1. The old woman was her stepmother
    2. The apple was poisoned

---

### Objective

1. Evaluate the possibilities that could occur if the treatment of animals in fairy tales were exchanged.

7. *Evaluation Level*

### Activity

a. Decide what would happen in each story if the characterization treatment of animals in "The Three Little Pigs" and "Puss and Boots" were exchanged.

---

### Assessment Checkpoint

This topic will assessed in the following way:
1. Teacher assessment for this topic will be based on: students

ability to discuss character growth and change, likenesses and differences in characters, and ability to compare and contrast the treatment of and placement of animals as characters in fairy tales.

---

### V. Topic: Events/Time Sequence

#### Objective

1. Observe how the plot develops in several fairy tales that your teacher has read to you.

1. *Knowledge Level*

#### Activities

a. Identify the scenes in sequence in "The Three Little Pigs," "Goldilocks and the Three Bears," and "King Midas."
b. Listen to the tape at the Learning Center that tells the story of Henny Penny out of sequence.
c. Watch the corresponding filmstrip.

---

#### Objective

1. Identify the order of events in some simple fairy tales.

2. *Comprehension Level*

#### Activities

a. Read several fairy tales that are more complex in nature.
b. Make a chart showing the sequence of events in one tale as compared to another.

---

#### Objective

1. Name as many events as possible in one fairy tale.

3. *Creative Thinking Level*

#### Activities

a. Brainstorm with a small group of children to fulfill the above objective.
b. Decide which events in your list will be good for a fairy tale and which can be deleted.
c. Write your own original tale using events from your brainstorming list—be original in your placement of events into a sequence.

---

#### Objective

1. Separate the various events in some fairy tales that you have read.
2. Categorize these events.

5. *Analysis Level*

## Activities

a. Prepare a graph that classifies the events in fairy tales into distinct categories. Use "Rapunzel," "The Golden Fleece," "The Little Match Girl."
b. Chart your results on a poster board.
c. Report your results to the class.

## Objective

1. Hypothesize what would occur if you could reorder events and time sequence in a fairy tale.

6. *Synthesis Level*

## Activities

a. Write a new short version to "The Elves and The Shoemaker" reordering events and time sequence.
b. Superimpose some events from "Goldilocks" on "Henny Penny" and create a new title.

## Objective

1. Discuss with the class the possibility of reordering events in fairy tales.

7. *Evaluation Level*

## Activities

a. Have a court trial "Changing Events and Time Sequences in Cinderella" versus "Not Changing Events and Time Sequences in Cinderella."
b. Conclude whether or not you feel the jury's verdict was right. Write your conclusion as a statement.
c. Write your conclusion as a letter to the judge.

## Assessment Checkpoint

This topic will be assessed in the following ways:
1. Teacher assessment for this topic will be based on: students' ability to discuss and show an understanding of time sequence in tales.
2. Self-assessmnt by students of their own efforts in writing original tales, making charts and graphs, and writing letters and statements.

## VI. Topic: Stereotypes

### Objective

1. Define the term *stereotype*.

1. *Knowledge Level*

2. Identify some stereotypes in fairy tales.

### Activities

a. Listen to the lecture on stereotypes.
b. Discuss with others in a small group stereotypes in tales.
c. Find some stereotypes in "Cinderella."

### Objective

1. Match similar stereotypes in several fairy tales.

2. *Comprehension Level*

### Activities

a. Watch the film on *Fairy Tale Stereotypes.*
b. Read some fairy tales that you have not read before and locate stereotypes in them.
c. Watch television during the week and see if you can find similar stereotypes.

### Objective

1. Relate your knowledge of fairy tale stereotypes to people in the news, radio, and television personalities.

3. *Application Level*

### Activities

a. Write a diary illustrating stereotypes you see each day via the media that compare to those you have met via fairy tales.
b. Illustrate your diary with caricatures of stereotypes.

### Objective

1. Imagine what would happen if your favorite TV character was the villain in a fairy tale.

6. *Synthesis Level*

### Activity

a. Produce a short play from your original fairy tale.

### Objective

1. Evaluate the importance of stereotypes in fairy tales. Are they an ingredient that must be included?

7. *Evaluation Level*

### Activities

a. Survey the class for their opinion on the question: Are stereotypes an element of fairy tales that must always be written in?

b. Conclude from the results of your survey if stereotypes are really necessary.

c. Make your own value judgment.

---

*Assessment Checkpoint*

This topic will be assessed in the following ways:

1. Self-assessment by students of their own creative efforts in writing tales, diaries, and plays.

2. Teacher assessment for this topic will be based on students' ability to identify and discuss the concept of stereotypes, and ability to transfer tale-type stereotypes to present-day stereotypes.

---

## Resource Books for This Unit

Baker, A. (1971). *Young years.* New York: Parents' Magazine Press.

Crosby, N. E., & Martin, E. H. (1981). *Fairy tales.* Cincinnati, OH: Education for Excellence, 7927 Hickory Hill Lane.

Crosby, N. E., & Martin, E. H. (1982). *Mysteries, mythology, fairy tales, fables, legends, the supernatural.* Buffalo, NY: DOK Publishers.

Crosby, N. E., & Martin, E. H. (1983). *Lucky legends.* Buffalo, NY: DOK Publishers.

Cushenberry, D. C., & Howell, H. (1974). *Reading and the gifted child.* Springfield, IL: Charles C. Thomas.

Hoomes, E. W. (1984). *Creat-a-fantasy.* Hawthorne, NJ: Educational Impressions.

Isabelle, J. (1974). *On children's literature.* New York: Schoenken Books.

Lipson, G., & Morrison, B. (1977). *Fact, fantasy and folklore.* Carthage, IL: Good Apple.

Polette, N. (1979). *Activities with folktales and fairytales.* O'Fallon, MO: Book Lures, Inc. P.O. Box 9450.

Polette, N. (1979). *Approaches to literature with gifted kids.* O'Fallon, MO: Book Lures, Inc. P.O. Box 9450.

Sale, R. (1978). *Fairy tales and after.* Cambridge, MA: Harvard University Press.

Stewig, J. W., & Sebesta, S. L. (1978). *Using literature in the elementary classroom.* Urbana, IL: National Council of Teachers of English.

---

## EXAMPLE 6.C Mathematical Inverses

### A Concept Unit for the Middle School

**John Hylkema**
**North Montgomery High School**
**Crawfordsville, Indiana**

## Introduction

This unit deals with the concept of balance, specifically as it relates to the idea of mathematical inverses. These can be thought of as quantities that cancel one another out, balance, are opposites, or are reciprocals. There are also inverse operations; these operations neutralize one another and, when performed successively, return action to the original state. The unit looks at the idea of neutralizing, opposing action as it is manifest in the statistical concept of inversely related variables, the economic concept of revenue neutral budgeting, and the science fiction topic of time and dimension travel. These topics are taken from many different disciplines in order to offer the gifted student the exploration of issues across traditional content boundaries indicated by the student's wide interest and need for an holistic outlook on knowledge. Among other possible areas of investigation are the balance formed by opposing political parties, moderation and balance in living our lives, the scales of justice, weight and measurement, and counterbalances used in engineering (e.g., drawbridge).

This unit is differentiated for gifted students in that it focuses on conceptual understanding in mathematics, not on mechanical skills. Students are also involved in creative thinking and problem solving as well as project activity. The material should be presented at a high level and fast pace. Finally, it is multidisciplinary so that gifted students can learn the concepts as they relate to several disciplines.

The unit is aimed at gifted students with above-average ability in mathematics, verbal, and creative skills working at *upper sixth- to lower ninth-grade levels.* Activities should cover a four- to five-week period; objectives easily break into instructional units of one to two hours. The activities involve a wide variety of instructional modes, including teacher lecture and optional individual or group work to match learner characteristics. Team teaching is a distinct possibility and would involve instructors familiar with math, statistics, economics, and creative arts. Evaluation of some objectives involve student and professional input.

## *Goals*

This unit deals with the concept of balance. Specifically, gifted students will be introduced to the subtopic of inverses and will be able to use them as they relate to mathematics. The student will also examine some analogous ideas from economics and creative arts. Gifted students will begin to examine the importance of balance in life and philosophy through equal but opposing quantities.

*Content Outline*

    I. Mathematics
        A. Algebra
            1. identities
            2. opposites
            3. reciprocals
            4. operations
            5. solving equations
        B. Geometry
            1. geometric transformations
                a. computer design

        C.  Statistics
           1.  graphing data
           2.  direct variation of variables
           3.  inverse variation of variables
  II.   Economics
        A.  Budget making
           1.  revenue neutral
  III.    Creative Arts
        A.  Representations of abstract ideas
           1.  literature
           2.  sculpture, drawing
           3.  writing
           4.  video, film, television

*Objective #1*
*Mathematics: Inverses (knowledge and comprehension)*

Students will be able to state the additive and multiplicative identities, tell how they relate to inverse, state the additive (opposite) or multiplicative (reciprocal) inverse of a number, and group the basic operations as inverse pairs.

*Activities*

1. Lecture on identities, inverse quantities, and inverse operations.
2. Divide students into small groups and assign a conservative assignment to reinforce lecture topics.

*Assessment Checkpoint*

1. Have students work in small groups and design a self-evaluation procedure for their understanding of the concepts.
2. Quiz on identities, inverse quantities, and inverse operations.
3. Help students who are not satisfied or comfortable with their knowledge level.

*Objective #2*
*Mathematics: Inverses (application, analysis, and synthesis)*

Students will be able to compare and contrast various experiences to the idea of inverse, and will develop a chess strategy based on that idea.

*Activities*

1. Brainstorm: "What are some things that happen every day that could be explained as inverses?" (The wind blows your hair; you comb it back to original. Your mom cleans your room; you make it comfortable again. You pay for something with a large bill; the cashier counts back change in a particular manner.)
2. Discuss and elaborate on each of the items developed from brainstorming.
3. Teach the rules of chess. Perhaps they could be presented by a knowledgeable student. Have students play one another until everyone has the basics.
4. Discuss manifestations of inverses on the chessboard.

5. Assign students to develop a strategy for chess based on "inverses."
6. Set up a chess tournament in class. Instruct students to attempt to apply and refine their strategy. Highly successful students should teach their strategies to other students.

*Assessment Checkpoint*

1. Did the student participate in brainstorming and discussions?
2. Student: Was your strategy successful? Were you able to change it to be successful?
3. Encourage self-evaluation by each student.

*Objective #3*
*Mathematics: Inverses (knowledge and competition)*
Students will be able to use the idea of inverse operation to solve linear equations.

*Activities*

1. Discuss/review the various operations involved in a linear equation and how they are manifested.
2. Brainstorm in small groups ideas for uses of inverses in solving linear equations. Examine promising student suggestions and direct discussion toward the preferred method.
3. Assign various equations to be solved by gifted students in small groups. Stress that students should be employing the idea of inverses.

*Assessment Checkpoint*

1. Have students develop one equation each to include on a test over this instructional objective.
2. Have students decide on grading levels after plotting the distribution of test scores.

*Objective #4*
*Mathematics (Geometry): Inverses (application)*
Students will be able to perform basic transformations and state the inverse of any given geometric transformation.

*Activities*

1. Discovery Lesson: This lesson will lead students through ideas of geometric transformations for a square. Students will be reminded of the topics of identities and inverses and asked for applications of those ideas to transformations.
2. Give students various objects, some of which are two-dimensional and others that are three-dimensional. Have them, individually or in small groups, experiment with transformations of their object looking for identity elements and inverses.
3. Students then will present their findings to the rest of the class and answer questions that arise.
4. Bring in a computer expert or engineer to discuss geometric transformation in computer graphics and computer aided design.

*Assessment Checkpoint*

1. The students will be given a teacher-prepared test to check on meeting the criterion. Students may elect to use a form of the test that utilizes objects.
2. After taking the test, each student is asked to identify his or her weak points and to devise a way of correcting the weaknesses.

## Objective #5
*Mathematics (Statistics): Inverses (application)*

Students will be able to graph data and differentiate between direct and inverse variation of variables.

*Activities*

1. Review/learn basic graphing of data.
2. Collect the following information to be graphed: (a) individual females' height and corresponding years in organized basketball and (b) individual males' height and corresponding years in organized basketball.
3. Collect data from the following game: Select 10 volunteers to shoot paper airplanes at the wastebasket. Begin close, then have volunteers move gradually backward, taking 10 shots at each distance. Plot the percentages made at each distance versus the actual distance.
4. Have students in small groups compare graphs of the data. How are they different? What do they show? How does the concept of inverse apply, if at all, in these instances?
5. Brainstorm for other instances where variables are related inversely.
6. Assign students in small groups to gather and present data relating any two variables, as was done in class. They should indicate whether there is inverse or direct variation and how they can tell.

*Assessment Checkpoint*

1. Do the students correctly graph the information in the assignment? Use small group mutual critiquing.
2. Do students correctly distinguish between inverse variation and direct variation? Use small group mutual critiquing.
3. Have students exchange and critique one another's projects.

## Objective #6
*Economics (Budget Marking): Inverses (evaluation)*

Students will be able to make a judgment concerning revenue-neutral budgeting—its viability, applicability, and reliability in various situations.

*Activities*

1. Over a period of two or three weeks, request that each student bring in articles from newspapers, magazines, and journals that deal with budget making at all levels of government.
2. Assign articles that deal with revenue-neutral budgets for student reading. Discuss revenue-neutral and other budget-making topics.
3. Divide students into small groups for the purpose of making budgets. Supply

each group with an actual budget that is currently in use. These could be budgets of the school departments, city, township, community organization, or any other group. Ask students to revise the budget for the next fiscal period. To do this, the students will have to investigate the group and its needs. This will be an ideal budget based on the percept that the group will be getting more funds. Next, have them develop a second budget based on the idea that no additional funds will be available. Both of these budgets should be sent to the groups involved.

*Assessment Checkpoint*

1. Was the group's budget well received by the institution involved? Did the institution use any of the ideas suggested? Were the students asked to provide more input into the budget process? Have each group of students, as organized for the activities, critique the budget plans of another group.
2. Close with a critique by the instructor and a discussion of concepts learned from the unit. Each gifted student contributes and is evaluated by the teacher.

*Objective #7*
*Creative Arts: Inverses (creativity and comprehension)*
Students will be able to creatively interpret the concept of inverse.

*Activities*

1. The students should view any or all of the following:
   *Star Trek*—various episodes involving dimension travel
   *Dr. Who*—episodes dealing with time and dimension travel
   *Back to the Future*—especially the transportation
   *Twilight Zone*—the movie and some of the TV episodes
2. Read science fiction involving time and dimension travel.
3. Assign the students to write a short story, draw a picture, make a sculpture, or produce a video using the idea of inverse as a starting point.

*Note:* These activities are aimed at science fiction. Students who feel more inspired by another area should be encouraged in that direction.

*Evaluation*

1. Products are to be judged on the basis of student- and teacher-generated criteria. Teachers should insist on evidence of the creative process and correct form depending on the medium.

*Chapter* 7

# Language Arts Curriculum for the Gifted

*JOYCE VanTASSEL-BASKA*

*There is no frigate like a book to take us lands away.*
*Nor any coursers like a page of prancing poetry . . .*
—*EMILY DICKINSON*

Although arguments for a high-quality liberal program of study in the language arts have been consistent over the past 10 years (Adler, 1982), the current state of language arts curriculum may be characterized as fragmented by both philosophical orientation and areas of emphasis. The whole-language movement has attempted to integrate language arts areas, to provide opportunities for interdisciplinary work, and to encourage "meaning-making" on the part of the learner (McKenna, Robinson, & Miller, 1990). The cultural literacy movement has attempted to stress the importance of students' developing a rich knowledge base in established works of literature and developing expository writing skills (Hirsch, 1989; Thompson, 1990). A third movement to include multicultural literature and a global perspective is also a primary orientation within the field. Although each of these orientations may be useful in the education of gifted learners, it must be stated that the language arts curriculum for them is as haphazard as it is for other learners. This is especially tragic since high verbal ability is a strong and early indication of gifted behavior. Lists of characteristics of the gifted population have always included several traits related to high verbal ability: early reading, large vocabulary, high-level reading comprehension, and verbal interests such as voracious reading on a wide variety of topics (Gallagher, 1985; Clarke, 1985).

Typical invervention provided for the verbally gifted has been an extension of what is offered to average students in the content area of language arts. Receptive experiences, such as the speaking and listening interactive process, form the core of such programs (Kaplan, 1979). Major differences between regular language arts programs and those for the gifted lie in methodologies and materials, open-ended activities, opportunities for student production, and interdisciplinary work. The combination of these four factors has represented a holistic view of a language arts curriculum for the verbally gifted.

A program emphasis on the concept of values education for those students gifted in the verbal areas was suggested by Gallagher (1985). He noted the need to develop interpretive and expressive skills through the world of literature, its cultural ramifications, and the value exploration that promotes self-awareness. He argued that verbal ability strengthens student understanding of complex ideas, which is a necessary base for values study and evaluating conflicting ideas.

General support for both formal study of language and classical subjects for the verbally able has been suggested by Ward (1981). The need to have gifted students study language is well expressed by the following general proposition of his differential education of the gifted: "the nature of language, its structures and functions, its integral relationship to thought and behavior should be part of the education of the intellectually superior child and youth" (p. 25).

A focus on language expression has been advocated through the informal teaching of linguistic elements by Arnold (1962). Some research has been directed toward the need to develop vocabulary in the gifted child as a way of improving overall language facility (Dale & Rozik, 1963) and as a way of enhancing verbal humor and the creative use of language (Pilon, 1975).

Many programs for the verbally gifted focused predominantly on developmental reading and literary discussion of ideas (Drews, 1972). Early programs in New York included biography as a genre for the gifted to direct their reading pursuits, partly out of a bibliotherapy motive (Hollingworth, 1926). California's approach to serving the verbally gifted was traditionally handled through a strong literature program developed throughout the grades (California Department of Education, 1979). Major objectives at each level stressed appreciation, understanding themes, and developing the tools of intellectual inquiry.

## Key Components of a Language Arts Program for the Gifted

Language arts is not a unified field of study; rather, it has evolved historically from a set of separate traditions and strands of learning. Therefore, it is important to see curriculum development in the language arts as progressing on parallel tracks that need to merge and criss-cross each other. Important strands include reading and literature, writing, language study, oral communication (speaking and listening), and foreign language.

### Reading and the Study of Literature

Studies of reading that have proliferated in the last 20 years have tended to focus on one of three areas: (1) the social world of reading with particular emphasis on the student as reader and teacher-child interactions (e.g., Cazden, 1988); (2) the basic mental processes of reading and textual features that address them (e.g., Palincsar & Brown, 1984); and (3) classroom-based research that advocates more time on task, among other recommendations (e.g., Carter, 1984). These three areas have not been addressed in a confluent way at the level of practice. The studies are not contradictory; rather, they center on different issues and priorities. However, the world of practice has embraced certain features of these studies. The Reading Commission of the National Council of Teachers of English (Davidson, 1988) recommended a deemphasis on the role of basals and standardized tests and a reconsideration of mandated curriculum. The State of California Framework (1987) and the NAEP report on reading (1992) both stress the need for a student-centered reading curriculum that focuses on shared inquiry discussion techniques of authentic and worthy texts. Such recommendations line up well with issues of teaching reading to high-ability learners.

The gifted child's major contact with the world of ideas is through literature. Books stimulate thought and provide the knowledge base required for creative thinking and problem solving. Intellectual growth in gifted children depends on their access to and regular involvement in the reading process. From the time of their earliest ability to read, they need access to a rich variety of fiction and nonfiction and opportunities to respond actively and creatively to what they are reading. Students should have abundant opportunities to discuss, analyze, and share the enjoyment of what they read with parents, teachers, and each other. Moreover, they need to be guided by adults who model the processes of analyzing and discussing reading.

Several authors provide excellent guidance for teachers about good literature for the gifted and how to teach it to optimize learning and love of literature. In *Books for the Gifted Child,* Baskin and Harris (1980), suggested the following criteria for finding the right books for the gifted:

1. *The language used in books for the gifted should be rich, varied, precise, complex, and exciting, for language is the instrument for the reception and expression of thought.*
2. *Books should be chosen with an eye to their open-endedness, their capacity to inspire contemplative behavior, such as through techniques of judging time sequences, shifting narrators, and unusual speech patterns of characters.*
3. *Books for the gifted should be complex enough to allow interpretative and evaluative behaviors to be elicited from readers.*
4. *Books for the gifted should help them build problem-solving skills and develop methods of productive thinking.*
5. *Books should provide characters as role models for emulation.*
6. *Books should be broad-based in form, from picture books to folktale and myths to nonfiction to biography to poetry to fiction. (p. 46)*

Polette (1982) and Polette and Hamlin (1980) also offered a wealth of ideas for structuring and conducting literature programs for the gifted. Literature programs at the high school level should involve gifted students in reading high-quality adult literature and should help them develop skill and enthusiasm in the intellectual and aesthetic experience of literature.

The literature program for the verbally talented child needs to be very rich from the beginning of the language arts experience in school. Children who are reading by kindergarten need a strong literature program at that stage of their development. The use of a basal reading series typically focuses too much time and attention on mastering the reading process, particularly phonics, rather than to allowing gifted students the opportunity for holistic reading of good literature. One way to combat this problem is to build a strong literature program for the gifted K–8, infusing the best and most challenging selections at each stage of development. Programs like *Junior Great Books* and *Paedaeia* offer the best of classical and contemporary literature selections for students through junior high school.

The literature program for the gifted should provide more than just reading lists and advanced selection, however. It should provide a context for discussion among students of key issues, ideas, and themes contained in literature and be a catalyst for student writing, drawing, and performing. It should provide the basis for the critical thinking component of the language arts curriculum, helping students sharpen their analytical, interpretive, and evaluation skills.

At the elementary level, gifted students can be given carefully selected lists for reading at home. Books should be selected with an eye to the intellectual criteria listed earlier. In addition, establishing in-class reading clusters is an important tool for discussion. Reading aloud is also a valuable adjunct to such a program. Small-group discussions about the following types of questions might be held at the primary level:

1. What happens in your book? Can you number the events? (sequencing)
2. Who is the most important person in the book? Why? Who is your favorite person in the book? (character development)
3. What new things did you learn from reading this book that you didn't know before? (concept formation)
4. What were your favorite words or sentences in the book? Why? (language awareness)
5. Good books make us feel as well as understand a story. What feelings did you have as you read the book? (identification)
6. How good was this book compared to others you have read? (evaluation) How would you rate it in respect to:
   a. interesting story
   b. characters I liked
   c. good ideas
   d. where it occurred was interesting
   e. new things to think about

Early readers should then be encouraged to read on their own and to think about their book through the way the small group discussions are conducted.

## Bibliotherapy

Bibliotherapy shares many of the components of a response-based literature program, and it can be an accessible, natural tool for teachers and librarians as well as counselors. Gifted learners may be particularly well suited to bibliotherapy, given their penchant for reading, their enthusiasm for asking questions, and their capacity for divergent thinking (Webb, Meckstroth, & Tolan, 1982). Only a few adaptations are necessary in a response-based literature program to address the personal and social needs of gifted learners.

Halsted (1988) identified three types of bibliotherapy—institutional, clinical, and developmental. In her construct, mental health professionals use institutional and clinical bibliotherapy with clients who have emotional or behavioral problems. Conversely, teachers, parents, librarians, and school counselors use developmental bibliotherapy to anticipate and meet needs before they become problems. Halsted has advocated bibliotherapy as a means of helping gifted learners recognize and articulate the difficulties that surround being different and of confronting their reluctance to use their abilities.

Central to using bibliotherapy is an understanding of what it does for a reader. Halsted describes the four stages of bibliotherapy as identification, catharsis, insight, and universalization. In the first stage, a reader identifies with a character in the book, recognizing personal similarities and caring about the character. Catharsis allows the reader to release empathetic emotions for the character. The third stage, insight, occurs when the reader applies the character's situation to his or her own life. Finally, universalization is the reader's recognition that difficulties and sense of difference are not his or hers alone.

An integrated literature model addresses an additional counseling need of gifted learners: communication of feelings. In isolation, bibliotherapy speaks to the reader's emotions and self-understanding. In the broader context of a response-based literature program, it provides a forum for practicing a range of communication skills. Students recognize, label, and honor feelings: They articulate fears, they listen and learn to reflect another's feelings, they work cooperatively, they learn to support a personal point of view, and they communicate formally with an audience through their presentation.

Halsted (1988) also cited important criteria for the emotional development of gifted students through assessing literature with an eye to its bibliotherapy value. These criteria are:

- *Characters should be coping with the same problems the readers are facing.*
- *The characters stand alone or in a small group for their convictions.*
- *A character may be different from his or her peers and learning to cope with the difference.*
- *The characters may be learning to accept someone else who is different.*
- *Adult characters should be present and supportive in at least some of the books.*
- *Some characters should be gifted adults.*
- *Some of the child characters should clearly be gifted themselves.*
- *Giftedness need not necessarily be labeled.*
- *Characters should be openminded, questioning, and have a passion for learning everything or devoted to one subject of intense interest.*
- *Characters should be struggling with issues of personal or moral courage, personal values, and moral and ethical choices.*
- *Some books should have humor of a high level.*

Such a set of criteria should be useful to practitioners in selecting emotionally rich reading material for gifted students.

## *Role of Libraries*

Able learners may be predisposed to use libraries for their early reading, their internal need for information, and their desire to communicate with the world. These children can be undemanding library clients, grateful for unfettered access to resources. Occasionally, one may discover a home-away-from-home and become a habitué of a particular library or find a special friend in the librarian. Librarians, on the other hand, appreciate having a self-motivated, intellectual clientele. The two groups often coexist peacefully but without a dynamic, interactive relationship. Ironically, librarians may be neglecting the children most likely to become active, mature library users.

Both the Association for Library Service to Children and American Association of School Librarians include in their missions the goal of meeting the individual needs of the child or student. Because gifted learners have unusual capabilities, they have specific intellectual, social, and emotional needs. These needs are best met through the collaborative efforts of parents, schools, and community agencies. Gifted learners need high-level, multifaceted programs in the community as well as in school.

Numerous opportunities exist to target gifted learners with library resources and to utilize the expertise of adults with the talents of children. Library-based programs offer children extended time to pursue an interest or idea in depth. They can assemble a peer group that can challenge one another to accomplish the best possible product (Boyce, Bailey, & VanTassel-Baska, 1990). Library workshops can offer children opportunities to link and synthesize their knowledge of literature with the writing process and book making to create an original product. Equally as important, such programs can harness the resources and expertise of librarians, teachers, and parents in offering programs for young people in a variety of settings.

The two companion units at the end of this chapter (Example 7.A) attempt to illustrate how gifted students might handle the concepts of form and function, first in poetry and then in the related art form of photography.

The use of a concept-oriented approach to teaching literature to the gifted is also most appropriate at all grade levels. Table 7–1 depicts six common themes or ideas found in great literature with some key literary selections that illustrate them. Structuring reading selections around such themes provides gifted students with a breadth of reading experiences not frequently encountered under other approaches, as well s a sense of the unity of key ideas across different works.

## *Writing and Composition*

Current National Assessment of Education Progress (NAEP) data in writing (1992) demonstrate limited emphasis on expository writing and greater emphasis on more creative forms, with the result being that writing samples of students' best work at grades 4 and 8 evidence mediocre control of the writing process and very limited competency in developing argument. Such a result might have been predicted from recent earlier studies. Applebee (1984) analyzed three popular high school writing texts and found that writing assignments were predominantly evaluative, seeking right answers rather than reflection from students and calling for limited responses. In a comprehensive survey of writing in high school, Applebee (1981) found only 10 percent of writing time being spent in

**TABLE 7–1   Literary Themes and Examples for Reading**

| Literary Themes | Comparative Examples for Student Reading |
|---|---|
| The role of the supernatural in human destiny (e.g., God, gods, fate, chance) | Greek, Roman, Egyptian, African myths (all levels) Sophocles, Euripedes, Aeschylus, (secondary) Thomas Hardy novels (e.g., *Mayor of Casterbridge*) (secondary) |
| Natural instinct vs. "civilization" influences | *Lord of the Flies*, William Golding (secondary) *Heart of Darkness*, Joseph Conrad (secondary) *Babbitt*, Sinclair Lewis (secondary) Wordsworth's "The World Is too Much with Us" (secondary) |
| Self-determination; individual control of destiny | *Bringing the Rain to Kapiti Plain*, Verna Aardema (primary) *The Odyssey*, Homer (middle school) *David Copperfield*, Dickens (middle school) *Sylvester and The Magic Pebble*, William Steig (primary) |
| Social justice | *To Kill a Mockingbird*, Harper Lee (junior high) *Black Boy*, Richard Wright (junior high) *Diary of Anne Frank*, (junior high) *The Pearl*, John Steinbeck (junior high) *You Be the Judge*, Sidney Carroll (intermediate) |
| Self-understanding, self-doubt, fears, anxieties | *Time to Get Out of the Bath, Shirley*, John Burningham (primary) *Ordinary Jack*, Helen Cresswell (intermediate) *Smith*, Leon Garfield (intermediate) *Catcher in the Rye*, J. D. Salinger (high school) *A Wrinkle in Time*, (middle school) |
| Ravages of time; loss of youth; growing old | *King Lear*, Shakespeare *The Picture of Dorian Gray*, Oscar Wilde *Ethan Frome*, Edith Wharton *Miss Rumphius*, Barbara Cooney (primary) *The Yearling*, Majorie Rawlings (intermediate) |

composing more than a paragraph. More recently, Cooper and Brennenan (1988) recommended more direct instruction in teaching writing and requisite thinking in order to master various forms, wide reading and analysis of texts, and sustained literacy programs for all. Thus, a critical issue to consider in the language arts is how to integrate a comprehensive writing program that provides extensive experiences in expository writing.

Writing opportunities for the gifted should begin early and provide an abundance of opportunities to write. Writing is a thinking process, and through writing experiences the gifted child can develop excellence in the capacity to think as well as to write. Very young children who may lack the motor coordination to write may nevertheless be engaged in writing-related activities through special teaching techniques such as tape recording, illustration, and invented spelling.

The fundamental skills associated with a process writing approach need to be used with gifted learners at all stages of development. Specifically these are:

Prewriting
Paragraph development
Theme development
Development of introductions and endings

Work on supporting details
Effective use of figures of speech
Editing
Teacher/peer conferencing
Revising
Rewriting

Also, important consideration needs to be given to the type of writing that gifted students are encouraged to master. A good balance needs to be struck between impressionist creative writing forms and analytic expository writing forms. Keeping the NAEP portfolio data in mind, all students are particularly weak in persuasive writing. As Marzano (1992) pointed out, there is a need for balance in how we assess the writing experience. Emphasis on quality of thinking as well as mechanics is required.

As with literature programs, writing programs for the gifted must begin as soon as they enter school. Recent research on emergent literacy (Sulzby, 1985) has stressed the importance of writing as a thinking process that clearly precedes the teaching of formal reading or handwriting in the primary curriculum. This issue is even more critical for gifted students. Although psychomotoric readiness to write may not be in place, young gifted children can clearly begin to conceptualize stories, sequence events, and present their feelings and experience through language. Consequently, an early focus on such writing behavior is important. Techniques for including writing as an activity for young gifted children include the following:

1. Have each child compose a story and transcribe it as it is being developed. Read it back for editing changes or additions and elaborations Share the stories in class.
2. Encourage parents to transcribe stories at home and ask the children to bring the stories to school for sharing.
3. Have students draw a picture to illustrate their story and develop a title for it.
4. Use tape recorders to initially record the story and then transcribe it later.
5. Have students compose a story at the computer or typewriter if they have mastered the device adequately enough.
6. Encourage free story building; provide students with a set of givens (e.g., characters, plot pieces, a setting).
7. Have students respond in writing to a piece of music, a picture, or a poem presented in class.
8. Allow young students the freedom to write without requiring accurate spelling and grammar.

As gifted students begin to handle cursive writing, teachers should encourage them to record their impressions or experiences in a daily journal. In this way, teachers can promote written fluency and handwriting at the same time. Encouraging creative responses to life experiences may also be helpful here. Using poetic form or a brief fable to relate a particular incident may be very stimulating and challenging to gifted students. The following represents a comparative sample of creative journal writing from a first-grader in a gifted program. The first sample was taken early in the school year when creative response was first being elicited. The second sample was done in the middle of the school year when the student had moved beyond simple visualization techniques into a more sophisticated approach to explaining natural phenomena through imaginative storytelling.

### Sample #1: The Magic Carpet

*If I had a magic carpet I could go to the desert. I would go because in the desert there are lots of pyramids.*

### Sample #2: How the Horse Got Its Mane

*Once upon a time horses didn't have tails. All the people thought the horses looked dumb, so the people sewed tails on the horses. But there was this one very dumb horseboy. All the horseboys were supposed to sew the tails on their horses. And when the horseboy was talking to his master, he was not looking where he was sewing. All of a sudden, the master had a smile on his face. The horseboy looked at his horse and he had sewed the tail on the neck. And that's how the horse got their manes.*

By the intermediate grades, gifted students need to master the basic skills and techniques of writing, at least as those skills apply to expository writing pieces. Collins (1985) pointed out that there are six critical strategies that are preconditions to a good writing program. These strategies should be used by teachers in an attempt to acclimate gifted students to the writing process. These six strategies are:

1. Provide opportunities for students to discuss and clarify writing assignments before they begin writing.
2. Provide opportunities for students to get more information about a topic before they begin writing.
3. Provide specific information about the criteria you will use to correct each assignment.
4. Provide opportunities for students to review and revise written work completed earlier in the year.
5. Encourage students to edit each other's papers before they are handed in.
6. Provide opportunities for students to read written work out loud to individuals or to small groups of students.

Donald Hall (Hall & Embler, 1976) remarked in one of his essays that "writing well is the art of clear thinking and honest feelings." For gifted students, learning these techniques is critical for improving their thinking and their self-expression. Perhaps no skill represents a greater deficiency for the gifted than does writing. Colleges have long complained of the lack of skill in this area, even among their best students. Thus, a rigorous program of teaching persuasive or expository writing skills seems crucial.

One very useful technique to incorporate into a writing program for the gifted is the workshop model. It is particularly useful for teaching editing, rewriting, and revision, as well as teaching the value of peer critique and the importance of evaluation in the writing process. One structure for the workshop technique follows, based on the Reynolds, Kopelke, and Durden (1984) text:

1. The class reiterates the objectives for a particular assignment.
2. Each student receives a copy of the essay and signs up to discuss a particular objective during the workshop.
3. The author reads the essay to the class and then remains silent until the end of the workshop.
4. Each student praises one aspect of the essay.
5. Each group discusses its designated objectives.
6. The author is given the opportunity to speak a one-sentence defense.
7. The class summarizes the techniques that appear to have worked in the essay.

There are many good texts available that stress language awareness through reading excellent prose selections. With older gifted students, where the goal of the writing program may be to develop a writing style, it may be useful to focus on models of writing to analyze and emulate according to such key issues. Thus, reading selections serve several simultaneous purposes:

1. They inform the student directly about an aspect of writing as well as a topic of interest.
2. They focus student attention on a distinctive style.
3. They serve as a model for analysis/emulation.

The following writing sample was obtained from a summer class at Northwestern University where writing models and a student workshop technique of group discussion and evaluation of individual writing were heavily utilized. The student writer is an eighth grader.

### Caught

*Sitting on the floor of a police station eating popcorn and crying once in a while, wasn't what I'd had in mind that frigid and bright blue Saturday morning.*

*Jason was too calm about being arrested. He just sat, relaxed with his legs spread wide apart. A silver earring pierced his image and his right ear. His head was cocked slightly upward and his mouth frozen tight with a sarcastic grin. I had just wanted to bash his clean head into the wall and break his image, but this was a police station.*

*The cops also picked up another guy from the El station. This one was from Milwaukee, and I had the experience of sitting next to him in the police car. Everything about him reeked of fermented piss; his clothes, his hair, his breath, and he probably had piss on the brain. The poor foreigner had gone up the wrong set of stairs and jumped the turnstile without realizing it was illegal. Jason and I weren't as creative—we did it on purpose.*

*I wanted to do it, but Jason didn't, which I thought was strange; he seemed to be so illegal. Jason carried a .38 with cartidges, that he showed me earlier that Saturday. The gun lay in his inside pocket, and with the moves of an expert gunsman, he showed me how to load the thing. Jason carried it for protection, from gangs I guess. He had recently gotten involved with a gang, and I saw the changes, but accepted them.*

*We went downtown to see a very bad Karate flick, which, ironically, we enjoyed, because we were friends. After the movie, we shot to get the sticky mountains of popcorn, which we loved so much, from a gourmet popcorn shop. It was probably Garrett's, but there's so many, who remembers?*

*No one was looking, I thought, and I didn't see the sense in paying for the train ride. I grabbed the sides of the turnstile where the prices were lit up and hoisted myself over; Jason followed. I felt like a criminal. I felt like I thought Jason felt. I was smiling, laughing, but Jason shrugged it off. I wanted to knock him off the platform. We were already up there.*

*The guy was a cop, so we never saw the nice blue suit. He was a plain clothes cop, who used words police officers didn't. "I saw you fucking kids jump that fucking gate." These words didn't freeze me at all, but seemed the proper greeting from a cop. The guy showed us his badge. We played along and looked scared, at least I did. He put the cuffs on and I begged a little, said I wouldn't do it again. Jason said nothing; did he want to get arrested?*

*The car was parked on the street, with every concerned person looking in. He started the report. I don't know how the watermelon got in my throat, but I was in the car, legs twitching violently, and waiting for the tears. I thought I had wet my pants; the smell shot through my nose and fell limp at the back of my head. It wasn't me. It was the guy from Milwaukee, just shoved in the car.*

*In between sobs in the cold car, I saw Jason looking out the window, unaffected. At the station his eyes searched towards the ceiling. I followed them to an eye chart on top of the far wall. I began to look at the chart, then at Jason and his coat. A thought kicked me, "would they search us?" The crying stopped, and I ate the popcorn; not tasting one kernel.*

*They didn't search us, but relief waited. Until my mother cautiously walked in, without an angry stare or disappointed look. Relief was the "Oh Well" smile, which she flashed at me. She simply walked over to the cop, and pointed out her kid. But how could I belong to this woman who forgave so easily?*

*Jason's parents couldn't be reached, so he left with me and the woman with the "Oh Well" smile. The lady asked a lot of questions, and I thought, "maybe she is my mother." But she didn't wait for the answers, which she seemed to know weren't coming. She couldn't be my mother.*

*I had cried in the police car and police station, but couldn't in front of this lady. I didn't say a word until Jason got out of the car, and then I spoke to the woman, "I know I'm bad, and it's okay if you don't love me anymore." The words just rolled out with no force or conviction behind them.*

*The woman's reply is something I don't remember, and I'm not sure that she did reply. I'm sure she sat a bag in my lap and said it had a grapefruit in it. It was yellow, but blushed sweetness. I peeled it methodically in silence, and my head rose to the mirror behind the sun shade. In it I saw the white outlines of dried tears, below my eyes, and the orange of my popcorn-stained lips. I peeled the grapefruit faster now, and ripped through the white skin to pinkness. The taste of popcorn was gone, and the orange lips returned to their orignial pink hue. Then they smiled, reluctantly, at my mother.*

*I knew then that Jason didn't have a blushing grapefruit waiting for him at home. It was already too late for him.*

This story shows an uncommon sophistication on the part of the young writer in his capacity to capture vivid detail and to let potent imagery tell the story. His choice of words, use of symbols, and direct style all reflect writing ability that has been shaped through internalizing the process of writing.

Another writing model that is important for the gifted to emulate is research writing or technical report writing. Since many of these students will be engaged in conducting research during their school years, it is important that they have the appropriate tools to frame a written research report of their efforts. Thus, teaching them the fundamental paradigm for a reseach paper should be a task of the writing program in tandem with the discipline under study for the project. As is often the case, science is the discipline, so collaboration with the science teacher is in order.

## Language Study

*I think that grammar is so lovely that even if it were utterly useless, one would still irresistibly explore it, as one explores chess, or architecture, or the spiral geometries of shells. Grammar is a sort of magic aesthetic lens, through which we can view the delicate structures upon which ideas rest. As scientists marvel at the silicate skeletal frames which support and form living organisms, through grammar we can view the delicate relationships which give form and pattern to the phenomena of the mind. If this comparison strikes you as idealistic and metaphorical, please consider it further. These relationships do exist, and they are beautiful. (Thompson, 1991)*

The language arts program for the gifted should offer opportunities to study the English language. Goals for this component of the language arts program should be to understand the syntactic structure of English (grammar) and its concomitant uses (usage); to promote vocabulary development; to foster an understanding of word relationships (analogies) and origins (etymology); and to develop an appreciation for semantics, linguistics, and the history of language.

Because gifted children exhibit individual differences in their mastery of the language skills of grammar, usage, and vocabulary, these segments of a program for the gifted must be highly individualized to accommodate individual levels of proficiency. Pretesting of skills and vocabulary always should be carried out, and instructional activities and materials should be determined diagnostically on the basis of pretest results.

In a language program for the gifted, clearly it is necessary to adopt a diagnostic-prescriptive approach to teaching grammar and usage since they are capable of mastering the language system much more rapidly than other learners and in a shorter time period than currently is allotted in the regular school curriculum. An overview of the syntactic structure by grade 6 would allow students time to master the parts within a year. A schemata such as Table 7–2 might be useful for that purpose.

The teaching of formal grammar is better handled through this matrix approach with gifted learners because:

1. It presents the entire system of English syntax to students holistically so that they can grasp immediately what they are seeking to learn.

**TABLE 7–2  A Matrix of Language Syntax**

| Forms | Function | Selective Combinations in Sentences |
|---|---|---|
| Nouns | Subject<br>Predicate nominative<br>Direct object<br>Indirect object<br>Object of preposition<br>Appositive | The *girl* went to the store. Mary, *the leader,* gave *Larry* her title. The teacher is my *friend.* |
| Verbs (principal parts, tense, voice, mood) | Infinitives<br>Active<br>Passive<br>Indicative<br>Subjunctive<br>Present/past/future<br>Present perfect/past perfect/<br>future perfect<br>Gerunds | The girl *walked* home. The girl *was walked* home by the boy. |
| Pronouns (*he/she/it*) | Replacement for nouns | *She* left *him* for *it.* |
| Adjectives (comparative) | Modifier of nouns | The *pretty* woman disliked the *sad* man. |
| Adverbs (*-ly*) (comparative forms) | Modifier of verbs, adjectives, and adverbs | We scored *poorly* on the test. Sara was *too* small for the task. She moved *very* slowly. |
| Conjunctions | "Binders" | We ate *and* slept. She went *but* I stayed. |
| Prepositions | Indications of place and time | He stood *in* the doorway. We left *at* six o'clock. |
| Multiple forms (more than one word) phrases, clauses, etc.) | Modifiers of nouns and verbs | Being *lonely,* she left. He wept *because he knew* the truth. |

2. It saves instructional time by reducing the need for reinforcement and repetition, which is a common approach used by textbooks to ensure mastery.
3. It allows students to focus their attention on what they do not know rather than remediating what they do know.

Thompson (1992) advocates having students diagram sentences as a tool for clarifying syntactic competency.

Another aspect of language study that is critical for the gifted is in the area of vocabulary development. A focus on the study of etymology, word roots, prefixes, and suffixes is an important part of their language learning. Use of vocabulary from foreign languages at the primary level enriches their vocabulary and builds an understanding of cognates in various languages. Learning root words from Latin through English, for example, can increase English vocabulary two-fold. The following list has been used in gifted programs:

| Sample English Words | Latin Root | English Meaning |
|---|---|---|
| Temporal, temporary | tempus, temporis | time |
| Belligerent, bellicose | bellum | war |
| Convene, venture | convenio | come together |
| Captivate, capture | captivs | prisoner |
| Terminal, terminate | terminus | end |
| Fortitude | fortis | brave |
| Perilous, peril | periculum | danger |
| Science | scio | know |
| Facile, facility | facilis | easy |

Working on analogies can also increase the students' vocabulary as well as deepen their understanding of word and syntax relationships. The examples that follow were taken selectively from the College Board's *10 SAT's:*

**yawn: boredom**   as   **smile: amusement**
Type of analogy: physical expression to feeling
Strategy: establish precise relationship between a given pair of words

**famine: starvation**   as   **deluge: flood**
Type of analogy: cause and effect
Strategy: make up a sentence using the given pair of words

**pride: lion**   as   **pack: wolf**
Type of analogy: group to a member
Strategy: explore multiple meanings and relationships for a given word

By modifying the nature of the language program for gifted learners, educators can focus on their capacity to become linguistically facile early on and to develop proficient use of language.

## Oral Discourse

Although it is common to find verbally talented students who have mastered the art of "glibness" without the substance of reflective and profound thinking, it is also common to find the direct teaching of oral discourse in its several forms to be sadly lacking from a verbal arts curriculum for the gifted. Most English classes for the gifted employ individual oral reports and panel presentations, but very few utilize debate, dramatics, and oral interpretation as lively expressive forms in their own right.

Debate is a particularly rigorous form of discourse that instills in gifted learners not only the skills of oral argument in the content of higher-level thought but also the metacognitive skills related to studying and thoughtful action. Figure 7–1 outlines the major elements of debate to be taught. These "active" expressive forms are extremely important for verbally talented students as skillful techniques to build higher-level thinking capacities and to integrate thought and feeling. Using creative dramatics in the classroom from kindergarten on seems most appropriate for these students. Formal debate

**FIGURE 7–1   Debate Outline**

I. Introduction
   A. Definition of terms: the proposition, the burden of proof, and status quo, the case, the constructive speech, the need argument, the evidence, the plan, the counterplan, the rebuttal

II. Preparation for Contest Debating
   A. Studying the subject
      1. Taking notes
      2. Selecting the main points
      3. Types and use of evidence

III. Aspects of the Debate
   A. Limitations of time
   B. Mechanics of presentation
   C. Selecting points for rebuttal
   D. Debate strategy
   E. Debate ethics

IV. Debate Structure
   A. First affirmative speech
      1. Introduction
      2. Statement of proposition
      3. Definition of terms
      4. Need arguments, 1, 2, and 3

   B. First negative speech
      1. Introduction
      2. Acceptance of, or redefinition of, terms
      3. General statement about the advisability of maintaining the status quo
      4. Disputation of the three affirmative need arguments

   C. Second affirmative speech
      1. Reestablishing the three arguments of need
      2. Presentation of the plan
      3. Implementation of plan to solve the deficiencies of the status quo
      4. Prospective application of the plan to the three affirmative need arguments

   D. Second negative speech
      1. Further disputation of the three affirmative need arguments
      2. The impracticality of the plan
      3. The new evils that implementation of the proposition and the plan will cause

*Sources:* Summers, H. B. (1934). *Contest debating: A textbook for beginners.* New York: H. W. Wilson. Haney, T. K. (1965). *An introduction to debate.* New York: Ginn.

can be introduced by fifth or sixth grade, and full-blown "dramatic performances" can be undertaken during the same time.

Focusing on oral communication will widen the scope of understanding the dramatic arts. The visual and auditory channels of communication now come into play in a visible way not found in the other components of an English/verbal arts curriculum, and students can begin to understand in a hands-on way the nature of interrelated arts. Therefore, equal time within the curriculum for these types of activities seems justified, rather than treating such areas as only electives within the larger school curriculum.

Oral mastery and use of language are critical parts of the language arts program. The thinking process involved in experiencing literature and in writing are linked intimately to and can be enhanced by oral language experience. Through planned experiences in discussion, debate, oral reading and interpretation, oral reports, dramatics, and panel presentations, gifted youth can learn to think effectively in and through the language, and they can learn to write more effectively.

At the primary and elementary levels, gifted children can learn to read aloud from storybooks with expressiveness, can learn to verbalize ideas through creative dramatics, and can begin to give oral reports and presentations. Beginning at the fourth or fifth level, they can engage in the more cognitively demanding activities of debate, acting, and research reporting. Middle school and high school classroom discussions can become strongly analytical, theoretical, and abstract and can deal with values and judgments. Improvisation and extemporaneous presentations, as well as formal debate, can provide high-level oral language experiences for the gifted.

Chaney (1992) emphasized the importance of developing critical listening and thinking skills as fundamental to engaging in oral presentations of any type. The following are major outcomes for high-ability students in this area.

*To Develop Listening/Oral Communication Skills:*
1. Discriminate between informative and persuasive messages.
2. Evaluate an oral persuasive message according to argument pattern, key strategies of persuasion, decision making, and credibility of speaker.
3. Develop skills of argument formulation (claim, data, and warrant).
4. Organize oral presentations, using logical ordering techniques, adequate supporting material, and structured arguments.

## Foreign Language

Historically, foreign language programs for the gifted have been viewed as an important part of the overall curriculum for the verbally able. These interventions are now supported by some research findings that suggest the importance of a threshold of mastery in one's own language as a prerequisite to second language learning, but that once the prerequisite is met, the second language is a major enhancement to linguistic competency (Cummins, 1979; Morris, 1971; Bartz, 1977). Foreign language was an integral part of the New York City rapid learner program at the Speyer School in the 1920s. French language and literature were introduced to gifted children, ranging in age from seven to nine years old, and taught to them for a full five years. The rationale for foreign language inclusion in the curriculum was that (1) early language study would foster future opportunities abroad, (2) early language study would produce early mastery for these students, and (3) early inclusion of foreign language would allow gifted students to take more languages during their school careers (Hollingworth, 1942).

The New York program and a program initiated in 1921 in Cleveland demonstrated great value in the inclusion of foreign language for the gifted child early in the elementary years, although they differed regarding whether it should be viewed as enrichment or as an opportunity for accelerative learning. The Cleveland program tended to blend both approaches in that it accelerated language learning by one year before ninth grade and it provided expanded activities and projects in French from second grade on. The New York classes, on the other hand, focused predominantly on enrichment aspects and did not offer a structured program that moved students ahead in the language. However, Hollingworth noted that the expectation was for students to pursue other foreign languages in high school.

In building a case for teaching Latin to verbally talented students, VanTassel-Baska (1987) cited valuable intrinsic features of the language itself. Reasons for the choice of Latin as an appropriate foreign language for the gifted are several:

1. Some 60 percent of English words are derived from Latin; thus, the study of this language greatly heightens vocabulary power in English.
2. Syntactic understanding is a major goal in learning Latin; it has added value in enhancing linguistic competence in English and in learning other languages.
3. The complexity of the language and its logical consistency make it a challenge to gifted students who enjoy learning new symbol systems, analyzing, and using deductive logic in solving problems.
4. The cultural heritage of the Western world is based on Greco-Roman traditions in art, music, literature, and language. To study Latin is to gain invaluable insight into the Western cultural system.
5. Latin stresses logical reasoning and analysis through an emphasis on translation and study of form changes at increasing levels of difficulty. Thus, it is an easy subject to modify for precocious students.
6. Unlike most languages, Latin has few irregularities.

Whatever the choice of a second language for the verbally gifted, it is important that they have the opportunity to learn one, and preferably much earlier than the typical school curriculum would allow. The primary grades are a good time to start a modern foreign language. Formal study of Latin or Greek can begin by fourth grade.

Programs of study in the English language can profit immensely from the existence of a concurrent foreign language study program or at least a study of vocabulary idioms and common phrases from other languages. Gifted children can also benefit a great deal from the study of a second language to enhance their grasp of the structure and semantics of their own language. Foreign language study may begin as early as kindergarten or first grade and be continuous throughout high school and into college. Mastery of a second (and third) language gives the gifted student a comprehensive understanding of the comparative structure of languages and their related cultures.

The major goals of a foreign language program for the gifted should be to develop proficiency in reading, speaking, and writing in two languages; to learn the culture and traditions that shape language; to be challenged by the interrelationships across languages with respect to form and meaning; and to appreciate and understand language systems. The rich opportunities for foreign language study closely follow these concepts.

## *Major Emphases Within Language Arts Curricula for High-Ability Learners*

Based on the current language arts issues, and an examination of the major strands of the language arts curriculum that might be emphasized, what are the issues that need special emphasis and attention for high-ability learners? The following emphases reflect a general philosophy of language arts curriculum for such students that can guide the process of curriculum development.

 • *Address the intellectual needs of high-ability students through selecting rich and rigorous reading materials.*

High-ability students, as all students, need to learn and master the content and the skills deemed by society as essential in order to be a good "participant" in the society. However, it is also true that basal reading materials are inadequate to guide high-ability students in the development of their potential. Language arts programs for identified high-ability students should provide rigorous opportunities for the development of their academic and intellectual potential in all major areas of the discipline. Thus, enhancing reading and literature programs through choice of substantive texts is a crucial component of appropriate curriculum.

 • *Foster critical and creative thinking.*

Although gifted students should have opportunities to understand the importance of performing the tasks and mastering the structures of traditional K–12 language arts curricula, they should also understand that mastery of a structure frees them to push beyond the boundaries and constraints of that form, to diverge into more creative patterns of thinking. Gifted students should not see mastery of standardized skills as an end, but as a means to more innovative thinking. Even the very youngest student should be given repeated opportunities to try out traditional and nontraditional modes of inquiry. The classroom must provide repeated opportunities for gifted students to engage in critical and creative thinking and inquiry that integrates the language arts.

 • *Incorporate whole-language, literature-based materials that emphasize the critical connection between reading and writing.*

Most students can profit from language arts programs that expose them to whole, meaningful works of literature. Since gifted students typically learn to read early and develop holistic reading strategies, early use of whole-language approaches seems particularly appropriate for them. Gifted students also can benefit from exposure to literature that demands their thoughtful interaction and that challenges their attitudes and beliefs. Recent research has demonstrated that the most fruitful type of interaction with texts occurs both receptively through reading and productively through writing. Students must be encouraged to see themselves as engaged in a continuing dialogue with exciting works of literature and great writers, and through thoughtful reading of and writing about those texts.

 • *Enhance the growth of metacognitive awareness and control.*

Among the special talents that gifted students possess is the early and heightened ability to think about their own thinking, or metacognitive awareness. Along with encouraging the students to interact thoughtfully with works of literature, language arts programs for high-ability learners should enhance the ability to examine critically their cognitive activities. In addition, then, to solving the problems involved in deriving meaning from a text or producing meaning through a text, gifted students should be encouraged to reflect on the ways that they plan, assess, evaluate, and revise their cognitive activities through meaningful research activities. Data on good readers indicate a high degree of metacognitive control over the basic skills or reading. Good readers possess positive habits and attitudes about reading; read with enough fluency so that they can focus on the meaning of what they read; use what they already know to understand what they read; form an understanding of what they read and extend, elaborate, and critically judge its meaning; use a variety of effective strategies to aid their understanding and to plan, manage, and check the progress of their reading; and read a wide variety of texts and read for different purposes (NAEP, 1992).

• *Encourage active learning.*

We make discourse; we do not just passively receive it. Too often students merely react passively to what they hear or read. High-ability students should be aware that they are active meaning makers not only in the stories that they create out of their own experiences but also in their reading of literature. They need to be encouraged to see themselves as active readers and shapers of language. We must make them aware of the processes that they use to speak, read, and write, and the role of their communities in those processes of producing discourse. We must make them aware of the various discourses that they use in several contexts.

• *Heighten students' awareness and appreciation of cultural diversity.*

It is critical that high-ability learners become especially sensitive to similarities and differences among and between cultures. Cultural diversity is a valuable resource, and exposure to such diversity can provide genuine opportunities for personal growth. Although not all materials in a language arts program will necessarily or explicitly explore cultural unity and diversity as a central theme, a special effort should be made to incorporate these materials. Given the importance of attitudinal factors in cognitive development, limited English proficiency students and students from minority groups within the dominant culture can be expected to benefit from the inclusion of materials that provide positive depictions of their cultural traditions. Moreover, students from the majority culture need a background in other cultures as well. Thus, the inclusion and focus on multicultural materials is critical to a strong language arts program for high-ability learners.

• *Use collaborative learning techniques.*

Since students are a valuable resource to each other, collaborative activities need to be fostered. Some of the most rewarding, unpredictable, and exciting learning occurs when peers collaborate on projects. Gifted students should be given opportunities to work on group projects where one student's ideas supplement, challenge, and redirect a classmate's work. In particular, students should be given opportunities to receive oral and written responses from their intellectual peers. They should come to regard themselves as members of a learning community, and they should come to consider their classmates as valuable sources of feedback and as co-learners. Use of discussion groups, workshop techniques for the writing process, panels, and debates are all strategies that can enhance collaborative learning.

- *Explore interdisciplinary applications by connecting literature to art, music, social studies, and other relevant areas of study.*

All students, but especially high-ability students, need exposure to material that helps them overcome narrow disciplinary constraints and that allows them to explore ideas in a number of areas. They should be exposed to the similarities as well as the differences among artistic media. They should explore the literacies of the written, visual, and performing arts and engage in the excitement of discovering the ways that one artistic medium defines the limits of or merges with another. How does an illustrator portray fantastic characters from a fairy tale? How might one go about setting a poem to music? How does gesture depict a description of an action in a short story? We should encourage gifted students to cross artistic boundaries and to apply the visual, musical, or dramatic to reading and writing. Beyond these applications, high-ability students can make interdisciplinary connections to an understanding of the cultural context within which a work of literature developed and to areas of study that use a common theme such as change.

- *Foster independence.*

By being both an innovative mentor and someone who knows when to let go, the ideal teacher provides the gifted student with a nurturing classroom of intellectual support as well as with the confidence to work on his or her own. The gifted student is thus encouraged to test out classroom instruction and to strike out, with the instructor's guidance, on his or her own. The instructor, then, often functions as a metacognitive coach who encourages students to take charge of what they have learned and to use their learning in independent ways.

- *Encourage the exploration of issues of significance, using a variety of research techniques.*

Students need to develop literary habits of mind that encourage them in using resources appropriately and effectively. Researching relevant issues of significance can be one avenue to develop such skills. By exploring an issue of real-world relevance and interest to the learner, students can learn how to organize data to support an argument, how to develop an argument, how to evaluate various perspectives on an issue, and how to present their findings in oral and written forms.

- *Develop authentic assessment strategies.*

If students are to believe that thinking and reflection are valued in a language arts program, then teachers must develop assessment techniques that honor that approach. Use of essays that challenge learners to explore new ideas and connections between ideas, journals that record thinking about reading, and other activity-based assessments are critical to a new language arts curriculum that is based on meaning and learner centered.

## Needs of At-Risk Gifted Children

Able learners, in general, show early signs of advanced verbal behaviors: early reading, strong interest in books and reading, fascination with words, and the desire and ability to express ideas in written form. These characteristics demand a responsive environment that can feed the child's intellectual needs. Libraries are the most natural resource for these children, particularly children who are educationally at risk. Children from low-income families, culturally diverse backgrounds, or dysfunctional families, or those who have physical or learning disabilities have an even greater need for libraries and specially tailored programs.

VanTassel-Baska and Willis (1988) documented a high incidence of gifted learners who, because of low socioeconomic conditions in their lives, are at risk of not being able to access educational opportunities important to college preparation. These students are unassisted in school for two reasons: (1) they are not eligible for Title I aid because they typically achieve above grade-level expectations and (2) they often do not qualify for special gifted programs because their scores on traditional intelligence measures are below program cutoffs. Consequently, they do not receive help from two key sources: those that provide assistance based on ability and those that provide assistance based on poverty conditions. Therefore, a community-based collaborative effort would assist in filling the program gap for these students.

Gifted programs are an important means for promising learners to access maximum educational opportunities, yet there is clear underrepresentation of promising low-income and minority students, particularly African Americans, in gifted programs in K–12 education. This disparity is an issue that cannot be ignored in a pluralistic society. A recent study of programs and services for disadvantaged gifted students nationally (Van-Tassel-Baska, Patton, & Prillaman, 1991) revealed that only eight states provide any form of differentiated service to low-income and/or minority children of promise other than what is provided in a regular gifted program. Fewer than 50 local programs are seriously addressing this issue; of these programs, only 6 are focusing on children below third grade.

Attention to tailoring the verbal arts curriculum more appropriately to meet the needs of at-risk learners may be necessary. Based on our current knowledge of successful interventions with these special populations (VanTassel-Baska, 1992), the following adaptations are suggested for classroom practice and parental/community follow up:

- *Presence of information on various cultural groups*
- *Contributions of minorities included*

- *Avoidance of cultural stereotyping*
- *Use of interactive strategies*
- *Use of expressive activities (oral language, movement, artistic)*
- *Use of analogical reasoning*
- *Use of creative synthesis activities*
- *Frequent positive reinforcement*
- *Enhancement of realistic perceptions of competence*

Such adaptations can prove helpful in enhancing the development of potential in at-risk learners whose needs require attention beyond those provided even to gifted students.

In the area of selecting appropriate multicultural literature for gifted students, Norton (1987) posed several questions that need to be asked in assessing the appropriateness of such materials. These questions include:

1. Are representatives of cultural groups portrayed as unique individuals with respect to character and physical appearance?
2. Does the author avoid stereotyping of cultural groups, including "model minority" and "bad minority" labels?
3. Is the culture of a minority group accurately portrayed and treated with respect?
4. In biographies, are people of color represented accurately with flaws as well as virtues?
5. In fiction, do minority group characters handle their own problems rather than exhibit dependency?
6. If dialect is used, does it have a legitmate purpose?
7. Does the book correct historical omissions and errors about minority groups?
8. Does the book reflect the changing status of women of color by providing appropriate role models for girls?

## Secondary Curriculum in the Language Arts

An important issue in building a secondary language arts program for the gifted is to recognize the interrelationship among the key components in the curriculum. The following sample, taken from an Advanced Placement examination in English, points out the degree of interplay among reading literature, composition, and language study. It also represents a good example of a high-level activity for gifted students in respect to analysis, interpretation, and evauation of an unknown problem. Such activity would be valuable for gifted students throughout the grades 7–12 continuum as an example of advanced content material being incorporated effectively into curriculum at an earlier stage.

> *Read the following poem carefully. Then write an essay in which you describe how the speaker's attitude toward loss in lines 16–19 is related to her attitude toward loss in lines 1–15. Using specific references to the text, show how verse form and language contribute to the reader's understanding of these attitudes. (Suggested time: 35 minutes)*

*One Art**

*The art of losing isn't hard to master;*
*so many things seem filled with the intent*
*to be lost that their loss is no disaster.*

*Lose something every day. Accept the fluster*
*of lost door keys, the hour badly spent.*
*The art of losing isn't hard to master.*

*Then practice losing farther, losing faster;*
*places, and names, and where it was you meant*
*to travel. One of these will bring disaster.*

*I lost my mother's watch. And look! my last, or*
*next-to-last, of three loved houses went.*
*The art of losing isn't hard to master.*

*I lost two cities, lovely ones. And, vaster,*
*some realms I owned, two rivers, a continent.*
*I miss them, but it wasn't a disaster.*

*—Even losing you (the joking voice, a gesture*
*I love) I shan't have lied. It's evident*
*the art of losing's not too hard to master*
*though it may look like (Write it!) disaster.*

The activity incorporates a strong emphasis on critical reading behavior, sensitivity to the structure and nuance of language, and using written form to express an evaluative judgment. As a test essay question, it allows teachers to evaluate the extent to which students have developed higher-level thinking skills and how well they can operationalize and transfer them to new materials. It could also be used effectively as a discussion or writing activity to help teach these skills.

Another way of treating the interrelationships within the verbal arts is to organize the curriculum according to the concept approach discussed in Chapter 1. In this model, the English program is built around key ideas that are valued in the context of society as well as the disciplines under study. The following outline, taken from a ninth-grade English program for gifted disadvantaged students, is exemplary of this approach.

### *Composition and Literature: Concepts from the (Phoenix Project) English Program*

*Search for Identity and Psychological Security*

> *This project is concerned with the needs of disadvantaged students with a potential for giftedness but who may be handicapped in skill and self-concept areas. This major theme, man's search for identity and psychological security, directly deals with self-concept. One of the major quests in the humanities, especially in the twentieth century, is this search. This unit will cover a variety of media that deal with self-awareness (i.e., art, poetry, essays, novels, filmstrips, values clarification techniques, and the examination of cultures, races, and life-styles).*

*Communications*

> *Communications is a second important concept, because it is basic and essential to dealing intelligibly with any other subject. Both nonverbal and verbal communication will be explored as well as ambiguities in language.*

*Power, Authority, and Justice*

> *Having explored his self-concept, the student moves to an exploration of power and authority. These forces often set parameters to his search for identity and fulfillment and are often determinants of his self-concept. The study of the use of power and authority leads into questions of justice and injustice, the ethical perspectives by which we assess the wielding of power and authority. Through literature, they can see microcosmic examples on a personal level of these same polarities.*

*Tolerance*

> *Justice is concerned with actions; tolerance with attitudes. The relationship of the two and of understanding is examined in this unit. Naturally, related topics are bigotry and prejudice, as well as apathy and indifference. Exposure to diverse cultures and religions will also be used as a springboard to understanding this concept.*

*Survival*

> *A sharpened awareness of the negative aspects of society leads into questions of chances for, and threats to, survival. Man's essential will to survive and his conquest of almost insurmountable obstacles to survival will be examined in this unit. Ecological problems as well as personal and societal ones are corollary topics in the survival quest.*

*Change and the Future*

> *Where do we go from here? How do we deal with rapid changes and what can we project for the future? The final unit logically looks ahead and attempts to provide tools to help deal with these questions and suggest possible answers.*

## Issues in Implementing Curriculum for the Gifted in the Language Arts

It may be useful to consider the following issues as one moves toward implementing a gifted curriculum for students in the areas discussed.

**1.** Helping students apply appropriate elements of reasoning to all of their work in the language arts is a necessary part of implementation. Using concept maps to describe difficult pieces of literature or to outline speeches and written compositions is a helpful technique to encourage reflective thought.

**2.** Grade-level designations should remain flexible with regard to the elements discussed in this chapter. Where possible, programs in the language arts should be cross-graded with appropriate testing rather than age determining placement in the curricular structure.

**3.** Achieving a balance among the verbal arts components is an important issue to consider. Typically, schools handle the problem by focusing differentially at different grade levels. Unfortunately, this approach tends to reduce the effort of a powerful verbal arts program. Flexible scheduling and varying time allotments for a given set of objectives would be one way of solving that problem. Foreign language learning, for example, could be reduced to two hours per week throughout the year. Teaching grammar could be condensed into one year, and four hours of instructional time in writing twice a week may be preferable.

**4.** Selecting teachers to work in verbal arts programs for the gifted is potentially difficult since one person may not embody all the expertise needed to handle the nature of the programs outlined in this chapter. Using teacher teams and outside resource professionals are two approaches to overcoming that problem. Older gifted students can also work with younger ones as another effective allocation of resources to meet the needs of the gifted. Bringing published authors in the classroom also can enhance the writing program.

**5.** Balancing the type of instructional activities in which gifted students engage is an important consideration. Writing, discussion, student performance, group problem solving, and reading are activities that need to be included in each week's instructional plan so that no one type of activity dominates the learning process in the language arts.

**6.** Use of wide-ranging materials is a critical implemenation issue. Basal texts and even a single anthology do not offer the rich literary selections needed by the gifted from kindergarten on. Much of the best children's literature is not incorporated into a single source. Thus, creating a multiple materials approach is crucial to carrying out the ideas expressed in this chapter.

**7.** Use of discussion-oriented inquiry techniques is a very critical part of a successful verbal arts program for the gifted. Questions that elicit thinking behaviors that are divergent, analytical, interpretive, and evaluative enhance a language arts program.

**8.** Good booklists should be available to the gifted at all ages, and teachers should actively encourage students to read particular selections. Examples of books for young gifted children (primary level) that are rich in idea, form, and illustration may be found in the resource section of this chapter.

**9.** As educators are in the process of developing curriculum for the gifted, it is important to attempt to keep a balance between developing objectives that focus on skill building and on idea building. Even in the area of higher-order skills, it may be useful to develop higher-order ideas as well.

**10.** The blend of content, process, and concept components in a language arts curriculum can only result in creating a more enriched, advanced, and personally relevant type of learning experiences for talented learners. Clearly, our objectives for these students need to reflect strongly the importance of these three dimensions. Figure 7–2 provides an example of such a blend in the literature domain.

## Conclusion

Language arts programs for the gifted should present opportunities for challenging curriculum throughout the K–12 continuum. One way to enhance such possibilities is to

**FIGURE 7–2   Examples of Objectives Generated by Content, Process, and Concept Perspectives**

The identified gifted learner will be able to:

### Content Objectives (Model A)

- Recognize various literary devices used by authors to explain mood, style, and purpose
- Identify the mythological allusions found in *The Odyssey*

### Process Objectives (Model B)

- Critique selected published works: poems, short stories, cartoons, art forms, and visual media
- Write a research paper that contrasts two authors' styles

### Content Objectives (Model C)

- Develop an understanding of satire through contemporary cartooning of literary works of the past
- Recognize that cultures reflect a unique view of human experience through their literature and art

---

redirect and refocus the traditional language arts strands in such a way as to make them more compatible with the characteristics and needs of the gifted learner at the appropriate stage of developmental readiness. Second, it is important to treat the strands of language, literature, writing, and oral discourse as separate domains of study as well as find suitable ways to interrelate them. Even gifted students need to feel they have gained some control over a tool skill such as the writing process or oral communications. The separate and integral study of language and literature again allows a level of competence to precede work in interdisciplinary areas. Third, educators in language arts programs for the gifted need to organize subject matter more carefully over the years these students are in school so that needless repetition and redundancy is removed from their curriculum experience. The results of such an effort would be to address the needs of the gifted population directly and in the process to upgrade the entire curriculum for all learners.

### Key Points Summary

- *The language arts need to be examined according to the subject matter strands that constitute them for purposes of curriculum modification for the gifted. These strands are literature, language (mother tongue and foreign), oral communication, and writing.*
- *Content acceleration can best be effected in the teaching of the vocabulary, syntax, and usage principles of a language, whether English or a foreign language.*
- *Process/product approaches to the curriculum are best carried out through the tool*

*skill programs of writing and composition as well as through forms such as debate and dramatics.*

- *Concept approaches to the language arts can best be enacted through the literature strand and its opportunities for the treatment of universal themes and the interrelated art forms of music and art.*
- *The goal structure for a verbal arts curriculum needs to have content, process/ product, and concept focal points so that the derived curriculum experiences can address differing needs of the gifted simultaneously: the need to move ahead at a rate determined by student capacity, the need to engage in problem-finding and problem-solving learning that leads to product development, and the need to explore ideas, themes, and issues within and across areas of knowledge.*
- *Providing a greater emphasis on the workshop approach to composition programs for the gifted will surely yield a greater return in terms of frequency of writing and mastery of fundamental persuasive writing skills at an earlier stage of development.*
- *Stress on learning vocabulary over spelling and learning writing skills over handwriting are important modifications in a language arts curriculum for the gifted.*
- *Early literature and writing experiences are necessary for the gifted child to thrive in the reading experience. These experiences should be standard in K–3 programs.*
- *The Advanced Placement Program of College Board in Literature and Composition provides an excellent basis for curriculum work in these areas of gifted students' programs as early as middle school. AP tests in these areas stress analytic and interpretive skills, the ability to generalize and synthesize information, and the capacity to evaluate effectively.*

## Selected Materials for Use in Language Arts Programs

### A Sampling of Books for Gifted Readers

Ahlberg, J., & Ahlberg, A. (1982). *The baby's catalogue.* Boston: Little, Brown.

Alexander, L. *Chronicles of Prydain.* New York: Holt, Rinehart & Winston. Titles include:

*The book of three* (1964)
*The black cauldron* (1965)
*The castle of Llyr* (1966)
*Taran wanderer* (1967)
*The high king* (1968)
*Coll and his white pig* (1967)
*The truthful harp* (1965)
*The foundling and other tales of Prydain* (1973)

Aliki. (1984). *Feelings.* New York: Harper and Row.

Anno, M. (1975). *Anno's counting book.* New York: Crowell.

Anno, M. (1978). *Anno's journey.* New York: Philomel Books.

Baskin, L. (1972). *Hosie's alphabet.* New York: Viking.

Bingham, M. (1989). *Berta Benz and the motorwagen: The story of the first automobile journey.* Santa Barbara, CA: Advocacy Press.

Bjork, C. (1987). *Linnea in Monet's garden.* New York: R. & S Books. Translated from Swedish by Joan Sandin.

Blumberg, R. (1985). *Commodore Perry in the land of the Shogun.* New York: Lothrop, Lee & Shepard.

Dickinson, E. (1978). *I'm nobody! Who are you?* Owings Mills, MD: Stemmer House.

Freeman, R. (1983). *Children of the wild West.* New York: Clarion Books.

Frost, R. (1982). *A swinger of birches.* Owings Mills, MD: Stemmer House.

Garza, C. L. (1990). *Family pictures/Cuadros de familia.* San Francisco: Children's Book Press.

Giblin, J. C. (1984). *Walls: Defenses throughout history.* Boston: Little, Brown.

Goodall, J. (1986). *The story of a castle.* New York: Macmillan.

Greenfield, E. (1988). *Grandpa's face.* New York: Philomel Books.

Hamilton, V. (1967). *Zeely.* New York: Macmillan.

Hamilton, V. (1971). *The planet of Junior Brown.* New York: Macmillan.

Hamilton, V. (1974). *M. C. Higgins, the great.* New York: Macmillan.

Hoyt-Goldsmith, D. (1990). *Totem pole.* New York: Holiday House.

LeGuin, U. K. (1976). *Very far away from anywhere else.* New York: Atheneum.

Macaulay, D. (1977). *Castle.* Boston: Houghton Mifflin.

Macaulay, D. (1990). *Black and white.* Boston: Houghton Mifflin.

Mahy, M. (1990). *The seven Chinese brothers.* New York: Scholastic.

Manes, S. (1982). *Be a perfect person in just three days!* Boston: Houghton Mifflin.

Moore, J. B. (1968). *The many ways of seeing.* Cleveland, OH: World.

Peet, B. (1989). *Bill Peet: An autobiography.* Boston: Houghton Mifflin.

Pinkwater, D. M. (1977). *The big orange splot.* New York: Hastings.

Singer, I. B. (1969). *A day of pleasure: Stories of a boy growing up in Warsaw.* New York: Farrar, Straux & Giroux. Translated from Yiddish.

Singer, I. B. (1976). *Naftali the storyteller and his horse. Sus and other stories.* New York: Farrar, Straus & Giroux.

Steptoe, J. (1987). *Mufaro's beautiful daughters.* New York: Lothrop, Lee & Shepard.

Tchudi, S., & Tchudi, S. (1984). *The young writer's handbook.* New York: Scribner's.

Van Allsburg, C. (1984). *The mysteries of Harris Burdick.* Boston: Houghton Mifflin.

Voight, C. *The Tillerman saga.* New York: Atheneum. Titles include:

*Dicey's Song* (1982)

*Homecoming* (1983)

*Solitary Blue* (1983)

*The Runner* (1985)

*Come a Stranger* (1986)

*Sons From Afar* (1987)

*Seventeen Against the Dealer* (1989)

Ward, L. (1973). *The silver pony: A story in pictures.* Boston: Houghton Mifflin.

Williams, T. T. (1984). *The secret language of snow.* San Francisco: Sierra Club/Pantheon.

Yolen, J. (1987). *Owl moon.* New York: Philomel Books.

## *Resources and Bibliographies*

Baskin, B. H., & Harris, K. H. (1980). *Books for the gifted child.* New York: Bowker.

*Books for the gifted child,* Vol. 2 (1988), by Paula Hauser and Gail A. Nelson. New York: Bowker.

Boyce, L. N., Bailey, J. M., & VanTassel-Baska, J. (1990). *Libraries link learning program and curriculum resource manual for use with at-risk gifted learners.* Williamsburg, VA: The College of William and Mary, Center for Gifted Education.

Cooperative Children's Book Center. 4290 Helen C. White Hall, University of Wisconsin-Madison, 600 N. Park Street, Madison, WI 53706. Bibliographies and newsletter devoted to multicultural children's literature.

Halstead, J. W. (1988). *Guiding gifted readers: From preschool to high school.* Columbus, OH: Ohio Psychology Publishing.

*Horn Book.* 14 Beacon Street, Boston, MA 02108. Magazine of articles and reviews devoted to quality children's literature.

*Scientific American.* December issue. Annual review of science books for young readers.

## *References*

Adler, M. (1982). *The paedeia proposal: An educational manifesto.* New York: Collier Books.

Applebee, A. N. (1981). *Writing in the secondary schools* (Research Monograph No. 21). Urbanna, IL: National Council of Teachers of English.

Applebee, A. N. (1984). *Contexts for learning to*

*write: Studies of secondary school instruction.* Norwood, NJ: Ablex.

Arnold, H. (1962). Useful creative techniques. In S. Parnes & H. Harding (Eds.), *A sourcebook for creative thinking.* New York: Scribner's.

Barbe, W. (1955). Evaluation of special classes for gifted children. *Exceptional Children, 22,* 60–62.

Bartz, W. (1977). *The role of foreign languages in gifted education.* Indianapolis: Indiana State Department of Public Instruction.

Baskin, B., & Harris, K. (1980). *Books for the gifted child.* London: Bowker.

Boyce, L. N., Bailey, J., & VanTassel-Baska, J. (1990). *Libraries link learning resource guide.* Williamsburg, VA: Center for Gifted Education.

California Department of Education. (1979). *Curriculum guide for teaching gifted children literature in grades 1–12.* Sacramento: California State Department of Education.

California Department of Education. (1987). *State of California language arts framework.* Sacramento, CA: Author.

Carter, L. (1984). The sustaining effects study of compensatory and elementary education. *Educational Researcher, 12* (7), 4–13.

Cazden, C. (1988). *Classroom discourse: The language of teaching and learning.* Portsmouth, NH: Heinemann.

Chaney, A. (1992). State of the art paper on oral communication. Washington, DC: Department of Education.

Clarke, B. (1985). *Growing up gifted,* 3rd ed. Columbus, OH: Merrill.

Collins, J. (1985). *The effective writing teacher: 18 strategies.* Andover, MA: The Network.

Cooper, C., & Brennenan, B. (1988). *Writing achievement of California eighth graders: A first look.* Sacramento, CA: California State Department of Education.

Cummins, J. (1979). Linguistic interdependence and the educational development of bilingual children." *Review of Educational Research, 49* (2), 222–251.

Dale, E., & Rozik, T. (1963). *Bibliography of vocabulary studies.* Columbus: Bureau of Educational Research and Service, The Ohio State University.

Davidson, J. L. (Ed.). (1988). *Counterpoint and beyond: A response to becoming a nation of readers,* Urbana, IL: National Council of Teachers of English.

Drews, E. (1972). *Learning together.* Englewood Cliffs, NJ: Prentice Hall.

Dudley, L., & Feracy, V. (undated). *Humanities.* New York: Macmillan.

Gallagher, J. (1985). *Teaching the gifted child,* 3rd ed. Boston: Allyn and Bacon.

Hall, D., & Embler, D. (1976). *A writer's reader.* Boston: Little, Brown.

Halsted, J. (1988). *Guiding gifted readers from preschool through high school.* Columbus, OH: Ohio Psychology Press.

Hirsch, E. D., Jr. (1987). *Cultural literacy: What every American needs to know.* Boston: Houghton Mifflin.

Hollingworth, L. (1926). *Gifted children.* New York: World Book.

Hollingworth, L. (1942). *Children above 180 I.Q.* New York: World Book.

Kaplan, S. (1979). Language arts and social studies curriculum in elementary school. In H. Passow (Ed.), *NSSE yearbook, The gifted and the talented.* Chicago: University of Chicago Press.

Marzano, R. (1992). *Cultivating thinking in English.* Urbana, IL: National Council of Teachers of English.

McKenna, M., Robinson, R., & Miller, J. (1990). Whole language: A research agenda for the nineties. *Educational Researcher, 19* (8), 3–6.

Morris, J. (1971). Barriers to successful reading in second language students at the secondary level. In B. Spolsky (Ed.), *The language education of minority children.* Rowlex: Newbury House.

National Assessment Governing Board. (1992). *Reading framework for the 1992 national assessment of educational progress.* Washington, DC: U.S. Department of Education.

National Center for Educational Statistics. (1992). *National assessment of educational progress 1990 portfolio study.* Washington, DC: U.S. Department of Education.

Norton, D. (1987). *Through the eyes of a child,* 2nd ed. Columbus, OH: Merrill.

Palincsar, A., & Brown, A. (1984). Reciprocal teaching of comprehension-fostering and comprehension-monitoring activities. *Cognition and Instruction, 1* (2), 117–175.

Pilon, A. (1975). Come hither, come hither, come hither: Words' worth. *Gifted Child Quarterly, 15* (1), 13–31.

Polette, N. (1982). *3 R's for the gifted: Reading,*

*writing, and research.* Littleton, CO: Libraries Unlimited.

Polette, N. & Hamlin, M. (1980). *Exploring books with gifted children.* Littleton, CO: Libraries Unlimited.

Reynolds, B., Kopelke, K., & Durden, W. (1984). *Writing instruction for verbally talented youth.* Rockville, MD: Aspen.

Sulzby, E. (1985). *Emergent writing and reading in 5–6 year olds: A longitudinal study.* Norwood, NJ: Ablex.

Thompson, M. (1990). *Classics in the classroom.* New York: Trillium.

Thompson, M. (1991). *The magic lens I and II.* New York: Trillium Press.

Thompson, M. (1992). *The state of the art in teaching language to high-ability learners.* Washington, DC: Department of Education.

Tschudi, S. (1991). *Planning and assessing the curriculum in English language arts.* Alexandria, VA: ASCD.

VanTassel-Baska, J. (1982). An experimental study on the teaching of Latin to the verbally precocious. *Roeper Review, 4* (3).

VanTassel-Baska, J. (1987). The case for the teaching of Latin to the verbally talented. *Roeper Review, 9* (3), 159–161.

VanTassel-Baska, J. (1992). *Planning effective curriculum for gifted learners.* Denver, CO: Love Publishing.

VanTassel-Baska, J., et al. (1988). *Comprehensive curriculum for gifted learners.* Boston: Allyn and Bacon.

VanTassel-Baska, J., & Willis, G. (1988). A three year study of the effects of low income on SAT scores among the academically able. *Gifted Child Quarterly, 31,* 169–173.

VanTassel-Baska, J., Patton, J., & Prillaman, D. (1991). *Gifted youth at risk.* Reston, VA: Council for Exceptional Children.

Webb, J., Meckstroth, E., & Tolan, S. (1982). *Guiding the gifted child.* Columbus, OH: Ohio Psychology Press.

## *Literature*

### *Literature: Uses of the Imagination*

Northrop Frye, supervisory editor. Will T. Jewkes, general editor. Harcourt Brace Jovanovich, 1972; 1973. *Primary audience: 7–12.*

> *Revolutionary in concept and technique, this paperback program for junior and senior high school guides students to discover recurring character, story, and image patterns, or archetypes, in the literature of all cultures and periods. With this approach, literature becomes more meaningful, more accessible as well as easier to teach. Poems, short stories, myths, parables, filmscripts, and songs are presented together with contemporary photographs, painting, posters, and cartoons to show the basic imaginative patterns all people share. For example, the archetype of the martyred hero is illustrated in Benet's "John Brown's Body," the myth of Prometheus, and a eulogy for Malcolm X by Ossie Davis; the rightful kingdom archetype in John F. Kennedy's Inaugural Address, the myths of Perseus, and the song "Aquarius" from Hair.*

### *Junior Great Books*

The Great Books Foundation, 40 East Huron Street, Chicago, Illinois 60611. *Primary audience:* elementary gifted students (1–6).

> *This program provides a structured collection of excellent classical and modern stories for students to read and discuss in the context of shared inquiry. Discussion leaders, teachers, or volunteers center discussion on problems of interpretation in a given selection. Students develop the ability to think reflectively and independently, to listen to and consider opinions other than their own. At the same time, they are exposed to excellent literature.*

## *Writing*

*The Elements of Style,* 3rd ed. W. Strunk, Jr. & E. B. White. New York: Macmillan, 1979.

> *Rules of usage of English language. Elucidates rules and principles of writing by concentrating on common violations.*

*The Lively Art of Writing.* Lucille Vaughan Payne, in 3 vols.: *Developing Structure, Effective Style, Understanding Forms.* Chicago: Follett, 1982.

> *Writing through development of mental pictures and distinct verb types, motion-picture verbs, soundtrack verbs, etc. Encourages students to think through writing to organize structure.*

*The Art of Styling Sentences.* M. L. Waddell, R. M. Esch, & R. R. Walker. Woodbury, NY: Barron's Educational Series, 1983.

> *Examples and diagrams of sentence patterns which form the basics of all good writing. Chapters and exercises in each chapter.*

*20 Questions for the Writer: A Rhetoric with Readings,* 4th ed. Jacqueline Berke. New York: Harcourt Brace Jovanovich, 1985.

> *Divides 20 questions into four categories: Imaginative, Informative, Analytical, Critical. Examples of each type of writing and exercises for same for students. Seven different ways of defining words and phrases. Appendices on sentence composition and review of punctuation.*

---

### EXAMPLE 7.A Sample Language Arts Teaching Units

This unit and the one following on photography have been developed to teach the genre of poetry and its relationship to other artistic forms. It is appropriate for gifted learners in several respects:

1. It engages students in generative learning immediately by having them "create" poems and photographs.
2. It uses selected poems intensively.
3. It focuses on higher-level thinking tasks about poetry and photography.
4. It uses an interdisciplinary approach.
5. It allows student choice in selecting activities.
6. It encourages original production.

> **Level:**   Middle school
>
> **Grouping:**   Special class of gifted/talented learners or cluster grouping

#### *Topic: Poetry as an Art Form*

*Objectives and Corresponding Activities*

1. Differentiate the form of poetry from prose.
   a. Share from well-known American poets (Emily Dickinson, Carl Sandburg, Robert Frost, Stephen Spender) several poems with the class by reading them, putting them on an overhead projector, and handing them out.
   b. Discuss differences in form and what helps constitute the form of these specific poems.

2. Interpret several poems appropriately, using analytical and aesthetic approaches.
   a. Through an inquiry approach, discover the meaning of each poem and how form contributes to meaning.
   b. Use a forced relationship approach to demonstrate ways to merge form and meaning.
3. Relate how the form of a poem reflects the meaning of a poem by using your favorite poem as an illustration.
   a. In small groups, have students use the creative problem-solving model to select and analyze a particular poem.
   b. Have students critique "favorite poems" in a group setting, citing form characteristics.
4. Using the poem "Jabberwocky," list examples that demonstrate the relationship of form and meaning.
   a. Have students brainstorm key phrases from the poem.
   b. Discuss the form of the poem.
   c. In small groups, utilize decision-making skills to determine relationship between form and meaning.
5. Utilize one form of poetry discussed and write your own poem.
   a. Review forms of poetry discussed.
   b. Practice writing a poem in class according to a particular form and idea.
   c. Share and critique with the class according to the stated parameters.
6. Set up criteria and judge the student poems in respect to form and meaning.
   a. Brainstorm criteria for judgment of student poems.
   b. Create an evaluation form for each student to fill out.
   c. Conduct poetry readings.
7. Create a poem by writing down an idea (in one line) and passing it on. When it comes back, finish the poem. (To be done in groups of four.)
   a. Group work on creating group poems.
   b. Share group poems and discuss how they differ from individual ones.
   c. Judge which group created the best group poem.

*Evaluation Design*

This topic will be evaluated through the following approaches:

1. Self-evaluation by students of their creative efforts in poetry and participation in group activities.
2. Class evaluation of original poems read (a total group score would be utilized here)
3. Teacher evaluation based on portfolio analysis

### Topic: Principles of Poetry

*Objectives and Corresponding Activities*

1. Identify principles of poetry by specific names: meter, rhyme, form, content, poetic devices.
   a. Read about characteristics of poems in John Ciardi's *How Does a Poem Mean.*

    b. Utilize five sample poems with the class to show how these characteristics are present and operate in the examples.
2. Compare and contrast two poems in respect to these principles.
    a. Read "Ulysses" by Tennyson and "Ozymandias" by Shelley.
    b. Write an essay describing similarities and differences in respect to poetic principles.
3. Read new poems and identify the principles represented.
    a. Read at least two poems by each of the following poets: Lao Tse; Shakespeare, Keats, Dickinson, Frost, Hughes.
    b. In groups, discuss the notion of the principles utilized by each poet and how it determines style.
    c. Present a panel discussion on this topic.
4. Compose a poem utilizing the major principles learned, and in the style of your favorite poet.
    a. Through inquiry, arrive at a definition of style and how it manifests itself in poetry.
    b. Brainstorm important steps in writing a poem.
    c. Create a "best list" of steps in poetry writing.
5. Judge whether the principles are appropriately utilized in each student's poem.
    a. Present poems to the class.
    b. Have the class guess what author's style is being imitated after each presentation.
    c. Discuss the poetic principles that are present.
    d. Utilize a discrepancy chart to show what might be missing from the poem that could have been included.
6. Create your own poetic principles and apply them to a poem that you write.
    a. Set up a list of steps to be followed in creating a new form of poetry.
    b. Read about creativity and the process of creativity.
    c. Practice poetry writing.
    d. Have a poet in residence share perceptions and insights with the class.

*Evaluation Design*

This topic will be evaluated through the following multiple approaches:

1. Essays will be evaluated on a scale of 1–5 (with 5 being high) according to the criteria of: applicability of content to the assignment, grammatical form, and fluidity of expression.
2. In-class presentations will be videotaped and critiqued by the class as a follow-up activity.
3. A guest poet will judge original poems.

### Topic: The Lives of Poets

*Objectives and Corresponding Activities*

1. Read biographies of two major poets.
    a. Brainstorm reasons for life history affecting artistic products.
    b. Through inquiry, discover the effects of the culture, the time period and other artists on any particular creation.

c. Choose two poets to study in regard to life and cultural milieu.
2. Explain what each poet's conception of the creative process is.
   a. Prepare note cards for an oral presentation on main aspects of biographies.
   b. Prepare oral presentation.
   c. Chart similarities and differences among the poets.
3. Apply conceptions of the creative process to the future.
   a. Do a small-group simulation, pretending students are poets in the year 2500. How would they speak about poetry and the creative process?
   b. Share preceptions of all groups.
4. What do poets see as vital components of their art? Analyze at least two biographies in this respect.
   a. Discuss the personal qualities that make a poet.
   b. Read about Blake and Eliot in this respect.
   c. Write an essay demonstrating your perception of the characters of these two poets. Hypothesize on what contributed to their nature.
5. Pretend you are a famous poet. Create your own epitaph based on how you've lived, what you've done, etc.
   a. Choose one of the poets studied.
   b. Write down important things you know about this poet.
   c. Read excerpts from Edgar Lee Masters' *Spoon River Anthology* for an understanding of poetic epitaphs.
6. Evaluate the lives of poets compared to nonartistic occupations; what differences exist? Chart the differences and indicate *your* values on each dimension.
   a. Develop an interview questionnaire regarding rationale for choice of occupation.
   b. Interview at least two people not in artistic fields.
   c. In small groups, discuss findings and use the creative problem-solving model to develop a chart of major results.
   d. Share group results and discuss.

*Evaluation Design*

This topic's objectives will be evaluated through the following procedures:

1. Class evaluation of oral reports via a structured instrument devised and field-tested by students themselves.
2. Teacher analysis of group interaction via a Flanders-type analysis on individual students.
3. Teacher-evaluated essay, on a 1–5 scale (5 being high) based on the criteria of: analysis of topic, synthesis of information, and evaluation of contributory factors to character formation of poets.
4. Have the class choose the five best epitaphs and critique them in respect to predetermined criteria.

### Topic: Photography as an Art Form

*Objectives and Corresponding Activities*

1. Understand the elements of photography.

a. Examine several photographs in class, taking notes on elements that interest you.
b. Discuss aspects of interest.
c. Categorize the areas of interest.
d. Show a set of slides and have the class pick out the key elements in each photograph.
2. Create a montage from a variety of photographs.
   a. In groups, build a montage around the theme of love.
   b. Use morphological analysis to determine a theme, a mode of treatment and resources to be utilized for individual montages.
   c. Provide an outline of project procedures.
3. Describe photographic materials and techniques.
   a. Introduce the tools of a photographer.
   b. Take the class on a tour of a dark room.
   c. Provide hands-on experience with developing techniques.
   d. Have a photographer discuss the technical aspects of his or her job.
4. Analyze photographs in respect to meaning, method, and use of symbols.
   a. Show slides of photographs and discuss how development techniques contribute to visual meaning.
   b. In small groups, prepare a series of photographs that demonstrate good fusion of aesthetics and technique along with a rationale for each.
   c. Individually, choose a favorite photograph and write an analysis of it, reflecting the issues discussed in class.
5. Judge the relative quality of photographs, given the criteria of technical competence, aesthetic content, use of symbols, clarity of ideas, and composition.
   a. Review and discuss terminology used in evaluation.
   b. In small groups, determine photographic quality in five photographs, using the stated criteria.
   c. Have groups present their decisions to the class.
   d. Debrief through a discussion of group differences in perception of quality.
   e. Assign selected readings from Robert Pirsig's *Zen and the Art of Motorcycle Maintenance* that deal with the issue of "quality."
6. Produce a photographic essay.
   a. Have students shoot a complete roll of 35mm film and develop it.
   b. Prepare a presentation for the class on the best series of pictures taken and what they represent.
   c. Conduct a contest and award 1st, 2nd, and 3rd prizes for the best photographs as judged by a class panel.

*Evaluation Design*

This topic will be evaluated through a three-tiered approach:

1. Level one evaluation will consist of each student completing a self-evaluation form for each major activity completed.
2. Level two evaluation will consist of teacher evaluations of all written and oral presentations.
3. Level three evaluation will consist of peer ratings on the photographic contest.

## Topic: Principles of Photography

*Objectives and Corresponding Activities*

1. Discern the principles of photography.
   a. Conduct a class discussion on *aesthetics* in respect to meaning and application; then discuss similarly the term *technique.*
   b. Write an essay describing how the principles of poetry and photography are alike and how they are different.
2. Create a photograph that allows you to analyze all the photographic principles.
   a. Do a group simulation on "If you were photographing a tornado that destroyed a town and claimed 100 lives, how would you organize for maximum effect?"
   b. Each group gives an oral report.
   c. Debrief around similarities and differences in interpretation of the event.
   d. Prepare a checklist of photographic procedures and principles to use in creating a picture.
   e. Submit completed checklist and sample photograph.
4. Select a theme and create a photographic essay around it.
   a. Brainstorm lists of possible subjects for photographic essays.
   b. Select a subject and outline alternative approaches to dealing with it photographically.
   c. Shoot and develop photos.
   d. Synthesize photo material for display.

*Evaluation Design*

This topic will be evaluated by the following devices:

1. Teacher rating sheet on group participation
2. Teacher rating of written essay on a 1–5 scale (5 being high)
3. Panel of three photographers (one professional and two amateur) to judge photo displays, utilizing a predetermined checklist
4. Peer evaluation of photographs illustrating basic principles

## Topic: Lives of Photographers

*Objectives and Corresponding Activities*

1. Understand the cultural and personal factors influencing the work of Steiglitz, Steichen, and Adams.
   a. Read biographical excerpts on each photographer.
   b. Prepare a group chart of major influences on each photographer.
   c. Share with the class and compare charts.
2. Compare the life and times of Steiglitz, Steichen, and Adams with their photographic style.
   a. Analyze the style of each photographer by listing special techniques or unusual, distinctive approaches to treatment of a subject.
   b. Compile a class list of these techniques.

    c. Write an essay reflecting on the relationship of style to personal and social factors.

    d. Compile and present a portfolio to the class that typifies each photographer's work.

    e. Evaluate the portfolio in respect to: adherence to style and comprehensiveness of the effort.

*Evaluation Design*

This topic will be evaluated by:

1. Teacher rating of portfolios
2. Peer judgment regarding charts of major influences
3. Checklist of biographic materials read, to be completed by the students

# Chapter 8

# Social Studies Curriculum for the Gifted

*JOYCE VanTASSEL-BASKA AND JOHN F. FELDHUSEN*

*Like Huck, we observed, we judged, we imitated and evaded as we could the dullness, corruption, and blindness of "civilization." —RALPH ELLISON*

Social studies curricula offer excellent opportunities to engage gifted and talented students in complex, challenging cognitive activities. Through reading, discussion, writing, and collaborative projects in the social studies, gifted and talented students can learn the skills of critical and creative thinking and the control functions of metacognition. They can also build powerful knowledge bases in subject matters that relate directly to their daily lives—political science, history, psychology, ecology, and so on.

Some students have natural talents for study and growth in the social studies. They should be identified early and guided into the most intensive experiences in the social studies throughout their school years. Other students' talents lie in other areas such as science, art, or music. They may be guided for their intensive educational experiences to other appropriate areas of the curriculum. However, they too need basic experiences in the social studies to develop their competencies and commitments as citizens and to develop the critical, creative, and metacognitive thinking skills of professionals, artists, and business leaders. All high-ability students need and can profit from educational experiences in the social studies.

## Conceptualizing the Social Studies

The framework for conceptualizing the social sciences is a key issue in making decisions about curriculum focus within this broad field for gifted learners. Scriven's model of the tripod is a useful image for perceiving the major areas of knowledge and how they relate to each other (see Figure 8–1):

> *I picture the social sciences as a rectangular surface supported on a tripod. The three legs are the three subjects that have some claim to being foundational social sciences, two of which have acquired a primary place in the curriculum. The three subjects are geography, history, and one that is primarily not in the secondary curriculum but in theoretical discussions of the structure of the social sciences—psychology.*
>
> *Now, why are these three primary? This is the reason: geography is the study of the spatial distribution of man and his large-scale effects on the earth. History is the study of his temporal distribution and achievements, and psychology is the study of the internal organization of the human entity. . . .*
>
> *On the tripod rests the surface that represents the standard social sciences of the academic curriculum: sociology, government, economics, and anthropology. They depend in varying ways on geography, history, and psychology, and I've tried to represent their varying degrees of dependency by their position.*

Scriven's model raises several issues of importance for decision making regarding curriculum for the gifted learner. The study of any part of the social sciences culminates in a consideration of ethics, which in turn provides the basis for social action. If we find Scriven's model representative, then a natural blend of content and idea can occur in the social science curriculum for the gifted. For all areas of study, ethical behavior becomes an integral part of the learning process. Furthermore, interdisciplinary curriculum efforts

**FIGURE 8–1   Model for the Social Sciences**

within the social sciences are essential to maintaining an appropriate perspective on any one area of study. Economics cannot be studied exclusive of its methodology, its relationship to government and other fields of study, and its impact in the social action arena. Thus, curriculum for the gifted learner must provide this mosaic of relationships. The implication of using this model as a guide for curriculum development is that all social science curriculum for the gifted should be treated in an interdisciplinary manner, regardless of the particular area under study.

Barr, Barth, and Shermis (1977) defined the social studies as "an integration of experience and knowledge from the social sciences and humanities for the purpose of citizenship education." Shermis (1989) also pointed out that three distinct historical traditions are linked to this definition: reflective inquiry, social sciences, and citizenship transmission. He argued that the first two of these three traditions offer unique opportunities to design appropriate instruction for the gifted in the social studies because of their capacity for high-level thinking activity and their need for engagement with high-level content from the social science disciplines.

There also abound other perspectives on what constitutes an appropriate approach to a social science curriculum. These perspectives may be characterized as:

- *The emphasis on history versus the emphasis on culture.* Those who argue for an historical emphasis in social science curriculum tend to view history as the centerpiece for study, thus inhibiting a broader range of knowledge exploration. Those who favor the cultural approach would relegate history to a less important role and emphasize particular cultures as the basis for study.
- *The emphasis on chronology versus the emphasis on systems.* The chronologists see history as the unfolding of events in absolute time, whereas those who favor the systems approach prefer viewing past time on the basis of major issues, ideas, or events that emerged out of a larger pattern.
- *The emphasis on content versus the emphasis on process.* Educators who favor strong content-based instruction in the social sciences view each area as capable of being mastered as a separate entity, whereas educators who favor the process approach believe that the fundamental learning for students from social science curricula is critical inquiry.

Based on the capacities of gifted learners to handle a blend of curriculum approaches, it is reasonable to suggest that distinguishing features of social science curricula for these students be in the scope of exposure to key areas of study, the understanding and concern for developing critical inquiry as the basis for ethical decision making leading to social policy, and the multiple perspectives view within and across each area of study. Key social studies goals for gifted programs might include:

1. To develop critical thought and the spirit of inquiry
2. To understand and develop a world cultures view
3. To appreciate the interrelationship of social science disciplines and institutions
4. To gain knowledge of significant developments in human history and the social systems of which they are a part
5. To develop research, discussion, and thinking skills
6. To develop skill in writing and project activities in the social studies domain

## Model Curricula in the Social Studies

Barr, Barth, and Shermis (1977) asserted that citizenship education is a major goal of the social studies. Thus, at any grade level the social studies curriculum should focus on issues central to life in the United States and in the world, and should prepare students to think through the major issues and problems facing our society. A knowledge base is implied in these assertions—students should know about the major concepts, principles, themes, problems, and issues that permeate our culture, and they should acquire the skills to analyze, evaluate, and synthesize ideas about them.

Shaver (1984) described the jurisprudential approach to social studies education. In this method and curriculum, students study, analyze, and evaluate major political ethical issues in our society. He argued that the approach is uniquely appropriate for the gifted because of their heightened capacity to read far beyond ordinary textbook content, to deal with moral and ethical issues at a high and abstract level, to use critical thinking skills in analyzing issues, and to verbalize their analyses in interaction with other gifted students. Shaver summarized the rationale for the jurisprudential approach as follows:

1. Social studies education is basically citizenship education.
2. Citizenship education ought to reflect the nature of the society and of the policy decisions to be made by the society.
3. Our society is pluralistic with a variety of frames of reference, resulting in continous disagreement over the political-ethical issues, which are at the heart of policy disputes.
4. Because political-ethical decisions must rest in part at least on one's view of what is morally desirable, values are crucial to their justification.
5. Values are defined differently and, when in conflict, weighted differently by people with different frames of reference.
6. Social studies education should, among other things, help students to analyze public issues in order to make better decisions as citizens; and an appropriate analytic frame must include consideration of values and value conflict, as well as questions of fact and language use.

Shermis and Clinkenbeard (1981) analyzed social studies texts and the study questions included in these texts. They concluded that although there was a shift over the years toward higher-level questions, there is still major adherence to questions at the knowledge and comprehension levels. Shermis and Clinkenbeard argued that gifted learners have a special need for high-level thinking experiences, and that social studies teachers must go beyond the standard text questions in designing discussion, case studies, and Socratic dialogues.

Schug (1981) argued that the whole community can be used as a laboratory to develop social studies curricula for the gifted. He suggested that social studies programs for the gifted should begin with a community advisory committee drawn from business, labor, agriculture, the arts, political parties, and so on. The curriculum can be developed around issues and problems in the community. The following are activities for civics and history courses:

### Civics

- *Visit or participate in meetings of the school board, city council, courts, public hearings, or state legislature.*
- *Interview public officials such as the mayor, county commissioners, city council members, school board members, or officials in local, state, or federal agencies.*
- *Invite a member of Congress or the state legislature as a class guest speaker.*
- *Do volunteer work at local political party headquarters.*
- *Conduct opinion polls about local public issues or candidates during an election.*
- *Establish a youth citizenship club whose goal is to encourage studying issues, candidates, and political participation.*
- *Interview candidates for office about their stands on youth-related issues.*

### History

- *Arrange field trips to local museums, historical societies, or historical sites.*
- *Develop oral history collections by doing tape-recorded interviews with senior citizens.*
- *Do volunteer work at local museums or historical societies.*
- *Write local histories based on written records, photographs, and interviews with resource people.*
- *Find and analyze historical artifacts such as weapons, tools, kitchen utensils, arrowheads, toys, clothing, letters, diaries, books, catalogs, or photographs (junk yards, garages, junk shops, and attics are often valuable sources of historical artifacts).*
- *Arrange a field trip to an old cemetery where students record dates of births and deaths and make inferences about past life spans, epidemics, and health care.*
- *Videotape interviews with senior citizens talking about life in the past.*

Barth and Shermis (1981) presented an extensive curriculum guide to social studies curricula for the gifted and talented. The guide presents material for social studies activities in grades K–12. After each section of activities, there is a section on differentiating to meet the specific needs and characteristics of gifted learners. Here, for example, is the learning objective and activity for an eighth-grade American History course whose overall goal is to "Develop a knowledge base for understanding the ever-changing relationship between human beings and their environment: past, present and future" (p. 40).

> *Learning Objective: Examine the status of blacks prior to and during the Civil War, and compare and contrast the status and role of blacks prior to, during, and after Reconstruction.*
>   *1. Learning activity: "Jim Crow and You"*
>       a. Duration of time: one or two sessions
>       b. *Materials: selections of Jim Crow laws, a student-made list of daily activities*
>       *Suggested readings:*
>       *The Reign of Jim Crow* (AEP)

*Impact of Our Past* (McGraw Hill)

*Promise of America* (Vol. 2 Scott Foresman)

c. *Description*

1) *Ask students to compile a list of activities they might experience during a typical day. (Example: riding a bus to school, buying lunch in the cafeteria).*

2) *After reading about Jim Crow laws, ask students to review their list and identify in some way those activities that would have been affected if the same Jim Crow laws applied to them today.*

3) *A reaction discussion on the students' feelings about Jim Crow laws could follow.*

4) *A coordinated activity could include posters, pictures, written articles, etc., on Jim Crow law and segregation.*

Here is a part of their discussion of how to use the activities with the gifted.

*How Do These Activities Work with the Gifted?*

*I Urge You* will involve gifted children in some risk-taking and unusual circumstances. While normal children will say "I urge Abraham Lincoln to free the slaves," one can reasonably expect gifted children to urge the appointment of Grant—a general with a superior sense of economic warefare—as General of the Army of the Potomac in 1861. The use of conventional categories in *What's In A Name* is a standard teaching strategy, but one can expect bright children to invent justifications for categories that are likely to go well beyond the conventional response. One can hardly predict what gifted children will do with *Jim Crow and You* which asks for a contemporary application of segregation laws. At the very least, gifted students will go beyond expressing feelings and deal with some of the complex reasons for racism, discrimination, bigotry, etc.; some will want to compare our experience with that of South Africa. (p. 45)

Flachner and Hirst (1976) developed curriculum guides for the Astor Program, an early childhood program for the gifted. *200 Years: A Study of Democracy* presents the outline for social studies activities in the program. One of the objectives states, "Children will learn that the United States developed from the combined skills and cultures of people from many levels" (p. 17). The unit begins with Walt Whitman's *I Hear America Singing* and then suggests the following activities:

**1.** What are some of the vocations and skills the colonists had? From what countries had they come? What work had they done in their former countries?

**2.** What contributions in skills and work did various ethnic groups make to the growth of America?

For each set of activities, quotations from relevant literature are included to be used as a basis for discussions and projects with gifted learners. The quotations are from excellent literature, which is much more advanced and complex than generally would be used at the early childhood level. Activities and questions for discussion are at similarly high levels. These guides can be used with young gifted children in various settings, including cluster groups and self-contained programs.

A number of curriculum guides have been developed, and operational program models have been implemented at the Burris Laboratory School at Ball State University, Muncie, Indiana, to serve the special needs of gifted learners. The operational model is generally in the form of a seminar for gifted students characterized by high-level discussions, attention to higher-level thinking skills, a focus on issues and problems, much in-depth research and project activity, and gifted learners reporting their studies in a variety of creative communication modes. In one of the curriculum guides "A Curricular Approach for Global Futures," Keener (undated) presented the complete curriculum for a futures-oriented course designed especially for gifted learners. Part of the outline for that course follows:

*Classroom Approaches and Generic Global Future Concepts*

*Reflective Thinking and Global Futures Concepts as Classroom Strategy*

*Global Futures Concepts as Content and Structure*
  Systems
  Interdependence
  Culture
  Life-style
  Dignity of Man
  Change
  Populations
  Scarcity/Allocation
  Energy
  Habitat
  Institution
  Sovereignty
  Conflict
  Power
  Communication

*Developmental/Investigative Activities*
  Individual or Small Group Investigation of an Alternative Global Future
  Delineating the Global Futures Investigation
  Reporting Research Theses in Global Futures
  Individualized Research Theses and Projects/Products
  Simplifying a Demographic Abstraction
  Nuclear Holocaust Survival Skills
  Appropriate Technologies for Developing Economies—Role-Playing

The closest curricular adaptation that has been made of the Scriven conceptual model of the social sciences is the K–12 gifted program used in Chicago Public Schools, Comprehensive Gifted Centers and Magnet High Schools. Because these programs are self-contained, the curriculum can differ substantially from the general curriculum for all students and can be effectively articulated across grade levels. Their social studies curriculum focuses on nine strands: geography, psychology, economics, history, political science, sociology, anthropology, philosophy, and research skills. These strands are targeted for different emphases at various grade levels from kindergarten through grade 12. The program takes a strong stance on providing students with a sense of the structural nature of the disciplines that make up the social studies, with a focus on the language of the discipline, its theories, and key concepts that define it. At no grade level is only one strand treated; rather, there is a multiple approach used at each. Only at the level of activities would a teacher make adaptations because the student is younger. The course descriptions present an intellectual purpose at each level of the curriculum. (See Example 8.A at the conclusion of this chapter for selected portions of this curriculum.)

## The Art of Inquiry

In the teaching of the social sciences, perhaps more than any other set of disciplines, the use of good inquiry techniques is vital since learner outcomes are dependent on developing a critical inquiring mind. Use of a questioning model (see Table 8–1) may be helpful in preparing social studies discussions. The instructor should be careful to include questions that require several types of thinking processes: memory/cognition, convergent, divergent, and evaluation. Yet, as the example illustrates, the questions are carefully

**TABLE 8–1   Varied Questioning Types and Examples**

| Question Types | Examples |
| --- | --- |
| *Memory/Cognition* | |
| These questions are typified by the characteristic of one right answer, are factual in nature, and begin with words like *who/what/when*. | Who directed Civil War activities for the North? What year did the Civil War begin? When did Lee surrender? |
| *Convergent* | |
| These questions are typified by multiple right responses that are analytical in nature, and tend to begin with *why/how*. | Why was the Civil War fought? How did the war begin? |
| *Divergent* | |
| These questions are hypothetical in nature, often creating scenarios or simulations for students to respond to. There are no right answers to this question type, which frequently begin with words like *what if/ pretend*. | What if the South had won the war; how would life be different today? Pretend you are a slave during the Civil War. What might you consider in deciding to join the abolitionist movement? |
| *Evaluative* | |
| These questions call for the exercise of student judgment and/or opinion. No right answers are anticipated, and questions begin with words like *in your opinion* or *which is best*. | Which policy is better: • to avoid war at all costs? • to fight for principles one believes in? In your opinion, is war a part of the human condition? |

structured to lead from concrete data to abstract speculating, from specific information about one historical event to an understanding of issues that apply to many events. A set of questions may be useful to consider in evaluating individual inquiry-based techniques to question posing:

1. Do the questions lead to problem formulation?
2. Do they aim toward *student* explication of the problem?
3. Are students called on to analyze their explanations and to test their hypothesis?
4. Are the questions open ended?
5. Are students able to formulate creative solutions?

The following questions have been developed around specific social studies topics to provide teachers of the gifted with a sense of the level, complexity, and nature of appropriate questions for gifted students. Each set of questions* represents a blend of convergent, divergent, and evaluative questions.

### American Studies

1. "The Crusades was the opening chapter in the story of the discovery of America." Explain this statement.
2. If you were a European of the sixteenth- or seventeenth-century period, why would you be willing to leave your home to come to a strange and dangerous New World?
3. The Constitution of the United States has been called "a bundle of compromises." Why?
4. You are a leader of a newly independent nation of Latin America. How would you feel about the issuance of the Monroe Doctrine?
5. An historian stated, "Geography determined which states would secede from the Union." What did he mean?
6. If you lived in the 1850s, would you have considered John Brown a hero or a murderer? Why?
7. Some historians believe that the Civil War could have been avoided; others feel it was inevitable. With which view do you agree? Why?
8. How may the art and literature of a period of American history give us a picture of life during that period? Give specific examples.
9. You are an urban planner. What problems must you solve to create cities in which people can live good lives?

### Ethnic Studies

1. The United States presents an example more of a "salad bowl" than of a "melting pot." Do you agree or disagree? why?
2. Why do you think African Americans have adopted more of the white man's customs and culture than the American Indians?
3. How are the problems of Mexican Americans similar to or different from those of African Americans and American Indians?

*These questions are adapted from *A Handbook for the Teaching of Social Studies,* 2nd ed., by The Association of Teachers of Social Studies in the City of New York/United Federation of Teachers. Copyright © 1985 by Allyn and Bacon, Inc. Reprinted with permission.

4. If you were a Japanese person living in California in 1942, how might you have felt if you had been placed in a relocation camp?

### *Government*

1. It has been said that the exposure of the Watergate conspiracy and its results prove that the American constitutional system works. Explain why you agree or disagree with this point of view.
2. If you had lived in the days of Hamilton and Jefferson, to which political party would you have belonged? Why?
3. It is argued that capital punishment is cruel and, therefore, unconstitutional. Do you agree with this argument? Why?
4. "Juvenile offenders should not be tried in separate courts; they should stand trial in regular courts and have all the protection given to adult defendants." Do you agree or disagree with this statement? Why?

These types of questions can frame spirited discussions with gifted students in a social studies classroom from the intermediate grades on, given appropriate background reading. The same approach, however, can be used with current events so that discussion is not dependent on prior reading. The emphasis is on the *meaning and process* of history, not the events themselves.

The teaching of interviewing techniques as a research tool in social science can also be stimulating for gifted students. One approach might be to interview mothers and grandmothers about their lives and perceptions they hold about growing up. Sample questions might include:

1. How did your parents discipline you?
2. What were your responsibilities in the household?
3. What expectations did your parents have for you?
4. Would you like to go back to childhood?

Other types of interviews of mothers or family members might center on some of these topics:

1. Interview grandparents or other family members about a particularly momentous historic time, such as World War II, the Depression, or the Civil Rights Movement. Some of the questions might concern the interviewee's view of the event or time period, and how or whether this event affected the interviewer or her family's lives.
2. Some interview topics concerning women in the family might also concentrate more on role differences, perceived or real, such as whether women's roles changed in various generations, or whether being female affected their roles or activities in a particular event.

Another favorite technique in gifted social studies programs is the use of simulations or scenarios that involve students directly in the ethical decision-making process. One example might be:

You are a school board member faced with allocating limited dollars to a special program. Six programs have been submitted for consideration, each carrying a political liability if you do not select it. What program will you fund and why? (Groups of five students review the set of programs proposed and deliberate.)

Through such a technique, gifted learners are placed in the role of decision makers, given ambiguous data, and forced to make a decision or formulate a plan or solution. Such real-life activities help students to understand how decisions are made in the real world and how to grapple with the problems inherent with decision processes.

## Teaching Models for the Social Studies

Four well-developed models of instructional programming are particularly relevant for teaching social studies to gifted and talented youth: Lipman's *Philosophy for Kids,* Kohlberg's moral dilemma and reasoning, Taba's teaching strategies, and Bruner's *Man: A Course of Study*. These models were all developed for general social studies classroom use, but with proper acceleration and enrichment and in the hands of perceptive teachers who have high expectations for gifted learners, the models offer unique opportunities to engage gifted learners in high level conceptual learning and in developing the skills of inquiry, research, writing, discussion, and project synthesis.

Lipman's *Philosophy for Kids* (Lipman, Sharp, & Oscanyan, 1980) is a comprehensive program for teaching methods of philosophic inquiry to students in grades K–12 through stories about children who encounter problems in school and in their daily lives and go about solving them with the skills of inquiry, thinking, and group discussion. In this program, children deal with both the content and modes of thinking with and about a world of ideas. Lipman and colleagues argued that their method of engaging students in thinking about and with content should be used in all areas of the curriculum. The story format with real characters at the age level of the students who are studying the material serves to motivate and model cognitive processing while helping children listen and study better, use more effective logic, and respect the world of ideas.

Kohlberg's (1978) philosophic analysis and developmental model of the stages of moral development were developed further into teaching methodologies to help youth progress to higher levels of conceptualization in dealing with moral and ethical issues. The essence of the methodology is the "moral dilemma." Students are confronted with situations calling for analysis of issues, weighting of conflicting values, evocation of philosophical principles, and decision making at a hypothetical level. The following is an illustration scenario:

Your friend is dying of inoperable cancer. She wishes to terminate her life. Her family, very conservative and fundamentalist in their religious beliefs, is irrevocably opposed to suicide. You have access to a lethal drug. Should you give it to your friend?

This dilemma offers abundant opportunity for analysis and delineation of issues and values, discussion of the implications of alternate courses of action, and decision making concerning the best possible course of action. Above all, the "moral dilemma" gives youth (and when carried out at high levels with complex dilemmas, gifted youth) excellent opportunities to deal with abstract philosophic concepts and grow in ability to deal with the world of ideas. Ethical and moral issues are suffused through all of the social studies and should be addressed, especially by the gifted as future leaders.

Taba's (1962, 1975) inquiry model for teaching stresses a dynamic, active role for the learners, and, in its cognitive emphasis, a uniquely relevant role for gifted learners. Based on the theoretical formulations of Dewey, Piaget, and cognitive development theory, the Taba model stresses four fundamental strategies: (1) concept development, (2) interpretation of data, (3) application of generalization, and (4) resolution of conflicts. In her book, *Teaching Models in the Education of the Gifted,* Maker (1982), an ardent proponent of the Taba model, suggested that teachers applying the Taba method must use careful sequencing in the presentation of content and thinking skills, open-ended questions, appropriate pacing, careful sequencing and patterning of questions, organized content, and a variety of well-rotated learning experiences. In the concept development stage, children are taught to discern relevant attributes of concepts, group common attributes of a concept, label the concept, and *subsense* it in larger or other conceptual contexts. In the second stage, interpreting data, students gather and make sense of information by use of listing, and by inferring causes and effects, drawing conclusions, and generalizing.

The stage of application of generalization involves teaching students to transfer generalizations to new situations. Finally, resolution of conflict is a process of learning to deal with feelings, emotions, attitudes, and values related to the concepts learned and generalizations derived.

The Taba model is not widely used in regular or gifted education. Its complexity, as well as its high cognitive level, probably precludes its use in regular classrooms. However, it is an ideal model for teaching and developing curriculum for gifted and talented learners in the social studies. Maker has done a valuable service to the field of gifted education in her promulgation of the Taba model.

Bruner's (1960) conceptions of curriculum and teaching as illustrated in the program *Man: A Course of Study* (MACOS) (Education Development Center, 1970) provide an excellent base for the development of instruction for gifted learners. Bruner has called for curriculum and teaching methodology that exposes students to the ideas and methods of scholars working in a discipline. He stressed that children should be active inquirers, emulating the search for understanding exhibited by scholars. Through such experiences, students move to increased levels of investigation in a field following a spiral curriculum of increasingly complex concepts and generalizations that constitute the structural organization of the field or discipline. In the early grades, the content is less complex but authentically representations of the field. Bruner proclaimed, "Any subject can be taught effectively in some intellectually honest form to any child at any state of development" (1960, p. 33). As Maker (1982) noted, the approach is often successful with gifted students but difficult with less able ones.

The Bruner model of curriculum development and instruction is uniquely relevant for gifted youth because it exposes them to the thinking and strategies of inquiry used by scholars in a field and gives them early opportunities to try operating within a discipline. Thus, the model has clear career education implications. Further, in its emphasis on discovery learning and disciplined inquiry, gifted students have a chance to develop their thinking skills to high levels. Finally, students come out of the learning experiences with well-organized, conceptual knowledge of a field. This knowledge base serves them well as they go on to higher-level studies in the same and related fields.

## Using a Concept Model to Organize Social Studies Curricula

Shane (1981) worked with scholars throughout the world in the social sciences to determine key ideas for infusion into a social studies curriculum for the year 2000. These ideas include the following:

- *Historical understanding of all the world*
- *Understanding of systems in the world*
- *Relationship of government and the governed*
- *Nature of power*
- *Sense of community*
- *The "trade-off"*
- *Economic equity*
- *An information economy replacing an industrial one*
- *Cultural pluralism*
- *Global interdependence*

Social studies programs for the gifted might be well served to treat these themes as central to their curriculum planning effort. The following course outline on peace studies (College Board, 1980) exemplifies a way to weave broad conceptual themes into the context of world history.*

### A Conceptual and Chronological Sequencing for Peace Studies

*Unit 1 (1st week): Introduction to Peace Studies*

**A.** Main Concept: Man reacts to conflict situations by virtue of conditioning and genetics.
**B.** Topics
    1. Theories of Aggression
    2. How Human Behavior Developed
    3. How We Study Human Behavior

*Unit II (2nd and 3rd weeks): Our Ancient Inheritance*

**A.** Main Concept: Men have gone to war for many reasons.
**B.** Topics
    1. Egypt—Territorial War at the Crossroads
    2. Sparta vs. Greece—Ideological War
    3. Roman Empire—Pax Romanum—Imperian War and Peace—War as It Contributes to Societal Decline

*From College Entrance Examination Board, 1980.

Also possibly:
Alexander—War and Cultural Diffusion
4. Judeo-Christian Concepts of War and Peace

*Unit III (4th week): Middle Ages*

**A.** Main Concept: The instinct of flight is cancelled by operant conditions such as loyalty and honor.
**B.** Topics
    1. Quest for Security—Feudalism
    2. Code of Chivalry
    3. Growth of Towns and Cities (theories of crowding and aggression)

*Unit IV (5th week): Renaissance and Reformation*

**A.** Main Concept: Religion has been a force both for war and for peace.
**B.** Topics
    1. The New Spirit of Man
    2. Diplomacy as Practiced in Italian City States—Machiavelli
    3. Wars of Religion
    4. Wars of Commerce

*Unit V (6th week): Age of Revolution*

**A.** Main Concept: Political revolutions have caused some of the bloodiest wars.
**B.** Topics
    1. Old Regime
    2. French Revolution
    3. Napoleonic Wars
    4. Congress of Vienna—Suppression of Nationalism

*Unit VI (7th week): World War I and Its Aftermath*

**A.** Main Concept: Modern warfare is hell.
**B.** Topics
    1. The Industrial Revolution and the Increase in Man's Ability to Destroy
    2. Causes of War
    3. Results
    4. The League and Its Failure

This outline presents a way to combine several approaches to organizing a social studies curriculum for the gifted. It presents the chronological approach so favored by many teachers, yet it gives the chronology a topical focus—namely, peace studies. Furthermore, it frames each unit with a key concept or idea that is representative of both the time period and the broad topic. The topic of peace and its antithesis war are viewed across time and culture so that key ideas can be highlighted at the moment of their greatest relevance. It is a good blend of content and concept considerations.

VanTassel-Baska and Feldhusen (1981) developed social studies units for the gifted around four main themes: change, signs and symbols, reason, and problem solving. These units were developed to be used in either pull-out programs or self-contained classrooms and have been field-tested in both. The primary unit for signs and symbols includes the following sample instructional objective and set of activities:

**Objective:** Gifted students will be able to analyze the history of writing and the development of the alphabet as a code.

**Activities:**

1. *Read, research, and report on the invention of the alphabet in the Middle East, Ancient land of Canaan, about 1000 B.C.*
2. *Study how Greeks adapted this alphabet and changed it to fit their language.*
3. *Make a scroll demonstrating Greek transformations of letters.*
4. *Create your own alphabet, and shape its features with your classmates.*
5. *Compose a twenty-word telegram using your own alphabet.*
6. *Make a scrapbook using photographs, drawings, cut outs, and so on, illustrating different methods of communication.*
7. *Choose one letter of the alphabet and research the development and significance of it. Share with classmates in an oral presentation.*

Using *Cities of Destiny* by Arnold Toynbee (1967) as a key resource, the "change" concept unit for intermediate grades focuses on the growth pattern of cities as a strategy for understanding the growth of societal institutions and social systems. Following is a content outline from that unit:

### *What Makes a Great City?*

*Prototype: Rome*

1. Structures
   A. Design
   B. Architecture
II. Societal Governance
   A. Classes
   B. Form of Government
   C. Influence of the Military
III. Sustenance Issues
   A. Food
   B. Clothes
   C. Work
IV. Science and Inventions
   A. The Balance
   B. Aqueducts
   C. Arches
V. The Arts
   A. Sculpture
   B. Drama
   C. Music
VI. Beliefs and Values
   A. Pagan → Christian
   B. Epicureanism/Stoicism

**VII.** Language
    A. The Oral Tradition
    B. The Written Record

Thus, students can come to understand the organism of a city and the degree to which great cities become cultural metaphors over time.

## Global Education Curriculum

With the political upheavals of the last decade has come an increasing need for gifted students to learn about the emerging trends and conditions in the world community. The opening of the Berlin Wall, the political reorganization of Eastern Europe, the invasion of and war in Kuwait, the Palestinian uprisings, the student revolution in China, the fall of communism in the former Soviet Union, and starvation in Africa are all massive new developments in our global society. Television news brings these major events to us within minutes of their unfolding. Never before has the United States been in a more central, political leadership role nor have we ever before had such an urgent need for leadership in all areas of our global functioning from commerce to the arts, but especially in political arenas. Our gifted students will be the leaders in dealing with emerging issues in the world community.

One of the major themes in the area of global education is global interdependence. Anderson (1990) suggested that interdependence is manifested in the need to study histories of other nations, geography and political reorganizations, the emerging global economics, world political systems, the internationalization of social interaction and sociological concepts, demographic migration of cultures and races, ecological systems of the planet, and emerging world cultures. There is also a special need to study the changing position of the United States from that of a hegemony to a position of decreasing dominance in the world setting. The economy of the United States, for example, is no longer controlled internally; rather, it is profoundly affected by economic tides in other nations and clusters of nations.

Tye (1990) cited a 1987 report from the Rockefeller Foundation in which a study commission recommended four major foci or emphases for the curriculum in American schools.

    *1. A better understanding of the world as a series of interrelated systems: physical, biological, economic, political, and informational-evaluative.*
    *2. More attention to the development of world civilizations as they relate to American history.*
    *3. Greater attention to the diversity of cultural patterns both around the world and within the United States.*
    *4. More training in policy analysis both of domestic and international issues. (Study Commission on Global Education, 1987, cited in Tye, 1990, p. 42)*

Lamy (1990) reported results of a conference at the Center for Human Interdependence at Chapham College in which Harvey's (1976) global education goals were embraced as appropriate curricular goals to prepare students for their future as world citizens:

1. *Perspective consciousness: An awareness of and appreciation for other images of the world.*
2. *State of the planet awareness: An in-depth understanding of global issues and events.*
3. *Cross-cultural awareness: A general understanding of the defining characteristics of world cultures. . . .*
4. *Systemic awareness: A familiarity with the nature of systems . . . in which . . . [we] are linked in patterns of interdependence. . . .*
5. *Options for participation: A review of strategies for participating in issue areas in local, national, and international settings. (p. 53)*

These emphases and goals guided, in part, the development of the following global education curriculum as reported by Anderson (1990) for the Chapham College Center for Human Interdependence:

### Elementary School Examples

1. *Grade: One*

   *Curricular areas: Language arts and social studies*
   *Unit title: First Graders Look at Community Members and Their Origins*
   Purpose/process: To have students understand that all Americans have an ethnic heritage and to provide opportunities for the students to understand the heritage and ethnic groups represented in their classroom, school, and community by interviewing and bringing into the classroom parents and people in the community who have come to make their home in Orange County.

2. *Grade: Six*

   *Curricular areas: Language arts and social studies*
   *Unit title: Overcoming Cultural Media Bias—Research and Application*
   Purpose/process: To have students evaluate if there is a cultural bias in television commercials. To explore the impact that television programs and their commercials have on children's perceptions of the world and on themselves.

### Intermediate School Examples

1. *Curricular area: General*
   *Unit title: Odd Man Out—The Ethnic Child in an Anglo School*
   Purpose/process: To have students of diverse ethnic backgrounds examine their roots, study schooling in the countries of their families' origins, and gain insight into the school environment as perceived by students of diverse ethnic heritages.
2. *Curricular area: English as a second language*
   *Unit title: Folk Tales Around the World*
   Purpose/process: After examining several books and other sources of folk tales, students put into practice language skills as they write their own folktale based

on their own ethnic backgrounds, which included Czechoslovakian, Chinese, Vietnamese, Hispanic, and Japanese.

### High School Examples

*1. Curricular area: Biology*
*Unit title: Population Issues in the Local and Global Community: A Program Stressing the Interdependence of Mankind*
Purpose/process: This unit was concerned with the growing problem of global population growth and its attendant problems of environmental degradation.
*2. Curricular area: U.S. History*
*Unit title: Global Awareness Through Family Histories*
Purpose/process: To help "American" students realize that they, too, were descended from immigrants; to help defuse racial tensions, eliminate racial and cultural stereotypes, and help the immigrant understand the "American" just a little bit better. (pp. 30–83)

Parker (1991) has delineated a number of plans for a comprehensive social studies curriculum appropriate to the rapidly emerging demands of the twenty-first century and for global education. Five major conceptual themes are presented to guide schools in developing such curricula:

1. *Interdependence. We live in a world of systems in which the actors and components interact to make up a unified, functioning whole.*
   *Related concepts: adaption, cause and effect, development, evolution, growth, revolution, time.*
2. *Change. The process of movement from one state of being to another is a universal aspect of the planet and is an inevitable part of life and living.*
   *Related concepts: adaption, cause and effect, development, evolution, growth, revolution, time.*
3. *Culture. People create social environments and systems comprised of unique beliefs, values, traditions, language, customs, technology, and institutions as a way of meeting basic human needs; shaped by their own physical environments and contact with other cultures.*
   *Related concepts: adaption, aesthetics, diversity, languages, norms, roles, values, space-time.*
4. *Scarcity. An imbalance exists between relatively unlimited wants and limited available resources necessitating the creation of systems for deciding how resources are to be distributed.*
   *Related concepts: conflict, exploration, migration, opportunity cost, policy, resources, specialization.*
5. *Conflict. People and nations often have differing values and opposing goals resulting in disagreement, tensions, and sometimes violence necessitating skill in coexistence, negotiation, living with ambiguity and conflict resolution.*
   *Related concepts: authority, collaboration, competition, interest/positions, justice, power, rights. (p. 121)*

It is clear that the rapid pace of change throughout the world and the changing relationship of the United States to emerging political, economic, social, and ecological conditions in other countries demands a complete reconceptualization of the social studies. Students must be given a new, larger, and more complex knowledge base, given a new set of thinking skills to deal with the information and the issues, and guided in the development of attitudes and values appropriate to a world perspective.

## Using Specific Topics to Organize a Social Studies Curriculum

Lebeau (1979) and Fearn and Fearn (1983) developed curricula for use with gifted students that focus on understanding law and its implications for citizenship, character development, and leadership. The course outline for a high school seminar for gifted students at Chelmsford High School (Massachusetts) in Comprehensive Law follows:

### Course Outline

I. *History of U.S. Jurisprudence*
   A. *Study of pre-Biblical and Mosaic Law and their moral and ethical contributions to standards of justice.*
   B. *Study of Greek and Roman Law and their contributions to a formalized legal code.*
   C. *Study of British Common Law as the foundation for the U.S. Constitution and civil jurisprudence.*
II. *The Bill of Rights*
   A. *The historic reasons for their inclusion in the U.S. Constitution.*
   B. *The application of Amendments I, IV, V, VI, VIII, IX, XIII, XIV, XIX.*
   C. *An in-depth study of the ramifications of the proposed Amendment.*
III. *Logic and Values*
   A. *Study and application of logic*
      1. *Syllogistics*
      2. *Judgments*
      3. *Moral Reasoning*
      4. *Analysis of data*
      5. *Cumulative arguments*
IV. *Supreme Court Decisions*
   A. *The process of judicial review and its application to the Constitution.*
   B. *The study of major Supreme Court cases, citing basic problem(s) for both defense and prosecution.*
   C. *The historic milieu in which the Supreme Court accepted the appeals.*
V. *Visits from Professionals in the Field of Law*
   A. *Attorneys*
   B. *Social Workers*
   C. *Paralegals*
   D. *Police Officers*

VI. *Independent Study*
  A. *Research on any court case of interest to students.*
  B. *In-depth investigation on the facts, issues, evidence, and testimony in the chosen case.*
  C. *Support of or opposition to the court's decision.*

## Elementary Programs in the Social Studies

Most elementary programs serve the gifted in the regular classroom or in a pull-out/resource room framework. In the regular classroom, the regular social studies curriculum serves all, but the gifted may be given opportunities individually or in small groups to study selected topics in depth and thereby learn special study, or library skills. In a resource room setting, the same opportunities may be provided but with more explicit guidance from the resource teacher. Developing or adapting specialized units of study in the social sciences may represent the most practical approach to curriculum development in these groupings. If grouping practices can be modified, it would be preferable for the gifted to have an instructional grouping in the social studies areas throughout the elementary grades.

The classic curriculum developed for use at the elementary level that provides for gifted learners in all key dimensions is Bruner's (1970) *Man: A Course of Study*. This curriculum has been used very successfully in school district gifted programs from grades 4 to 8. It offers learners an opportunity to explore differences in values, beliefs, and attitudes across cultures. Rich in the variety of activities it provides, MACOS also has films that depict the cultural life studied.

## Secondary Programs in the Social Studies

At the middle school level, gifted students either get individualized treatment and special project opportunities in the regular classroom comparable to the elementary model, or they are enrolled in a special honors class or seminar for gifted learners. In the latter case, a greater exposure to the content of the disciplines is possible, along with a strong emphasis on inquiry activities focused on major themes, issues, and concepts in selected disciplines (e.g., history, psychology, economics). At the high school level, gifted learners may be enrolled in an honors section or a College Board Advanced Placement class (e.g., American history or European history) in which the major focus is on the discipline and its methodology, with an emphasis on discussion, research, and problem solving. Gifted students can also elect to take social studies courses early and thereby accelerate their program in this area. This approach provides time to participate in special programs like the Executive Internship Program, headquarterd in Springfield, Illinois, which invites able seniors to spend a semester working in state government and participating in a weekly seminar regarding their experiences.

## Comprehensive Curriculum

A sound curriculum plan for gifted and high-ability learners and for students with special talents in the social studies integrated with students' complete school program, K–12, would incorporate experiences of all the types presented in the chapter, would be based on a set of goals like those presented earlier in this chapter, and would call for teaching strategies of the type advocated by Bruner, Kohlberg, Lipman, and Taba.

Planning the optimum curriculum requires much systematic, collaborative effort among teachers, department heads, and curriculum specialists. They must be well versed in the content or knowledge base of the social studies disciplines, knowledgeable about new methodologies for teaching the social studies, and cognizant of the special characteristics and needs of gifted learners.

In Example 8.A at the end of this chapter a comprehensive social studies curriculum plan for gifted learners is presented. It was developed by Yossel Naiman and teachers for the gifted program in Chicago Public Schools.

## Issues in Implementing Curricula for the Gifted in Social Studies

Developing and implementing a curriculum for the gifted in social studies involves *a priori* decisions concerning program goals, program models, meeting individual student needs, the role of the disciplines, and the commitment to acceleration and enrichment approaches. But at the stage of implementation, there may be a need to confront other issues as well.

**1.** Finding a balance between enrichment and acceleration in the social studies seems judicious. Enrichment in the social studies can often come as a result of acceleration through basic social studies courses, which then frees the gifted student for specialized learning activities. Students who complete the American history material in less time can be freed for an in-depth study of the historical antecedents of the War in Vietnam. Or students may undertake an extended study of current political organization in African governments and how those structures grew out of the large infusion of financial aid from European countries, Canada, and the United States.

**2.** Another implementation issue deals with the modification in the instructional processes needed to move toward actualizing the goals stated at the beginning of this chapter as important for social science programs for the gifted. In order to accommodate content, process, product, and concept goals, the teacher must ensure that instructional time is used effectively and that content material is organized well. Otherwise, the differentiation for gifted learners is lost. At the secondary level, to group gifted learners for American history and then do nothing to modify the curriculum and instructional approach is to defeat the purpose of having a special program. Modifying material without also altering instructional technique is also insufficient.

**3.** Since using the inquiry approach and teaching research skills are viewed as important goals in social science programs for the gifted, the issue of staff development is crucial. Teachers need to be trained to use inquiry techniques and to be monitored on their implementation with students in the classroom through videotape and playback techniques or another form of peer evaluation. Training in the research methodology of the social sciences would also be useful for teachers who will be engaging students in these procedures.

**4.** The use of cooperative units of study with teachers from other departments should be considered one way to enhance the study of cultures and their underlying systems. Using foreign language teachers, English teachers, and art and music teachers to reflect perspectives on a given cultural period may contribute greatly to the education of gifted learners.

**5.** Choice of effective outside speakers is another issue to consider at the implementation stage of social science programs. Too often choices are made based on the general field that an adult in the community happens to be practicing in, rather than selecting speakers who can address the impact of social policy in a particular field of the social sciences. Establishing criteria for speakers who come into gifted programs is important:

    a. Speakers should be knowledgeable on issues or problems that the group is studying.

    b. Speakers should be willing to engage gifted learners in discussion about this topic.

    c. Speakers should be attuned to the conceptual level at which gifted learners can function and gear their presentation accordingly.

    d. Speakers should help meet a predetermined learning objective rather than only be used as an additional resource.

    e. Speakers should be willing to follow-up on their topic with materials, a visit to the workplace, a return engagement, or individual consultation with a student.

**6.** How to evaluate student learning is a critical issue. A strong focus on the well-organized essay as a grading standard in social science programs should be considered. Not only does this approach lend itself well to the interdisciplinary nature of the material but it also prepares gifted learners in expository writing skills that are necessary to articulate concepts at high levels of abstraction. Portfolios of student essays and projects can also provide breadth in the evaluation of student learning.

## Conclusion

Gifted students can experience high-level, challenging interactions with the world of ideas and learn the skills of critical, creative, and logical thinking in the social sciences. There is an abundance of material in the social sciences to provide enriching experiences beyond the regular curriculum, but, above all, that curriculum must be fast paced and accelerated to provide appropriately challenging learning experiences for the gifted.

### Key Points Summary

- *The major goals of a social science curriculum for gifted learners are to (1) develop critical thinking and inquiry, (2) understand world cultures, (3) appreciate the relationships among social science disciplines, (4) know major developments in history, and (5) be skilled in social science research.*
- *Social science curricula for the gifted can be organized by either content topic, a set of broad concepts, or a key area for study within the structure of the discipline.*
- *An inquiry approach to instruction is most appropriate for teaching the social science curriculum.*

- *Many model programs in social science for the gifted stress topics such as global interdependence, futures study, law, and leadership.*
- *Implementation issues to consider include maintaining a balance between accelerative and enrichment practices, modifying curriculum and instructional processes rather than just materials, staff development, interdepartment planning at the secondary level, selecting speakers, and using the essay as a principal evaluation tool.*

# *References*

Adams, J. E. (undated). *Environmental studies from a global perspective.* Muncie, IN: Ball State University (Burris-Ball State School Corporation).

Anderson, C. C. (1990). Global education and the community. In K. A. Tye (Ed.), *Global education, from thought to action* (pp. 125–141). Alexandria, VA: Association for Supervision and curriculum Development.

Anderson, L. F. (1990). A rationale for global education. In K. A. Tye (Ed.), *Global education, from thought to action* (pp 13–34). Alexandria, VA: Association for Supervision and Curriculum Development.

Association of Teachers of Social Studies in the City of New York. (1977). *A handbook for the teaching of social studies.* Boston: Allyn and Bacon.

Barr, R. D., Barth, J. L., & Shermis, S. S. (1977). *Defining the social studies.* Washington, DC: National Council for the Social Studies.

Barth, J. L., & Shermis, S. S. (1981). *Teaching social studies to the gifted and talented.* Indianapolis: Indiana Department of Public Instruction.

Bloom, B. S. (1956). *Taxonomy of educational objectives, Handbook I, Cognitive domain.* New York: Longmans, Green.

Bruner, J. (1960). *The process of education.* Cambridge, MA: Harvard University Press.

Bruner, J. (ed.). (1970). *Man: A course of study.* Washington, DC: Curriculum Associates.

College Entrance Examination Board. (1980). *Beginning an advanced placement course in European history, Edition C.* Princeton, NJ: Educational Testing Service.

Education Development Center. (1970). *Man: A course of study.* Washington, DC: Curriculum Development Associates.

Fearn, L., & Fearn, C. (1983). *Citizenship and character development.* San Diego, CA: San Diego Unified School District.

Flachner, J., & Hirst, B. (1976). *200 Years: A study of democracy.* New York: Astor Program.

Harvey, R. (1976). *An attainable global perspective.* Denver, CO: Center for Teaching International Relations.

Keener, C. (undated). *A curricular approach for global studies.* Muncie, IN: Ball State University (Burris-Ball State School Corporation).

Kohlberg, L. (1978). The cognitive-developmental approach to moral education. In F. Scharf (Ed.), *Readings in moral education* (pp. 36–51). Minneapolis: Winston.

Lamy, S. L. (1990). Global education: A conflict of images. In K. A. Tye (Ed.), *Global education, from thought to action* (pp. 49–63). Alexandria, VA: Association for Supervision and Curriculum Development.

LeBeau, M. (1979). *Comprehensive law.* Chelmsford, MA: Chelmsford High School.

Lipman, M., Sharp, A. M., & Oscanyan, F. S. (1980). *Philosophy in the classroom.* Philadelphia: Temple University Press.

Maker, C. J. (1982). *Teaching models in the education of the gifted.* Rockville, MD: Aspen.

Parker, W. C. (1991). *Reviewing the social studies curriculum.* Alexandria, VA: Association for Supervision and Curriculum Development.

Rattes, L. E., Wasserman, S., Jonas, A., & Rothstein, A. (1986). *Teaching for thinking, theory, strategies, and activities for the classroom.* New York: Teachers College Press.

Schug, M. C. (1981). Using the local community to improve citizenship education for the gifted. *Roeper Review, 4* (2), 22–23.

Scriven, M. (1964). A model of the social sciences. In J. Schwab (Ed.), *Education and the structure of knowledge.* Chicago: Rand McNally.

Shane, H. (1981). *A study of curriculum content for the future*. New York: College Entrance Examination Board.

Shaver, P. (1984). Social studies education for the gifted. *Roeper Review, 7* (1), 4–7.

Shermis, S. S. (1989). Teaching students gifted in social studies. In R. M. Milgram (Ed.), *Teaching gifted and talented learners in regular classrooms* (pp. 249–268). Springfield, IL: Charles C. Thomas.

Shermis, S. S., & Clinkenbeard, P. R. (1981). History texts for the Gifted: A look at the past century. *Roeper Review, 4* (2), 19–21.

Taba, H. (1962). *Curriculum development: Theory and practice*. New York: Harcourt, Brace and World.

Taba, H. (1975). Learning by discovery: Psychological, educational rationale. In W. B. Barbe & J. S. Renzulliu (Eds.), *Psychology and education of the gifted* (pp. 346–354). New York: Irvington Press.

VanTassel-Baska, J., & Feldhusen, J. (1981). *Concept curriculum for the gifted*. Matteson, IL: Matteson School District #162.

Toynbee, A. (1967). *Cities of destiny*. New York: Weathervane Books.

Tye, B. B. (1990). Schooling in America today: Potential for global studies. In K. A. Type (Ed.), *Global education, from thought to action* (pp. 35–48). Alexandria, VA: Association for Supervision and Curriculum Development.

## EXAMPLE 8.A  Gifted Social Studies Syllabus: Chicago Public Schools Gifted Program, K–12

*Yossel Naiman, Developer*

### *Kindergarten*

#### *Geography*

Gifted kindergarten geography curriculum encompasses study of the physical world through the examination of maps and globes. It is expected that children in gifted programs exit with the ability to recognize the name and locations of the world's continents, major oceans, major rivers, the States of the Union, the City of Chicago, the poles, the climate zones, the equator, the hemispheres, the major longitudinal and latitudinal lines of demarcation, and the concepts of right, left, horizontal, vertical, above, below, and up and down.

#### *Psychology*

It is expected that children in gifted kindergarten programs exit with the ability to differentiate between needs and wants of both the individual and family and to identify the various roles and behaviors of family members and their interdependent relationships.

#### *History*

Students will exit kindergarten with a conceptual framework for past, present, and future, the history of their families, and minimal awareness of current events. They will be able to perceive the relationship between past events, present events, and the implications for future events.

## First Grade

### Geography

Gifted children will leave the first-grade level able to define, locate, and give examples of the following topographical terms: desert, forest, island, lake, mountain, peninsula, plain, river, valley, and volcano. They will exit first grade with the ability to read map symbols related to elevation, population, transportation, resources, industries, and topographical features.

### Economics

Gifted students at the first-grade level will define and give examples of the following terms: production, distribution, and consumption; producer, distributor, and consumer; goods and services; technology, and commerce; and the divisions of agriculture, manufacturing, transportation.

### History

History will be examined by the students from two perspectives: that of the individual and that of the communities from which they emanate. Students will examine and discuss community events, past and present. They will write their personal history. They will survey the history of Chicago covering major topics beginning with early settlement, the advent of the city charter, industrialization, waves of immigration, urbanization, and the major personages.

### Sociology

Students will discuss roles within the school, community, and neighborhood. They will learn of the hierarchies of administrations that exist within each of the three and show the interrelationships that exist. Beginning with the students' immediate classroom, students will expand knowledge of their school, and community organizations such as the student council, the PTA, the Advisory Council, block clubs, and other organizations.

### Anthropology

Students will locate the points of origin of racial groups on a world map. Using the class's ethnic composition, students will locate the points of origin of each of the ethnic groups represented on a world map. They will classify those groups according to their language families. After defining the term, students will examine the customs, traditions, and folkways of the groups studied.

## Second Grade

### Psychology

The students will define the following terms associated with the growth and development of personality: peer group, identity, self-concept, environment, interaction, and leadership. The students will explore the conflicts that affect the development of their identity and self-concept; individual vs. society, individual vs. nature, individual vs. self. The students will recognize the interplay of aggression, ambition, dominance, and reward/punishment.

*History*

The students will trace the history of Illinois from early explorers, settlement, Indians, statehood, immigration, Lincoln, Civil War, famous people and growth of Chicago to the present day. Their studies will include identification of Illinois borders, neighboring states, bodies of water, population centers (including the capital), distribution of resources, and recreational areas. Students will write a family history in narrative form covering two generations. The concepts of ancestry and genealogy will be introduced and defined.

### Third Grade

*Geography*

A continuing focus of the geography strand of the social studies program concerns the study of the various regions of the Western hemisphere in respect to the distribution of natural resources, the climates, the industrial development, the cultures represented, the governmental structures in place, and the economics of each of those regions. In that study, students will compare and contrast single product and diversified economies.

*Psychology*

Continuing in the psychology strand, students will discuss values, beliefs, attitudes as they have observed them. Questions will be presented such as: What beliefs do you have that affect your life? What do you value? What attitudes do you have as a result of the beliefs and values you have? Students will list characteristics of leadership and examine specific types of leaders and leadership. Using what they have learned about beliefs, values, attitudes, and leadership, the students will develop a basic understanding of group dynamics.

*Research Skills*

In order to prepare for research assignments, the students will read and analyze statements for examples of bias, assumption and generalization, conclusion, and clarity.

### Fourth Grade

*Geography*

Geography will include the study of the following regions: Europe, North Africa/Middle East, Sub-Saharan Africa, Asia, Australia/Indonesia. Students will compare and contrast the distribution of natural resources, climates, industries, and economies. Students will examine, in-depth, cultures, governmental structures and economies of a country representative of each region, distinguishing between diversified and single product-based economies.

*History*

In a survey of world history of early man to the decline of the Roman Empire, the students will study the following units: (1) Prehistoric Man, (2) Early River Valley Civilizations of the Near East and Far East, (3) Later Civilizations of the Near East, (4)

Aegean World/Greece, and (5) Roman Civilization to Constantine. The students will develop an understanding of the political, social, and economic structures and cultural aspects of the respective units.

*Sociology*

Students will define these terms: conflict, conformity, interaction, leadership, perception, prejudice stereotypes, bias, and propaganda. They will explore how conflict, conformity, and types of leadership affect group interaction. Questions to be addressed are: What determines who succeeds as a leader? What determines which leaders a group will accept or reject? Does communication help a group achieve its goals? Why do people conform? When can conformity be good? bad? Can conflict be both positive and negative?

*Research Skills*

Students will select a topic, use appropriate sources, organize information, and produce a written report for oral presentation.

### Fifth Grade

*Philosophy*

In their introduction to philosophy, the students will explore philosophy and establish it as a discipline which attempts to explain the human condition. The students will define ethics and examine ethical theories and representative theorists. The following theories and theorists should be included: Aristotle, Plato, Hedonism (Epicurus), Stoicism (Epictetus); Relativism (Spinoza); Utilitarianism (Mill), Naturalism (Rousseau); Pragmatism (Dewey); Existentialism (Sartre) and K'Ling Fu-Tiu Confucius. Questions to be studied will include: (1) What is a good life? (2) How should man behave? (3) What is a good society? (4) Which is the higher virtue—truth or justice? (5) Upon what premise do each of the philosophers base their conclusions?

*Research Skills*

Students will select a topic, use a variety of sources, organize information, and produce a library research project. It is expected that the student will also review political and physical geography as it pertains to the historical topic being considered.

### Sixth Grade

*History*

In a survey of world history from 18th Century Political Revolutions to the present, students will study the following units: (1) Nonpolitical Revolutions (Industrial, Scientific and Age of Reason); (2) Napoleonic Era; (3) National Independence Movements—Italy, Germany, South America; (4) Building of Empires; (5) World War I; (6) Russian Revolution; (7) Chinese Revolution; (8) Rise of Fascism; (9) Worldwide Depression; (10) World War II, (11) Cold War; (12) Emerging Nations.

The students will develop an understanding of the political, social and economic and cultural aspects of the period. It is expected that students will also review the physical, political, and economic geography as it pertains to the historical topic being considered.

*Philosophy*

The philosophy strand continues as the students define "politics" as a discipline. They will study the following theorists: Plato, Aristotle, Confucius, Machiavelli, Hobbes, Spinoza, Locke, Rousseau, Burke, Mill, and Marx. The students will seek the answers to these questions: What is the ultimate justification for any form of government? Who should rule? What should be the limits of governmental power (individual liberty)? For whose benefit? Within this strand, the students will select a topic, use a variety of sources expressing opposing viewpoints, organize the information, and produce a library research report.

### Seventh Grade

*Anthropology*

The students will compare and contrast various cultures throughout history, specifically:

At least two of the following: Tasaday, Netsilik, Australian Aborigine, Kalahari Bushman, Hebrews and Sioux.
Mayans with one or more: Iroquois, Pueblo, Kwakiutl, and Norman England.
Periclean Athens with one or more: Ancient Ghana, Ancient Maili, Ancient Songhai, Kush and Axum.
Minimally two of the following: Asoka India, Chou Dynasty, Tokagawa Shogunate, and Arman Egyptian.
Minimally two of the following: the Kenyatti Kenyan Revolution, Ghandi's Indian Revolution, the Castro Revolution of Cuba, Juarez's revolution in Mexico.
Postwar Japan with one or more: Mao's China, Modern Brazil and Stalin's Russia.
Renaissance Venice with one or more: Byzantine Empire, the Abbasid Caliphate, the Mongol Empire and Moorish Spain.

The following topics will be covered: social organization, economic organization, political organization, moral and ethical behavior; education, expression of aesthetic needs, communication, and leisure-time activities.

*Philosophy*

The students will define "aesthetics" as a discipline. They will study the following theorists: Plato, Aristotle, George Santayana, Alexander Baumgarten, Thomas Monroe, Benedito Croce, and John Dewey. The students will seek answers to the questions: What is beauty? Where does beauty reside? What is art? What is the purpose of art? What is the value of art?

## Eighth Grade

### Political Science

Students will analyze the federal and state constitutions, comparing and contrasting the structures and functions of the three branches of the various levels of government. They will analyze and evaluate the effects of the following on government: media, peer pressure, political parties, public opinion, surveys, and voter participation. Students will compare and contrast the structure and function of the following governments: Great Britain, France, and the former Soviet Union with that of the United States.

### Philosophy

In an introduction to semantics, the students will study logic as a means of argument. The students will analyze propositions for truth, validity, and soundness, and they will study inductive and deductive reasoning. They will study the medium of language in terms of the relationships between language and thought, speech and language, signs and symbols, and words and things. The students will be introduced to the informal fallacies of ambiguity, presumption, and relevance.

## Ninth Grade

### Sociology

One semester in the ninth grade will be spent in the discipline of sociology. Students will interpret major theorists, including Durkheim, Summer, Ward Reisman, Owen, Marx, Parsons, Boaz, Mead, and the social criticism of Jonathan Swift and Jane Addams. Students will study the methodologies of language factor, participant observation, comparison of institutions, sample survey, contrasting methods, and cummunity studies. They will use those methodologies in analyzing the following topics: aging, hunger and population, ethnic minority groups, family and marriage, urban problems, social stratification, and mobility.

### Macroeconomics

The other semester in the ninth grade will be spent in the discipline of macroeconomics. Students will interpret major theorists, including Barbara Ward, J. K. Galbraith, P. Samuelson, Robert Browne, J. S. Jevous, and Karl Marx. They will utilize the vocabulary and the concepts presented by the theorist plus factors of measurement in analyzing changing conditions. They will analyze the interdependency of national markets with a global perspective. They will examine within the same framework specific issues, i.e., gold and silver markets, prime interest, lending rates, oil pricing mechanisms, etc. They will examine the economics of capitalist, socialist, communist, and third-world developing countries, analyzing the influence of politics and political philosophy on the allocation of scarce resources.

## Tenth Grade

### Theory of Knowledge

In one semester of the tenth grade, the students will investigate the Theory of Knowledge (Epistemology) branch of philosophy by examining how selected philosophers answered these questions: What are the sources from which man derives knowledge? What can man know? What is the nature of truth? What are the standards or criteria by which man can reliably judge the truth or falsity of our knowledge? The philosophers to be studied include Aristotle, Plato, Descartes, Auguste Comte, Bertrand Russell, and J. S. Mill.

### Law

The other semester of the tenth grade will be devoted to the study of law. A study of the history of the Supreme Court will enable students to determine how the Supreme Court operates, how the concept of judicial review was developed, how justices are selected, how the Court has influenced and affected American life, and how decisions are implemented. The students will analyze and interpret selected Supreme Court cases.

## Eleventh Grade

### Modern European Studies

The eleventh-year program is Modern European Studies, incorporating history at the college level that will prepare students if they choose to take an advanced placement modern European History examination. The course will focus on the interpretation of historical philosophers such as Spengler, Toynbee, Hegel, Marx, Croce, Ranke, Gibbons, Durant, and de Tocqueville. Students will write interpretive essays, research papers from original documents, and will take notes from lectures and printed sources. Students will analyze major historical themes in Modern European History. In addition to the political approach, students will analyze significant work of individuals and then works in science, art, architecture, music, and literature. They will examine the impact their contributions have had on the development of modern European History.

## Twelfth Grade

### American Studies

In the twelfth grade, students will study advanced placement American history. In making demands on the students equivalent to those of a full-year introductory college course, the focus will be to weigh the evidence and interpretations presented in historical scholarship and to arrive at conclusions on the basis of informed judgment. Students will be provided with the analytical skills and factual knowledge necessary to deal critically with the themes of American history. This course will prepare students if they choose to take an advanced placement examination. In addition to political themes, students will analyze significant works of individuals in science, art, architecture, music, and literature. They will examine these people and the impact of their contributions to the development of American history.

# Chapter 9

# Science Curriculum for the Gifted

*JOYCE VanTASSEL-BASKA*

*Between impulse and action, to interpose evidence, reason, and judgment.*
—*PAUL BRANDWEIN*

Perhaps no curriculum area better captures the natural curiosity and intellectual spirit of gifted students than does science. It is the basic area of interest for many gifted children from their earliest years on. Blurton (1983) reviewed the literature on the early backgrounds of famous scientists and found the majority of studies showed childhood interest in science by the age of five years. Also present in their histories was an early home laboratory. However, this early interest of the gifted in science is rarely matched with an appropriate curriculum within the school context.

Given the current outcry regarding the lack of good general science education in our schools, it may be difficult to convince educators of the need to focus on a differentiated science program for gifted learners. In some respects, if the general science program were upgraded, it would result in more appropriate curricular intervention for the gifted to the levels being recommended by national groups.

Science education is currently experiencing several major and interrelated problems in this country. Current national reports recommend a major shift in the organization of science curriculum from a content emphasis to a focus on key concepts and scientific principles taught through hands-on, real-world, problem-solving approaches (AAAS, 1989, 1990; Bennett, 1986; Hilton et al., 1989; National Science Board Commission, 1983; NAEP, 1988). Major curriculum reform efforts emanating from several disciplines have highlighted the need for curriculum change that moves away from the teaching of discrete facts toward the organization of significant content by concepts, away from content coverage toward selective examples to support principles, and away from passive learning toward hands-on inquiry-based learning experiences (ASCD, 1990).

Current curriculum and instructional problems, combined with the need to develop a literate scientific citizenry, create a special kind of dilemma for science education. School organizational structure at all grade levels is too inflexible to accommodate serious science study. Laboratory time and hands-on classroom experiments require longer time periods than are typically allocated (NAEP, 1988). Moreover, science instructional time is significantly less than amounts allocated to reading and math. Combined with the instructional time issue is the lack of training of teachers to do science with children in an appropriate way (AAAS, 1989; Bennett, 1986; National Science Board Commission, 1983). Most elementary and middle school teachers rely heavily on textbook worksheets and canned experiments for conveying what science is. Because science is poorly and infrequently taught at the elementary level, it has failed to sustain the involvement of all but the most science-prone students and those who may have extracurricular resources to spark their continued interest in science. The most tragic loss of continued involvement in science is among girls and minorities, as well as other high-ability learners lacking opportunity (Hilton et al., 1989).

An interrelated part of the problem is the failure to treat science as active inquiry and students as real investigators in the process of making meaning of their world. In order for science to be viewed as real inquiry, it must be taught in a way that demonstrates a strong emphasis on science concepts, investigation of real problems, and the integration of science with other disciplines.

The needs of science education may be perceived as complex, requiring solutions on several fronts simultaneously. These need areas may be delineated as:

1. The development of model curricula that reflect the elements of the new science and standards appropriate to high-ability learners
2. Changes in the selection of curriculum materials and how they are used
3. Instructional strategies that complement the new science and demonstrate effectiveness with a variety of learners
4. Teacher attitudes and behaviors that accept the importance of curriculum and instructional change and are capable of implementation
5. Authentic assessment approaches that focus on open-ended tasks, problem-solving, and portfolio models
6. Systemic change models that allow these dynamics to work together

These general concerns about the state of science curriculum in our schools are felt keenly by educators of high-ability learners. The data clearly indicate that our top students are not ready to compete at world-class levels (NAEP, 1990; Stevenson, 1992). It is critical that high-ability students have a functional knowledge of science, even if they do not enter careers directly related to scientific research or teaching. In our complex society, with the increasing involvement of science in matters of health, the economy, and national security, the general population needs to have a better understanding and appreciation of science, mathematics, and technology. Many high-ability students do not experience an appropriately accelerated and enriched science curriculum during their elementary and middle school experiences; often science is not even taught systematically at the elementary level. Yet, high-ability learners, including the intellectually gifted and the science prone, exhibit an unusual readiness to engage in inquiry and exhibit intense curiosity about the world around them, eager to participate in more concept-based work in science. It is also at elementary and middle-grade levels that independent investigations involving science can most easily be initiated and scientific processes explored in an interdisciplinary framework. However, in the majority of U.S. school districts, the textbook approach is the major delivery system for science curriculum, used primarily as a passive learning tool where children read and answer factual questions. Consequently, many gifted learners face boredom and demotivation in this critical field of inquiry.

Gifted learners in science, then, need a curriculum that is sufficiently advanced and challenging, offering a sequence of tasks that extends their knowledge base. They also need a curriculum that provides opportunities for original investigations in science, using real-world problems as a point of departure. Lastly, they need to study important scientific concepts that allow for making connections within science areas and across to other areas of study.

## Key Components of a Science Curriculum for Gifted and High-Ability Learners

By overlaying the concerns of general science education with the special learning needs of gifted learners, we see common issues emerging: how to infuse the curriculum with appropriate content and methodology; how to positively impact on science and technology literacy, especially among high ability students; and how to motivate students to see the joy of engaging in science inquiry. This blending of science education interests and gifted education needs led to the consideration of the following six key components necessary to curriculum development work that seeks to wed principles of the new science to curriculum principles for gifted learners:

**1.** *Developing an understanding of scientific concepts.* In a world of fragmented information and knowledge explosion, there is a need to organize subject matter more effectively. One of the most powerful ideas that emerged from a study of 120 scholars conducted by Shane (1981) was a recognition among leading scientists that students need to understand key concepts in science more than specific facts and that scientists could agree on what these concepts were. Judson (1980) also used key science concepts to develop his powerful curriculum *The Search for Solutions,* and concluded his text material with a set of unanswered scientific questions. Focusing on scientific concepts is also a cornerstone of new work in science curriculum, most notably *Science for All Americans* (Rutherford & Ahlgren, 1989).

**2.** *Developing scientific inquiry skills in collaborative settings.* Just as one considers a shift in the organization of science curriculum toward key concepts, so too there needs to be a shift toward the student as investigator. Sternberg (1982) has outlined this major focus for gifted learners as the importance of engaging in problem finding, problem solving, problem evaluation, and scientific reporting.

An appropriate science curriculum should reflect an emphasis on more independent laboratory work, more extensive reading, more authentic library skills, and more true experimental work (Brandwein & Passow, 1988). Cothron, Giese, and Rezba (1989) suggested the use of a four-question strategy to help students internalize experimental design procedures, asking what materials are available for conducting experiments on a particular phenomenon, how a phenomenon acts, how one changes the set of materials to affect an action, and how one measures or describes the response to the change.

Closely related to an understanding of doing real-world science is the ability to work collaboratively in a research team. Given the nature of the knowledge explosion, no one is capable of grasping all content knowledge for purposes of generating new knowledge. Consequently, an important model of science for the high-ability learner to understand is that of collaboration. In the world of scientific research, many breakthroughs are made by scientific teams made up of individuals with specialized backgrounds, but with a scheme for working together on current scientific problems that requires combinational knowledge from several areas. Work in biochemistry is a good example of this, for biologists and chemists routinely address key research questions together. Even the recent practice of awarding the prestigious Nobel Prizes in the sciences is toward a joint award to a team that has made a major contribution. Mentorships and internships both offer structured program opportunities for gifted students to appreciate the nature of collaborative work in the sciences.

**3.** *Developing a knowledge base in science areas.* Another key component to an appropriate science curriculum for high-ability learners is the opportunity to learn significant content in science areas. Emphasis on equal exposure of students to content in the biological, physical, and geological sciences is also necessary to ensure that intradisciplinary understandings are developed. In an analysis of the effects of curriculum materials, it was found that students generally learned the specific content areas of science (biology, chemistry, etc.) to which they were exposed. However, in the case of selected National Science Foundation curriculum materials, which are strongly content oriented and include BSCS biology, Chemistry study, IPS Science, and PSSC Physics, students improved more in the areas of process skills, analytical skills, and creativity when compared to students using other curricula (Welch, 1984). It appears that the science curriculum that has a significant content base organized conceptually can enhance the development of skills critical for doing science. Where high-ability students are exposed to a heavy content emphasis, as is still the case with some basal text materials, it is critical that opportunities for testing out of content already mastered are provided along with opportunities for advanced work in science topics. Rutherford and Ahlgren (1990) integrated scientific knowledge requirements into a set of scientific views of the world. These include:

> *a. The structure and evolution of the universe*
> *b. The general features of the planet earth*
> *c. The basic concepts related to matter, energy, force, and motion*
> *d. The human organism as a biological, social, and technological species*
> *e. The human life cycle through all stages of development and maturation*
> *f. The basic structure and functioning of the human body*

The emphasis on learning an appropriate knowledge base in the sciences is then shaped by these views that guide the teaching of more discrete content.

**4.** *Developing interdisciplinary connections.* In the last half of this century, we have come to recognize the awesome connection between scientific discovery, technological development, and direct impact on society (Kuhn, 1970; Bronowski, 1978). Perhaps the development of the atom bomb was the first time this connection was truly etched on our collective consciousness. Since that time, however, the connections have been repeated over and over again. Consequently, to teach science as a totally objective set of processes is to misrepresent the role of science in today's world. High-ability students need to be exposed to the social issues surrounding the scientific enterprise and to develop a philosophy of science and a code of ethics that includes concerns for the moral and ethical dimensions of doing science.

Infusion of technological advances into the curriculum should be a two-pronged approach: use of technological tools that aid learning (e.g., computer simulations, video discs, CD-ROMS) and inclusion in the curriculum content of the technological advances that affect society (e.g., telephone, laser, or medical technology). In each case, it is important for students to see the application of these advances and not just know of their existence.

Making the connection between science concepts and other areas of inquiry such as the social sciences, mathematics, and language is also crucial to meaningful science learning. As students study the concept of scientific systems, for example, it is helpful to link that study to systems of government, systems of economics, and various communication systems. This forging of deliberate connections to other disciplines of study provides a richer and more complex curriculum for high-ability learners.

**5.** *Developing investigations of real problems.* Integral to considerations in developing an appropriate science curriculum framework is the role of the learner and his or her sense of connectedness to the enterprise of doing science as scientists themselves do. Traditional curriculum structure has a well-established order of instruction: information comes first, followed by questioning to determine student understanding, and ending with some sort of problem-solving activity. While this approach is very systematic and easy for teachers to manage, it does not reflect the kind of learning that takes place in the real world, and especially in the science professions. The goal of problem-based learning—one technique to engage learners in real problem solving—is to make learning in school more closely parallel the life-long learning that occurs in adulthood (Barrows, 1985).

With laboratory experiences carefully structured within the investigation of the problem, problem-based curriculum becomes an encapsulation of the entire process of scientific thought, investigation, and impact. Moreover, problem-based curriculum has the advantage of easily incorporating study and discussion of the interrelationship between science and social structures such as government and economics.

**6.** *Developing scientific habits of mind.* Welch (1984) has noted the importance of understanding the activities, beliefs, and personal traits of scientists in order to make appropriate inferences about science curriculum. Most scientists share a common set of fundamental beliefs about the natural world. These include such ideas as the existence of universal physical laws, the Copernican theory, and the belief that living things evolved over a long time period from simple to more complex forms. Such shared beliefs, unlike religious beliefs, are subject to question and can radically change if experiment or observation of the world indicates that they do not accurately reflect the true nature of things. Thus, science is uniquely dependent on experiment and inquiry. It is therefore important to convey both the fundamental ideas of science and the methods by which they are tested and refined to learners.

Welch also noted that certain personality traits seem to characterize the more success-ful scientists. Welch provided us with important guidance on the appropriate way to structure a science program for high-ability learners. The particularly important character-istics that scientists exhibit have been identified by Brandwein (1955) and Klemm (1977) as curiosity, creativeness, and commitment. Table 9–1 reflects these salient features of the domain of science inquiry.

Science curriculum for high-ability learners, then, must incorporate the following goal structure:

- *To study broad scientific concepts of merit that have meaning in all domains in science*
- *To engage in scientific investigation*
- *To provide in-depth opportunities to learn special topics in science*
- *To understand the role of science in society, including the relationship of science to all other areas of the human enterprise*
- *To foster curiosity about the world of science through the application of problem-based learning*
- *To master the tools of science by understanding the activities, beliefs, and character-istics of scientists*

Although there is considerable overlap in the proposed exemplary science curriculum for all learners and curriculum differentiation issues for the gifted, there still remain two

**TABLE 9–1   Domains of Science Inquiry**

| Activities | Beliefs | Personal Traits |
|---|---|---|
| | About Nature | |
| Observation | Intelligible | Curiosity |
| Measurement | Causal | Creativity |
| Experimentation | Noncapricious | Commitment |
| Communication | | |
| Mental Processes | About Method | |
| Induction | Objectivity | |
| Deduction | Skepticism | |
| Form hypotheses | Replication | |
| Create theories | Parsimony | |
| Analysis | | |
| Synthesis | About Knowledge | |
| Extrapolation | Structure | |
| Evaluation | Explanation | |
| Estimation | Prediction | |
| Speculation | Tentative | |

*Source:* Welch, W. W. (1986). A science-based approach to science learning. In D. Holdzkom & P. Lutz (Eds.), *Research within reach: Science education.* Washington, DC: National Science Teachers Association.

issues that must be accounted for in working with the gifted. The differentiation for these learners in such a model must still emanate from a clear understanding of the capacity of such learners at a given grade level to engage in a faster pace of learning at an advanced level. Moreover, high-ability learners require access to more sophisticated curriculum treatment at earlier stages of development. Consequently, curriculum expectations for these students need to reflect such adaptations at advanced and world-class levels.

## Using a Synthesis of Curriculum Models to Develop Science Curriculum

This book has delineated in Chapter 1 three models of curriculum development that have been used successfully in gifted education: a content model, a process-based model, and a concept-based model. Recent curriculum development work in science would suggest that a synthesis of these models may be most appropriate in creating a coherent curricular structure.

VanTassel-Baska, Gallagher, Sher, and Bailey (1992) engaged in an 18-month curriculum development project funded through the U.S. Department of Education that implemented the recommendations just cited for "new science" in schools and at the same time differentiated products for high-ability learners at the K–8 levels. The curriculum work began by focusing on the most important concepts in science.

A series of papers that describe a number of broad, overarching, scientifically grounded concepts common to many branches of science were developed by the scientist working with the project. They were chosen with reference to the concepts selected by Rutherford and Ahlgren in *Science for All Americans* (1989), those adopted by the California Department of Education (1990), and those selected by Judson for his book *The Search for Solutions* (1980). Additional criteria applied to selecting the concepts in this project were (1) ease of applicability to all science areas, (2) numerous valid connections to nonscience domains of inquiry, and (3) concepts found highly workable to demonstrate content manifestations at the unit level of analysis.

Of all the concepts referred to in other works, six were chosen for explication in the project: scale, models, change, systems, evolution, and reductionism. In addition, during the course of the project, a general description of the scientific process that would be useful for teachers to follow was developed along with a description of useful ways to incorporate laboratory work for high-ability learners. Finally, an applications paper containing implementation suggestions was developed for teacher use in teaching the specific scientific concepts.

The overall purpose of the concept papers was to aid teachers in understanding the key components and generalizations that are critical to specific science concepts as well as to see ways these concepts can be applied to high-ability students' learning science in the classroom. Moreover, by providing a rich bibliography of further readings on each concept, teachers are encouraged to engage in the first step of the scientific process: learning as much as possible about what they are expected to teach.

A scope and sequence model for K–8 science curriculum was developed that selected a particular concept and developed it systematically from generalizations to learner outcomes to content applications to interdisciplinary applications at the specific grade levels of K–2, 3–5, and 6–8. The scope and sequence model provided an organizing structure for the development of teacher units around the concept. In science the concept was "systems."

This concept was developed through the process of (1) stating generalizations, (2) applying those generalizations to a set of generic concept outcomes, (3) applying the generic outcomes to specific science content, and (4) applying the outcomes to specific content from other disciplines (see Figure 9–1). An example of these transitions in concept development follows.

### *Application of the Model*

*Generalizations*

- *All systems have identifiable elements and boundaries.*
- *All systems experience input and provide output.*
- *Systems are characterized by the nature of their internal interactions.*
- *Systems display predictable behaviors.*

*Concept Outcomes*

For any given system, the student will be able to:

- *Describe the important elements of the system.*
- *Delineate the boundaries of the system.*
- *Describe input into the system and evaluate its effects on the system.*
- *Describe the output from the system and evaluate the impact of the system on the outside world.*
- *Analyze important interactions among system elements that give rise to overall system behavior.*
- *Use the language of "systems" to describe components of a new system under study.*
- *Transfer knowledge about one system studied to other systems.*

**Figure 9–1  A Model for Developing Concepts in Science**

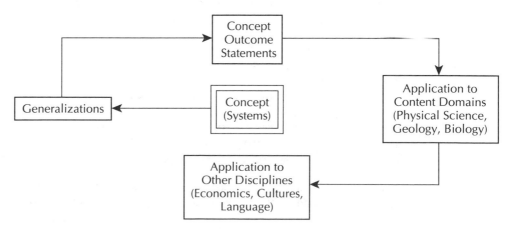

### Application to Content Topics

*Lab and Field Geology*

For a local site of geological interest, the students will be able to:

- *Identify the most common minerals through standard classification methods (including simple chemical tests, when appropriate)*
- *Identify different types of geological materials (silt, shale, aggregate, etc.)*
- *Map the distribution of the different minerals and different types of geologic materials present at the site*
- *Relate the materials present in the site of geologic interest to the geological processes that are operating at the site or that operated at the site in the past (for example, gravel pits are full of many different types of rocks; how did they get there?)*

### Application to Other Disciplines

*Cities as Systems*

All cities can be thought of as systems whose elements include both the physical structures and systems present (buildings, roads, parks, sewers, electrical and gas lines, and so on) and the human components present (individuals, families, neighborhoods, political control systems, school, businesses, and so on).

The students will be able to:

- *Describe the elements that make up a city.*
- *Understand the functioning of the city as a whole.*
- *Analyze important interactions among the city's elements that keep the city functioning.*
- *Demonstrate the importance of input into the city (food, energy, materials, people).*
- *Analyze city output and its varied effects on the outside world (products, information, people, trash, etc.).*

*Economic Systems*

For a variety of different economic systems (for example, capitalism as practiced in the United States, democratic socialism as practiced in Sweden, command economy socialism as practiced in the former USSR), the student will be able to:

- *Describe the important elements of each economic system.*
- *Describe the interactions between system elements that determine the overall behavior of the economy.*
- *Analyze the interactions of the economy with outside forces.*
- *Compare and contrast the ability of the different economic systems to innovate, to provide products and services to the people in each system, and to respond flexibly to internal and external challenges.*
- *Analyze the effects that each system has on the world economy as a whole.*

A set of exemplary science curriculum units were then developed for primary, intermediate, and middle school levels. These units were generated from the project's selected concept of "systems," followed the concept and research process outcomes, and were evaluated according to the project criteria for exemplary science curriculum materials. The list of unit titles and the specific systems studied by grade level clusters was:

### Sample Systems Units

| Grade | Unit Topic | System Studied |
|---|---|---|
| K–2 | Small Ecosystems | Plant growth system<br>Effects of altering the system<br>Effects of introducing new elements into a system |
|  | Small Animal Community | Ant farms<br>  labor system<br>  communication system |
| 3–5 | Kitchen Chemistry | Chemical reaction system<br>Ecosystem |
|  | Archaeology | System of scientific research |
| 6–8 | Pollution of Chesapeake Bay | Chemical system<br>Agricultural system<br>Bay life system<br>Regulatory system |
|  | Nuclear Power | Environmental system<br>Regulatory system<br>Human health system<br>Power generation system<br>Waste disposal system |

In addition to the conceptual development of "systems," another major strand of the science curriculum work was to delineate and develop an equal emphasis on science process. Scientists working with the project collaborated on how best to represent the way scientists do there work. Sher (1993) defined *scientific process* as:

1. *Learn a great deal about your field.*
2. *Think of a good (interesting, important, and tractable) problem.*
3. *Decide which experiments/observations/calculations would contribute to a solution of the problem.*
4. *Perform the experiments/observations/calculations.*
5. *Decide whether the results really do contribute to a better understanding of the problem.*
6. *Communicate your results to as many people as possible. (pp. 3–5)*

This process description then led to the development of generic outcomes for students that incorporated all of the important process on doing science. These outcomes were:

*Generic Scientific Research Outcomes*
Students will:

- *Explore a scientific area.*
- *Identify meaningful problem for investigation.*
- *State an hypothesis.*
- *Work through a preplanned experiment or demonstration or aid in the development of an experiment.*
- *Make appropriate observations.*
- *Create a simple graph or chart. Label diagrams appropriately.*
- *Record data in appropriate format.*
- *Analyze experimental data: data tables, graphs.*
- *Perform appropriate calculations by hand.*
- *Evaluate experiment results in light of the original problem.*
- *Make predictions about similar problems.*
- *Communicate using posters, oral communication, brief lab reports.*

These outcomes frame the scientific research work from kindergarten through eighth grade and are infused in each of the teaching units as well.

Finally, the project ensured that an appropriate science content emphasis was present through several approaches:

1. Involving university and practicing scientists as a part of the working team who could offer content-based suggestions throughout the development process.
2. Listing criteria developed by scientists that spelled out the specific science content emphases they felt high-ability learners needed in a curriculum at K–8 levels. These criteria are:
   a. Content base in key areas of science that provide the fundamentals of basic science
   b. Content base in key areas of technology
   c. Inclusion of current science/technology content
   d. Inclusion of historical and current science/technology issues
   e. Topics linked to broad scientific concepts
   f. Balance of qualitative and quantitative information
   g. Balance of theoretical and practical science
   h. Presence of moral and ethical dimensions of science and technology to society and to developing nations
   i. Science is accurate and presented understandably
   j. Important science concepts are covered in depth
3. Cross referencing the development work to existing textbooks and guides that primarily focused on content at K–8 levels of development.

A synthesis approach such as this merges the concerns for reform of science curriculum and provides the necessary curriculum differentiation for gifted learners while addressing the need for higher standards for all students.

## Secondary Science Curriculum for the Gifted

Over the last 50 years, the United States had taken a livelier interest in science offerings for its most able population than it has in any other curriculum area at the secondary level. The perception of this country's world standing is frequently equated with how well students are provided for in the basic sciences. Thus, it is not unusual to find long-standing and intensive science programs for the gifted having been successful over a period of years.

The Bronx High School of Science has a 50-year tradition in offering excellent science opportunities for highly able students in New York City. While the focus of the school's nomenclature centers on science, it offers an excellent program to gifted students across the curriculum. Thus far, the program has produced three Nobel laureates in the sciences and it has a long list of distinguished graduates who have gone on to make outstanding science contributions. The ingredients of success for the school's strong science effort rest on three variables: the quality of the student, the quality of the teaching staff, and the strong curriculum in science. Students at the school take four years of science and are exposed to a heavy emphasis on inquiry training in the scientific process. In essence, they learn how to think about science and how to question. The Bronx High School offers a full complement of Advanced Placement courses in the sciences, including AP Biology, AP Chemistry, and AP Physics. In addition, it provides specialized courses that allow students to pursue their own independent work in science, both during the academic year and in the summer. An innovative curriculum was developed in 1975 to foster creativity in science at the school (Galasso, 1977). It has proven to be especially successful with younger science students who need the motivational focus that the curriculum provides. The features of the school curriculum are carefully structured to provide multiple student outcomes. Listed below is an outline used for developing curriculum at the School:

### Features of a Science Lesson

1. *Philosophy*
   a. Comparison with other subject areas
   b. Problem solving
2. *Lesson Structure and Lesson Planning*
   a. Motivation—aim sequence
   b. Gathering and/or giving information
   c. Hypothesizing
   d. Testing hypotheses
   e. Summaries
   f. Homework
   g. Instructional objectives
   h. Reading and writing skills
   i. Demonstrations
3. *Other Types of Lessons*
   a. Laboratory lesson

b. Reading lesson
c. Review lesson

The North Carolina School of Math and Science represents a more recent intensive focus on the sciences for gifted learners. Begun in 1980 at the behest of the governor as a device to upgrade education in the state as well as provide exemplary programming to the most able, the school already has distinguished itself as a landmark institution. The quality of graduates is high, and they have enjoyed successful placement in the prestigious world of higher education. Furthermore, the school is proving itself to be a successful economic development tool for the state, luring high-powered scientists to work in the research triangle and creating a whole new generation of students who will wish to remain in the area.

Key features of this school in respect to its science curriculum include:

- *Up-to-date scientific equipment available for student use*
- *Access to practicing scientists in the research triangle area surrounding the school; internships with selected scientists is an integral part of the program*
- *Employment of scientists as instructors for special courses in the sciences*
- *A thematic orientation to much of the school's coursework, blending biology, chemistry, and physics together in one unified course around basic scientific principles, for example*

New efforts based on the North Carolina model have also developed in other parts of the country. The Louisiana School of Math, Science, and the Arts is flourishing, and the Illinois Math and Science Academy (IMSA) has made major strides in curriculum development over the past seven years of operation. It now houses a national Center for Problem-Based Learning, which evolved out of the development of a specialized team-taught course on science and society. Curriculum development efforts at the school in all subjects have emphasized conceptually based interdisciplinary curriculum for use with its gifted population. Located in proximity to two national laboratories, Argonne and Fermilab, IMSA has also developed its curriculum to take advantage of the high technology and human resources available from both of these laboratories.

The Indiana Academy of Arts and Sciences also has an impressive curriculum plan, although only in operation for a few years. One distinctive approach used at this specialized school for gifted students on the campus of Ball State University is a research seminar taken by all students at the school. The seminar emphasizes important elements of reasoning within the framework of science, research procedures, and ethical implications of research. An outline of this seminar model follows:

1. *Problem finding* involves helping students locate or isolate a problem. Problem identification, establishment of limitations, and problem statement are stressed.
2. *Research design* includes an overview of relevant research, methdologies, and development of an appropriate research design.
3. *Reference sources* acquaints the student with the tools of scholarship necessary to conduct a comprehensive review of professional literature on a given topic. Special attention is given to specialized indices and electronic data retrieval systems.

4. *Data collection* introduces students to methods for observing phenomena or obtaining evidence necessary to the investigation. Techniques can range from the use of scientific instruments to case studies, depending on the nature of each student's project.

5. *Analysis and interpretation of data* continues skills introduced in the fourth component, giving special attention to application of microcomputers. Again, methods are diverse. Since the research seminars are grouped by student interest, each group can focus on techniques directly applicable to its specific projects. Students will be introduced to various computer applications.

6. *Drawing conclusions* stresses the application of logic and the standards of scholarship in the development of the final product of research.

7. *Technical writing* focuses on the written exposition of the research report. Students are introduced to the various style manuals that apply to scholarly writing, and they begin to prepare drafts of the parts of their reports that are near completion.

8. *Ethical issues in research* is a topic with two perspectives. First, students consider the ethical implications of the consequences of their research, and the ethical implications of various research methodologies are discussed. Second, students consider the ethical issues related to the academic integrity of their research.

9. *Presenting findings* is the culminating phase in the research competency program. Students prepare their reports for presentation or exhibition through appropriate refereed outlets. Use of computer-assisted graphics and audio-visual materials in preparation for presentation or exhibition is included. Students are assisted by faculty in searching appropriate outlets to publish or exhibit their work.

VanTassel-Baska, Landau, and Olszewski (1985) presented a possible scope and sequence of courses in the physical and life sciences covering grades 6 through 12 that would be appropriate for academically gifted students. Science courses that are typically available to high school students (i.e., biology, chemistry, and physics) are included in this curriculum; however, students would begin the formal study of specific science subjects such as biology and physical science at the junior high level, allowing them to take more science courses and to achieve advanced placement credit for more science subjects during high school. This curriculum in its entirety is particularly appropriate for students who wish to enter honors science programs at the university level, for students who wish to pursue further study in an integrated science program at the university level (involving more than one science subject), for students who plan a career that involves major intensive study in several science fields (e.g., biophysicist), and for students who plan to pursue study in a science field to the doctoral level.

By the time they reach middle school, students who have outstanding abilities in science are ready for a program that fosters an in-depth understanding of the major science areas while emphasizing that science is a dynamic, creative field (Martin, 1979). Rapid change, advanced technology, and the use of more sophisticated science must be incorporated into the curricula while retaining a strong conceptual focus and an emphasis on problem finding, problem solving, evaluation, and reporting. The overall aim, then, is the development of a curriculum that will factilitate the learning of both the content and methods of the sciences.

## *Curriculum Materials in Science*

Excellent science curriculum materials were produced in the 1960s, including BSCS biology, chemistry study, and PSSC physics at the secondary level, and AAAS science and EES science at the elementary level. Unfortunately, the science curricula, like the mathematics curricula, have slowly been replaced by less and less rigorous and challenging materials. The "new science" materials were regarded as inappropriate for most students; the emphasis on learning by *doing* was time consuming, the reading was too demanding, and the conceptual orientation of the materials was too difficult. These shortcomings of the 1960s curricula are precisely the characteristics that make them an appropriate foundation for science curricula today.

It is equally important to recognize the fundamental importance of teacher training in the use of these materials in order to render programs effective. Existing materials must also be adapted to reflect the accelerated rate of development of new information in the sciences that has resulted from the enormous technological advances of the intervening decades. Furthermore, the role of technology as a tool for gifted learners must be considered.

The National Curriculum Development Project in Science conducted by VanTassel-Baska and colleagues (1992) engaged in an extensive evaluation of existing science curriculum materials and developed a useful assessment model. Promising science curriculum materials for high-ability learners were reviewed according to a curriculum evaluation system that developed criteria for judging exemplary science curriculum. By delineating a set of curriculum standards, the evaluation system provided schools with a template for reviewing any new science curriculum materials that are teacher-made or commercially developed according to general curriculum design features, exemplary science features, and tailoring for high-ability learners.

Specifically, evaluation criteria for the review of curriculum materials included an assessment of the general curriculum design features (rationale and purpose, content, and responsiveness to developmental needs); classroom design features (instructional objectives, activities, instructional strategies, assessment procedures, materials resources, and extension ideas); and technology features at Phase I. A second review addressed issues of exemplary science inquiry, including both science content and science process features at Phase II. The last phase (Phase III) of the review process focused on differentiation for high-ability learners. This segment of the review process also examined more specifically issues of curriculum responsiveness to intellectually gifted learners, science-prone students, girls, minorities, and students with disabilities. These criteria have been coalesced into rating forms, described and presented in a product entitled *Curriculum Assessment Guide* (CAG) (Boyce et al, 1992b).

Initially an annotated bibliography of 62 science materials were compiled using a variety of data sources to locate the most promising ones. From this list, ultimately 26 sets of curriculum materials were reviewed, culminating in a product entitled *A Consumer's Guide to Science Curriculum for High Ability Learners, K–8* (Boyce et al., 1992a).

Three reviewers with different expertise and perspectives evaluated each curriculum by using the CAG. First, a materials specialist conducted a thorough review of the entire curriculum by applying all three sections of criteria (Phases I, II, and III). The general curriculum features were rated on a scale of 1–3, a discrimination judged sufficient by the review team for the general curriculum features of materials. The sections that address exemplary science features and tailoring for special populations were rated on a scale of 1–5, allowing for greater discrimination on key features. In addition, specific examples of how the curriculum met or failed to meet certain criteria were noted during this part of the review.

Finally, a narrative review was written that provided (1) a thorough description of the curriculum material, (2) an analysis of its strengths and weaknesses, and (3) a conclusion that pinpointed recommended use.

The annotated resource list that follows was bound to meet more of the exemplary criteria used in the curriculum evaluation than other materials and was recommended for use with high-ability learners. For a complete set of reviews, refer to *A Consumer's Guide to Science Curriculum for High Ability Learners, K–8* (Boyce et al., 1992a).

### *Key Resources in Science Curriculum for Gifted High-Ability Learners*

*Challenge of the Unknown.* (1986). Seven-part film series produced by J. J. Crimmins, New York; Teacher's manual published by W. W. Norton, New York. (*Challenge of the Unknown* is available to schools on free-loan videocassettes, with permission to copy and keep the copied sets; a free teaching guide is included. For this service, contact Karol Media, Wilkes-Barre, PA.)

> Challenge of the Unknown *seeks to enable students to use math as a problem-solving tool in the real world. The seven segments of the series, which encompass* problem creation *as well as* problem solving, *include Situation, Information, Restatement, Outcomes, Management, Estimation, and Argument. Although math applications receive primary emphasis, the materials demonstrate scientific inquiry in action. Grades 5–8.*

*Chemical Education for Public Understanding Program* (CEPUP). (1990). Berkeley, CA: Lawrence Hall of Science, University of California. Distributed by Addison-Wesley.

> *The CEPUP materials integrate chemical concepts and processes with societal issues through inquiry-based activities that emphasize problem solving and decision making. As of April 1991, eight modules comprise the program, covering such topics as a chemical survey, solutions and pollution, threshold limits, risk comparison, groundwater, toxic wastes, plastics, and chemicals in food. The CEPUP manual and kit are designed for nonlaboratory settings. In this program, students collect and process scientific evidence and use it to make decisions about chemicals in the context of society. Grades 7–9.*

Cothron, J. H., Giese, R. N., & Rezba, R. J. (1989). *Students and Research: Practical Strategies for Science Classrooms and Competitions.* Dubuque, IA: Kendall/Hunt.

> Students and Research *is a manual for teachers that provides an extensive curriculum designed to promote scientific literacy via scientific experimentation. Divided into four parts—basic principles of experimental design and analysis, advanced principles of experimental design and analysis, management strategies for classroom and independent research, and strategies for successful science competitions—the authors believe that the necessary skills to develop problem-solving abilities may be gained through implementation of their program. Encompassing product, process, and values as the three aspects of science, the manual attempts not only to provide a broad knowledge base developed through independent investigation but to frame that knowledge within societal values and expectations of science. Grades 4–12.*

*Full Option Science System* (FOSS), (1989–1991 under development). Berkeley CA: Lawrence Hall of Science, University of California.

> FOSS *is a hands-on science program for grades 3–4 and 5–6 organized under the four topic strands of scientific reasoning and technology, physical science, earth science, and life science. For each strand, there are two activity modules. Each activity module includes content background information, ideas for preparing and managing the activities, detailed lesson plans, discussion questions, and interdisciplinary extensions. Conceptual themes such as systems and interaction, patterns of change, evolution, and models are integrated into the content strands. Grades 5–6.*

*Great Explorations in Math & Science* (GEMS). Berkeley, CA: Lawrence Hall of Science, University of California.

> GEMS *publications include teacher's guides, assemble presenter's guides, and exhibit guides. The publications integrate math with life, earth, and phyical science, using a "guided discovery" approach to learning. The teacher's guides, which include student materials, encompass 2 to 15 class sessions that can be integrated into a curriculum or stand alone. Grades K–10.*

*Insights: A Hands-On Elementary Science Curriculum.* (1991 under development). Newton, MA: Education Development Center. Distributed by Wings for Learning, Scotts Valley, CA.

> Insights *is an inquiry-based program consisting of thematic modules. When the project is completed, the modules can be used together as a complete curriculum or as individual modules to supplement an existing curriculum. The major organizing themes of systems, change, structure and function, diversity, cause and effect, and energy are infused throughout the modules. Three modules are available as of May 1991: Myself and Others, Bones and Skeletons, and Circuits and Pathways. Grades K–6.*

Iozzi, L. A., & Bastardo, P. J. (1990). *Science-Technology-Society: Preparing for Tomorrow's World. Decisions for Today and Tomorrow.* Longmont, CO: Sopris West.

> Science-Technology-Society *is a teaching module divided into three main parts. Part A provides the necessary background information for the successful presentation of the module. Part B contains the specific teaching directions and suggestions for the 12 activities offered. Part C consists of the master copies of the student readings and student activities. The areas of exploration include technological advances, genetic engineering, artificial intelligence, nuclear energy, acid precipitation, hazardous wastes, food and agriculture, organ transplants, transportation, robotics, and technology and decision making. Grades 7–12.*

Judson, H. F. (1980). *The Search for Solutions.* New York: Holt, Rinehart & Winston. (1980 edition is out of print. An abridged edition without illustrations and captions is available from John Hopkins University Press, 1987. *Search for Solutions* videocassettes are available to schools on free-loan with permission to copy; a free teaching guide is included. Contact Karol Media, Wilkes-Barre, PA.)

> The Search for Solutions *explains in detail how science is done and distinguishes between good science, bad science, and nonsense. Judson incorporates aesthetic criticism in this book, based on his intimate knowledge of the laboratory. After discussing "The Rage to Know" as the basis for investigation, Judson considers patterns, change, chance, feedback, modeling, strong predictions, evidence, and theory as ways of searching for solutions. He concludes with eight problems in search of solutions, including origins of the universe, evolution, and aging and death. Grades 6–12.*

*LEGO TC Logo.* Enfield, CT: Lego Systems

>  LEGO *TC Logo is an interdisciplinary activity series that can be used to integrate science, mathematics, design, and engineering. By using LEGO blocks as construction material interfaced with a computer and a special version of Logo computer language, children invent, engineer, and operate model machines. Grades 4–8.*

Based on the thorough review of existing science materials, it appears appropriate to underscore the extent to which cost-effective exemplary curriculum materials are readily available for use in classrooms. One problem uncovered, however, was the very limited use those materials were receiving, even in schools and districts that have purchased them. Some of the best materials may be characterized as unleveled in respect to grade, interdisciplinary in orientation, and comprised of multiple modes of learning, usually including video or computer technology as a key feature. It is paradoxical that the very curricular components that we value for their appropriateness with high-ability learners are overlooked when they are "packaged" into ready-made curriculum materials. If this science project provides any lesson, it is that we already have excellent curriculum for high-ability and other learning groups; the problem rests with (1) continuing the developmental process through extending and refining that which is already available using existing frameworks and (2) removing barriers to getting the new curriculum institutionalized in classroom practice, such as lack of experimental materials and/or equipment and lack of human resource assistance in implementing classroom science procedures.

*National Geographic Kids Network.* (1990, in development). Washington, DC: National Geographic.

>  *Using* National Geographic Kids Network, *students conduct original research, use a computer to record data, and then use a modem and telecommunications to share their findings with "research teammates" across the United States and the world. A National Geographic scientist examines the data on-line and coaches the students in their study. Some of the units that are available are "Hello!" "Acid Rain," "What's in Our Water?" and "Weather in Action." Grades 4–6.*

*Science and Technology for Children* (STC). (1991–1994). Washington, DC: National Science Resources Center, Distributed by Carolina Biological Supply, Burlington, NC.

>  *STC is a new modular, hands-on science program built around four central themes: observing, measuring, and identifying properties; seeking evidence and recognizing patterns and cycles; identifying cause and effect and extending the senses; and designing and conducting experiments. The themes are woven through a sequence of life science, earth science, physical science, and technology units. Several units are available: plant growth and development, electric circuits, microworlds, life cycles of butterflies, experiments with plants, and magnets and motor units. Grades 1–6.*

*Science Teaching Through its Astronomical Roots* (Project STAR). Cambridge, MA: Harvard-Smithsonian Center for Astrophysics. Distributed by Learning Technologies., Cambridge, MA.

>  *The complete STAR curriculum—including a test, a teacher's guide, two sets of videos, and the STAR activity manual and activity kits—are currently available. The activity manual with 21 astronomy activities includes hands-on exercises, homework problems, and extension activities. Each activity begins with a section that gives students a chance to explore their own*

> preconceptions or "naive theories" that can become barriers to the understanding of science. The STAR materials and activities then provide opportunities for students to replace their theories with more powerful, accepted ideas. Grades 10–12.

*The Voyage of the Mimi* (1984–date) and *The Second Voyage of Mimi* (1989–date). New York: Bank Street College of Education. Distributed by Wings for Learning, Scotts Valley, CA.

> *The* Voyage of the Mimi *is a multimedia, interdisciplinary curriculum that centers around a 26-part video story of the crew of the 72-foot ketch* Mimi *and their whale research. Topics covered in the curriculum include whales, maps and navigation, and ecosystems. In addition to the video series, extensive print materials for students and teachers, and computer software with probes support related classroom investigations. Grades 4–10.*
>
> *In the second voyage, the* Mimi *sails off the coast of the Yucatan Peninsula of Mexico where archeologists study the ancient Maya civilization. This curriculum focuses on the Maya civilization, archeology, the Maya base-twenty nunber system, and the astronomy of the earth and sun. Grades 4–10.*

Major publishing companies also need to be aware of the extent to which their existing materials are inadequate for the task of curriculum reform. No basal text reached the level of being recommended for use with high-ability learners with the exception of the BSCS biology program originally developed in the 1960s. If the use of basals continues to be school practice, there is clearly a need to convince textbook publishers to restructure their materials based on the more powerful curriculum models.

Clearly, the major thrust in curriculum reform in science education for high-ability learners must be in the arena of teacher training. The need for specific subject matter training is great if the findings of this project regarding the convergent areas of science reform and curriculum efforts for the gifted are to be understood and implemented in all classrooms at the K–8 levels. In science, all teachers are teachers of the high-ability learner, except in special schools or self-contained classes. Thus, the need to engage with general science educators in their attempts to reform science education for all learners is a crucial part of our role as educators of the gifted.

Teacher training efforts for gifted learners need to target the following areas over the next several years. In respect to curriculum in general, preservice and in-service work needs to focus on how to implement discipline-specific models of curriculum and instruction that are responsive to the underlying needs of gifted learners, how to engage learners as investigators providing the tools and processes used by real-world problem solvers, and how to raise standards and expectations for gifted learners in regular classrooms.

There are also many fine reference books on science already available that organize science ideas according to conceptual themes. One such example is Judson's (1980) book called *The Search for Solutions*. This text organizes scientific ideas according to nine key issues and themes.

1. Investigation: The Rage to Know
2. Pattern
3. Change
4. Chance

5. Feedback
6. Modeling
7. Strong predictions
8. Evidence
9. Theory

Using exemplary photographs, paintings, and diagrams to illustrate these key ideas in science as well as featuring interviews with current scientists, Judson creates a "feeling" for science in his readers that deepens their understanding of science as the art of knowing. Filmstrips and teaching guides have also been developed for use with the text.

Another book and former PBS television series that has a strong conceptual organization is *Connections* by James Burke (1978). He has chosen to focus on eight recent inventions that account for phenomenal change in our modern environment and daily lives: the atomic bomb, the telephone, the computer, the production-line system of manufacture, aircraft, plastics, the guided rocket, and television. Burke links each of them, however, to earlier inventions that take the reader back to ancient times. These "chains of discovery" allow students to understand the nature of scientific and technological breakthroughs over time and culture.

A third example of such materials is the fine intellectual masterpiece by Jacob Bronowski, *The Ascent of Man* (1976). His work chronicles the progress of man according to key scientific discoveries, yet the text also bridges these discoveries to issues of social progress. His description of our current conception of science and its relationship to an earlier view of architecture is typical of the interplay of ideas he uses throughout the text:

> *The fact of the matter is that our conception of science now, towards the end of the twentieth century, has changed radically. Now we see science as a description and explanation of the underlying structures of nature; and words like* structure, pattern, plan, arrangement, architecture *constantly occur in every description that we try to make. . . . The spiral structure of DNA has become the most vivid image of science in the last years. And that imagery lives in these arches.*
>
> *What did the people do who made this building and others like it? They took a dead heap of stones, which is not a cathedral, and they turned it into a cathedral by exploiting the natural forces of gravity, the way the stone is laid naturally in its bedding plane, the brilliant invention of the flying buttress and arch and so on. And they created a structure that grew out of the analysis of nature into this superb synthesis. The kind of man who is interested in the architecture of nature today is the kind of man who made the architecture nearly eight hundred years ago. There is one gift above all others that makes man unique among the animals, and it is the gift displayed everywhere here: his immense pleasure in exercising and pushing forward his own skill. (pp. 112–113)*

The Bronowski work can be used as a teacher reference for organizing an interdisciplinary program in science or as a direct teaching tool with students from sixth grade on. A PBS film series highlights each section of the book.

The three examples provided here are excellent beginning resources in building a conceptually based science program that could focus on some of the most fascinating scientific ideas of our time.

## *Curriculum Development in Technology*

Science curriculum for the gifted should include a strong component on technology, its history, and its development as a field. This component could emphasize the linkages among advances in science and technology. That is, since science typically provides the underlying knowledge base for technology, each science content area—physics, biology, and chemistry—would include units focusing on the technological advances that have been possible as a result of specific discoveries within that content area. These units could be developed independently so as to be easily integrated into the study of the content area where appropriate (i.e., when students have sufficient knowledge of the underlying scientific basis to permit a thoughtful and indepth examination of some of the technological results). The impact of technology on furthering scientific discoveries that make a contribution to the knowledge base—or the reciprocity between science and technology (e.g., the telescope causing a revolution in astronomy)—could also be examined. An example would be a unit on the atom bomb (a technological result of the field of chemistry). An understanding of the periodic table and the patterns and regularity within it as a result of the structure of the atom and its properties would be necessary before one could proceed to the topic of nuclear fission and the results of this process on the element of plutonium. This topic could be introduced in the chemistry curriculum at the point where students have the prerequisite knowledge to fully understand its evolution within the content area.

Woven throughout such units would be an emphasis on overarching and recurrent themes and issues that relate to the field of technology as a whole and to specific technologies somewhat more cogently or urgently. These include the power of technology as a force that causes exponential growth; the impact of technology on society—movement from an industrial society to an information society; the results of technology—societal progress versus societal regression; the effects of technological advances on the quality of life; and the strategies that society and individuals can employ (problem solving, problem prediction, decision making) to cope with the rapidity of changes wrought by technological and scientific advances and their potential results. Key areas of societal impact to include in a curriculum might be:

1. Environmental pollution through toxic wastes, acid rain, etc.
2. The beginning and ending of life through in vitro fertilization techniques, life support systems, organ transplants, etc.
3. National defense through nuclear arsenals, STAR wars, etc.
4. Improved medical treatment through laser surgery, CAT scans, etc.
5. Improved communication access through computer mail, videotape, etc.
6. Improved transportation networks through structural redesign and computerized systems

## Women and Minorities in Science

Although current theory and research provide a direction for establishing sound science programs for gifted and high-ability students at a general level, there is a need to focus more sharply on the plight of women and minorities in science. The National Science Foundation noted in its 1986 biennial report, *Women and Minorities in Science and Engineering,* that minority students' lower participation in advanced precollege math and science courses is the most crucial immediate concern of minorities. The basic precursor to poor science performance in college was found to be elementary and secondary school preparation in math and science (Chipman & Thomas, 1984). Thus, curriculum implications for encouraging girls and minorities to continue studying mathematics and science have continued as a major issue over the last two decades.

Several studies have cited the lower incidence of women in advanced coursework in these areas and fewer women in careers related to science. Whereas reasons for this discrepancy may be found in the social (Eccles, 1984), psychological (Astin, 1969), and biological (Benbow & Stanley, 1980) milieus, it is a difficult discrepancy to ignore when addressing the needs of gifted females and minorities. Consequently, it may be important for curriculum planners to be conscious of the need for emphasizing appropriate approaches in nurturing gifted girls and minority students in the context of a science program.

The literature suggests several strategies for maintaining female and minority interest in the sciences:

- *Provide information about contributions of women and minorities in science.*
- *Help girls and minorities understand the effects of sex-stereotyping and bias in science and career materials on their self-perceptions.*
- *Present information about women and minorities who have careers in science and technology.*
- *Explain the projections for science and engineering careers over the next decade.*
- *Relate the changing roles of men and women to the career potential for women in science.*
- *Select materials that avoid sex and minority stereotypes in their illustrations (e.g., pictures in which women are actively engaged in science, outdoors as well as indoors, and in which as many men are looking over women's shoulders and vice versa).*
- *Invite women and minority scientists into the classroom to talk about relevant topics.*
- *Encourage all students to develop manipulative hobbies, such as butterfly collecting, photography, computers, or constructing models and radios.*

Another way to deal with some gifted girls' lack of self-confidence may be to use bibliotherapy techniques that focus on reading biographies of women scientists and/or other works that they may have written. The following is a list of famous women scientists, about whom much has been written.

Elizabeth Blackwell (1821–1910): Physician. First woman in United States to become a doctor; established the New York Infirmary for Women and Children;

organized Women's Central Relief Association which trained nurses; assisted in developing examinations long before they were compulsory; founded the New England Hospital for Women and Children in 1859.

Rachel Fuller Brown (1898–1980): Organic chemist. Co-developer with Elizabeth Lee Hazen (1885–1975) of Nystatin, the first antifungal antibiotic for use in human disease; received the Squibb Award in Chemotherapy and was the first woman to receive the Chemical Pioneer Award of the American Institute of Chemists.

Mary Bunting (1910–    ): Microbiologist. First woman member on the Atomic Energy Commission; made discoveries on the effects of radiation on bacteria.

Eleanor M. Burbridge (1919–    ): Astronomer. First woman Royal Astronomer at the Royal Greenwich Observatory in England.

Rachel Carson (1907–1964): Biologist. Alerted the country to the dangers of pollution through her book *Silent Spring*.

Gerty Cori (1896–1957): Biochemist. First American woman to receive the Nobel Prize in Medicine/Physiology in 1947; researched carbohydrate metabolism on how the body uses its fuel supply of starches and sugars as related to certain hormone secretions.

Marie Curie (1867–1934): Chemist. First person to receive two Nobel Prizes: Physics in 1903 for the discovery of radium and Chemistry in 1911 for her research into radioactivity.

Lilian Gilbreth (1878–1972): Industrial engineer. Developed time and human motion studies to reduce waste and increase efficiency in the office, factory, hospital, and home settings.

Hetty Goldman (1881–1972): Archeologist. Interpreted the stages of prehistoric life in Greece; first woman professor at the Institute of Advanced Study at Princeton.

Jane Goodall (1934–    ): Animal behaviorist. Conducted detailed studies to show that chimpanzees are intelligent, tool making, social animals.

Dorothy Crowfoot Hodgkin (1910–    ): Crystallographer. Received the Nobel Prize in Chemistry in 1964 for research on the crystal structure of biochemical compounds, particularly penicillin.

Hyatia (c. 370–415): Mathematician. Mathematics and philosophy professor at the University of Alexandria in Egypt; developed the astrolabe and planesphere, instruments used for studying the stars.

Shirley Jackson (1946–    ): Physicist. First and only black woman currently in theoretical physics; participant in the International School of Subnuclear Physics in Italy.

Irene Joliot-Curie (1897–1956): Physicist. Received the Nobel Prize in Chemistry for discovering a technique for making artificial radioactive elements.

Maria C. Mayer (1906–1972): Physicist. Received the Nobel Prize in Physics in 1963 for her work during World War II on isotope separation for the atom bomb.

Barbara McClintock (1902–    ): Research scientist. Received the Nobel Prize in Medicine/Physiology in 1983 for her research in the cytogenetics of maize.

Margaret Mead (1901–1978). Anthropologist. Studied and wrote on the cultures of the South Sea Island, childbearing, and the role of woman in society.

Florence Sabin (1871–1953): Physician. Teach of anatomy and histology at the Johns

Hopkins University; discovered the origin of red corpuscles and made contributions to tuberculosis research; received the National Achievement Award in 1932.

Rosalyn Sussman Yalow (1921–    ): Medical physicist. Received the Nobel Prize in Medicine/Physiology in 1977 for the discovery of randioimmunology, a method of measuring minute concentrations of hundreds of substances in body tissues important in determining the differences between diseased and normal tissues.

## Implementation Issues in Science Programs

The issues associated with implementing a sound curriculum for gifted students in science are clear in terms of understanding what the goals of such a curriculum should be, based on the characteristics and needs of able learners as well as the nature of the activities, beliefs, and characteristics of successful scientists. What remains more difficult to handle from an administrative perspective are the resource needs to carry out such an ambitious program. Perhaps it would be useful to focus on some of these needed resource areas and how they might be handled.

**1.** *The choice of teacher.* It is vitally important that the teacher of gifted students in science know science. This is as important in the elementary-level program as it is in a secondary one. The individual should have advanced content knowledge in science but also have the skills to manage a science classroom effectively. Using high school staff to work in an elementary science program may be one way of getting the level of expertise required. Another way would be to differentiate the teaching staff so that one individual teaches predominantly science. Use of student help from universities as well as scientists in the area also may enhance the learning process for these students.

**2.** *The scientific environment.* Up-to-date science equipment in a laboratory that is conducive to conducting group and individual experiments is vital to carrying out the nature of the programs suggested in this chapter. For young students, in particular, collecting and analyzing the natural world is a wonderful context for scientific inquiry. Thus, classrooms need not be equipped with everything to make science viable. However, the need to create a conducive environment for doing science is a vital aspect of implementation.

**3.** *The emphasis on problem finding and problem solving rather than merely "problem doing."* Although canned experiments are easier to use in a classroom setting, they do little to instill a love of science in the gifted or to further the cause of real scientific inquiry. Engaging students in original research questions is an important aspect of implementing a successful science program for them. Using everyday tools, simple designs, and curiosity about natural phenomena constitute the best resources for students indulging in problem-finding behavior.

**4.** *Selection of texts that focus on broad conceptual issues rather than isolated topics or skills.* Several texts that are organized by key themes in science, such as *Connections* and *Ascent of Man,* have been discussed in this chapter. Moreover, a list of high-powered resources to help implement a science program for high-ability learners has been suggested. These materials in combination are superior to existing basal texts for use with all learners.

**5.** *Opportunity for individual scientific research work through hosting science fairs and junior science symposia.* Encouragement in scientific investigation can be enhanced by deliberately structuring an event to display and evaluate student work and utilizing scientists from the community as participants and critics. Programs like Science Olympiad or science fairs provide a chance for students to test themselves against other students who have similar interests and abilities as well as tap into the ideas of real practicing scientists.

**6.** *Connections to the real world of science through mentorships and internships.* Having students assigned to a hospital laboratory or a corporate research lab is one way of their gaining valuable insights into science as a profession. Such placements also enhance understanding scientific inquiry as an internalized process.

## Conclusion

In order for the United States to be first in the world of science and mathematics, our education system must place greater emphasis on science as an important area of study from an early age. Coupled with such an emphasis must be a rigorous curriculum that prepares students well for the society of the next century. Understanding the most relevant scientific concepts, applying the scientific research process, and grappling with the ethical issues of science and technology are the cornerstone pieces of such a world class curriculum. Original work in science conducted by the students themselves from an early age should be carefully nurtured so that scientific curiosity is stimulated and not extinguished. It will likely take scientsts some time to solve problems like those cited by Judson (1980) as the critical eight currently in search of solutions.

1. *What was the origin of the universe?*
2. *Needed: a unified theory in physics for four kinds of observable forces—weak, strong, electronagnetic, and gravitational.*
3. *What was the origin of the solar system?*
4. *What is the origin of life?*
5. *Establishing the quantitative bases of natural selection and evolution.*
6. *What are the controlling processes that cause the fertilized egg to become the organism?*
7. *What are the mechanisms by which aging and death occur?*
8. *How does the human nervous system perceive, think, and process information? (p. 200)*

Effective science programs for gifted learners, however, can begin to nuture the process.

### Key Points Summary

- *Science programs for the gifted should emphasize important scientific concepts, inquiry-based activities in a research mode, opportunities for modeling scientific behaviors, and an appreciation of the interplay of science and technology.*

- *Gifted students should understand and emulate the total domain of science inquiry: the activities, beliefs, and personal traits of scientists.*
- *Elementary science programs for the gifted should stress problem-based learning in science, both in small groups and independently.*
- *High school programs for the gifted should focus on more opportunities for real-world connections to practicing scientists, to the community, and to the ethical and moral considerations underlying scientific discovery.*
- *Excellent materials for use as curriculum for the gifted in science already exist; however, teachers must be trained to use them.*
- *Interdisciplinary materials can assist in teaching gifted students the serious implications of science study in our world.*
- *Minorities and gifted girls need special encouragement to continue in science programs and to relate to the field as a potential career path.*

## References

*Academic preparation for college*. (1982). New York: The College Entrance Examination Board, Education Equality Project.

American Association for the Advancement of Science. (1989). *Science for all Americans*. (AAAS Publication 89-01S). Washington, DC: Author.

American Association for the Advancement of Science. (1990). *The liberal art of science*. (AAAS Publication 90-13S). Washington, DC: Author.

Association for Supervision and Curriculum Development. (1990). *Update*. Alexandria, VA: Author.

Astin, H. (1969). *The woman doctorate in America*. New York: Russell Sage.

Barrows, H. S. (1985). *The tutorial process*. Springfield; Southern Illinois University of Medicine.

Benbow, C., & Stanley, J. (1980). Sex differences in mathematical ability: Fact or artifacts? *Science, 210*, 1262–1264.

Bennett, W. J. (1986). *First lessons: A report on elementary education in America*. Washington, DC: U.S. Government Printing Office.

Blurton, C. (1983). Science talent: The elusive gift. *School Science and Mathematics, 83* (8), 654–664.

Boyce, L. N., Johnson, D., Sher, B., Bailey, J., & VanTassel-Baska, J. (1992a). A consumer's guide to science curriculum for high ability learners, K–8. Washington, DC: U.S. Department of Education.

Boyce, L. N., Johnson, D., Sher, B., Bailey, J., & VanTassel-Baska, J. (1992b). *Curriculum assessment guide*. Washington, DC: U.S. Department of Education.

Brandwein, P. F. (1955). *The gifted student as future scientist*. New York: Harcourt, Brace, and Jovanovich.

Brandwein, P. F., & Passow, A. H. (Eds.). (1988). *Gifted young in science: Potential through performance*. Washington, DC: National Science Teachers Association.

Bronowski, J. (1976). *The ascent of man*. Boston: Little, Brown.

Burke, J. (1978). *Connections*. Boston: Little, Brown.

California Department of Education. (1990). *Science framework for California schools K–12*. Sacramento, CA: Author.

*A celebration of teaching high schools in the 1980s*. (1983). Reston, VA: The National Association of the Commission on Educational Issues of the National Association of Independent Schools. A Study of High Schools, NASSP.

Chipman, S., & Thomas, V. (1984). *The participation of women and minorities in math, science, and technical fields*. Office of Naval Research.

Cothron, J., Giese, R., & Rezba, R. (1989). *Students and research*. Dubuque, IA: Kendall-Hunt.

Eccles, J. (1984). Sex differences in mathematics participation. In M. Steinkamp & M. Maehr (Eds.), *Women in science*. Greenwich, CT: JAI Press.

*Educating Americans for the 21st century: A report to the American people and the National Science*

*Board.* (1983). The National Science Board Commission on PreCollege Education in Mathematics, Science, and Technology, Washington DC.

Galasso, V. (1977). *Model program for developing creativity in science.* Washington, DC: U.S. Office of Education, Office of Gifted and Talented.

Gallagher, J. (1966). *Ethics and moral judgment in children: A pilot investigation.* Boston: Unitarian Universalist Association.

Harms, N., & Yager, R. (1981). *What research says to the science teacher* (Vol. 3). NSTA Monograph. Washington, DC.

Harré, R. (1981). *Great scientific experiments.* New York: Oxford University Press.

*High school: A report on American secondary education.* (1983). The Carnegie Foundation for the Advancement of Teaching, supported by the Atlantic Richfield Foundation and the Carnegie Corporation of New York.

Hilton, T. L., Hsia, J., Solorzano, D. G., & Benton, N. L. (1989). *Persistence in science of high-ability minority students.* Princeton, NJ: Educational Testing Service.

Holdzkom, D., & Lutz, P. B. (1984). *Research within reach: Scienced education.* Charleston, WV: Appalachia Educational Laboratory.

International Association for the Evaluation of Educational Achievement. (1988). *Science achievement in seventeen countries: A preliminary report.* Oxford: Pergamon Press.

Judson, H. (1979). *The eighth day of creation.* New York: Simon and Schuster.

Judson, H. (1980). *The search for solutions.* New York: Holt, Rinehart and Winston.

Klemm, W. R. (Ed.). (1977). *Discovery processes in modern biology.* Huntington, NY: Robert E. Krieger Publishing.

Klopfer, L. E. (1969). The teaching of science and the history of science. *Journal of Research in Science Teaching, 6,* 87–95.

Kuhn, T. (1970). *The structure of scientific revolutions.* Chicago: University of Chicago Press.

Lockard, J. D. (Ed.). (1977). *Twenty years of science and mathematics curriculum development: The tenth report of the international clearinghouse on science and mathematics curricular developments.* College Park, MD: The International Clearinghouse, Science Teaching Center, University of Maryland.

Lockwood, A. T. (1992). The defacto curriculum. *Focus in Change, 6,* 9–11.

Martin, K. (1979). Science and the gifted adolescent. *Roeper Review, 2* (2), 25–26.

National Assessment of Educational Progress. (1988). *Science learning matters.* Princeton, NJ: Educational Testing Service.

National Science Board Commission. (1983). *Educating Americans for the 21st century.* Washington, DC: National Science Foundation.

Rensberger, B. (1986). *How the world works.* New York: William Morrow & Company.

Rutherford, F., & Ahlgren, A. (1989). *Science for all Americans.* New York: Oxford University Press.

Shane, H. (1981). *A study of curriculum content for the future.* New York: College Entrance Examination Board.

Sher, B. (1993). *Guide to science concepts.* Williamsburg, VA: Center for Gifted Education.

Sternberg, R. J. (1982). Teaching scientific thinking to gifted children. *Roeper Review, 4* (4), 4–6.

Stevenson, H. W., & Sigler, J. W. (1992). *The learning gap: Why our schools are failing and what we can learn from Japanese and Chinese education.* New York: Summit Books.

VanTassel-Baska, J., Landau, M., & Olszewski, P. (1985). Toward developing an appropriate math/science curriculum for gifted learners. *Journal for the Education of the Gifted, 8* (4), 257–272.

VanTassel-Baska, J., et al. (1992). *Developing science curriculum for high ability learners.* Washington, DC: Department of Education.

Welch, W. (1984). *Proceedings from the National Institute of Education, National Conference on Science.* Washington, DC: National Institute of Education.

## Example 9.A A Science Unit on Change*

*Developed by Dr. Gerald Krockover*
*Purdue University*

### Introduction

Everyone makes many observations every day, but only a few people make scientific observations. Scientific observations are made to obtain information. With the information, the scientist attempts to answer questions raised by ideas using special procedures called experiments.

In an experiment, a scientist is interested in changes–before, during, and after the experiment has been conducted. Once it has been established that a change has occurred, the scientist is almost certain to be curious about what is responsible for the change.

This unit explores the differences between physical and chemical changes, the effect of change overtime, and identification of the components of an observed change.

### Primary

*Motivation:* Have students experiment with food coloring to make different colors. What combinations result in certain colors such as orange, purple, etc.?

*Objective:* Gifted students will be able to observe and distinguish between physical and chemical changes.

*Activities:*

**1.** Give students an ice cube and have them weigh and observe it. Record what happens to the ice cube after 1 minute, 5 minutes, 10 minutes, 50 minutes (or every 5 minutes for 50 minutes). What caused the ice cube to change? Collect the water from the melting ice cube and weigh it. Does the mass of the water equal the mass of the ice cube? Why or why not? Pour the water into a container and refreeze it. Does the mass of the "new" ice cube equal the mass of the original one? Why or why not? This is an example of a physical change. Design an experiment to illustrate a chemical change. Hint: what if the water evaporated?

**2.** Take a sheet of paper and cut off a corner. How has the paper changed? Put the paper back to its original shape. What other physical changes can be used to illustrate that it can be returned to the original state? Try crushing a can versus a sheet of paper or aluminum foil. Next try mixing finger paints. Mix yellow and red—what color results? Separate the resulting color back to red and yellow—if this cannot be done, is this an irreversible chemical change?

*Objective:* Gifted students will be able to identify the physical and chemical changes that occur in one's envirionment.

*Source:* Adapted from "A Guide for Teaching the Concept of Change in Science," by Gerald H. Krockover, Purdue University, West Lafayette, Indiana 47907. Adapted with permission.

*Activities:*

**1.** Have students select a deciduous tree to observe over a period of time. Have them prepare observation charts based upon the tree characteristics that they wish to observe. Point out that the observations should be quantified if at all possible. Variables that could be selected include: number of leaves, tree height, number of limbs of a certain size, tree girth, or leaf colors. Identify the changes (physical) that have taken place based upon the variable(s) selected. Prepare a graph of the variable used over time. Locate other physical changes that are related to the changes observed for the tree. What chemical changes can be identified for investigation. Why do leaves fall off some trees and not off others? What makes leaves fall off? Why don't leaves fall off evergreen trees?

**2.** Discuss what is needed for a plant to grow. Soak lima (either yellow or white) or mung beans overnight (clean first with a bleach solution). Place one dry and one wet seed on a paper towel. Observe the differences with a hand magnifying glass. Plant both seeds in separate cups. Set the cups in the sunlight and water them as required. Observe their growth. Record the growth pictorially or cut strips of paper to record the growth of the plant and glue the strips on construction paper each day. Next select a garden site, prepare it and decide upon the garden seeds to be used. Plant the seeds, care for the garden and observe its growth over time.

*Objective:* Gifted students will be able to observe and describe the changes that take place in organic material over time.

*Activities:*

**1.** Collect a series of photographs of famous movie or television stars over time (watch "Face the Music" to get the idea). Observe the photographs and try to identify the famous person. Why do physical changes take place as one gets "older"? Have children bring in a series of photographs of parents, grandparents, themselves, pets, etc., that show a change over time. What changes are most noticeable? Least noticeable? Next try products and how their advertisements have changed over time. Try Coke, Pepsi, or McDonalds. Have children illustrate how they will look when they are 10, 20, 30, 40, 50, 60, and 70 years old.

*Authentic Assessment*

**1.** Provide students with pictures that illustrate a sequence of events and have the students order the pictures. Try plant growth, seasons, or events.

**2.** Have the students design two experiments that illustrate change using an apple. One experiment should illustrate a physical change and the other experiment should illustrate a chemical change. Have them graph their results.

**3.** Provide pictures or samples of unpopped and popped corn, bread and toast, cake and cake dough, burned splint and unburned splint, etc. Have students match changed and unchanged materials and describe the properties changed. Then have the students prepare five of their own examples.

### *Intermediate*

*Motivation:* Have students select five objects that they think will change when water is added. Have them test their predictions.

*Objective:* Gifted students will be able to identify the physical and chemical changes that occur in one's environment; observe and describe the changes that take place in organic material over time; solve genetic problems involving single dominant recessive traits.

*Activities:*

**1.** Prepare a fruit fly culture. When it is one week old, have the students observe the larvae. The second week have the students observe the increase in population and the need for food refills. Record changes in the life cycle. Predict how many flies there will be by the fourth week. Make a fruit fly graph over a period of six weeks. Count the fruit flies by laying the glass vial containing the fruit flies on the overhead projector and projecting the image on a sampling grid drawn on the chalkboard. The record will probably show a population increase and decline over the six weeks. Have students identify habitat factors which cause change such as: sunlight, air, water, food, space, pollution, soil, etc. Identify factors which are necessary for the survival of the fruit fly, beans, dogs, people, frogs, etc. Using the fruit fly graph, discuss why the population decreased. Next relate the fruit fly experiment to the problem of endangered species. Discuss: Is man an endangered species? Why or why not?

**2.** These activities illustrate the fact that only some chemical changes can be reversed. Begin by pouring water into two small containers. Pour enough bromothymol blue into each container to get a strong blue color. Blow through a straw into one of the containers. The observation should be that the color changes to yellow or green. Infer why the color changes. Leave both containers overnight and compare the colors the next day. Both containers will be blue again—an example of a reversible chemical change.

Pour clear soda water into a container. Pour an equal amount of water into another container. Put several drops of bromothymol blue into each container. Note that the soda water turns yellow or green while the plain water turns blue. Find out what soda water contains that causes this chemical change. Is it the same material as that in the first experiment? Prove your answers.

To illustrate irreversible chemical changes weigh a sheet of paper on a gram scale or balance scale. Place the paper in a pie tin. Burn the paper (carefully and use caution) and weigh the remains. Observe the color, odor, texture, thickness, and mass of the product. Where did the lost mass go? Design an experiment to collect this lost mass.

Place an ordinary iron nail and a painted (use waterproof paint) iron nail into a clear container of water. Observe what happens for one week. Find out the chemical reaction that is taking place.

Place a ball of wet steel wool into a test tube. Invert the test tube in a tray of water that is only a few centimeters deep. Observe what happens to the water as the steel wool "rusts" over time. Graph the change in water level over time. Infer that the water has taken the place of something (oxygen in the air) which has combined with the steel wool to form "rust." Test the inference by placing a glowing splint into the test tube (a lack of oxygen will make the splint go out).

**3.** Test a number of household and school substances (Caution: make sure that they are safe to test) with litmus paper of pH Hydrion paper to determine whether the materials are acidic, basic, or neutral. Students should record the original color of the litmus paper and the materials used. It is a good idea to use only one drop of solution in the center of the litmus paper. Solids must be mixed with neutral (distilled) water. Have the students also try "homemade" indicators such as beet juice, cherry juice, grape juice or red cabbage juice. Add the juice (one teaspoon to a half glass of water) and note the color changes. Test all the foods eaten for a specific meal, Tums, Rolaids, aspirin, vitamins, etc.

Using an eyedropper as a titration, test how many drops of a certain combination are needed to make a solution neutral. Try lemon juice and baking soda; vinegar and soap; vinegar and household ammonia (use caution for the fumes); and orange juice and garden lime.

*Authentic Assessment:*

**1.** Collect photographs of people in a variety of environments such as: after earthquakes, in drought areas, crowded cities, etc. Discuss and predict what changes may happen to the future populations and why. Relate these changes to the fruit fly experiment.

**2.** Obtain brine shrimp eggs and prepare the brine shrimp water by placing tap water in a container and letting it stand for one day. Add about 30 ml of rock salt to 1 litre of water. Put 50 to 100 brine shrimp eggs into a vial of brine. Cap and observe for a few days. After 3 days, count the hatched brine shrimp by using a sampling technique. One sampling technique might be to place a clear plastic container over graph paper. Pour the content of the vial into the plastic container. Count the shrimp in one square of the graph paper and multiply by the number of squares covered. Record the data. Compare the number of hatched shrimp to the number of unhatched shrimp to determine a hatching ratio.

Then predict the change in the brine shrimp population when the environmental conditions are changed (heat in this case). Cut a circle (37 cm in diameter) out of stiff cardboard. Draw concentric circles at regular intervals from the center of the circle. Glue aluminum foil to the bottom side of the circle. Trim the edges. Cut the top off of a small cardboard box. Place a lamp with a 25 watt bulb in the box (observe caution when using this apparatus due to the heat developed). Cover with a coffee can which has had both top and bottom removed and holes punched along the ridges of the top and bottom (see figure).

Place the circle on top of the box. Place brine shrimp vials in various concentric circles. Record the number of shrimp hatched every day and from which circle they came. Thermometers can be used to measure the heat output at each location. (Note: keep tops on vials.) State conclusions based upon a graph of the data collected. Investigate the effect of factors other than heat upon brine shrimp such as: detergent, bleach, or ammonia. No brine shrimp? Try fruit flies or mealworms. What do brine shrimp eat? Try one grain of yeast per vial per day.,

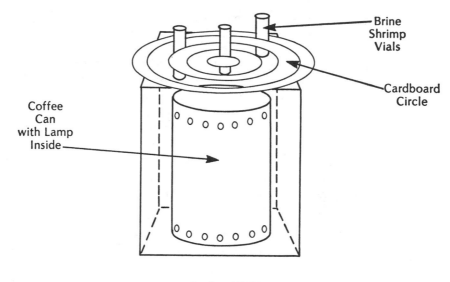

*Brine Shrimp Vials*

*Cardboard Circle*

*Coffee Can with Lamp Inside*

### *Junior High*

*Motivation:* Using litmus or pH paper, have the students classify common household items into acids or bases. Students could make predictions first and then record their observed results.

*Objective:* Gifted students will be able to observe and describe the changes that take place in organic material over time.

*Activities:*

**1.** Obtain a variety of seeds such as mung beans, lima beans, green beans, pumpkin, etc. Design an experiment to test the effect of the germination rate of seeds in a water and detergent combination using no phosphate and low phosphate detergents. Remember to use a control for the experiment and to identify the manipulated (independent) and responding (dependent) variables. Discuss the effect of detergents with and without phosphates upon the germination of primary producers in our ecosystem. Should phosphate be banned from all detergents used in the United States? Why or why not? Find out which states ban phosphates in detergents and which do not. Design a plan to change your state from its present stance.

**2.** Set up a culture of Daphnia (water fleas). Sample a preselected quantity at specific intervals, for example, one eyedropper full every 24 hours. Count the number of Daphnia to obtain an estimate of the population increase. Graph the results.

*Objective:* Gifted students will be able to record and organize weather data over a period of months.

*Activities:*

**1.** Recognize and organize weather data based upon the following variables: temperature, barometric pressure, precipitation, relative humidity, cloud type, wind speed and directions, and dew point. Prepare a weekly weather observation chart to observe the weather for one month using the above variables. Then design the weather instruments needed to measure the variables stated above. Once data are recorded, students should draw inferences related to the relationship between weather changes and *each* of the above variables. To illustrate some of the weather observation techniques students should visit the nearest office of the National Weather Service to learn how weather data is received and so that they can learn to read surface weather maps and teletype printouts. Furthermore, students can check their weather data by using a NOAA Weather Radio. A subscription for the monthly weather data for your area from NOAA should also be purchased.

Students should prepare their own weather reports including extended weekend forecasts. All measurements should be made in both the Imperial and metric systems of measurement. If only one measurement system is used, it should be the metric system.

*Activities:*

**1.** Construct a material tester by using a light bulb in a socket (use caution) set at a fixed distance from a slot into which materials can be placed. Use equal area and thickness squares of different materials such as fiberglass, wood, and ceiling tile. Construct a thermometer holder so that it can be placed against the tile at the same spot for each test. Test the temperature change when the light bulb is turned on for a specific period of time such as one or two minutes. Test the effect of thickness and air space. Test the effect of color by using the same material painted different colors.

Then design experiments to measure sound conductivity through different materials and/or heat conservation in a home.

*Objective:* Gifted students will be able to identify the components of a characteristic property for a given material.

*Activities:*

**1.** Obtain marble chips, iron filings, and lead shot or equivalent substitutes. Prepare a data table similar to the following one for each of the three materials previously stated:

*Marble Chips*

*Mass, grams*_____*Volume, millilitres*

Weigh six samples of marble chips and then record the corresponding volume displacement. Use a graduated cylinder and read an initial water volume and then a final water volume with the marble chips immersed in the water. The difference in water level is the volume of the marble chips. Repeat this for six samples of iron filings and for six samples of lead shot.

Graph the resultant data using one pencil color for marble chips, another for lead shot, and a third color for iron filings. Use the x-axis for volume (ml) and the y-axis for mass (g). Note that each material data set falls into a certain area of the graph. Calculate the slope of each line drawn for each of the three materials used,

|  | $\dfrac{Y\ (g)}{X\ (ml)}$ |
|---|---|
| Marble Chips | 2.9 |
| Iron Filings | 6.8 |
| Lead Shot | 10.8 |

The accepted values are given above for comparison. The ratio of mass to volume that we have used is called the *density* of an object. This experiment illustrates that density is independent of the amount of material involved. Thus, changing the amount of material does not change its density. This property of a material is called a characteristic property. Other characteristic properties which could be investigated include: color, odor, hardness, electric conductivity, and ability to flow. Mass and volume, on the other hand, are properties of a material which can change from one object to another.

Is temperature a characteristic property? Why or why not? Try graphing water temperature (y-axis) to find out. Start with an ice cube and stop when the water is boiling. Did you find out that temperature is both? The characteristic property part of temperature is that part between the melting point of a solid and the boiling point of a liquid called the liquid range.

*Authentic Assessment:*

**1.** Design and conduct an experiment to determine whether or not plasticene clay (nonwater soluable) can be used to demonstrate the characteristic property of density.

## *References for Example 9.A*

Bainbridge, J. W., et al. *Weather Study: An Approach to Scientific Inquiry,* Methuen Educational Limited, 11 New Fetter Lane, London EC4, England, 1972.

Berger, Gilda and Melvin Berger. *Fitting In: Animals in Their Habitats,* Coward McCann and Geoghegan, 200 Madison Avenue, New York, NY, 10016, 1976.

Crocker, Robert K. *Elementary Science Curriculum Study,* Volumes 1 and 2, McGraw-Hill-Ryerson Limited, Toronto, Canada, 1973.

*Crustal Evolution Education Project Modules,* Wards Natural Science Establishment, Rochester, NY, 1980.

Davis, Hubert, ed. *A January Fog Will Freeze a Hog and Other Weather Folklore,* Crown Publishers, One Park Avenue, New York, NY, 10016, 1977.

DeVito, A. and Krockover, Gerald H. *Activities Handbook for Teaching Energy Education,* Goodyear Publishing Company, Santa Monica, CA, 1981.

DeVito, A. and Krockover, Gerald H. *Creative Sciencing: Ideas and Activities for Teachers and Children,* Second Edition, Little Brown and Company, Inc., Boston, 1980.

Elementary Science Study Unit on *Change,* Webster Division, McGraw-Hill Book Company, New York, NY, 1976.

*Growth Implications and the Earth's Future,* Education Development Center, 55 Chapel Street, Newton, MA, 02160, 1977.

Hounshell, Paul B. and Ira R. Trollinger. *Games for the Science Classroom,* National Science Teachers Association, 1742 Connecticut Avenue, N.W., Washington, DC, 20009, 1977.

Intermediate Science Curriculum Study, *Investigating Variation Minicourse,* Silver Burdett Company, Morristown, NJ, 1977. (also *Winds and Weather Minicourse,* 1977).

Lawrence Hall of Science, *Outdoor Biology Instructional Strategies,* University of California, Berkeley, CA, 1976.

*New UNESCO Source Book for Science Teaching,* UNIPUB, Inc., 650 First Avenue, New York, NY, 10017, 1973.

Pringle, Lawrence. *Death is Natural,* Four Winds Press, 50 West 44th Street, New York, NY, 10036, 1977.

Sagan, Carl. *The Dragons of Eden,* Ballatine Books, New York, NY, 1978.

*Think About,* Agency for Instructional Television, Box A, Bloomington, IN, 47402, 1979. (Sixty 15-minute color programs)

Troyer, Donald L., et al. *Sourcebook for Biological Sciences,* Macmillan, Inc., 866 Third Avenue, New York, NY, 10022, 1972.

Utgard, Russell O., et al. *Sourcebook for Earth Sciences and Astronomy,* Macmillan, Inc., 866 Third Avenue, New York, NY, 10022, 1972.

Wentworth, Daniel F. et al., *Examining Your Environment Series.* Toronto: Holt, Rinehart and Winston of Canada, Limited, 1976.

Wichers, David and John Tuey. *How to Make Things Grow,* Van Nostrand Reinhold Books, 120 Alexander Street, Princeton, NJ, 08450, 1972.

Wichers, David and John Tuey. *How to Be a Scientist At Home,* Van Nostrand Reinhold Books, 120 Alexander Street, Princeton NJ, 08450, 1971.

# Chapter 10

# Mathematics Curriculum for the Gifted

*DANA T. JOHNSON*

*I do not know what I may appear to the world, but to myself I seem to have been only like a boy playing on the seashore, now and then finding a smoother pebble or a prettier shell than ordinary, while the great ocean of truth lay all un-discovered before me.—ISAAC NEWTON*

Recent reports from the National Assessment of Educational Progress (NAEP) tell us that students in the United States are woefully behind students in other countries in science and mathematics performance (NAEP, 1988). This is due in part to the fact that schools in this country have moved toward heterogeneous grouping models as part of an emphasis on social and personal development as opposed to academic achievement (Gallagher, 1991). Many bright students are suffering frustration and boredom as a result of nonchallenging mathematical work (Vance, 1983). Boredom and lack of academic challenges will hinder progress toward the national goal of first-place status in mathematics and science by the year 2000. Even though curriculum for all learners needs attention in light of reform efforts, differentiated experiences for mathematically gifted learners should be even more carefully considered because of the unique needs and extraordinary potential of this group.

Much debate has taken place about the relative merits of acceleration (providing higher-level concepts sooner) versus enrichment (more detail and breadth) with no definitive conclusion. The discussion is especially relevant to mathematics education because of the sequential nature of skills taught, thus making acceleration an apropriate option. Proponents argue that acceleration allows the gifted to learn more efficiently

(Feldhusen, Proctor, & Black, 1986), increases effectiveness (Davis & Rimm, 1988), and exposes gifted students to a new group of peers (Clark, 1988). Despite the consistent research that supports acceleration for the gifted (Kulik & Kulik, 1984; Brody & Benbow, 1987), practitioners often view it as a practice that can be potentially hazardous to the social and emotional adjustment of students (Southern, Jones, & Fiscus, 1989). Renzulli (1977) has favored an enrichment model that takes advantage of students' interests and preferred learning styles. Worcester (1979) suggested that enrichment has obvious value but cautions that busywork is sometimes confused with enrichment. Stanley (1980) suggested that acceleration and enrichment are not mutually exclusive as "properly conducted acceleration tends to be enriching, and appropriate enrichment is deliberately accelerative" (p. 9). The needs of individual students as well as groups must be considered in planning mathematics curriculum for the gifted; thus, a combination of approaches is necessary.

## Goals for a Differentiated Program for Gifted Learners in Mathematics

Programs for the gifted often emphasize creativity or general thinking skills without attention to specific content domains. Stanley (1980) suggested that creativity should be handled through subject areas. Learners who are gifted in mathematics require special attention within the mathematics classroom. An appropriate program for these students should adopt the following goals:

1. *To provide a context for gifted students to learn as much as possible about mathematical concepts, ideas, and skills.* Since gifted students have the capacity to learn more than is usually presented in standard courses, adjustments in curriculum must be made.
2. *To prepare mathematically gifted students to be creative and independent thinkers.* Mathematics provides an environment for stimulating creative thought and developing the high potential of these students to become problem solvers of the highest caliber.
3. *To help mathematically gifted students appreciate the beauty of mathematics.* Through its study, gifted learners are more likely than other students to comprehend, value, and find meaning in mathematics as the study of patterns and as the language of the universe.

Appropriate adjustments in mathematics curriculum for gifted students is essential to reaching these goals. Opportunities for these students to develop their talents usually do not arise spontaneously in their environment and need to be provided through careful consideration and planning on the part of educators who are responsible for curriculum development. Special attention should be given to those students who possess extraordinary talents even among the gifted population.

A combination of approaches is needed in order to reach the preceding goals. Figure 10–1 expresses the relationship of these goals to the three curriculum models outlined in Chapter 1.

**Figure 10–1    The Relationship of Program Goals and Curriculum Models for Mathematically Gifted Learners**

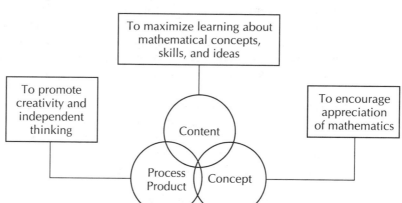

## *Using the Content Model to Organize Mathematics Curriculum*

Appropriate curriculum and instruction for mathematically gifted learners cannot be delivered only through a supplemental program or enrichment materials. The core curriculum for these students must be modified so that the daily exposure to mathematics is more closely aligned with their abilities. In the elementary grades, it is estimated that more than half of the material included in a basal mathematics curriculum is review (Hirschhorn, 1986). For a mathematically gifted student, this can be agony. There are a number of ways to remedy this.

The most typical modification of mathematics curriculum for high-ability learners is acceleration. Acceleration can be done in several ways. A frequent model is the one in which a student is placed in the course for the next higher grade level (a linear shift). However, if the curriculum material is not altered significantly in pace or depth, it will not meet the needs of high-ability students.

Through faster pacing, students are sometimes permitted to move through the standard mathematics curriculum in a shorter period of time. Appropriate pacing can be aided by using a diagnostic testing procedure to assess what students already know and proceeding with only those skills and concepts that remain unmastered (Stanley, 1980; Lupkowski, Assouline, & Stanley, 1990). A good rule of thumb for gifted students is that two years of standard content can be covered in one year (VanTassel-Baska, Landau, & Olszewski, 1985). Compacting of a particular course can be accomplished, thereby allowing more time either for additional enrichment topics or for moving on to the next year's work. Within an acceleration model, students may complete all math courses in the school before their senior year. It is imperative that these students not be allowed to give up the study of mathematics. Rather, an arrangement should be made for coursework at a local college or for working with a mentor.

Mathematically gifted learners exhibit characteristics such as speed in reasoning and ability to form comprehensive generalizations (Krutetskii, 1976; Heid, 1983). Research suggests that mathematically gifted students reach the formal operations stage of reasoning in mathematics earlier than other students (Feldman, 1982). There is some support for the practice of acceleration in mathematics at all levels of instruction.

Although the National Council of Teachers of Mathematics (NCTM) is supportive of acceleration, it is much more conservative about the number of students who might benefit from it. The NCTM policy statement on vertical acceleration (1983) recommends

> *that vertical acceleration be considered only for a limited number of highly talented and mathematically creative students whose interest and attitudes clearly indicate that they have the ability and perseverance to complete a carefully designed sequential curriculum. For all but this select group, a strong, expanded program emphasizing mathematics enrichment is preferable.*

Yet, more recent work on cooperative learning and grouping gifted students encourages the use of acceleration with gifted students as the preferred model of curricular differentiation (Slavin, 1990). No studies indicate that acceleration is harmful, and many demonstrate that it is beneficial (Southern, Jones, & Fiscus, 1989).

Appropriately chosen curriculum materials for gifted learners will greatly enhance their learning experiences. Traditionally, textbooks have been the main teaching materials. Good materials should avoid an emphasis on rote learning and memory-recall questions; rather, they should emphasize higher-order thinking skills (analysis, synthesis, and evaluation). Presentation of new concepts should be thorough enough to represent real depth of content. Possibilities for extensions should be included. Since textbooks will not provide all of the desired features, teachers will have to seek out other materials as supplements or be prepared to write some of their own.

The core content of a course in mathematics can be modified through enrichment. This can be (1) enrichment of the course with additional topics or (2) in-depth study of course concepts. The first is done more easily in courses prior to algebra due to relative flexibility in curriculum content. Hersberger and Wheatley (1980) argued that the heavy computational emphasis in elementary school math classes can be replaced by inclusion of topics such as probability, statistics, problem solving with a computer, and spatial visualization; these topics are not usually available in most precollege curricula. In Algebra I and higher-level courses, where there is less flexibility in terms of course topics, enrichment can be done primarily within the course as the content lends itself to infusion of more rigor and emphasis on higher-order thinking skills. For example, in the high school geometry course, an in-depth unit on non-Euclidean geometries should be included. In other more standard chapters, challenging problems should be favored over the routine ones and proofs should be included. When standard mathematics content in a high school course is addressed at a fast pace and at a suitably complex level of thought, it can be an enriching experience for the gifted learner without the introduction of supplementary topics.

Manipulatives should also be used as an integral part of mathematics learning for gifted students. Difficult puzzles such as the Chinese Ring puzzle and the Tower of Hanoi will appeal to and challenge many gifted learners. Hands-on activities should be used with open-ended problems, such as the geoboard activity described in Figure 10–2.

**Figure 10–2    Area on a Geoboard**

*Objective:* Students will find the area of a polygon (constructed on a geoboard) for which the lengths of the sides are not known.

*Activity:*

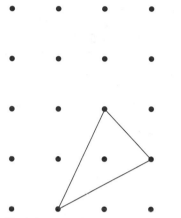

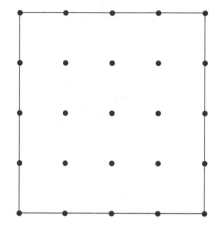

1. Find the area of this triangle. Describe how you arrived at your solution.

2. Inscribe a square inside the square above or on a geoboard. Find the ratio of the area of the inscribed square to the area of the original square. Compare your results to those of your classmates. Discuss any possible generalizations.

**Extension**

*Objective:* Students will generate a formula for finding the area of any polygon that is constructed on a geoboard based on the number of pegs on the perimeter and the number of pegs in the interior of the polygon.

*Activity:* Working in a small group, make polygons on a geoboard. Collect the appropriate data in the table below. See if you can write a formula that gives the area of the polygon as a function of the number of pegs that lie on the perimeter and the number of pegs in the interior of the polygon.

| Polygon | No. of pegs on perimeter | No. of pegs in interior | Area |
|---|---|---|---|
|  |  |  |  |

## *Exemplary Programs That Use the Content Model*

A model program that is exemplary in its use of acceleration, compression, and a diagnostic-prescriptive approach is the Center for Talented Youth (CTY) program of the Johns Hopkins University and replications of that model at other university-based programs (Moore & Wood, 1988). Students who have previously scored in the top 3 percent on any standardized test may take the SAT at the January testing date of their seventh-grade year. A math score ≥500, along with a combined score ≥930, or a verbal score ≥430 and a Test of Standard Written English score ≥35 makes a student eligible to register for a three-week summer program at a number of colleges on the East coast, in California, or in Switzerland. Among the course offerings is the Precalculus Mathematics Sequence, which is designed to allow students to study mathematics at an individual pace. It employs a diagnostic test to assess the appropriate starting point for each student within Algebra I, Algebra II, Algebra III, Geometry, Trigonometry, and Analytic Geometry. Most students complete the equivalent of one year of high school mathematics in a three-week summer session (*CTY Summer Program Bulletin, 1992*).

An example of an elementary program that is based on the content model is the Individual Progress Program (IPP) that was developed in the Seattle Public Schools. Gifted students study mathematics, language arts, and reading through an accelerated and individualized curriculum. Students are given a diagnostic test at the beginning of each school year to determine placement levels in each subject. They accelerate through the subject at a pace that is comfortable for them.

## Using the Process/Product Model to Organize Mathematics Curriculum

The process/product model of curriculum involves not only mathematical processes but also others such as organizational and research skills. The teaching of content is not the goal of this model; rather, it emphasizes problem finding and solving and product development. Problem finding is cited by Sternberg (1982) as a characteristic that distinguishes gifted scientists who make significant contributions to their fields; he has advocated the teaching of scientific thinking to gifted children in anticipation of their roles in future careers. In the process/product model, student interest influences project choice and direction. Work can be done cooperatively in small groups, individually, or under the direction of a mentor.

This model works well for implementing enrichment topics that supplement core content in cases where mathematically gifted students are pulled out of regular class for enrichment or are enrolled in a self-contained program. Several examples of project ideas include the following:

- *Researching the history of a mathematical idea*
- *Learning to make Escher-type drawings*
- *Computer modeling of a student-generated problem*
- *Analyzing and inventing mathematical games or puzzles*
- *Studying conic section applications in astronomy*
- *Constructing and studying applications of spirals*
- *Investigating mathematical patterns in string designs*
- *Looking for examples of mathematical sequences that occur in nature*

### Exemplary Programs That Use the Process/Product Model

An example of a model curriculum of the process/product type is *The Challenge of the Unknown*. This is a video-based problem-solving curriculum that features examples of real-world problem solvers, many of whom are scientists or who use the skills commonly associated with scientific endeavors. The program can be used with students as young as grade 3 but as old as high school age. References are provided for further background of a topic and activities are suggested in an accompanying teacher's guide. The problems presented are highly motivational for pursuit of further individual or cooperative problems that exhibit similar properties. Examples of extension projects are the study of fractals, design and implementation of a school census as a model of a national census, and the study of vectors in relation to a building demolition problem.

The following elements of exemplary curriculum for the mathematically gifted are included in the *Challenge* program: problem solving as a focus; interdisciplinary features, including mathematical modeling; use of technology (video, examples of computer modeling such as fractals); a high level of abstraction of concepts in problem solving; and identification of new problems in terms of the seven types identified in the program (situation, information, restatement, outcomes, management, estimation, and argument).

In the section of *The Challenge of the Unknown* that deals with *restatement* problems, which includes modeling, the students view a video segment about a paleontologist who has attempted to determine the running speed of various dinosaurs by using a mathematical model that was developed by British biologist R. McNeill Alexander. The model is a formula that uses stride length and hip height as variables. Figure 10–3 includes an activity for elementary students is based on that portion of the *Challenge* program.

## Figure 10–3   Modeling the Running Speed of Students

*Objective:* To evaluate the Alexander model for computing the running speed of animals by comparing actual speeds of students to those predicted by the model.

*Activity:*

1. Give each student a head start to get up full speed, and clock how long it takes to run 100 meters. Calculate the actual running speed, $R$, using the $D = RT$ formula.

2. Find the average stride length, $s$, for each student. Find the hip height, $h$ (from hip bone to floor).

3. Use the Alexander formula, $v = \dfrac{.78s^{1.67}}{h^{1.17}}$, and a calculator to

   calculate the prediction that the formula makes for each person's speed.

4. Graph the set of all pairs $(R,v)$. If the formula is perfect, all points will lie on the line $R = v$.

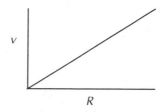

5. What can you conclude about Alexander's formula based on your data? What could you do to check it further? Imagine that you are in charge of Model Verification for the government Great Ideas in Math and Science office. Write a report evaluating the Alexander model.

## Using the Concept Model to Organize Mathematics Curriculum

A third model for organizing curriculum in mathematics is the concept model. It uses themes or key ideas as organizers for areas of study. Traditionally, mathematics curriculum has been selected and arranged according to content, which is most often presented in cookbook fashion with a "recipe" or formula and emphasizes basic skills. An advantage of the concept model is that it tends to emphasize abstract concepts and modes of thinking. It is interdisciplinary in its orientation and helps students appreciate the workings of mathematical ideas.

Some examples of themes as organizers might include the following:

- *Proof.* This includes deductive, inductive, and indirect proofs. A unit on proof can be intradisciplinary, including algebra (prove that $0.9999 \ldots = 1$), geometry, number theory, topology (the four-color problem as an example of computer verification), and calculus (prove that the sum of the series $\frac{1}{2} + \frac{1}{4} + \frac{1}{8} + \ldots$ is 1). The history of famous theorems can be studied; the famous unsolved conjectures can be posed. An example is Goldbach's Conjecture, made in 1742, which suggests that every even integer greater than two is the sum of two primes.
- *Patterns in nature.* Some examples are spirals in shells and pine cones, planetary motion, flower petal arrangements, and weather patterns.
- *Space.* For example, tesselations can be studied and drawn in the second dimension. Archimedean solids can be constructed. The story of *Flatland* (Abbott, 1952) can be used to discuss multidimensional perspectives.
- *Mathematical models.* The real number system can be modeled. Examples from applications of math are modeling the running speed of dinosaurs and economic models expressed in terms of algebra. A sample activity that invites students to design a model is described in Figure 10–4.
- *Systems.* Systems may include the study of modular number systems, ancient number systems, and number systems with bases other than ten. For secondary students, an introduction to groups, fields, and rings can be used.
- *Problem solving.* Figure 10–5 includes a sample of an activity that was written for a unit on problem solving. It does not deal with specific content, but instead allows for a wide range of possibilities for solving variations of the problem.

### Exemplary Programs That Use the Concept Model

The Unified Modern Mathematics program (Fehr et al., 1972) is an example of a concept model program. It is a middle school to high school program that does not separate mathematical branches such as algebra and geometry but rather integrates them.

Another example is *Mathematics: A Human Endeavor* (Jacobs, 1982), which is a textbook that is organized under the conceptual framework of appreciation of mathematics rather than the teaching of skills. The first chapter in the book is called "Mathematical Ways of Thinking" and includes not only inductive and deductive reasoning but also discusses the patterns of movement on a billiards table. Some of the other chapters are

**Figure 10–4   The Three Door Quiz Show Problem**

Here is an example of a problem that will generate many interesting results from students. It involves math as science as well as probability and modeling.

*Objectives:* (1) Students will design a model that will assist in solving a problem. (2) Students will clarify assumptions in a problem and investigate how any changes in assumptions can change the solution to the problem. (3) Students will compute the probability of an outcome.

Marilyn Vos Savant (who supposedly has the highest IQ of anyone in the United States) was asked this question in her "Ask Marilyn" column in *Parade Magazine* that is included in many Sunday newspapers. "Suppose you're on a game show, and you're given the choice of three doors. Behind one door is a car; behind the others, goats. You pick a door, say No. 1, and the host, who knows what's behind the doors, opens another door, say No. 3, which has a goat. He then says to you, 'Do you want to pick door No. 2?' Is it to your advantage to switch your choice?"

Marilyn claimed the correct answer was "Yes." Following publication of this problem, the columnist was swamped with letters, some from mathematicians, that said she was wrong. Was she?

1. Support your answer with a written explanation. State any assumptions that you made about the conditions of the problem.
2. State the probabilities that you will be right if you switch and wrong if you switch.
3. If you change your assumptions, how is your conclusion changed?
4. Design and implement a model that will verify your conclusion. Summarize and communicate your results to the class.

Marilyn responded in her column several times and eventually encouraged her readers to experiment with three cups and a coin. She kept track of the responses and reported, "From academic institutions, about 71% now believe you should switch, compared with only 35% before. Many of them commented that it altered their thinking dramatically, especially about the state of mathematical education in this country" (*Parade,* July 7, 1991, p. 29).

---

entitled "Number Sequences," "Symmetry and Regular Figures," and "Methods of Counting." The topics included in each chapter are related to the real world. Jacobs communicates enthusiam for all ideas presented. This book would be appropriate for use with middle school gifted learners. Figure 10–6 is an example of an activity that comes from a chapter on counting.

## *Key Issues in a Program for Gifted Learners in Mathematics*

There are several key issues that should be considered in developing a mathematics program for gifted learners. The first of these is the scope of content covered, which must be as broad as possible. In the elementary grades, most mathematics content in standard courses is focused on arithmetic and often emphasizes drill and practice. Middle and high school courses do not often go beyond minimum state standards. Textbooks are usually organized with the most interesting material at the end, which is reached by few teachers. This is not appropriate for mathematically gifted learners who are capable of and usually interested in doing much more.

The following emphases should be included in the years before the study of algebra by weaving them throughout the mathematics curriculum:

## Figure 10–5  Krypto

The game of Krypto is a card game that uses a deck of cards numbered 1–25 (three each of cards 1–10, two each of cards 11–17, and one each of cards 18–25). A hand of five cards is dealt, then a sixth card that serves as a target number is dealt. The object of the game is to use all five cards in any order combined with any of the operations of addition, subtraction, multiplication, and/or division to obtain a result that is given by the number on the target card. Solutions may not be unique. Some hands may be unsolvable (packaging indicates this is the case in about 1/3,000 hands).

*Example*: Hand dealt:  | 5 | | 12 | | 3 | | 7 | | 20 |

Target card:  | 2 |

*Possible solution:* $12 \div (3 \times 7 - 20 + 5)$

*Objectives:*
1. Students will practice mental arithmetic skills.
2. Students will write Krypto solutions in correct algebraic notation.

*Activities:*
1. Play Krypto with a partner or small group. Call "Krypto" when you think you have a solution, then present it orally. Keep track of how many hands you win.
2. If your partner or group agrees that your solution is valid, write it out in correct algebraic notation.
3. Deal a five-card hand. Do not deal a target card. Number a sheet of paper from 1 to 25 and use each of these numbers as a target. Write out all solutions in correct notation.

*Extensions:*
1. Consider the following theorem about Krypto. Try it on 10 hands and see if you think it works. Can you prove that it works?

$S$ = the sum of the 5 cards in the hand
$T$ = the value of the target card

A Krypto hand is solvable using only the operations addition and subtraction if and only if (the parity of $S$) = (the parity of $T$) and $(S - T)/2$ can be obtained by addition of some subset of the 5 cards.
2. Write a computer program to generate Krypto hands.
3. Design and carry out a Krypto tournament for your class.
4. How do you think the developers of the game concluded that about 1 in every 3,000 hands is unsolvable?

- *Problem solving.* The entire mathematics curriculum should function under the umbrella of problem solving, particularly including examples of real-world and interdisciplinary applications.
- *Estimation.* A unit each year would be appropriate, while estimation should be encouraged in all computational work throughout the year.
- *Mental arithmetic.* The use of mental arithmetic requires deep understanding of number relationships rather than mechanical algorithms. This skill should be encouraged continuously beginning in the preschool years.
- *Spatial visualization.* A short unit should be included every year with special materials and problems available in learning centers for self-paced exploration.

**Figure 10–6  Telephone Wires**

The Bell Telephone companies use a color code to keep track of the wires in their cables. The cables contain 50 wires, each of which is coded with two colors. The two colors appear as stripes on the wires: one color as a wide stripe and the other as a narrow one. The list below shows the colors of the wires with the color of the wide stripe listed first. Can you figure out the system by which the colors are paired? If so, what is it and why are there exactly 50 possibilities according to the system?

| | | |
|---|---|---|
| 1. blue-white | 18. blue-yellow | 35. gray-black |
| 2. gray-yellow | 19. black-gray | 36. black-brown |
| 3. black-blue | 20. white-orange | 37. white-green |
| 4. orange-purple | 21. brown-purple | 38. green-purple |
| 5. green-purple | 22. gray-white | 39. red-blue |
| 6. yellow-orange | 23. orange-red | 40. blue-red |
| 7. brown-black | 24. purple-green | 41. red-green |
| 8. orange-white | 25. brown-yellow | 42. gray-red |
| 9. red-orange | 26. orange-yellow | 43. green-red |
| 10. blue-black | 27. yellow-brown | 44. green-black |
| 11. white-gray | 28. red-brown | 45. blue-purple |
| 12. purple-orange | 29. purple-blue | 46. red-gray |
| 13. brown-white | 30. yellow-green | 47. purple-gray |
| 14. white-blue | 31. black-green | 48. white-brown |
| 15. black-orange | 32. brown-red | 49. gray-purple |
| 16. yellow-blue | 33. yellow-gray | 50. orange-black |
| 17. green-yellow | 34. purple-brown | |

*Source:* From *Mathematics: A Human Endeavor* by Harold Jacobs. Copyright © 1982 by W. H. Freeman and Company. Reprinted with permission.

- *Computational skills with fractions, decimals, and integers.* These are basic skills that are essential for work with many higher-level concepts. Proficiency should be required but not belabored in emphasis.

The following emphases are more topical in nature and can be treated in discrete units:

- *Percent.* Mathematically gifted students should be introduced to percents by third grade. They should be reinforced through relevant applications with absolute proficiency assured by seventh grade.
- *Geometry.* A unit on geometry should be included each year. Variations should include transformational, plane, solid, and coordinate geometries.
- *Computer programming.* Types of programming such as LEGO Logo should be introduced in the primary grades. By fourth grade, a unit on BASIC programming should be taught with extended topics in the following years.
- *Number theory.* Introductory topics such as prime numbers may be taught in the primary grades with a thorough treatment around sixth grade.
- *Probability and statistics.* Major units should be covered in the two years preceding Algebra I.
- *Structure and properties of the real number system.* Some elements of the real number system are presented through the introduction of whole numbers, fractions,

and decimals in the early grades. However, a very thorough unit emphasizing the concept of a system should be included along with the teaching of irrational numbers in the year before algebra.

A key component necessary in a curriculum for gifted learners is greater depth of content and higher level of complexity combined with abstraction of concepts. The level of challenge should be sufficiently high, both in curriculum content and in assessment instruments. Assessments should not necessarily expect 100 percent proficiency (the ceiling effect) but perhaps could assign the highest possible grade for 80 to 90 percent proficiency. This would assist students in stretching their thought processes. However, this may require some modification in the grading system of a school where a rigid grading scale may be in effect. In standard mathematical content, abstraction is often overlooked in favor of a straightforward definition, formula, or shortcut. Elementary mathematics classes focus primarily on computation and rote procedures. More depth needs to be infused to sufficiently challenge the gifted. For example, students are taught for many years that addition is a commutative operation, but the presentation is at the level of a fact or vocabulary item. An appropriate extension for gifted learners to the development of commutativity and other properties would be to present the students with an abstract operation and system of elements such as the one given in Figure 10–7.

Another element in an exemplary mathematics program for gifted learners is a discovery orientation that allows for exploration of concepts. Students should build understanding for themselves or construct it (Wheatley, 1988). While this is desirable for all students, it is essential for the gifted, as they will be more likely to extend this discovery process beyond the boundaries of the classroom assignment. Gifted students often discover atypical algorithms and/or solutions that are mathematically sound and are personally meaningful; students should be encouraged to individualize skills and processes. Hersberger and Wheatley (1980) suggested a flexible grading system for classwork and homework so that exploration and divergent thought are encouraged. Gifted students also are more likely to see relationships on their own without direct instruction from the teacher or text. Concepts that are internalized in this way are more likely to be retained in the long term. For example, when $\pi$ is first introduced, students should be given a large collection of circular objects and told to investigate the relationship between the circumference and the diameter of any circle. They should be expected to write up their data and conclusions in a report.

**Figure 10–7   An Abstract Problem on Properties**

| Δ | A | B | C | D | |
|---|---|---|---|---|---|
| A | C | B | A | D | 1. Is operation Δ commutative? |
| B | B | A | D | C | Explain your answer. |
| C | A | D | C | B | 2. Is there an identity element for |
| D | D | C | B | A | operation Δ? How do you know? |

A fourth key element of curriculum for the mathematically gifted is a focus on problem solving. Appropriate problem solving for the mathematically gifted provides opportunities for higher-order thinking skills in a context of real-world, interdisciplinary applications. Nonstandard problems should be used to replace and/or supplement the usual textbook variety. Problems from contests such as Mathematical Olympiads (for sixth grade and under) and the American High School Mathematics Examinations are a good source of nonstandard problems. However, they tend to be abstract in nature. For example, if *A, B, C,* and *D* represent different digits and *(ABC)(D)* = 1771, what number is *ABC?* Inclusion of real-world problems is desirable but sources are not as abundant. There is a need for curriculum development in this area.

A number of open-ended problems should be included. These problems may have multiple solutions or many paths to a unique answer may exist. Students should be encouraged to find problems in their environment (or their minds) and attempt to solve them. They need to get to the point where they can wonder about a problem or relationship, formulate the problem, and generate a solution.

A fifth key element is a metacognitive approach to solving problems. The Polya problem-solving model (Polya, 1971) is helpful in organizing thought processes for solving mathematical problems: (1) understand the problem, (2) make a plan to solve it, (3) carry out the plan, and (4) look back to evaluate the process and the solution. Exemplary curriculum for the gifted should emphasize the question, How did you arrive at that conclusion? Both oral and written expressions of those answers should be included. The "Gifted Decks" of the *Techniques of Problem Solving* cards (Greenes, Immerzeel et al., 1980) provide an excellent source of appropriate problems for this purpose in elementary or early secondary grades. They can be used by individuals or in small groups, and/or can be placed in learning centers. The level of challenge can be adjusted to suit the learner.

A final element that should be included in curriculum for the mathematically gifted is interdisciplinary connections. There are a number of ways that mathematics can be connected to other disciplines. Some examples include the following:

- *Since mathematics is considered by some to be the "queen" of the sciences, the processes of science are relevant to the study of mathematics. The process of observing, forming a hypothesis (often called a conjecture), and experimentation is also commonly done in mathematics. This can be done in relation to theoretical mathematical ideas. This process could be used to investigate the following question: Given an integer,* n, *what is the greatest possible divisor that must be checked to determine whether* n *is a prime number? Such a technique also incorporates the notion of allowing learners to discover truth for themselves.*
- *Here is a real-world example: In the grocery store, is it better to get in a long line at the "express" cashier or a short line with many items in the carts? To answer this question, students need to observe, hypothesize, collect data, display data, draw conclusions, and revise the hypothesis. Math projects of this type should also be encouraged as science fair entries.*
- *The relationship of mathematics to science is symbiotic. Science can be a great motivator to the development of mathematical ideas. Mathematics is an essential and powerful tool that enables science to function as it does. Many of the new curriculum projects capture this relationship (GEMS: Great Explorations in Math and Science,*

*AIMS: Activities in Math and Science, TIMS· Teaching Integrated Math and Science). Some of the science curriculum projects from the 1960s, such as the Elementary Science Study (ESS) and Science—A Process Approach (SAPA), heavily integrate mathematics into their programs. All students should be required to support their scientific study with mathematical skills. However, this can be done with gifted learners even more extensively, and modeling can be a powerful tool. For example, population growth can be modeled; on a primary level this could entail diagrams, whereas older students could provide an exponential function model. Formulas should not merely be handed to students but should be developed or "discovered" by them to suit the problem at hand.*

- *To round out the skills of a student who excels in mathematics, it is essential to develop oral and written communication skills. The demands of the workplace in the twenty-first century will require them. For decades (perhaps centuries) in this country, students have submitted written answers to math problems. Beyond basic arithmetic problems, the emphasis should be on solutions that spell out the reasoning behind the answers. In addition, precision and clarity should be the standard. Sound curriculum materials are needed to model this practice. In addition, oral presentation should be required of less routine problems. Students should be expected to use correct mathematical terminology comfortably. Classroom activities and assessments should include writing about mathematical ideas.*

- *Biographies of the men and women of mathematics and science can serve as role models to students who have these talents. Certain stories from the history of mathematics can be inspirational for any student, but would be especially appreciated by those who have an interest in and understanding of mathematical ideas. An example is the story of Karl Gauss (considered to be one of the three greatest mathematicians of all time) who, as a young student, was told to add all the integers from 1 to 100. Gifted students may recognize the notion of this intended "busywork" exercise and should be appreciative of Gauss's success at thwarting the schoolmaster's assignment by producing an ingenious and instantaneous solution. He used the fact that there are 50 sums of 101, as noted in the following pattern:*

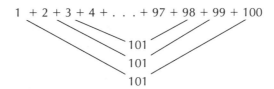

- *The study of mathematics should include historical perspectives on the development of ideas over time and geography (e.g., the development of calculus in both England and Germany in the late seventeenth century; was the Pythagorean Theorem discovered by Pythagoras?) The study of some famous mathematicians will shed light on the interdisciplinary nature of mathematics as other fields of interest of these people, such as philosophy and astronomy, are encountered. Highlights such as the "Eureka" moment of Archimedes should be experienced by all students but with the gifted, the moment should be extended into a discussion and follow-up work related to the nature of discovery.*

- *The applications of mathematics to other disciplines are important. For example, in art, geometric ideas can be explored. These include tessellations, the golden proportion, symmetry, proportional drawing, and dimensions. In social studies, the rates of change in populations can be graphed and studied and predictions can be made about the future. Concepts such the multiplier effect and statistics can be studied as they are applied to the economic functioning of the United States. Mathematics provides support for these areas while they, in turn, provide motivation for the development of mathematics as a set of tool skills.*

Thus, an ideal curriculum for the mathematically gifted incorporates multiple perspectives both within the discipline and in relationship to other disciplines and real world problems. A broad scope and depth of content combined with discovery, problem solving, and metacognitive strategies will enrich mathematical curriculum experiences for these students.

## The Role of Technology in Mathematics Education for the Gifted

Curriculum for the mathematically gifted should be well supported by technology. Even though these tools are useful in the teaching of all students, they empower gifted students to investigate higher-level concepts and provide creative solutions to advanced problems. Appropriate uses of several of these tools are discussed next.

### Calculators

Simple arithmetic operations should be done mentally. If the objective is to practice or demonstrate facility with basic skills, pencil and paper should be used. Curriculum activities should provide differentiated problems that assume the use of a calculator but emphasize higher-level thinking and minimize arithmetic. A sample activity for elementary grades is: About how long will it take to count to one billion? Students should be required to explain or write out their solution. Secondary students should use a computer or calculator for data analysis in special statistics or other mathematics-related projects. The College Board has announced a change in the SAT within the next few years that will permit the use of a calculator on some portions of the test.

There is controversy about whether time should be "wasted" learning arithmetic facts since all adults use a calculator for anything beyond the most basic calculations. However, for the gifted, math facts are patterns that should be absorbed easily if attention is given to personalizing the internalization of the process (metcognition) rather than treating it as a rote memory exercise. Number "facts" are relationships that will be required as part of pattern recognition in higher-order mathematical processes. For example, to factor the quadratic expression, $x^2 - 5x - 24$, one must *know* the set of factors of 24 rather than reconstructing them from scratch each time they are needed.

Students should be required to use calculators in elementary, middle, and secondary grades for some part of their mathematical experience. Correct and efficient use should be emphasized. Appropriate situations for the use of a calculator include the following:

- *Manipulation of numbers in problem-solving activities where the numbers and operations are burdensome and the object of the activity is not to practice arithmetic skills. Mental estimation of answers should be emphasized.*
- *Discovery lessons where many computations need to be done quickly and accurately in the process of observing a pattern and calculating by hand would only be busywork.*
- *Practice in estimation where students estimate answers to arithmetic problems and assess their accuracy using a calculator.*
- *Obtaining information that was found in tables in a precalculator age, such as square roots, logarithms, and values of trigonometric functions.*

### *Computers*

A computer can be a very powerful teaching and learning tool that enables the undertaking of tasks that are much more complex than could otherwise be attempted. The power of the technology must be unleashed in creative ways that cannot be replicated or would be more difficult to do without the use of this technology. To access the power of the computer, all students in a program for the gifted should learn programming skills before entering high school. A computer literacy course is not sufficient. Gifted students should then be called on to draw on those skills as they would be asked to read, write, use an encyclopedia, or carry out arithmetic computations. Examples of computer use in mathematics curriculum include the following:

- *Concepts such as "limits" and "convergence" can be explored at a very early age. The following question could be answered by computer programming and exploration: Determine whether each series converges. If so, explain why and determine to what number it converges:*
  *a. $1 + \frac{1}{2} + \frac{1}{3} + \frac{1}{4} + \frac{1}{5} + \ldots$*
  *b. $1 + \frac{1}{4} + \frac{1}{2} + \frac{1}{8} + \frac{1}{16} + \ldots$*
- *Assume a middle school class is doing a unit on democracy and would like to investigate the effect of different voting mechanisms on election outcomes. Student-written programs could be run to model voting behaviors under different systems of choice.*
- *Software programs, either commercially available or student-written, can be used creatively to avoid time-consuming calculations on questions such the example in Figure 10–8.*

### Figure 10–8   IRAs and the IRS

Compare and contrast possible advantages and disadvantages to an individual and to the government under each of these IRS options for an Individual Retirement Account (IRA). An individual may contribute up to $2,000 to an IRA account each year:

*Plan A:* While deducting the $2,000 on his or her tax return; the interest accumulates tax-free until retirement at age 65.

*Plan B:* While not deducting the $2,000 on his or her tax return; the interest accumulates tax-free until retirement at age 65.

- *The use of the computer in a classroom only to provide drill and practice should be avoided. This reduces the technology to an expensive alternative to a worksheet.*
- *A computer can enhance data analysis and display. Graphs and tables can easily be constructed and comparisons of data can be made. Higher-order thinking skills can be encouraged through the use of the computer as an electronic data manipulation tool.*
- *Textbooks (at the level of pre-algebra and above) often include computer options at the end of chapters but, in general, few classes take advantage of them. These could be a beginning but should not be the totality of computer assignments in differentiated math classes for gifted students.*
- *A unique computer program that would be beneficial and appealing to mathematically gifted students in elementary grades through high school is the use of LEGO Logo. This program combines the familiar plastic building blocks with the Logo programming language. Students build machines with the blocks, sensors, and motors and then program them to perform several functions.*

### Videotapes

Another area of technology that supports mathematical thought is the use of videotape materials to convey concepts visually. Experiences that are not usually available to students can be shared and ideas for further exploration can be stimulated. However, for gifted students, the viewing of the film should not be the entirety of the activity but should be the basis for discussion, a follow-up activity, and perhaps a project. The Disney film, "Donald in Mathmagic Land," is an example of one that could be shown for entertainment purposes or as the basis for in-depth inquiry about mathematical ideas. The former experience is inappropriate for the gifted; the second would be a rich experience for them.

## Essential Topics for Mathematically Talented Students

The National Council of Teachers of Mathematics *Curriculum and Evaluation Standards* (1989) outlines curriculum goals in mathematics (see Figure 10–9). These goals constitute a reasonable emphasis for talented learners as well as average learners. Differentiation for the talented learner would lie with how the topics are treated, the level of the problems used, pacing, and the depth at which the concepts are addressed.

## Issues for Curriculum Implementation

A number of issues accompany the implementation of appropriate curriculum experiences for mathematically gifted learners. Among them are concerns about instructional grouping and affective issues of acceleration. The lack of appropriate curriculum materials is frequently a problem, while teacher preparation and in-service training are also often lacking. Administrative support is necessary to facilitate a program that properly addresses the needs of these students.

Since there is little research on the direct effects of ability grouping for gifted

**Figure 10–9   NCTM Standards**

*(Grades K–4)*

Mathematics as Problem Solving
Mathematics as Communication
Mathematics as Reasoning
Mathematical Connections
Estimation
Number sense and numeration
Concepts of Whole Number Operations
Whole Number Computation
Geometry and Spatial Sense
Measurement
Statistics and Probability;
Fractions and Decimals
Patterns and Relationships

*(Grades 5–8)*

Mathematics as Problem Solving
Mathematics as Communication
Mathematics as Reasoning
Mathematical Connections
Number and Number Relationships
Number System and Number Theory
Computation and Estimation
Patterns and Functions
Algebra
Statistics
Probability
Geometry
Measurement

*(Grades 9–12)*   These curriculum topics define a core curriculum that will apply to *all* students with a few additions for college-bound students. Within the core, content differentiation should occur to address the needs of varying ability levels.

Mathematics as Problem Solving
Mathematics as Reasoning
Algebra
Trigonometry
Probability
Conceptual Underpinnings of Calculus
Geometry from a Synthetic Perspective

Geometry from an Algebraic Perspective
Mathematics as Communication
Mathematical Connections
Functions
Statistics
Discrete Mathematics
Mathematical Structure

learners, Gallagher (1991) suggested that "one is forced to rely upon experience and expert testimony" (p. 16). Most practitioners would agree that it is nearly impossible for a teacher to cope with the vast range of abilities that is found in a typical heterogeneous classroom. In order to implement curriculum that is designed with appropriate depth and breadth for gifted learners, the best possible mathematics classroom arrangement is to group these learners in self-contained classrooms. This allows the syllabus to be compacted, appropriate supplemental experiences can be more easily incorporated, and students can be provided with an opportunity to interact with peers in collaborative groups. Since the NCTM *Standards* advocate for all students coverage of many of the topic areas that have traditionally been recommended for the gifted, it is imperative that a differentiated experience still be provided for gifted learners through a high level of abstraction and pacing of the material.

Another issue that arises is the extent and type of acceleration that should be used as some modes may affect the psychological well-being of individual students. Whenever possible, it is best to maintain a group of gifted students who can be accelerated together within a grade level. In general, these students support each other both mathematically and psychologically. However, when this is not possible, individual acceleration should be considered for those qualified students who desire it. If an appropriate course is not available or if a student is not comfortable moving out of his or her grade level for a higher-level class, independent study work can also be considered but should be well supported by guidance from a teacher or mentor. If the work is easy enough that it can be accomplished without any guiding attention, the curriculum is not challenging enough to serve the needs of the student. An exemplary mentor model was developed for the Study of Mathematically Precocious Youth (SMPY) at Johns Hopkins University (Lupkowski, Assouline, & Stanley, 1990). It employs diagnostic testing followed by prescriptive instruction and has been very successful with highly gifted students.

Lack of appropriate curriculum materials can be an impediment to implementing appropriate strategies for mathematics instruction for the gifted. Currently, it is difficult to find a match between students and existing materials. In a review of 10 sets of mathematics materials for gifted elementary students, Ferguson (1991) found that no single set included all necessary elements for the mathematically gifted. The basal texts reviewed were found to be only minimally effective for use with gifted learners. The most highly rated materials were *The Challenge of the Unknown, Mathematics: A Human Endeavor,* and *Techniques of Problem Solving: Gifted Secondary Deck.* (These materials have been described in greater depth at earlier places in the chapter.) New materials under development should be more closely aligned with the new NCTM *Standards.* However, even when those are available, they may not contain sufficiently high-level options for the mathematically gifted. The implication of this lack of suitable materials is that teachers who work with the mathematically gifted should be prepared to modify and write curriculum. At the very least they should be able to adapt and accelerate existing curriculum.

Special care should be taken in assigning teachers who are adequately prepared in both content and teaching strategies. To be able to teach more advanced content, teachers need a firm foundation in mathematics. Secondary certification usually requires this, yet the trend in middle schools is to do away with subject matter specialists; therefore, it may be even more difficult to ensure availability of mathematics specialists in the future. Both elementary and middle school teachers should have some college-level mathematics courses beyond those required for teacher certification as well as a keen interest in and enjoyment of the subject as prerequisites for teaching mathematics to the gifted. Ongoing mathematics training and support is necessary for teachers who work with mathematically gifted students and can come about in the form of in-service training, college coursework, or resource support from school district staff.

In order to carry out any of the differentiated curriculum practices discussed here, it is necessary to have the support of the school and school district administration. Flexibility is needed for scheduling, acceleration, and grouping. A comprehensive scope and sequence for mathematically gifted students should be planned jointly by gifted and mathematics curriculum coordinators so that all students who deserve attention in this area receive a quality education rather than a patchwork attempt at meeting their needs.

## Conclusion

In the twenty-first century, who will push the boundaries of knowledge forward in mathematics, science, and technology? Gifted students of today will be the solvers of vital problems of tomorrow. But they need to be given opportunities, through appropriate and challenging curriculum, to develop their talents and interests so that when they stand on the shore of the "great ocean of truth" they will dive in rather than merely stroll obliviously down the beach.

Standards for all students will be moving in the direction of less emphasis on rote learning and more emphasis on communications, interdisciplinary connections, and problem solving. These are areas that have traditionally been encouraged for the gifted. How, then, will curriculum for the gifted differ? It must still allow for content coverage at a faster pace; it must allow for greater depth and abstraction; it must allow for appropriately differentiated materials; and it can best be accomplished when students are grouped together for instruction.

### *Key Points Summary*

- *Acceleration and enrichment are both viable approaches to use with gifted students in mathematics.*
- *No single curriculum model alone will meet the needs of the mathematically gifted. A combination of the content, process/product, and concept models is suggested.*
- *No single set of curriculum materials can adequately meet the needs of gifted learners. Multiple resources are essential.*
- *There is a need for curriculum development in mathematics for the gifted. This needs to be done on several fronts: by major curriculum development projects, school districts, and individual teachers.*
- *Even among the population of gifted learners, there is a great deal of diversity. Therefore, appropriate learning experiences need to be tailored for each student. The highly gifted need more services that are intensive in nature.*
- *Technology should support mathematics curriculum. All gifted students should learn the basics of computer programming before entering high school and should be required to use these skills in the solution of complex problems.*
- *Students with similar mathematical abilities should be grouped together.*
- *Problem solving, discovery, and hands-on approaches should be used to maximize the learning potential of gifted learners.*
- *Highly qualified teachers are essential to deliver a challenging mathematics curriculum to gifted learners at all grade levels.*

## *Materials and Resources*

Abbott, E. (1952). *Flatland*. New York: Dover Publications.

Bartkovich, K., & George, W. (1980). *Teaching the gifted and talented in the mathematics classroom*. Washington, DC: NEA.

Bell, E. T. (1965). *Men of mathematics*. New York: Simon and Schuster.

Black, H., & Black, S. (1981) *Figural analogies*. Pacific Grove, CA: Midwest Publications.

Charles, R., & Lester, F. (1982). *Teaching problem solving: What, why, and how*. Palo Alto, CA: Dale Seymour Publications.

Daurio, S. P. (1979). Educational enrichment versus acceleration: A review of the literature. In W. C. George, J. J. Cohn, & J. C. Stanley (Eds.), *Educating the gifted: Acceleration and enrichment* (pp. 13–63). Baltimore: The Johns Hopins University Press.

Elementary Science Study. (1984). *Attribute games and problems*. Nashua, NH: Delta.

Gardner, M. (1975). *Mathematical carnival*. New York: Knopf.

Greenes, C., Immerzeel, G., et al. (1980). *Techniques of problem solving (TOPS)*. Palo Alto, CA: Dale Seymour Publications.

Haag, V., Kaufman, B., Martin, E., & Rising, G.

(1987). *Challenge: A program for the mathematically talented.* Menlo Park, CA: Addison-Wesley.

Harnadek, A. (1990). *Math mind benders.* (Vols. Warm up 1, Warm up 2, A1, A2, B1, B2, C1, C2). Pacific Grove, CA: Midwest Publications.

House, P. (April, 1983). Alternative education programs for gifted students in mathematics. *Mathematics Teacher, 76* (4), 229–233.

*LEGO TC Logo.* Lego Dacta, 555 Taylor Road, Enfield, CT 06082.

Maddux, H. C. (Ed.). (1986). *The Challenge of the Unknown.* New York: W. W. Norton. (Videotapes available from Karol Media, P.O. Box 7600, Wolkes-Barre, PA 187773-7600).

Mathematical Association of America. *The Contest Problem Books I–IV.* MAA.

Mathematical Olympiads for Elementary Schools. SUNY, College at Old Westbury, P.O. Box 190, Old Westbury, NY 11568.

Middle Grades Mathematics Project. (1986). In Fitzgerald, W., Lappan, G., Phillips, E., Shroyer, J., & Winter, M. Factors and Multiples; Mouse and Elephant: Measuring Growth; Probability, Similarity, and Equivalent Fractions; and Spatial Visualization. Menlo Park, CA: Addison-Wesley.

Papert, S. (1982). *Mindstorms: Children, computers & powerful ideas.* New York: Basic Books.

Payne, J. (1981). The mathematics curriculum for talented students. *Arithmetic Teacher, 28* (6), 18–21.

Pratscher, S., Jones, K., & Lamb, C. (1982). Differentiating instruction in mathematics for talented and gifted youngsters. *School Science and Mathematics, 82,* 365–372.

Stanley, J. (1991). An academic model for educating the mathematically talented. *Gifted Child Quarterly, 35,* 36–42.

Trafton, P. (1981). Overview: Providing for mathematically able students. *Arithmetic Teacher, 28* (6), 12–13.

Wheatley, G. (1983). A mathematics curriculum for the gifted and talented. *Gifted Child Quarterly, 27* (2), 77–80.

Wolfle, J. A. (1986). Enriching the mathematics program for middle school gifted students. *Roeper Review, 9* (2), 81–85.

*Sources of Manipulative Materials* (such as geoboards, krypto cards, pattern blocks):

Creative Publications
5005 West 110th Street
Oak Lawn, IL 60453
1-800-624-0822

Dale Seymour Publications
P.O. Box 10888
Menlo Park, CA 94025
Outside California    1-800-USA-1100
Inside California    1-800-ABC-0766

Delta Education
P.O. Box 950
Hudson, NH 03051-9924
1-800-442-5444

# References

Brody, L. E., & Benbow, C. P. (1987). Accelerative strategies: How effective are they for the gifted? *Gifted Child Quarterly, 31* (3), 105–109.

Clark, B. (1988). *Growing up gifted* (3rd ed.). Columbus, OH: Merrill.

*CTY Summer Programs Bulletin.* (1992). The Center for Talented Youth. Baltimore: The Johns Hopkins University Press.

Davis, G. A., & Rimm, S. B. (1988). *Education of the gifted and talented* (3rd ed.). Englewood Cliffs, NJ: Prentice Hall.

Fehr, H., et al. (1972) *Unified modern mathematics,*

*courses 1–6.* New York: Columbia University Teachers' College Press.

Feldhusen, J. F., Proctor, T. B., & Black, K. N. (1986). Guidelines for grade advancement of precocious children. *Roeper Review, 9* (1), 25–27.

Feldman, D. H. (1982). A developmental framework for research with gifted children. In D. H. Feldman (Ed.), *Developmental approaches to giftedness and creativity* (pp. 31–45). San Francisco: Jossey-Bass.

Ferguson, B. (1991). *A differentiated curriculum model for gifted learners in elementary mathematics.* Unpublished master's thesis, College of William and Mary, Williamsburg, VA.

Gallagher, J. (1991). Educational reform, values, and gifted students. *Gifted Child Quarterly, 35,* 12–19.

Heid, M. K. (1983). Characteristics and special needs of the gifted student in mathematics. *Mathematics Teacher, 76,* 221–226.

Hersberger, J., & Wheatley, G. (1980). A proposed model for a gifted elementary school mathematics program. *Gifted Child Quarterly, 24* (1), 37–40.

Hirshhorn, D. (1986, November). *The University of Chicago School Mathematics Project.* Presentation of the National Association of Gifted Children, Las Vegas.

Jacobs, H. (1982). *Mathematics: A human endeavor.* New York: W. H. Freeman.

Krutetskii, V. A. (1976). *The psychology of mathematical abilities in schoolchildren.* (J. Teller, Trans.). Chicago: The University of Chicago Press.

Kulik, J. A., & Kulik, C. C. (1984). Synthesis of research on effects of accelerated instruction. *Educational Leadership, 42,* 84–89.

Lupkowski, A., Assouline, S., & Stanley, J. (1990). Applying a mentor model for mathematically talented students. *Gifted Child Today, 13* (2), 15–19.

Moore, N. D., & Wood, S. S. (1988). Mathematics with a gifted difference. *Roeper Review, 10* (4), 231–324.

National Assessment of Educational Progress. (1988). *Science learning matters.* Princeton, NJ: Educational Testing Service.

National Council of Teachers of Mathematics. (1989). *Curriculum and evaluation standards for school mathematics.* Reston, VA: Author.

Polya, G. (1971). *How to solve it.* Princeton, NJ: Princeton University Press.

Renzulli, J. (1977). *The enrichment triad.* Wethersfield, CT: Creative Learning Press.

Slavin, R. (1990). Ability grouping, cooperative learning and the gifted. *Journal for the Education of the Gifted, 14,* 3–8.

Southern, W. T., Jones, E. D., & Fiscus, E. D. (1989). Practioner objections to the academic acceleration of gifted children. *Gifted Child Quarterly, 33* (1), 29–35.

Stanley, J. (1980). On educating the gifted. *Educational Researcher, 9,* 8–12.

Sternberg, R. J. (1982). Teaching scientific thinking to gifted children. *Roeper Review, 4* (4), 4–6.

Vance, J. (1983). The mathematically talented student revisited. *Arithmetic Teacher, 31* (1), 22–25.

VanTassel-Baska, J., Landau, M., & Olszewski, P. (1985). Toward developing an appropriate math/science curriculum for gifted learners. *Journal for the Education of the Gifted, 7* (4), 257–272.

Vos Savant, M. (1991, July 7). Ask Marilyn. *Parade Magazine,* pp. 28–29.

Wheatley, G. (1988). Mathematics curriculum for the gifted. In J. VanTassel-Baska, J. Feldhusen, K. Seeley, G. Wheatley, L. Silverman, & W. Foster (Eds.), *Comprehensive curriculum for gifted learners.* Boston: Allyn and Bacon.

Worcester, D. (1979). Enrichment. In W. George, S. Cohn, & J. Stanley (Eds.). *Educating the gifted: Acceleration and enrichment* (pp. 98–104). Baltimore: The Johns Hopkins University Press.

## EXAMPLE 10.A Sample Lesson Plan on Estimation from *The Challenge of the Unknown*

  **I.** Rationale
   A. Estimation is an essential skill.
   B. The usual mathematics curriculum does not include enough.
   C. Students need to see more examples of real-world problem solving.

II. Objectives for the *Challenge* program
   A. Students will improve their problem-solving skills.
   B. Students will observe how others use problem-solving skills to solve real-world problems.
III. Objectives for lesson on estimation
   A. Students will identify situations where an estimate is appropriate.
   B. Students will improve their estimating skills.
   C. Students will participate in new techniques for estimating tag and recapture and grid-like estimation.
IV. Activities
   A. Preassessment: Estimate the number of styrofoam pieces in a given box.
   B. View video segment on shark population estimates.
   C. Estimate the number of salt crystals in a packet using a grid-like technique.
   D. Simulate the tag and recapture procedure for sharks by using the box of styrofoam pieces.
V. Possible extension activities
   A. More proportion problems related to tag and recapture; what can be done to improve the estimate?
   B. More estimation problems such as estimating how long it would take to count to one billion or estimating the number of leaves on a tree.
   C. Projects such as designing a way to estimate the dog population in your school or district; the number of customers that shop at a certain store; or the number of people attending a pep rally.
VI. Evaluation
   A. At the end of the lesson have students estimate the number of styrofoam pieces in the box; compare to original estimates.
   B. Have students write a paragraph explaining what is meant by the statement from the shark film: "Two guesses are better than one."
   C. Have students do a project such as those suggested under possible extension activities.
   D. Ask students to collect examples from newspapers and magazines and explain why estimation was an appropriate technique in each situation.

---

**EXAMPLE 10.B Sample Objectives and Activities in Mathematics**

### *Problem Solving*

*Goal:* Students will develop strategies for solving nonroutine problems.

*Activity:* Organize the class into groups of three. Give each group one copy of one problem. Sample nonroutine problems are provided below. Provide time for the groups to work. Then have representatives of each group present to the class their solutions and strategies.

*Problems:*
1. The product of three numbers is 6783 and their sum is 57. What are the three numbers?

2. The surface of Clear Lake is 35 feet above the surface of Blue Lake. Clear Lake is twice as deep as Blue Lake. The bottom of Clear Lake is 12 feet above the bottom of Blue Lake. How deep is Blue Lake?

3. When asked how old she is, a teacher responded with this riddle: "My age is a two-digit number. When multiplied by seven, the result is a three-digit number. When the digit six is written after the three-digit number, that number is increased by 1,833." How old is the teacher?

4. Two flagpoles are each 100 feet high. A rope 150 feet long is strung between the tops of the flagpoles. At its lowest point, the rope sags to within 25 feet of the ground. How far apart are the flagpoles?

5. In a game of simplified football, a touchdown results in 7 points and a field goal results in 3 points. What is the largest game score for a team *not* possible?

6. A printer uses 837 digits to number the pages of a book. How many pages are there in the book?

7. Which sums are most likely to occur in adding two numbers?
   a. The 50 numbers shown below were taken from the last two digits of a listing in a phone book.
   b. Find the sum of each pair of digits.
   c. Arrange the sums so that you can see the number of times each sum occurs.
   d. Are all sums just as likely to occur?
   e. How many ways can a sum of 8 occur?
   f. Form a generalization about the pattern of sums and explain.
   g. Obtain a phone book and pick 100 names in a row.
   h. Copy the last two digits and repeat the experiment.
   i. Did your results agree with the first experiment?

| | | | | | |
|---|---|---|---|---|---|
| 63 | 36 | 95 | 63 | 85 | 37 |
| 59 | 21 | 35 | 84 | 79 | 96 |
| 70 | 58 | 43 | 27 | 36 | 28 |
| 33 | 72 | 96 | 48 | 22 | 49 |
| 55 | 37 | 03 | 43 | 35 | 81 |
| 71 | 67 | 63 | 34 | 84 | 48 |
| 05 | 68 | 35 | 59 | 49 | 96 |
| 47 | 42 | 14 | 23 | 91 | 95 |
| 01 | 39 | | | | |

**Numeration**

*Objective:* Write numerals in base five.

*Activies:*

Given the set of xs shown below, we usually write 12 for the number of objects.

This representation uses a group size of ten. Let us see what happens when we use a different group size. Suppose we use a group size of five. The grouping is shown below.

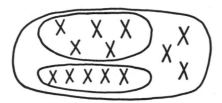

We can write 23 (base five) to show that there are two groups of five and three more.

The system of numbers we usually use is a base ten system. The system used above is a base five system.

We can write 23 (base five) = 12 (base ten).

Write the base five numeral for each set shown on page 000.

Any number can be chosen for the group size. Thus, we could write numerals in many different bases. For example, let's choose a group size of three. Write the base three numeral for each of the previous sets.

Choose other base sizes and write the numerals in those bases.

*Objective:* Write the base five numerals to 444 (five). How can you be sure your work is correct?

*Activities:*

It is interesting to count in other bases. For example, to count in base five, we only use the symbols 0, 1, 2, 3, 4.

To count in base five we say,

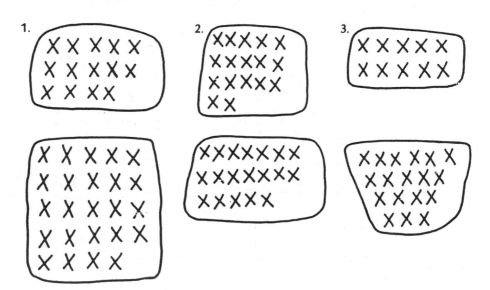

1, 2, 3, 4, 10, 11, 12, 13, 14, 20, 21
Continue counting in base five until you reach 44 (base five).
What comes next?
What is the base ten numeral for 44 (five)?

*Objective:* Convert from one base to another.

*Activities:*
To convert from base five to base ten we use the group size.
  Example:
    Write the base ten numeral for 34 (base five).
      34 (base five) = 3 × 5 + 4 = 19 (base ten).
      243 (base five) = 2 × 25 + 4 × 5 + 3 = 73 (base ten).
    Write the base ten numeral for each of the numerals below.
      a. 41 (base 5)    b. 24 (base 5)    c. 110 (base 5)
      d. 100 (base 5)   e. 444 (base 5)   f. 1000 (base 5)
      g. Choose six other base 5 numerals and change them to base ten.

*Objective:* Perform computations in different bases.

*Activities:*
Try adding, subtracting, multiplying, and dividing in base 5.
  Sample tasks:

a.   12 (five)    b.   43 (five)    c.  312 (five)    d. $4\overline{\smash{\big)}\,132}$ (five)
   +32 (five)       +24 (five)        × 3
   ─────────        ─────────        ─────────
    (five)           (five)           (five)

How can you be sure your work is correct?

*Objective:* Write numerals in other bases.

*Activities:*
Write the base eight numeral for each set shown below.

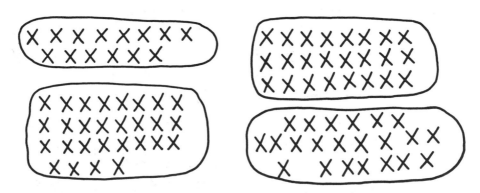

Try counting and adding in base eight.
Can you change numerals from base eight to base five? base ten?
Write the base ten numeral for each:

a. 17 (eight)    b. 36 (eight)    c. 203 (eight)
    Now make up 10 (eight) problems of:
d. your own and solve them!
e. 17 (eight)    f. 36 (eight)    g. 111 (eight)
h. Now make up 10 (eight) problems of your own and solve them!

*Objective:* Invent a numeration system.

*Activities:*
Other symbols than 1,2,3 . . . can be used to build a numeration system. Use the symbols A,B,C,D,E to write the first twenty base 5 numerals. If you use $A = 0$, $B = 1$, $C = 2$, $D = 3$, $E = 4$ you should find that 16 (base 10) is *DB* and that 23 (base 5) is *CD*.

Use the symbols, $\ulcorner$, $\urcorner$, $\llcorner$, $\lrcorner$ to write the base four numeral for the first twenty numbers.

Make up symbols and write the base eight numerals for the first thirty numbers.

*Objective:* Describe the binary system (base two).

*Activities:*
Look up the binary system and study it. Learn to count and add in the binary system.

*Objective:* Write a computer program to convert from one base to another.

*Activity:*
Do it!

*Evaluation:*
1. What comes after 24 (five)?
2. 42 (five) = _____ (ten).
3. 102 (five) – 43 (five) = _____ (five).
4. 36 (eight) = _____ (ten).
5. 20 (eight) = _____ (five).

## Measurement

*The Wick Experiment*

*Goal:* Determine a pattern of change.

*Materials:* Wick (blotter paper, chromotography paper), container (drinking glass), pencil, watch with second hand.

*Procedure:*
1. Mark off seven or more dots on the wick at 5 mm intervals with a felt tipped marker (not a pencil or ball point).

| 0 | 1 | 2 | 3 | 4 | 5 | 6 | 7 | 8 | 9 |
|---|---|---|---|---|---|---|---|---|---|
| • | • | • | • | • | • | • | • | • | • |

2. Prepare a glass with about two centimeters of water.

**3.** Suspend the wick from a pencil across the glass so that it just touches the water. DO NOT put the wick in the water until you are ready to begin timing.

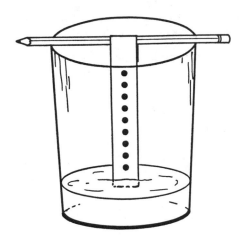

**4.** Using a table like the one below, record the time in minutes and seconds when the water reaches each dot.

| | Watch Reading | Time |
|---|---|---|
| 0 | Ex. 15:00 | Ex.  0 |
| 1 | 15:07 | 7 |
| 2 | 15:37 | 30 |
| 3 | | |
| 4 | | |
| 5 | | |
| . | | |
| . | | |
| . | | |

**5.** Make a graph of the pairs of data as shown below.

*Mark Number*          *Time*

      1
      2
      3
      4
      5
      6
      7

Your graph should be prepared like the one shown on page 259.

*Questions:*

**1.** Does the water rise at a constant rate? Explain.

2. Does the water slow down or speed up as it rises? Explain.
3. Try changing certain parts of the experiment.
   a. Suppose the wick is thinner. Will the curve be the same?
4. Suppose you try a different type of wick. Will the results change?
5. Think of other things to vary.

*Comment:* You will probably wish to repeat the experiment several times to be sure of your results. Scientists usually do an experiment many times to be sure of their findings.

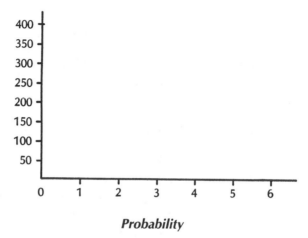

### *Probability*

*Objective:* Gifted students will be able to describe the meaning of the word *random.*

*Activities:*

1. Look up the word *random* in several reference books. Write a definition of the word.
2. Ask a high school math teacher what *random* means.
3. Check the reference manual for a computer and find out the command to generate a random number from 0 to 1 (for example, 0.4325678). What is the command to generate a random whole number from 1 to 10? Use this command to pick a random number from 1 to 20.
4. What does it mean to draw a ball from a jar at random?
5. In the State Lottery, the winning numbers are drawn at random. What does this mean?

*Objective:* Gifted students will be able to determine the chance of an event that cannot be predicted.

*Activities:*

1. What is the probability a thumbtack will land point up? Unlike a coin experiment, it is impossible to predict the chance of this event. However, we can estimate the chance by trying the experiment. Obtain 10 thumbtacks, all alike. Toss the ten tacks and record the number with point up. Repeat this experiment for a total of 10 tosses. This is like tossing one tack 100 times. Write the fraction

of the tosses on which the tack landed point up. This is an estimate of the chance of the tack landing point up. Compare your results with others. How did your answer differ?

2. Carlos wants to get all six baseball cards available. Each pack of gum contains one card. Question: On the average, how many cards must be purchased to get all six different cards?

The answer to this question can be estimated by conducting an experiment. Use a regular six-sided die with sides numbered one through six. (You could also use a computer to pick random numbers from one to six.) Roll the die until you have gotten each side. Make a chart for recording your tries. Repeat this experiment 10 times and then average the results. By using a larger number of tries, you obtain a better estimate of the answer.

A faster way to conduct this experiment is to program a computer to roll the die for you.

3. Problem: Three coins are tossed. What is the chance they will land with exactly 2 heads showing? Try to reason through the answer. Next, perform an experiment to estimate the chance. Prepare a recording sheet with number of tosses down the left and number of heads (0,1,2,3) across the top.

4. Toss three coins 40 times. Record the number of heads on each toss. Based on your findings, what is your estimate of the chance of getting exactly two heads?

Sue Ellen thought about the experiment and said that the chance of getting one head is the same as the chance of getting two heads. Is she correct? Explain.

Pat found a way of computing the chances in the problems above. He made a list of the ways each coin can land. His work is shown below.

Possible Outcomes:
H H H
H H T
H T H
T H H
H T T
T H T
T T H
T T T

There are eight possible outcomes. Since there are three outcomes with two heads, the chance of getting exactly two heads is $\frac{3}{8}$. Use this information to find the chance of getting three heads. One head. No heads.

5. Repeat this experiment with four coins. Estimate the chance of getting 0 heads, 1 head, 2 heads, 3 heads, and 4 heads. Look for a pattern in your results.

6. Draw a graph of the results in number 3 and 4.

7. Based on your work, predict the chance of 2 heads in the toss of five coins. Estimate the chance of 0 heads, 1 head, 3 heads, 4 heads, and 5 heads.

8. Write a computer program to simulate a probability experiment.

9. To determine whether a game is fair, try selected games. In each case decide whether the game is fair. By a fair game, we mean that each player has an equal chance of winning.

**10.** Select 10 activities from the book, *What Are My Chances?* (Book A and Book B, by A. Shute and S. Choate, Creative Publications, 1977, Palo Alto, Calif.). Complete the activities.

*Evaluation:*

Have students generate three probability experiments and present one to the class. Peer critique should follow.

### Spatial Visualization

*Goal:* Students will develop spatial reasoning by determining and comparing constructed geometric shapes.

*Activity:*

Provide cubes of some sort, Multi-link Blocks work well. Pose the following problem: How many *different* shapes can be made with five cubes? Each cube must share a face with at least one other cube. This is a challenging problem. There is no mathematical formula—the possibilities must be analyzed and a system for determining all shapes constructed. There are 29 different shapes. Have groups compare results as needed. Challenge students to draw the 29 shapes. Ask students to formulate interesting follow up questions.

    Examples:

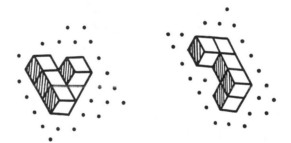

# The Study of the Humanities

*JOYCE VanTASSEL-BASKA*

> *It is not enough to teach an individual a specialty. Through it he may become a kind of useful machine but not a harmoniously developed personality. It is essential that the student acquire an understanding of and a lively feeling for values. He must acquire a vivid sense of the beautiful and of the morally good. Otherwise he—with his specialized knowledge—more closely resembles a well-trained dog than a harmoniously developed person.—ALBERT EINSTEIN*

If the proper study of humankind is men and women, as the poet Alexander Pope has intoned, then perhaps the humanities constitute the most important areas of study for any student since such study uses humankind as the source of inspiration. A reasonable definition of the humanities then might be: The humanities are comprised of all formal and informal acts of humankind that have resulted in creative products that deliberately attempt to portray and enhance the human condition in some form. Thus, a child's drawing would be an appropriate object for study, whereas a garbage heap would not. The child's drawing represents a deliberate act of expression, whereas the garbage heap is a destructive product created haphazardly and without artistic intent.

Although this definition is rather broad, it has the advantage of allowing educators a wide degree of latitude in structuring humanities programs and hopefully allows for a revision of thinking regarding this important area of the curriculum. Too often, the definition of the humanities has been limited only to the study of the fine arts. Consequently, the power of the humanities for integrating human experience was viewed as a formal amalgam of specific subjects in the curriculum. How can we successfully develop a humanities curriculum?

One theoretical reference point for the teaching of the humanities on this grand scale would be the work of Phenix (1964), who categorized all bodies of knowledge into broad realms of meaning that reflect all of the diverse acts of humankind:

*Symbolics* are concerned with our invention and use of various symbol systems. These would include spoken languages (native, foreign, and computer), mathematics, and nonverbal symbolic forms such as gestures, sign language, etc.

*Empirics* are knowledge areas in which we are concerned with abstract phenomena and human behaviors and the need to generalize about them. These areas include science, psychology, and the social sciences.

*Esthetics* focus on our desire to create new forms and perceive objects in particular ways. These areas include music, the visual arts, the movement arts, and literature.

*Synoptics* allow us to reenact the past and seek ultimate answers related to life's purpose. These areas of study would include history, religion, and philosophy.

*Ethics* focus on our need to make judgments of good and evil and therefore are concerned with moral knowledge.

*Synnoetics* are concerned with our relationships to other people and therefore focus on personal and interpersonal knowledge.

Use of this model would allow all of curriculum to be subsumed under its broad categories and would provide a reconceptualized view of what should be learned in schools at a broad level.

Another overarching model to consider for conceptualizing humanities curricula was represented by Brandwein (1971). He probed the meaning of five core concepts as they are perceived and expressed by humankind:

| | |
|---|---|
| Truth (consistency, relevance, reality) | Individuals search for and express the reality of their experience. |
| Beauty (significant form, ideal form) | Individuals perceive and express the beauty of experience. |
| Justice (compassion, mercy) | Individuals seek and express the ideals of justice. |
| Love (loving-kindness) | Individuals seek and express love. |
| Faith (ultimate concern, commitment) | Individuals seek and express their faith. |

Use of this model would allow curriculum to be organized thematically around core concepts of human experience still at a broad enough level for inclusion of all traditional subject matter areas. Thus, such a humanities orientation to curriculum provides the needed organizing structure for real interdisciplinarity.

The primary modes of expression used to communicate human experience are described: art, movement and dance, play and drama, music, and language. Individuals then can move through levels of expression within and across modes in search of higher levels of meaning. This model is very useful in integrating separate fine arts areas of the curriculum around key concepts and levels of experience.

## Rationale

Why are the humanities so important as an area of study? There are several reasons that curriculum planners need to consider when organizing curriculum experiences:

1. The humanities, by their very nature, provide a perfect union of cognitive and affective elements, thus providing students with curriculum experiences that directly engage them in equally high-level intellectual and emotional activity.
2. Intellectually gifted children have unusually keen powers to see and understand interrelationships; therefore, the humanities are useful curricular tools, for their whole structure is based on constantly interrelating form and content across knowledge bases.
3. Humanities are an enrichment tool in the highest sense, for they provide an intellectual framework not available in studying only one content area that exposes students to many areas of curriculum not traditionally studied.
4. The humanities provide a basis for understanding the creative as well as the intellectual process through being actively engaged in the creative process and analyzing and evaluating the creative products of others.

Based on this rationale, goals for humanities programs for the gifted might be:

- *To enhance students' understanding of the power and good in the creative acts of humanity*
- *To provide opportunities for students to integrate ideas across broad fields of study*
- *To develop a sensitivity to the process of knowledge production and utilization in the real world*
- *To appreciate their own and others' capacities for creative production*
- *To provide a framework for understanding systems of knowledge and their organization*

These are K–12 goals that can be addressed through a total framework of study or through carefully weaving this perspective into all curriculum areas. Although the importance of using the humanities as a focal point for providing curriculum for the gifted may not be in question, how those humanities experiences for the gifted are organized is an area lacking consensus. There are several ways that school districts and other educators have approached the task:

1. Focus on the past, using chronology, to note the important contributions of men and women across history and fields.
2. Focus on the present and future, using the perspective of contemporary society. Who are we and where are we going (with some homage paid to where we've been)?
3. Focus on universal themes or ideas. Topics like War or Love are popular, yet more intellectually stated topics are also used (e.g., Justice in nineteenth-Century British Society: A Study of Cultural Values).
4. Focus on the common elements across humanities subject areas. For example, the use of theme and symbol as they are expressed in literature, art, and music.

In any of these orientations to organizing a humanities curriculum, it is important to note the charaterics of a sound humanities program. Lindsey (1981) listed six important variables to consider in building such programs.

| | |
|---|---|
| **Value Focused** | The Humanities look at man in the world as his actions reflect his more significant commitments. |
| **Interdisciplinary** | The Humanities take their subject matter from all the discrete disciplines—history, literature, the arts, philosophy, theology, etc.—and fuse these into illustrations of Man in the World. |
| **Topical** | The subject matter of the Humanities is organized into topical units for study. *The Nature of Honor,* for instance, might address this idea from our time into deep antiquity. David, Peter, Brutus, Don Quixote, Lancelot, Antigone, Nat Turner—all these personages might be used to illustrate the concept. |
| **Student Centered** | In the Humanities, learning outcomes are the result of a rich and meaningful exploration by teacher and student together. Thus, everyone continues to grow and develop as a result of the learning. |
| **Intellectual** | Study in the Humanities is the manifestation of *intelligence manifest in a healthy on-going curiosity about oneself. . . .* Minds that are intellectually alive continue the quest for knowledge, truth, beauty, wisdom. |
| **Creative** | The Humanities allow the gifted to synthesize existing knowledge into novel and improved models for the future. |

Can the humanities be taught earlier than secondary level? Several theorists have argued that the integration of subject matter disciplines must be preceded by a firm grounding in at least one of those disciplines. Students developmentally may not be ready to function at such abstract levels at earlier ages (Piaget, 1962). Yet, we know that even young gifted children can make extraordinary conceptual connections on their own without a formal learning environment. Clearly, there is much that can be done with a humanities program at all grade levels.

Should the humanities be seen as an area of exploration only for gifted learners during the K–12 years in school? Certainly, the humanities are appropriate for all learners. Yet, students may require a threshold competence in core domains of inquiry before they might profit from an intellectually rich interdisciplinary exploration of the humanities. In the final analysis, how the humanities are defined and approached will best determine which students might profit most from such a curriculum. What is clear is that gifted learners can profit immensely from such curriculum approaches. Therefore, why not begin with this population and translate to other levels as it seems appropriate and feasible?

## Humanities as Concept-Based Curriculum

The humanities provide the focus on key ideas, issues, and themes that have haunted humans over the centuries and that have expressed themselves in various forms—literature, art, mathematics, and the social sciences. The task of organizing concept curriculum, even once you have made a decision on an ongoing organizational model, is very complex. VanTassel-Baska and Feldhusen (1981) used Adler's *Syntopicon* as a large universe of ideas from which to choose a select few to develop interdisciplinary humanities curriculum at the K–8 levels. The key concepts used were change, reasoning, and signs and symbols. Table 11–1 shows the way each of these concepts was interpreted in core domains of study.

The next task was to write curriculum guides that flowed from these myriad interpretations of the three concepts. These guides were formalized by grade-level clusters, K–3, 4–6, 7–8, according to each of the concepts. This approach to concept curriculum making provided a broad unifying framework within which objectives and activities were developed for the requisite levels and content fields.

Another approach to concept curriculum was used in the Phoenix Project curriculum in Toledo, Ohio (VanTassel, 1974). This program was developed to integrate curriculum experiences for disadvantaged gifted learners at the high-school level, grades 9–10. The

**TABLE 11–1   Matrix of Key Concepts by Subject Area**

| Key Concept | Langage Arts | Social Studies | Mathematics | Science |
|---|---|---|---|---|
| Change | *Seasonal change as viewed in children's literature *Life cycle issues in literature | *Differences between peoples of the world *Growth of cities as cultural centers *The evolution of major cultures | *Modeling Theory *Techniques for representing changes: graphing | *Differences between physical and chemical changes *The effects of change over time *Methods for describing observed change |
| Reasoning | *Discrimination of fact from fiction *The relationship of syntax to meaning in literature | *The power of reason: critical thinking *The collapse of reason in advertising and propaganda *Applications of reason in the twenty-first century | *Probability reasoning *Prediction theory | *Reasoning as the scientific art of problem solving *Reasoning as a scientific attitude |
| Signs and Symbols | *Punctuation *Literary symbols *The conversion of symbol to theme | *Common nonverbal signs and symbols in everyday life *Learning language systems as a code to culture *Symbols within a culture | *Numeration systems as symbols in mathematics *The computer as a tool to manipulate symbols | *Symbols as communication in science *Archaelogy as a study of symbols *Maps as symbols of the real world |

*Source:* J. VanTassel-Baska and J. Feldhusen, *Concept Curriculum for the Gifted.* Matteson School District, Matteson, Illinois, 1981.

techniques employed to achieve this integration were through the organization of the program and cooperative staff planning as well as through writing integrated curriculum. The curriculum used special projects, field trips, and speakers at agents of unification. An example of the project unification approach follows:

*Phoenix Curriculum Areas*  *Planned Projects*

Math

Science

Social Studies

English

1. A project that focuses on showing the relationship of equality and inequality in each of the content domains.
2. A paper that describes the use of symbol in all knowledge areas.
3. A seminar that explores issues of space according to the perspective of a mathematician, scientist, social scientist, and writer.

A key integration technique used in Phoenix was team teaching and team planning, carried out on a block-scheduling model. Each of the four Phoenix teachers was assigned four Phoenix periods, back to back, within which the team could make decisions on daily time allotments. Typically each teacher taught for three periods and planned with at least one other team member for the fourth, accommodating a total of 60 students in the process. Consequently, long-term projects could be planned that involved all areas of the curriculum. The project model for unifying ideas and concepts could be implemented in other school contexts as well at both elementary and secondary levels.

Another approach to humanities education for the gifted has been through the incorporation of philosophy as a core element in the curriculum experience. The teaching of philosophy as an integrated learning experience for the gifted was first suggested by Ward (1961), and used as the "cement" to hold together the North Carolina Governors School's course structure, later popularized by Matthew Lipman's fine national program, *Philosophy for Children.* It currently enjoys prominence in an International Baccalaureate program, a rigorous course of study for secondary students that uses the theory of knowledge as an organizing principle.

If we view the humanities as the seamless web of human experience embodied in works like the *Great Books of the Western World,* then we must recognize the importance of logic as a tool skill for understanding and interpreting such experience. Schroeder (1981) has incorporated this idea into the study of philosophy as a subject for the gifted by fourth grade. He advocated the teaching of a continuum of concepts around the subject area core shown in Table 11–2.

The seminar model represents an excellent approach to the delivery of a humanities curriculum. Typically special seminars for the gifted are held biweekly or even monthly and are scheduled for three- to four-hour sessions. Topics are delineated for the year and may be loosely linked to a single concept or may explore several concepts. Frequently, outside speakers are employed to provide indepth commentary on a particular idea or issue. Examples of seminar topics and speakers in the humanities follow:

*Humanities Topic*  *Seminar Leader*
Urban Architecture  Urban planner
Comtemporary Art Forms  Local artist

| The Work of Hemingway as an Example of 20th Century Alienation | Writer-in-the-schools |
| Cultural Archetypes: The People of Chicago | Studs Terkel, Chicago philosopher |
| Conservation: The Key to Survival in the Future | Futurist |
| The Search for Meaning: Developing a Philosophy of Life | Humanities professor |

## Key Questions Regarding the Humanities

Some key questions for curriculum developers may be helpful to consider in planning a humanities curriculum:

**1.** *How broadly do you want to organize humanities experiences?* The examples cited thus far in this chapter range widely in terms of scope. School districts can start with any of the approaches cited but need to consider carefully how to broaden the scope of their humanities opportunities to students over the years of K–12 education.

**2.** *How do you want to ensure that a study of the humanities is considered basic for the gifted learner?* One way of ensuring the inclusion of the humanities perspective is to see that any curriculum that is implemented for gifted learners contains a concept strand, an aspect that addresses big ideas, issues, and themes. In the teaching of algebra, for example, ensure that there is some focus on the idea that algebraic notation is one of several symbol systems within mathematics, the idea that mathematics is an invented system, and the idea that mathematics shares many formal characteristics with music and art. Also ensure that students learn about the people who do mathematics, the process they use, the way they think, and what mathematics means to them. By including such an emphasis in the curriculum, students are assured of gaining insights into the larger issues in mathematics, well beyond individual problems assigned from the book.

**TABLE 11–2  Philosophy Continuum for the Gifted by Grade Levels***

| 4th Grade | 5th | 6th | 7th | 8th | 9–12th | 13+ |
|---|---|---|---|---|---|---|
| Formal Logic | Syllogism | Verbal & Rhetorical | | Classics of Philosophy & | | Ethics Aesthetics |
| | | Fallacy | | Persuasian | | Religion |
| Philosophy for Children | (Lewis Carroll's silly syllogisms) | (use in politics, advertising, etc.) | | (Plato, Descartes, Berkeley, Hume) | | |
| Program | Fallacy (Darryl Huff's *How to Lie with Statistics*) | | | | | |

*Source: Adapted from F. Schroeder, "Trends for the Future in Humanities for the Gifted Student," *Roeper Review* 4(2).

**3.** *What are some curriculum examples of integrated work in the humanities?* Using the humanities to structure an integrated curriculum is a very powerful way to address the needs of the gifted. Incorporating history, literature, philosophy, art, and music into a curricular whole can provide gifted students with an extraordinary grasp of how integrated knowledge really is, and the various forms in which it is effectively utilized. The matrix chart from the Phoenix Program employs a thematic structure superimposed on a chronological time frame in order to generate sample readings, artworks, and musical pieces (see Table 11–3).

Another example from a high school seminar for gifted students illustrates the role of the arts in expressing cultural values. In this curriculum, overall goals, objectives, and a course syllabus are articulated from a broad themes perspective (see Figure 11–1).

An eclectic approach to organizing a humanities curriculum for the gifted was taken in the Portland, Oregon, Parkrose School District. Educators decided to treat the humanities as their program core for grades 7–12 and to integrate English, social studies, and career education across the secondary span. Each year of study carried a theme:

Grade 7: The Individual in Society
Grade 8: National Perspectives
Grade 9: Global Perspectives
Grade 10: National Prospectives II
Grade 11: Comparative Governments
Grade 12: Independent Study of Current Issues

Several subthemes or topics were then carefully selected under each year's course of study. A sample concept teaching guide is included here for the ninth-grade theme of Global Perspectives with a subtheme of Power Conflicts.*

### The Global Perspective: Concept Teaching Guide

*1. Power Conflicts: Talk Solfty . . . but Carry a Big Stick*

    A. *Theme: Why and how do human power conflicts develop?*

    B. *Introductory Unit: Students compare and contrast conflicts in their lives, especially* vis à vis *parents, teachers, other adults, peers, and younger children.*

    C. *Introductory Case Study:* Power Conflict in the Raw: Military Conquest *(at least one is chosen for past and present)*

        *1. Present: Nazi Invasion of Europe, Korean War, Soviet Invasions of Hungary (1956) and Czechoslovakia (1968), Russo-Japanese War, World War I, etc.*

        *2. Past: Mongol Invasion, Attila the Hun, Tamer Lane, Alexander the Great, Napoleanic Wars, etc.*

        *3. Analysis of past and present military conflicts to show causes, effects,*

*(text continues on page 275)*

---

*Reprinted with permission from Parkrose School District No. 3, *Academic Excellence in the Humanities.* Seattle: The Northwest Clearinghouse for Gifted Education, 1982. Available through the Clearinghouse, 1410 South 200th St., Seattle, Washington, 98198.

**TABLE 11–3  Phoenix Curriculum in the Humanities**

Humanities—Aspects for Integration—Literature

| | Communication | Search for Identity and Psychological Security | Power and Authority | Justice | Tolerance | Survival | Change |
|---|---|---|---|---|---|---|---|
| Man Emerges from Nature Pre-410 A.D. | •Socratic method<br>•Cicero's orations<br>•"Pyramus and Thisbe" myth | •Pericles—"Funeral Oration"<br>•Romulus and Remus myth<br>•Virgil (*Aeneid*)<br>•Ovid | •*Antigone*—Sophocles<br>•"Ozymandias"—Shelley | •Oresteian Trilogy<br>•Parable (Matt 18: 23–35)<br>•Myth | •Parable (Luke 10:30–37)<br>•Medea Euripides | •The *Odyssey*<br>•Aeneas, Jason, Theseus, Hercules as heroes | •*"Genesis"*<br>•Plato "Allegory of the Cave" and *The Republic* |
| Man Fashions Security with Faith (410–1453) | •Trombador and Trouvere stories, songs, poems | •*Everyman* (film-record)<br>•"Our Lady's Juggler" | •St. Thomas (Proofs of the existence of God) *Summa Theological*<br>•"Sir Patrick Spens" (anon. form) | •Dante's *Inferno*—"Third Canto" | •"Prodigal Son" (Luke 15) | •"Lord Randal" (anon. poem) | •"Song of Roland"<br>•Alchemy<br>•Gold Art |
| Man Rediscovers His Freedom (1453–1650) | •*Romeo and Juliet*—Shakespeare | •"Letter to Posterity"—Petrarch<br>•*Voices* | •Machiavelli—excerpts from *Voices*<br>•*Canterbury Tales*—Chaucer<br>•*Julius Caesar*—Shakespeare | •"Mother Goose Rhymes"<br>•*Voices* | •Luther—Osborne<br>•"Musee des Beaux Arts"—Auden<br>•"No Man Is an Island"—Donne | •"Of Warfare" | •"Shall I Compare Thee to a Summer's Day?"—Shakespeare<br>•"Even Such Is Time"—Raleigh<br>•"To The Virgins"—Herrick |

| | | | | | | | |
|---|---|---|---|---|---|---|---|
| Man Attempts to Order His World (1650–1900) | •*Gulliver's Travels*—Swift •"There is No Frigate Like a Book" and "I Would Like to See It Lap the Lillies"—E. Dickinson | •"Essay on Man" (Epistle II, 1)—Pope •"Songs of Myself"—Whitman | •"Eve of Waterloo"—Byron | •"Rime of the Ancient Mariner"—Coleridge •"Civil Disobedience"—Thoreau | •*Declaration of Independence* •"The Quaker"—Hawthorne •*Letters from the Earth*—Twain •"On Tolerance"—Thoreau •*Billy Budd*—Melville | •Spenser and Darwin—Laws of the Universe •*Great Expectations*—Dickens •*Swiss Family Robinson*—film •"The Outcasts of Poker Flats"—Harte | •"Essay on Man" (Epistle I)—Pope •Thoreau and Emerson Poetry •*The Time Machine* and *War of the Worlds*—Wells |
| Man Fragmentizes His World (1900–?) | •*The Miracle Worker*—Gibson •"Paul's Case"—Cather •"Too Early Spring"—Benet •*A Doll's House*—Ibsen •"Invictus"—Henley •"The Road Not taken"—Frost •*A View from the Bridge*—Miller •*A Raisin in the Sun*—Hansberry •*The Glass Menagerie*—Williams •*Catcher in the Rye*—Salinger •*The Learning Tree*—Parks | •*1984*—Orwell •"The Catbird Seat"—Thurber •"The Lottery"—Jackson •*Lord of the Flies*—Golding •*Occurrence at Owl Creek*—Bierce •*A Different Drummer*—Kelley | •"Cask of Amontillado"—Poe •"The Coup de Grace"—Bierce •"Richard Cory"—Robinson | | •*Who's Afraid of Virginia Woolf*—Albee •*Of Mice and Men*—Steinbeck •"The Baby Party"—Fitzgerald •"And the World Will Be Purified"—Pegler •"Go Tell It On the Mountain"—Baldwin | •"Flight" and *The Pearl*—Steinbeck •"Death in the Woods"—Anderson •"To Build a Fire"—London •*Diary of Anne Frank*—Frank •*Hiroshima*—Hersey •*The Uprooted*—Hamlin | •"The Second Coming"—Yeats •"By the Waters of Babylon"—Benet •*Chariots of the Gods*—Damiken •*2001 Space Odyssey*—Clarke |

**TABLE 11-3** *(continued)*

### Humanities—Aspects for Integration—Arts and Music

| | Communication | Search for Identity and Psychological Security | Power and Authority | Justice | Tolerance | Survival | Change |
|---|---|---|---|---|---|---|---|
| Man Emerges from Nature (per–410 A.D.) | •Catacomb art<br>•Greek music (Seikilos song) | •Parthenon<br>•Romulus and Remus and Wolf (statue)<br>•Colossus (Rhodes)<br>•Statue of Liberty | •Egyptian sculpture<br>•Pyramids<br>•Athena | •Laocoon (statue) | •Dying Gaul (statue) | •Pont du Gard (Roman bridge)<br>•Appian Way (Roman highway) | •Depiction of human figure: 600 B.C. |
| Man Fashions Security with Faith (410–1453) | •Gothic sculpture<br>•Illuminated manuscripts | •Medieval Walled City<br>•Ptolemic concept of universe—*Basis for Divine Comedy* | •Gothic architecture<br>•Charlemagne's throne, church, etc., at Aachen<br>•van Eyck's *Adoration of the Lamb* | •Gregorian chant (Kyrie Elison) | •Walled City concept | •Mont St. Michel | •Romanesque vs. Gothic styles of architecture |
| Man Rediscovers His Freedom (1453–1650) | •African drum music<br>•Ghirlandajo—"An Old Man with His Grandson" | •Copernican concept of universe<br>•"Pieta"—Michelangelo | •"Last Supper"—DaVinci | •El Greco—"Laocoon"<br>•Michelangelo—"Last Judgement" | •Bruegel—"Fall of Icarus" | •Michelangelo—"Pieta" | •Development of harmony<br>•Josquin—"Ave Maria"<br>•Transition: God-centered and man-centered art |

| | | | | | | |
|---|---|---|---|---|---|---|
| Man Attempts to Order His World (1650–1900) | •Rembrandt—"Descent from the Cross"<br>•Goya—"Disasters of War" Series | •Picasso—"Tragedy"<br>•Rodin—"The Thinker" | •Bach—"Passacaglia C Minor"<br>•Versailles | •David—"Death of Socrates" | •Bach—"Crucifixion from St. Matthew's Passion"<br>•African sculpture<br>•Japanese woodcuts | •Gericault—"Raft of the Medusa" | •Development of painting (Baroque-Impressionism) |
| Man Fragmentizes His World (1900–?) | •Abstract painting<br>•Jazz | •Tooker—"Government Bureau," "Subway," "Waiting Room" | •Leadbelly—"John Henry" | •"Sacco and Venzetti" (painting) | •Picasso—"Guernica" | •"Red Staircase" (painting) | •Modern architecture<br>•*Duke Ellington's* "Kyrie and Credo" (Jazz and Credo) *Jazz Suite on Mass Texts* |

## FIGURE 11–1   Gifted Humanities Seminar

PART I: Long-term Goals
1. To understand that the search for knowledge is unending and natural
2. To understand the concepts of art, science, knowledge, beauty, and truth
3. To understand how the individual functions within American culture

PART II: Objectives
1. The student will be able to compare ideas about the individual's role in society.
2. The student will be able to understand various perspectives about knowledge, art, and science.
3. The student will be able to grow in his or her appreciation of the arts.
4. The student will be able to understand the role of art in a technological world.

PART III: Course Outline
  I. The Individual: An Examination of Values
    A. The individual and experience
      1. What are values?
      2. What role does experience play in the formation of values?
      3. What causes values to change?
    B. The individual and knowledge
      1. What is the relationship between knowledge and experience?
      2. Is empirical knowledge the best kind of knowledge?
      3. Does knowledge help one attain happiness?
    C. Knowledge and wisdom
      1. Is there a relationship between knowledge and wisdom?
      2. Which is preferable, knowledge or wisdom?
      3. As one grows in knowledge or wisdom, do values change?
  II. The Individual: An Examination of Ideas
    A. Discussions of philosophy
      1. Basic philosophical concepts
        a. What is philosophy?
        b. How can we distinguish between Eastern and Western philosophy?
        c. What are the universal qualities of philosophy?
    B. Discussions of underlying ideas
      1. The nature of science
        a. What is science?
        b. Are there similarities between art and science?
        c. Are there dangers in placing more emphasis on either art or science?
      2. Science and knowledge
        a. What is the relationship between science and knowledge?
        b. Is scientific knowledge the same as technology?
        c. Does man control technology or does technology control man?
      3. The nature of art
        a. What is art?
        b. How can we distinguish between good art, bad art, and non-art?
        c. What are some differences between Eastern and Western art?
      4. Art and knowledge
        a. What is the relationship between art and knowledge?
        b. Is man's need to know similar to his need to express?
      5. Quality
        a. What is quality in life? In art?
        b. Does everyone recognize quality?
 III. The Individual: The Role of the Individual in Society
    A. The individual as autonomous
      1. Is man basically a social creature?
      2. How important is conformity to most humans?

3. In what ways are values dictated by society so that pressures are placed on the individual?
4. What, other than society, may motivate human beings?

B. The individual as a part of society
1. Is it natural for an individual to want to contribute to his society ?
2. Is man basically a product of his society?
3. What must humans do to insure the survival of their society?
4. What conflicts does the individual face as a member of society?

---

*and relationships, to lead the students to form generalizations about the causes and types of power conflicts*

D. *Concept Generalizations: Using military conquest as a base, students construct an analytic framework of global power conflicts, which should include the following categories:*

1. *Causes (overpopulation, value conflicts, militarism, self-protection, imbalance of power, economics, and others)*
2. *Types (military conquest, revolution, civil war, terrorism, genocide, peaceful compromise, passive resistance, submission, and others)*

E. *Student Case Studies: Using the concept generalizations discovered in step "D," the students investigate and analyze specific types of power conflicts in their historic settings to discover additional generalizations about the concept in its different manifestations. Following teaching model step #4, these types should be investigated:*

1. *Military Conquest (e.g., Nazi, Japanese, European, Barbarians, Islamic, Mongol, Napoleonic, Norman French, Roman, Byzantine, Incan, Mayan, Aztec, Alexandrian, and others)*
2. *Revolution (e.g., American, French, Russian, Irish, Hungarian, Greek, South American, Boer, Chinese, and others)*
3. *Civil War (American, Russian, Spanish, Chinese, Irish, Indian/ Pakistani, and others)*
4. *Terrorism—Subversive and despotic (Leftist, Rightist, Irish, Vietnamese, Moslem, Palestinian, Japanese, Nazi, South American, Soviet, African, American Radical, and others)*
5. *Genocide (Nazi, Soviet, American, Indian, Chinese, Biblical and others)*
6. *Peaceful compromise (Munich, SALT Talks, Cold War, Holy Alliance, Three-Emperors League, Soviet/Finnish)*
7. *Passive Resistance (India, Denmark in WWII, American War-Resisters, Quakers, and others)*
8. *Submission (Czechoslavakia in 1938, 1948, and 1968; Austrian Anschluss; (Anglo-Saxon submission to Norman French)*

F. *Concept Analysis: following the final step of the teaching model, the students will, in writing, analyze, synthesize, and evaluate what they have discovered about power conflicts, focusing especially on why there are power conflicts, how they come about, and what might be future developments. In addition, students should attempt answers to the "what if's" of past, present, and future power conflicts.*

This approach to planning and implementing humanities curriculum provides guidance to the teacher on how to structure the teaching-learning process for a given unit of study. It also provides an overarching scheme for several years of productive study for the gifted learner.

It is important to note the commonality of each of these treatments of the humanities in school-based programs; they share a common focus on humankind, our issues and concerns, and our creative products. Thus, any subject area could be transformed into a humanities approach, for such a focus underlies the framework of all knowledge. By providing students with insights into the person or the culture behind the idea, invention, or the artist's rendering, we have made visible an important perspective in the quest for educational relevance.

Recent general trends in humanities education also provide support for broadening the base of what the humanities might be. Humanities educators have cited the importance of stressing interpretive skills rather than direct recall of names and facts; making connections among the arts; placing greater emphasis on nonverbal arts, such as architecture, painting, dance, and symphonic music; placing more emphasis on non-Western arts; and placing new emphasis on emergent and popular arts, such as film, jazz, and science fiction.

## The Learner in the Context of the Humanities

Just as the curriculum in the humanities is integrative and focused on large ideas and concepts, so too must the perspective of the learner shift from a focus on a right or wrong answer to a position that recognizes the relativistic nature of the world. Not that this shift is unimportant in other areas of study, but in the humanities it is vital to the acquired learning stance that students must make.

Perry (1970) has researched learner positions among college students and has developed an epistemological framework to account for them:

Position #1: *duality* (the student sees everything in black and white terms)
Position #2: *multiplicity* (the student is able to entertain the idea that people could have more than one point of view about the same event)
Position #3: *subordinate relativism* (the student sees that some truths are based on the perspective of the viewer and the circumstances surrounding events)
Position #4: *relativism* (the student recognizes that all truth is relative to situations and circumstances and the perceptual field of the viewer)

This model represents one paradigm that may be useful in describing the nature and the direction of the change necessary for students to make in their thinking as they are exposed to humanities education over their years of schooling. The goal of such an education is to lead a student to an ever-increasing level of perception about the nature of the world and what is meaningful in it.

## Creativity and the Humanities

If the study of humankind and our accomplishments is to have real meaning in the lives of students, will they not have to experience the creative impulse for themselves? It seems quite reasonable that the answer to this question is a resounding "yes." One curriculum that addresses creativity in its various components and also uses the context of the humanities for its examples is *Creativity: The Human Resource* developed by Chevron Research Company (1980). A filmstrip and teacher's guide were developed around the following aspects of creativity with corresponding activities. A sample from this curriculum follows:

| *Creativity Components* | *Corresponding Activity* |
|---|---|
| Recognizing Patterns | Ask students to bring objects to class that are interesting to them in some way. List properties of selected objects; guess objects correctly from properties. |
| Making Connections | Listen to two different pieces of symphonic music. Draw the "feeling" of the music on $9 \times 12$ construction paper. Discuss relational outcomes. |
| Taking Risks | Have students go on a "smelling" tour of unseen odors. They should write down: how the odor makes them feel, what colors it reminds them of, whether it is pleasant, whether it reminds them of any personal experience in their past. |
| Challenging Assumptions | Have students plan a school without teachers. Have them write an essay describing a favorite class in such a school. |
| Taking Advantage of Chance | Have students think up unexpected events that could happen. List the consequences of each, as many as possible. Discuss. |
| Seeing in New Ways | Have students choose a picture and view it only in $2'' \times 2''$ frames. Choose a frame that is visually pleasing, cut it out, mount it, and write about it. |

The filmstrip that accompanies this curriculum depicts visual images that reflect each of these creativity components. For example, Buckminster Fuller's geodesic dome is used to illustrate risk taking and Duchamp's work is used to illustrate the challenging of assumptions.

Another approach to the exploration of creativity within humanities programs is to have students engage in the "making" of an actual product within each area studied. Thus, the following list of creative tasks could be generated for each of the humanities areas named:

| | | |
|---|---|---|
| Visual Arts | $\rightarrow$ | Create a photographic montage. |
| Music | $\rightarrow$ | Write and perform a musical composition. |
| Poetry | $\rightarrow$ | Write an original poem about humankind and our environment. |
| History | $\rightarrow$ | Research and write the history of a small town nearby. |

| Science | → | Design an experiment to answer a question you don't understand; carry out the experiment. |
| Mathematics | → | Create a mathematical model to represent how something of interest to you works. |
| Philosophy | → | Develop your own philosophy of life and articulate it on paper. |

Such product development opportunities may give students a worthwhile experience of creation that strengthens their appreciation for the creative contributions of others.

More extended manifestations of these ideas can be carried out in long-term individual and group projects within the humanities program. Many gifted students have prepared films, art portfolios, and musical scores; written books; and conducted original research—all within the framework of a humanities program. Thus, the teaching of creativity embedded in broad subject matter is a reasonable approach to employ.

Another perspective on the teaching of creativity and its inclusion in a curricular structure comes through the work of Piechowski (1990) and Piirto (1992). They have advocated the use of biography and autobiography of eminent individuals as tools to understanding the creative personality, the creative process, and creative products. While this approach has been advocated in curriculum for the gifted over the past 60-plus years (e.g., Hollingworth, 1926), study of biography has rarely been employed as a way to explore the humanities. Yet, the lives of the eminent may provide the richest and most challenging material for gifted students to use in their quest for understanding the best works of humankind.

## Issues in Implementing Humanities Curricula for the Gifted

As with any aspect of a curriculum for the gifted, there are special issues and concerns that must be considered at the stage of implementation. In some respects, the issues are more problematic in the humanities than they are in the other individual domains of study because of the inherent organizational change that is required to adopt a humanities perpective in schools. The integration of subject matter requires a breaking down of the current school operation: scheduling, staffing, and curriculum planning being primary considerations.

**1.** Selecting the right teachers to work with a humanities curricula is perhaps the most fundamental issue. Qualifications to work with such curriculum include the following: (a) a genuine enthusiasm for viewing knowledge in an integrated way, (b) strong training in one area of the humanities, (c) avocational involvements that show interest in other humanities topics or areas of study, (d) flexibility in teaching style, and (e) a strong desire to learn from colleagues also working in this area. It is also useful to consider teachers based on their willingness to engage in team teaching as well as team planning. The complexity of the effort to structure a humanities curriculum requires the combination of conceptual strengths with flexible, open personalities.

**2.** Scheduling a humanities program is a critical dimension of implementation. Two scheduling models seem particularly facilitative. One is block scheduling that allows periods for humanities work to be scheduled back to back. This model aids students and teachers in terms of coordinating and integrating both the concepts and the logistics of such a program. Another helpful scheduling model is a school within a school that allows identified students and their teachers to be scheduled separately from the total school. This model allows for maximum flexibility in time to be allocated and limits the effects of irregular scheduling on the total system.

**3.** Whereas the large issues of planning and implementing a humanities curriculum have been addressed throughout this chapter, it is useful to comment on some common organizational difficulties that tend to emerge:

a. At the secondary level, the issue of credit to be given for humanities coursework is often a barrier to implementation. It usually is easiest if one, but preferably two, core departments are willing to award credit for the coursework. Typically these are the social studies and English departments. Although fine arts departments are often willing to award credit, the importance of those credits for graduation and college is not seen by gifted students or their parents as highly valuable.

b. Deciding on the organizational approach to humanities work may be extremely difficult in some school contexts. Strong proponents of theme-oriented curriculum often clash with those who prefer more traditional orientations such as the study of cultures. Since it is important for the institutionalization of the program to build consensus, one way to handle differences is by compromise. Since all humanities work involves several levels of study and analysis, it is possible to accommodate global themes and cultural studies in a loose fit; conversely, it is possible to fit themes within the broad context of cultural study.

c. Although it is tempting to allow a humanities program to utilize many outside speakers and community resources, it is dangerous to have the overriding impression of the program be one of a potpourri of topics and presentations that do not necessrily fit together except at a very general level. Consequently, guarding against the reliance on outside instructors may be important to ensure that you are building a rich tapestry of understanding of an idea at several levels and not just superficially exposing students to many different stimuli.

## Conclusion

As educators of the gifted, we can point to many noble experiments with these learners that have appeared to succeed. We speak often of their need to understand themselves, other people, and other ways of life. We also anticipate their future "greatness" as creative producers in whatever their chosen fields. And we value their potential contribution to making a better society in which to live. Yet these worthy expectations can only be adequately addressed in a humanities curriculum that deliberately integrates thought and feeling, skill and idea, and subject and object. For it is in this context that the power of the individual can be developed—the character as well as the intellect.

### Key Points Summary

• *At the most abstract level of Phenix's "acts of man," the humanities provide an integration of all domains of study.*

- *Humanities approaches need to be incorporated at all stages of development and levels of K–12 schooling.*
- *Important characteristics of humanities study is that it is value focused, interdisciplinary, topical, student centered, intellectual, and creative.*
- *Humanities curriculum exemplifies the best of concept curriculum in its orientiation to interdisciplinary work that is organized around important ideas.*
- *The program models for integrating humanities curriculum include school-within-a-school programs, seminars, separate courses, the teachers of philosophy, and individual thematic units of study.*
- *Humanities teaching and learning is concerned about drawing out the learner to recognize multiple and relative perspectives on issues, themes, and problems.*
- *The humanities provide an appropriate context in which to teach the heuristics of creativity and to practice the construction of personal meaning through product generation.*

## Selected Materials for Use in Humanities Programs for the Gifted

*Philosophy for Children program.* c/o Matthew Lipman, Montclair State College, Montclair, NJ. *Primary audience:* intermediate middle-school gifted students.

> *This set of reading materials that focus on students caught in common human dilemmas emphasizes a philosophical orientation to student discussions that promote an examination of values and their role in human decision making. Used as a literary tool, the selections lend themselves well to student understanding of human motivation, conflict, and common literary themes and issues. The program also constitutes a strong critical-thinking vehicle for teaching and learning in that domain.*

*The Humanities* (undated). Louise Dudley and Austin Faricy. New York: McGraw-Hill. *Primary audience:* secondary.

> *This humanities text focuses on literature, the visual arts, and music, and attempts to conceptually present the humanities as the artistic creations by all people at all times, stressing that art lives because it is appreciated and enjoyed at an experiential level. The book is organized around key concepts in the arts: subject, function, medium, organization, style, and judgment. Powerful examples from various art forms are used to illustrate ideas. This is an excellent resource for the teacher in a humanities program.*

*Civilization.* Kenneth Clark. New York: Harper and Row. *Primary audience:* secondary.

> *This classic book blends the traditional art forms with a strong sense of historical context as a basis for the dicussion of what constitutes a civilization. Useful in humanities programs for the gifted, the book also could be used as a social studies text from the perspective of world cultures. It is a compendium of scholarly references and archetypal concepts. A PBS television series captured salient elements of the book and is available on videotape.*

*Concept Curriculum for the Gifted.* Joyce VanTassel-Baska and John Feldhusen. c/o Keystone Consortium, P.O. Box 2377, West Lafayette, IN 47906. *Primary audience:* elementary and junior high.

> *This set of units is organized around four concepts: change, signs and symbols, reasoning, and problem solving in each of the core subject matter areas, including language arts, social*

*studies, mathematics, and science. Developed for use in pull-out or self-contained programs, the curriculum is organized by primary, intermediate, and junior-high levels.*

*The Discoverers.* (1985). Daniel Boorstein. New York; Vintage Books. *Primary audience:* secondary.

*This book provides teachers and students with a perspective on world history frameworks according to important ideas and policies rather than people and events. A more current book by the same author,* The Creators, *is also an excellent source of ideas about creativity.*

# References

*Academic excellence in the humanities.* (1982). Seattle WA: The Northwest Clearinghouse for Gifted Education.

Brandwein, P. (1971). *The permanent agenda of man: The humanities.* New York: Harcourt, Brace, and Jovanovich.

*Creativity: The human resource.* (1980). VanNuys, CA: The Chevron Research Company.

Hollingworth, L. (1926). *Gifted children.* New York: World Book.

Lindsey, B. (1981). Cornerstones and keystones: Humanities for the gifted and talented. *Roeper Review, 4*(2), 6–9.

Perry, W. G. (1970). *Forms of intellectual and ethical development in the college years.* New York: Holt, Rinehart, and Winston.

Phenix, P. H. (1964). *Realms of meaning.* New York: McGraw-Hill.

Piaget, J. (1962). *Plays, dreams and imitation in childhood.* New York: W. W. Norton.

Piechowski, M. (1990). Eleanor Roosevelt: Portrait of self-activation. In D. Ventis & J. VanTassel-Baska (Eds.), *Developmental perspectives on the gifted.* Williamsburg, VA: College of William and Mary, Center for Gifted Education.

Piirto, J. (1992). *Understanding those who create.* Columbus, OH: Ohio Psychology Press.

Schroeder, F. (1981). Trends for the future in humanities for the gifted student. *Roeper Review, 4* (2), 12–15.

VanTassel-Baska, J. (1974). *The Phoenix project curriculum guide.* Toledo, OH: Toledo Public Schools.

VanTassel-Baska, J., & Feldhusen, J. (1981). *Concept curriculum for the gifted.* Matteson, IL: Matteson School District.

Ward, V. (1961). *An axiomatic model for educating the gifted.* Columbus, OH: Charles Merrill.

Chapter *12*

# Arts Curriculum for the Gifted

*KENNETH SEELEY*

> *Art is not a mirror held up to reality, but a hammer with which to shape it.*
> *—BERTOLDT BRECHT*

The educational world of most students is comprised of compartmentalized, segmented, and arbitrarily assigned academic domains of study that are taught separately, often in courses by different teachers, from different departments, in different classrooms, at different times of the day. This organization of learning and knowledge may promote efficient schedules for mass education, but it gives little time and attention to aesthetics or the relatedness of knowledge in various disciplines. Given this structure and its inertia, we as educators need to examine alternatives that provide bridges among knowledge, experience, and awareness. It is the arts as well as the humanities that offer such bridges.

The overall goal of teaching the arts to gifted learners is to help these students scrutinize the knowledge, experience, and values they derive from all of their studies and to translate them into unique and satisfying portrayals and explanations of their existence. In order to achieve this broad and complex goal, we must create arts experiences that are:

1. *Interpretive or integrative* of the student's knowledge and experience
2. *Normative* in helping the student move toward an understanding of art forms and the student's own appreciation of these forms
3. *Critical* in strengthening the student's ability to question, confront, deliberate, judge, and create alternative forms

It is also important to adopt a philosophy regarding the arts that will provide the basis for curriculum development activities. Much has been written about the philosophy of art.

282

In his landmark work, *Art as Experience,* originally published in 1934, Dewey provides an excellent philosophical beginning for our treatment of the arts experience. Dewey states,

> *The real work of art is the building up of an integral experience out of the interaction of organic and environmental conditions and energies. . . . The thing expressed is wrung from the producer by the pressure exercised by objective things upon the natural impulses and tendencies. . . . The act of expression that constitutes a work of art is a construction in time, not an instantaneous emission. . . . It means that the expression of the self in and through a medium, constituting the work of art, is itself a prolonged interaction of something issuing from the self with objective conditions, a process in which both of them acquire a form and order they did not at first possess. (pp. 64–65)*

The inferences drawn from Dewey's philosophy about "real art" might be summarized as:

- *Art requires an integrating and interactive process to produce it.*
- *Art uses emotion ("natural impulses and tendencies") combined with objective materials and forms.*
- *Art takes a prolonged period of time to produce.*
- *Art is an expression of self into a chosen work.*
- *Art results in both the artist and the medium for the art acquiring characteristics that are new and perhaps unique.*

Dewey's philosophy can be used as a point of departure for curriculum developers to refine their own philosophy and values. The philosophy for curriculum development must address a differentiation of arts for *all* versus arts for the *gifted.* This is not intended to diminish the importance of existing arts curricula. Rather, it implies that an arts curriculum for the gifted must extend and enrich what exists because the potential of the gifted student is to become a real artist. Certainly, art, theater and music classes, art appreciation, and aesthetics should be integral parts of a good school curriculum. These activities can serve to identify those students with exceptional potential who need their talent developed through specialized experiences.

## What Can the Arts Provide?

As advocates for the gifted, we must also become advocates for the arts if we are to have our children move from the focus on the head to the heart and soul of human experience which make a whole individual. Education focuses on the average head. Gifted education focuses on the superior head. The arts give us an opportunity to move beyond the narrow intellectual pursuits of even "good" schooling. Specifically, the arts provide:

1. A universal means of communication as both creator and observer
2. A mechanism to transmit and understand a culture across generations

3. A means to understand the underlying concepts of many subjects in the curriculum through the elements of sound, movement, color, mass, energy, space, line, shape, and language
4. The medium for expressing deep emotions in verbal or nonverbal forms
5. An integrating force that weaves through the humanities and provides emotional voice and insight to knowledges
6. A connection to play and childhood essential to the development of sensitivity and creativity which can be applied to any human endeavor irrespective of age
7. Attention to personal observation, self awareness, and self-expression which is important in the development of self-esteem
8. A sense of pleasure, challenge, and mystery that can bring learning to life

In 1988, The National Endowment for the Arts released the results of a study of the state of arts education in the United States. The report defines four parts of a national mission for arts education:

1. To give our young people a sense of civilization
2. To foster creativity
3. To teach effective communication
4. To provide the tools for critical assessment of what one reads, sees, and hears

The report goes on to summarize that basic arts education does not exist in the United States today. There is little to indicate that anything has improved between this 1988 report and today. The budgetary crises at all levels and the lack of inclusion of the arts in the president's national goals for education promote a back-to-basics mentality and continued erosion of support for arts curricula.

In an address to the President's Committee on the Arts and Humanities, Harold Williams, of the Getty Trust, outlined three major reasons why the arts continue to be ignored by schools. (Williams, 1991). First, the arts are seen as dealing with emotion and not the development of the mind. Second, arts are not formally assessed, and consequently do not promote a student's academic upward mobility. Finally, Williams asserted that the arts are ignored because art educators focus almost exclusively on developing students' creative talent.

The idea that the arts address only emotional expression fails to take into account the appropriate role of the arts in using inventive problem solving, developing analytic and synthetic reasoning ability, and refining of critical thinking and judgments. Further, the lack of formal assessment devalues the arts as serious fields of study. This may change in that mainstream approaches to student assessment are adding portfolio assessment. Serious artists have used this form of outcome evaluation to present themselves and their work for centuries. Finally, arts educators must move beyond merely creative talent and deal with issues of substance such as aesthetics, thinking skills, art history, and criticism in the arts curriculum. While the arts can provide much substance in a curriculum for gifted learners, we function in an educational context that examines the larger picture of arts education.

## The Arts for Whom?

Given the reality of limited funding for education, it is important to define early the role of the arts for various types of learners in schools. Early exposure to the arts is important if we are to find talent and develop it. This implies a curriculum philosophy of arts for all students as a means of finding potential talent. In later years of schooling, the instruction needs to become more intense and specialized. Unfortunately, the arts suffer from a value system that sees this area of the curriculum as a frill or fad. As an advocate for the arts, Lorin Hollander, a concert pianist who started as a prodigy with the New York Philharmonic at age 12, has some important words:

> *A back to basics mentality in the schools, if it weren't so tragic, would be ludicrous. But that's what they're doing. How dare they? How dare they trust whatever common denominator came up with this theory: that the arts and arts education are expendable to mankind. This is criminal. It is not intelligent. I believe that if arts education is not handled with creativity and care and brilliance in the public schools, then we are asking for severe mental disturbance in our communities. How will people touch, spiritually embrace? We are equipping kids with words and numbers and strong legs and arms, and then they confront each other, spout at each other, have no sense of the humanity in each other, like two points of triangles, with their feelings behind them, never learning how to use them, and these feelings are then turned inward.*

If we are to find and develop young artists, we must have active arts programs in schools. This chapter focuses on the arts for talented children, but we must be advocates of a firm general curriculum base in the arts from which to build specialized curriculum. An arts curriculum is essential for the talent development of children with high potential, whether artistically gifted or academically gifted. It heightens sensitivity and creative ability. It provides emotional outlets and a medium for expression that words and numbers cannot. The arts also provide a new means of understanding and explaining complex phenomena of human endeavor and human motivation.

In order to answer the question, Arts for whom? it is important to wrestle with the value questions of how public education views the arts. If, as Hollander (1978) has suggested, the arts are seen as expendable, then it may require a course of action that limits arts to the gifted education curriculum, if they are to be included at all. Even within the field of gifted education, the arts are typically given short shrift. It appears at this juncture that in most school settings it will be an uphill battle. However, the struggle must continue if we value the intellectual and emotional well-being of our children. The education of gifted children is a logical vehicle for developing a meaningful arts curriculum in unique ways.

However, it is necessary to address some of the political realities of public education. It is unlikely that public schools would ever offer sufficient curriculum in all areas of the arts to challenge the most talented students. Indeed, families often need to support the talent development of their children through private study with artists, yet some families may not be able to do so because of economic disadvantage. However, the schools can provide an important set of basic arts exposures from which future opportunities at least have a chance to flower because the talent becomes identified.

## *Outcomes of a K–12 Arts Curriculum*

The College Board (1985) has defined a set of outcomes for arts curriculum by the end of grade 12 that provide an important beginning for considering gifted curriculum experiences. These outcomes can frame the development of specific arts curriculum for gifted students at each grade level; however, it would be preferable to integrate these outcomes into interdisciplinary classroom experiences.

Preparation in the arts will be valuable to students whatever their intended field of study. The actual practice of the arts can engage the imagination, foster flexible ways of thinking, develop disciplined effort, and build self-confidence. Appreciation of the arts is integral to the understanding of other cultures sought in the study of history, foreign language, and social science. For some, such college-level work will lead to careers in the arts. For many others, it will permanently enhance the quality of their lives, whether they continue artistic activity as an avocation or they learn to appreciate the arts as observers and members of audiences.

All able learners will benefit from the following general preparation in the arts:

- *The ability to understand and appreciate the unique qualities of each of the arts*
- *The ability to appreciate how people of various cultures have used the arts to express themselves*
- *The ability to understand and appreciate different artistic styles and works from representative historical periods and cultures*
- *Some knowledge of the social and intellectual influences affecting artistic form*
- *The ability to use the skills, media, tools, and processes required to express themselves in one or more of the arts*

Students also will profit from more intensive preparation in at least one of the four areas of the arts: visual arts, theater, music, and dance.

If the preparation of students is in the *visual arts,* they will need the following knowledge and skills:

- *The ability to identify and describe—using the appropriate vocabulary—various visual art forms from different historical periods*
- *The ability to analyze the structure of a work of visual art*
- *The ability to evaluate a work of visual art*
- *To know how to express themselves in one or more of the visual art forms, such as drawing, painting, photography, weaving, ceramics, and sculpture*

If the preparation is in *theater,* they will need the following knowledge and skills:

- *The ability to identify and describe—using the appropriate vocabulary—different kinds of plays from different historical periods*

- *The ability to analyze the structure, plot, characterization, and language of a play, both as a literary document and as a theater production*
- *The ability to evaluate a theater production*
- *To know how to express themselves by acting or improvising in a play, by writing a play, or by directing or working behind the scenes of a theater production*

If the preparation is in *music,* they will need the following knowledge and skills:

- *The ability to identify and describe—using the appropriate vocabulary—various musical forms from different historical periods*
- *The ability to listen perceptively to music, distinguishing such elements as pitch, rhythm, timbre, and dynamics*
- *The ability to read music*
- *The ability to evaluate a musical work or performance*
- *To know how to express themselves by playing an instrument, singing in a group or individually, or composing music*

If the preparation is in *dance,* they will need the following knowledge and skills:

- *The ability to identify and describe—using the appropriate vocabulary—dances of various cultures and historical periods*
- *The ability to analyze various techniques, styles, and choreographic forms*
- *The ability to evaluate a dance performance*
- *To know how to express themselves through dancing or choreography*

## Differentiating Curriculum in the Arts

For the purposes of discussion in this chapter, "the arts" refer to the major fine and performing arts, including visual arts, dance, music, theater, and creative writing. Curriculum development that addresses all of these areas is based on the general model presented in Chapter 1. The model suggests three areas of curriculum differentiation: modifying the core curriculum, extending the core, and integrating the curriculum areas. There is great variation both within and across public schools on core curriculum in the arts. Within schools the variation is usually by level. Secondary schools typically have more highly developed offerings in the arts than at the elementary level. This variation is particularly problematic for talented young children, but it could be mediated by allowing such children access to secondary classes on a part-time basis. The variation across school districts has to do with the nature and extent of the curriculum offerings in the arts. For instance, some school districts have no special art teachers or music teachers at the elementary level. It is also rare to find specialized drama classes at the elementary or middle-school level. Also, the level of instruction in the arts in public schools is typically too broadly based to challenge the very talented young artist. Therefore, the modification of the core curriculum in the arts for the talented student is very situation specific. In some instances there is no curriculum to modify.

The following strategies are suggested for modifying the core curriculum:

1. Allow talented elementary students to attend secondary arts classes.
2. Cluster talented students by using magnet schools and offer advanced instruction such as master classes and individualized approaches.
3. Articulate existing school arts programs for individual talented students who are studying privately.
4. Utilize the artists-in-the-schools program for some specialized offerings for the most talented students.

In order to consider the concept of an extended core curriculum for the arts, it is necessary to do an extensive needs assessment of individual students. Once there is a determination of the talent areas, level of ability, and location of the students, the extended curriculum can be developed. If the strategies suggested for modifying the core are in place, it is much easier to begin the extension process. Programs for gifted young artists need a process/product extension that typically goes beyond what most schools offer. Differentiating curriculum at this stage requires some or all of the following alternatives to be considered:

1. Create master classes in each art area for the most talented students, based on ability and irrespective of age.
2. Utilize community mentors/artists to provide individual talent development on an ongoing basis.
3. Create alternatives within each art area that are not found in the typical core curriculum such as music composition, conducting, theatrical directing and producing, use of nontraditional art media, writing novels or extensive works, or choreography.
4. Generate real audiences and outlets for the students' products or performances such as commercial gallery exhibits; solo or ensemble performances with adult dance, music, or theatrical groups; or submitting creative writing for publication.
5. Develop collaboration efforts in the arts.

## Considering the Visual Arts

Special attention is given here to the visual arts because they are typically not well addressed in the curriculum for talented youth, nor is there as much private instruction available in this area as in the other arts. Outlets for the performing arts are more common, and creative writing is often well developed in both regular and gifted education. However, the recognition and specific development of young visual artists rarely occurs in school, even though it is important to find these students at an early age.

Gardner (1980) stated, "For it is in the activity of the young child, his preconscious sense of form, his willingness to explore and to solve problems that arise, his capacity to take risks, his affective needs, which must be worked out in a symbolic realm—that we find the crucial seeds of the greatest artistic achievement."

Typically, the first artistic activity that children are exposed to is drawing. Gifted young visual artists often will skip or accelerate through the normal stages of drawings that are described in most art education texts. However, there has not been a visual arts equivalent of a prodigy who achieved adult eminence as we might find in music, drama, or verbal areas. This phenomenon may relate to the development of fine motor skills and visual-spatial ability required for accomplished visual art. It may also be related to lack of opportunity for intense and sustained instruction in visual art. At present, this is merely speculation, but it would certainly make for an important research project to see if accelerating visual art instruction results in precocious ability as in other areas.

Identifying young visual artists for a special program is typically done by three different approaches similar to identifying all gifted children. A product review of the child's art work by artists (typically accompanied by an interview) is a common approach. Another way is to have a special art program open to anyone who wants to come as a means of exposing children to serious peers with opportunities for focused art activities. Finally, there is a self-nomination process after the child has a clear understanding of the program.

Some specialized tests have been developed that may help in the identification. After nine years of research of artistically gifted students, the Wilson Cognitive Instrument was developed, in which a self-evaluation Likert-type scale is used. Wilson (see Hurwitz, 1983) developed another art test—the National Assessment of Art Test for students ages 9 to 17 years, which provides standards for teachers to use in evaluating children's art.

Hurwitz (1983) provided an informative handbook for those who would plan programs for talented students in the visual arts. He has given excellent exemplary program descriptions, such as self-study units for the Gifted in Art from Worcester, Massachusetts. This is an upper-elementary art program that allows the artistically talented students to work in their own regular classrooms on specially designed independent study units. Another example of an elementary-level program is Aesthetic Education for the Intellectually Gifted at William Ward School in New Rochelle, New York. Here, a team of artists (art, dance, drama, and media) worked with intellectually gifted students in a year-long pull-out program. A high school exemplary program is described at the Milwaukee Art Center (a city museum), which operates a studio course for high school credit over a semester for a daily two-hour program. Hurwitz has also recommended the Advanced Placement Program in art areas.

## Curriculum Integration in the Arts

The integration of the arts may represent the most appropriate area for gifted education curriculum development, in that most skill development in individual areas is done by specialists or through private study. This section focuses on collaboration in the arts as a means of integration. Other means of integration can be done in more verbal areas such as art history, philosophy of art, aesthetics, and art appreciation.

Collaboration in the arts is often misunderstood as one art form being an adjunct to another. Some examples are the relationship of music as background for dance, or visual art as scenery background for theater. This is not collaboration, however; it is merely a layering of art forms. Collaboration requires an interweaving of the arts to meet the following criteria: (1) each art form must have its own integrity and be able to stand alone, (2) there must be common elements in each art form that relate to the other, and (3) the whole must be greater than the sum of its parts. Collaboration is both a process and a product. As a process, it has artists working together as equals in the development of the ideas and concepts as well as the techniques to implement those ideas. One artist is not more important than the other in the process. The collaborative product must meet the above three criteria and create a unique impact on the audience that would not happen if the individual art pieces were presented by themselves.

Collaboration in the arts is not widely done nor is it easy to do. It requires of artists an openness and vulnerability that may be uncomfortable. The creative writer who writes lyrics with a composer needs to analyze the music critically as it relates to the words, and the musician must do the same with the words as it relates to the music. The teamwork required can be trying and at times a battle of wills between and among artists. It is this human dynamic that makes the collaborative process difficult and has probably limited the number of significant collaborations in the world of art.

Collaboration makes the student think critically about the arts. Criteria are established by which to evaluate a collaboration critically. Three questions are used to analyze each collaborative effort:

1. Does the collaboration find common elements in each discipline? A successful collaboration somehow identifies an idea, a theme, a word, a concept—something about which each discipline has something to say.
2. Can the separate elements from each discipline stand on their own? A successful collaboration is made up of parts from each artistic discipline that have their own integrity and quality.
3. Are the separate elements of each discipline even better for being part of the collaboration as a whole? A successful collaboration is a whole that is greater than the sum of its parts.

Having these defined criteria by which to judge a collaboration, the students develop a critical vocabulary that can also be applied to individual disciplines. Students gain confidence in their own ability to speak critically about the arts, and they learn that criticism is not a personal judgment but rather a constructive tool in the creative process. Criticism is an integral part of any collaboration; it provides the direction and structure for revision and refinement of the work in progress. The students learn to view their work as a work in progress rather than as a final statement that has no room for change or improvement.

Collaboration also contributes greatly to the development of the individual. Interpersonal skills come into play as students learn to interact effectively with a group as the group works toward a common goal. Each student must identify and defend his or her own values and learn how to stand up for those values in the creative process. There is a give and take in the process of collaboration that helps students recognize when to acquiesce and when to stand firm for a given idea or principle. It is through this interaction that a student begins to understand his or her own creative process within the larger context of the group. Students learn how to be supportive as well as critical of one another.

The process of collaboration involves first identifying a common idea or theme that relates in some way to each artistic discipline. Then each discipline is explored to find how it can contribute to the creation of the work, maintaining the integrity of its own expression while going beyond itself to find a unified expression of all of the artistic disciplines involved in the process.

Through the process of collaborating with artists from other disciplines, the student must first define and articulate the concerns and unique qualities of his or her own discipline. Only then is the student able to begin to search for the common ground between artistic disciplines. Indirectly, collaboration embodies the quest for self-expression and the development of the individual that is at the center of the arts.

In order to establish similarities between artistic disciplines, the student must examine the language used in each discipline to try to find a common vocabulary to describe the concerns of each discipline relative to a common goal. Conversely, the student also discovers through this process the differences between disciplines, finding that each discipline has its own unique concerns and language that have no application to other disciplines.

## Application of the Collaborative Process

To translate this process into a gifted education program, it is important to discuss the concept at length and build on the student artists' creative powers. Three elements are recommended as an approach to teaching collaboration:

1. Develop a common vocabulary across the arts involved.
2. Teach the basics of artistic criticism as a constructive process that leads to the final element.
3. Employ revision and refinement over time.

Gibson (1986) has developed a glossary of art terms that provide a mechanism for teachers and students to integrate the arts through a common vocabulary used across them. It is an example for a teacher to use, change, or add to with students as an important exercise to broaden perspectives. If a musician can understand what a visual artist means by *space,* what a creative writer means by *space,* and what a dancer means by *space,* the common understanding is the basis for good collaboration. More than an exercise in general semantics, the vocabulary-building activity among student artists can help them understand their own art better, as well as other arts.

The second element of criticism is greatly aided by having a common vocabulary and also identifying any vocabulary that is unique to one art form. This understanding facilitates critical analyses of collaborations that may be used as examples, such as professional exhibits and performances in the community. It further facilitates the criticism expressed between student artists about their developing collaborative ideas and products. Formal instruction in criticism would be helpful, particularly in assisting in the development of careful observation and listening skills. This may be introduced as a unit on aesthetics that incorporates the vocabulary-building exercises, all as a prelude to the collaboration effort.

The most difficult of the three elements to communicate to young artists is the final concept of revision. There is a widespread myth that the most creative productions are spontaneous or instantaneous. These creative "Aha's!" are seen as the final product. As Dewey (1934) aptly pointed out in his philosophy, "A work of art is a construction in time, not an instantaneous emission" (p. 65). Too often the young artists immediately transform their creative ideas into a product and believe they are done. The initial product must be seen as a beginning—not an end. Teachers of the gifted can present many case studies of great artists, writers, dancers, and musicians who take long periods through many iterations and revisions to reach what they felt was close to a final product. Revision must be viewed as a necessary part of the creative process if the product is to have significance and meaning. Revision does not diminish the importance of the initial creative idea. It should be seen as enriching and developing it in a cycle that may generate many products and take many turns over time. This is particularly true for the performing arts, although visual artists may view a completed painting as only one product along the way of the development of their original creative idea. They do not feel "done" even though the canvas or the sculptured piece is on display in a gallery.

When teachers of the gifted attempt this integration of the arts idea by using art teachers or artists from the community, they should not expect an enthusiastic response. Most artists are invested in their own art medium and view integration as one art serving as handmaiden to another. The teacher of the gifted can play the unique role of facilitator and "integrator" among the student artists and adult artists.

## Collaboration by Arts Disciplines

In order to move from the collaborative process discussion to the real world of instructional settings, a number of artists were asked to share their thoughts about collaboration as they have experienced it in their classes. The following sections, organized by arts areas, contain the key ideas of artists who have taught in the Clayton Foundation Collaborative Arts Program (1991).

### Dance

Collaboration best occurs in dance classes when the students are ready—that is, when they have a knowledge base and experience to draw on and when their critiquing skills are sharp. Self-esteem and trust should have been established as well. The students must realize they are ready to expand and merge notions of dance with perspectives of other art forms. They must have matured beyond the making of "pretty" dances and be willing to take risks trying new things. Space, too, is important. Dancers must have room to move. Dance, however, as it deals so effectively with the abstract—through theme, gesture, emotion—readily complements the other arts, yet protects its own integrity.

Dance can build self-esteem through a step-by-step process:

1. Always teach class warm-ups in such a manner that everyone can complete the tasks. Let students feel success immediately.
2. Any critiques offered during warm-ups should be geared toward showing what is good in an individual's work, how it could be made better, and how it could be expanded more fully to say what is intended.
3. The instructor should take time to talk about and practice critiquing skills with the class.
4. Skills for expanding movement should then be practiced in the second half of the class and might best be called the "crafts of choreography."
5. Students must collaborate among themselves in their own discipline before integrat-

ing their efforts with students from the other arts. Keep assignments simple in the beginning. Make them precise, clear studies.

6. The actual seeding and planting of collaborative opportunities is most effectively achieved if students choose topics close to their hearts and at the same time somewhat universal (for example, emotions, fears, yearnings, and so on).

Each dance collaborator needs to sit out and observe a piece in progress in order to sense its wholeness and life. The mystery and miracle of the piece itself will emerge—if given a chance. The basis for collaboration using dance might be defined as the ability to escape technique by mastering it so the students can move on to more original expressions of movement. In addition, it is centrally important that the collaborating artists occasionally step back and allow the materials and the process to breathe, to gain new life.

### Music

Collaboration with other disciplines seems to nurture the music composition process in the beginning experimental stages, both as a stimulus to improvisation and as a guideline for musical structures. There are many ways to stimulate this collaboration. Importantly, though, one should begin each session with warm-ups deliberately structured to facilitate making connections between the arts. For instance, visual images, perhaps taken from a painting by a student in the class, can be used to suggest different emotions, which are translated into purely musical motifs, spontaneous sounds, rhythms, and pitches that correspond with the students' inner impressions of the observed work. Impressions of stories, movements, and different kinds of visual art can be expressed successfully with group efforts, group improvisations, and group composition.

One can derive musical phrases from technical influences. Assign scale values to the digits of a student's phone number. Turn everyone's number into a melody, then choose appropriate instruments, tones, and cadences. The teacher can also encourage students to compose music to reflect the character of videos observed without sound. More and more, image and sound are being combined by our culture; such a drill would allow students to participate in this trend.

Collaboration simply denotes two or more art forms stimulating each artist's perceptions and working together to create a single form. Not all the brainstorming done at the beginning of the collaborative process needs to be verbal. Improvisation and more unconventional processes can also be implemented to start the process along.

### Theatre

In many respects, collaboration is the foundation for the community art form—theatre. The collaborative process is basic to building theatrical productions, with one major exception. When a team of designers, technicians, and actors work together, their creative process and contribution must fall within the parameters of the director's interpretation and focus on the script.

One of the first things to do with a group of students is to review the basic rules of brainstorming: (1) all ideas are good/valid, (2) do not judge or put down any of them, (3) remind students of the amount of time devoted to the process, and (4) ask what is important in their lives and experiences.

The next goal is to focus the ideas and weed out ones the group is most interested in exploring. It is important to determine what is appealing to her or his sensibilities for further work. Next, we look for patterns and ties in the ideas. Also important to remember is that you are asking students to share very private, personal information; so there has to be respect for those who are open and for the fact that the information gathered is confidential. Collaboration of anything personal must be created with some privacy, trust, and time. Certainly, collaborations can be built in a more public, short-term way, but they will have a different texture, message, and feeling.

At the end of each session, determine what the next day's goals for collaboration would be. The students should discuss and decide what needs to be done. As the collaborations develop, the techniques of critique and revision are used, stressing the importance of examining what is good and strong.

### Visual Arts

In collaboration, the visual arts best function when the artists involved are open to direct, clear observation; when they are capable of reflecting the moment and translating it into a visible language and remain open to revision; and when collaboration is *not* so performance oriented as to force exhibitionism and pretentious activity.

Some teaching hints to keep in mind when collaborating using the visual arts include the following:

1. Teach and model flexibility.
2. Make your product strong and resilient.
3. Remember that the art element of the collaboration should be able to stand on its own.
4. Develop with the students continuing lists of possible places where exciting art environments could be created.
5. Ask devilish questions.
6. Help set goals and deadlines.

### Writing

Collaboration is most easily prepared for in young writers by practicing writing in what rhetorical jargon calls "their own voice." That is to say, most of the young writers have spent a good deal of their time, as writers, imitating others. And, of course, this is a wonderful exercise. When James Joyce does it, we crank out papers about "influence." In addition, imitation creates fluency and confidence. But, relying too often upon copying models in order to create product can also generate whole classrooms full of people all writing the same tidy little parodies. Writing this kind of imitated material will not prepare one to collaborate with other young artists and teaches nothing about the process of how writers actually do write.

The creative writing process begins by focusing the different kinds of voices available from open and closed poetic forms. On the other hand, we study poetic lives like those of William Carlos Williams or John Skelton. By contrast, we study the ballad, and then write some about school, friends, and skateboards. We do controlled two and three beat lines; we experiment with rhyme schemes. Then, try to get out of the way and assign writing tasks that make the students choose how a given emotion or idea might best be captured for an audience. They must decide whether to use prose or poetry, and be able to tell why. If they are using prose, they must be able to describe what exactly they want the parts of their piece to do, to create, to picture. Regarding their poetry, they must be able to talk about why it rhymes or does not, why it has the stress patterns it does.

All of these kinds of drills will prepare students to adapt to the flow of collaborative endeavors. Unless they are prepared to adapt, unless they are allowed to think about intent and reaction and about the limits of parody, young writers may find working in collaborative projects frustrating. Everyone else will be off down the road, while the writers are still trying to figure out how to write something they have already seen or done.

## *Aesthetics*

Technology in general and television in particular have induced dramatic changes in people's perceptions of time and of effort. Not so long ago, pace of life was measured; housework took time, travel took time, and food wasn't fast. People listened to each other, read out loud, and listened for hours to oratory. Later, people listened to the radio, creating pictures with their minds. They *expected* that everything took time and required physical or mental effort. Not so today: Television gives easily understood information instantaneously. If you don't get it right away, change the channel. Attention span is geared to the eight minutes between commercials. Watching television is passive; no response is required. You are not imaging much or learning much because you are not creating what you see—it is given. Moreover, the familiar and readily available television fare crowds out other forms of entertainment—our students literally don't know what they are missing.

Certainly, they are missing a great deal. The pleasures and stimulation offered by the arts in general are lost to them. They miss catharsis and emotional quiet—and just at the stage when they most desperately need them. Indeed, they are missing a sense of connection to others.

As a result of their contemporary lives, students need to understand a few basic concepts about art:

1. Art is universal in some form; art has been created in every human place and culture.
2. Each culture has its own artistic preferences, reflecting its own views.
3. Art survives because people like it. Art adds meaning to their lives.
4. Art is not nature. Art is deliberate selection, rearrangement, ordering, and intensification.
5. A work of art is created over time. A well-documented moment of inspiration is usually preceded by intense immersion of the artistic problem.

Building on these key ideas, teachers make use of guiding questions that encourage students to take a closer look at art. Here are some good ones:

1. What is it about? Representational art often has a subject; nonrepresentational many times does not.
2. What is it for? Crafts are the most likely arts to have functions; poetry and painting often have the least. Picasso's antiwar painting is a strong exception to the rule.
3. What is it made of? The medium is the raw substance of art.
4. How is it done? Style often reflects a particular shared point of view or the personality of the maker.
5. How is it put together? Form, genre, and elements are all aspects of art organization.

When using such cues, students will need to develop a common vocabulary to think and speak clearly one with another. Aesthetics is best taught in ways that generally work well with students by using (1) active participation, (2) links with one's own concern, (3) vivid humor, (4) peer interaction, and (5) variety and tangible support.

The process of aesthetics education consists of repeated and varied experiences in seeing and hearing, doing, and responding to art. The interplay of all three kinds of experience will stimulate aesthetic appreciation. Being able to explore many types of art by doing is extremely important. Creating art allows students to be active, work with peers, express their individuality and perhaps their emotions, and produces a tangible product. Experiencing the process allows them to appreciate the work of artists more fully. They begin to think as artists do. They learn about the elements and nuances of making art.

Thus, we see the essential role of collaboration in aesthetics. It is the conduit whereby aesthetics can efficiently enter the classroom. Moreover, it confronts a series of school issues, such as the fragmentation caused by short time blocks and rotating schedules; devaluing of art education that results in cuts in arts programs; the "we/they" relationship between academic and "exploratory" teaching. Aesthetics education incorporated into schools has the power to cure these ills and to make all of school teaching more effective.

## Magnet Schools in the Arts

Some large cities offer a specialized high school in the arts. (Certainly this concept was popularized by the movie and television series *Fame*.) This type of school is a fine resource for meeting the needs of secondary talented students. It has also opened up the world of the arts to less affluent students who could not afford private specialized instruction. One case study is presented here of the New Orleans Center for the Creative Arts (NOCCA) to provide a good example of such a magnet school.

Opened in 1974, NOCCA offers professional arts training in dance, theater, music, writing, and visual arts. It is operated by the New Orleans public schools for 250 students who attend on a half-day basis, spending the other half day in their home schools. The teachers who staff the school are professional performers who work in their arts discipline; they are not typical classroom teachers. Students are selected by audition, interview, and product reviews, with the understanding that they wish to pursue a career in the arts. NOCCA prepares students after three or four years to enter the arts profession for which they were trained. Students also must be academically successful in their home schools to qualify for selection.

Like most arts schools, this magnet school is more rigorous than the normal high school. Balancing the normal academics with the specialized arts classes is extremely demanding. In a way, it helps to screen out the less committed students. The world of fine and performing arts is very competitive, and only those who are absolutely committed to their craft have a chance for success.

A recent study of the students at NOCCA was reported by Kauffman, Tews, and Milam (1986). They summarized their findings as follows:

1. Students appear to enjoy and benefit from the depth, breadth, and qualitative differences in their arts training.
2. Students in disciplines that appear to be less academic (dance and visual art) need to be sensitized to the intellectual and academic aspects of their art.
3. Many students experience isolation or rejection as a result of their artistic endeavors.
4. The development of self-esteem and future goals can be among the most significant outcomes of an arts training program.

## A Framework for Developing a Magnet School

The basics in creating a magnet school in the arts includes developing a rationale, goals, organizational pattern, and curriculum. The following were used in the development of the Denver School for the Arts:

### Rationale for a Magnet School

1. Bring a sense of pride to students and the community. It will increase the self-esteem of middle school students.
2. Create a greater awareness and understanding of the performing and visual arts in a community.
3. Increase accessibility to all sectors of the community to various art forms.
4. Elevate opportunities for training and performing for artistic children, showcasing their talents.
5. Provide opportunities to explore new ideas and programs in education.
6. Foster a merger of the various artistic communities already in support of young artists with a school system.
7. Provide an educational program designed to provide a broad intercultural and arts-related vocational program with the overall goal of having each student achieve his or her maximum potential artistically and academically.
8. Create opportunities to work with professional artists that will provide students a perspective of working artists, their technical expertise, and their commitment to their art form.

### Sample Goals

- *To attract a student population from diverse ethnic, cultural, and economic backgrounds on the basis of related interests in the arts*
- *To provide a multicultural educational curriculum*
- *To stimulate community support and involvement in the arts*
- *To develop artistic talents and interests of each student to the maximum*
- *To create equal educational opportunities in both the basic skills and the arts areas*
- *To experience learning through inquiry, experience, and experimentation*
- *To build technical and artistic skills necessary to achieve and perform in specific arts disciplines*
- *To utilize practicing artists and arts agencies in the community*
- *To establish excellence in the arts and acquire scholarships and entrance into institutions of higher education*

- *To provide a bridge into conservatory and highly acclaimed arts programs*
- *To offer exposure to all areas of art and specific areas of concentration*
- *To emphasize collaboration in the arts*

### Typical Organizational Pattern

- *Special classes for novices and masters in specific arts areas*
- *Special evening and weekend classes*
- *Instructional media center supplied with equipment and resources geared to the arts*
- *Professional artists used as teachers and resources*
- *Specialized equipment for production of art works*
- *Existence of varying performing groups for differing levels of accomplishment*
- *Touring companies for outreach*
- *Juried exhibitions of visual art*
- *Introduction to career opportunities related to the various art fields through cooperative programs*
- *Extracurricular programs*

### Sample Curriculum

Visual arts, dance, theatre, vocal music, instrumental music, and creative writing will be the foundation of the arts curriculum, with specialized courses to develop and enhance the talents and interests of the students. Visual and performing arts will be integrated into the content areas of reading, language arts, math, science, and social studies. Arts activities will be selected on the basis of individual interests, needs and skills. An interdisciplinary approach will prevail in all the classes.

Although lacking in number, magnet school programs are valuable models. However, there are many alternatives that smaller communities can develop. A "school within a school" concept that allows flexible scheduling for blocks of time can also provide a viable arts program. Programs with universities and museums can also be developed to provide the specialized arts training for talented high school students.

## Implementation Issues in the Arts

Implementation of arts programs for the gifted present a set of unique issues that require the thoughtful consideration of program and curriculum planners.

**1.** As in the other content areas, a curriculum in the arts for gifted students should extend from the core curriculum. Implementation becomes problematic when there is not a sufficiently rich core curriculum to use as a beginning point for the arts curriculum development. Such situations require teachers and coordinators to create specialized curriculum unique to the gifted program.

**2.** Utilization of arts resource people can pose implementation problems, depending on availability, cooperation, and costs. Artists in the community may be available, but schools may not have sufficient funds to bring them into the classes. Other communities may not have artists available in certain disciplines, or arts resource people within the school may not wish to cooperate with the gifted program. Gaining parental support can be helpful in finding resource people and/or sponsoring fund-raising activities for an artist-in-residence program.

**3.** Developing internal resources to the schools is important if an arts program is to be sustaining and articulated from elementary to secondary levels. Developing and implementing a model curriculum in one area of the arts is helpful in gaining internal support to move to other arts areas. Involving school arts personnel in planning for gifted students is a good way to develop ownership and future cooperation in implementing curriculum.

**4.** Joining forces with arts organizations in the community for advocacy purposes can assist in gaining broader-based support for arts programs in schools. Such relationships can also lead to mentorships for artistically talented students. The overall advocacy effort should help the general climate for the arts in the community.

## Conclusion

Although teachers of the gifted are often called on to be a jack of all trades, they can develop an integrated arts curriculum without being artists. Interdisciplinary approaches are implicit to any quality curriculum for the gifted; the arts are no exception. They provide fertile ground for high-level, challenging learning experiences. The preceding information is built on the curriculum development processes presented in an earlier chapter and provides for the beginning of an integrated arts curriculum for artistically gifted students. These ideas and strategies have been implemented and field-tested with elementary and middle school students in Colorado as part of a state-supported program development effort in gifted education. There is also evidence that these ideas would work with high school students and could provide an additional dimension to arts magnet schools that have traditionally been single-discipline oriented.

### Key Points Summary

- *The development of arts curriculum for the gifted should begin with a philosophy of art that is broad so as to demonstrate the value of arts for all gifted students. The philosophy should also be specific enough to guide curriculum for the most talented in the arts disciplines.*
- *A good basic arts curriculum in the elementary grades is important if we are to find potential art talent, particularly in visual art.*
- *Curriculum in the arts varies greatly among schools and the most talented students often must rely on private instruction to be sufficiently challenged.*
- *Schools can offer many alternatives to talented students by allowing access to secondary school instruction for elementary students, and offering advanced placement programs in the arts to secondary students.*
- *Arts curriculum for gifted students can focus on collaboration and integration with the teacher of the gifted providing facilitation among the artists.*
- *Collaboration in the arts offers many exciting opportunities for talented students to expand beyond their own discipline into new understandings of art in its broadest sense.*

- *Criticism and aesthetics are important elements of arts curriculum from which all gifted students can benefit.*
- *The concept of revision is important to challenge talented students in the arts who have often been praised for a first effort as a final product.*

## References

Clayton Foundation. (1991). *Collaborative arts program.* Denver, CO: Author. College Board. (1985). *Academic preparation for college.* New York: College Board.

Dewey, J. (1934). *Art as experience.* New York: Capricorn Books.

Eisner, E. W. (1972). *Educating artistic vision.* New York: Macmillan.

Gardner, H. (1980). *Artful scribbles: The significance of children's drawings.* New York: Basic Books.

Gibson, R. (1986). A glossary of arts terminology. Clayton Institute for the Arts in the Humanities (occasional paper).

Hollander, L. (1978). Keynote Presentation at the National Forum for the Arts and the Gifted (U.S.O.E., Dept. of H.E.W.), Aspen.

Hurwitz, A. (1983). *The gifted and talented in art.* Worcester, MA: Davis Publications.

Kaufmann, F. A., Tews, T. C., & Milam, C. P. (1986). New Orleans Center for the Creative Arts: Program description and student perceptions. *Gifted Students Institute Quarterly, 11* (3).

Stein, L. (1986). Artists as teachers. Clayton Institute for the Arts and Humanities (occasional paper).

Stein, L. (1986). Collaboration in the arts. Clayton Institute for the Arts and Humanities (occasional paper).

Williams, H. (1991). *The language of civilization: The vital role of arts in education.* New York: President's Committee on Arts and Humanities.

*C h a p t e r* *13*

# Thinking Skills and Curriculum Development

*JOHN F. FELDHUSEN*

*Some problems are so difficult they can't be solved in a million years—unless someone thinks about them for five minutes. —H. L. MENCKEN*

The terms *thinking skills* and *process skills* are often used interchangeably in the field of gifted education. Although there is still very little research to support the teachability of thinking skills, educational practitioners enthusiastically embrace new materials and methods for teaching in this area. Much of the impetus for teaching thinking comes from educational programs to teach creative thinking to children in regular classrooms and from more recent emphases on teaching creative thinking in gifted programs. Although the research evidence is questioned, there certainly is some reason to believe that creative thinking can be enhanced (Tannenbaum, 1983; Feldhusen & Clinkenbeard, 1987). Feldhusen and Treffinger (1975) also reported survey research showing that a vast majority of elementary teachers claim to be teaching creative thinking in their classes.

The pioneering work of Guilford (Guilford & Hoepfner, 1971) paved the way for many of our approaches to the assessment of thinking skills and to conceptions of how to teach them. While focusing our attention on divergent thinking, Guilford also stressed a number of other cognitive skills in the structure of intellect operations (cognition, memory, convergent production, and evaluation) and on reasoning and problem solving. Meeker (1982) continued the work of Guilford and greatly extended it to school applications in both diagnostic testing and curriculum materials to enhance thinking skills. Torrance and Myers (1970) and Williams (1972) carried out extensive curriculum development projects in the area of divergent and creative thinking, which led to widespread acceptance of the concept of teaching thinking skills to children in all subjects and from grades K–12.

The impetus to incorporate thinking skills goals in gifted programs also emerges from the widespread availability of instructional materials that purport to teach thinking skills. *Philosophy in the Classroom* (Lipman, Sharp, & Oscanyan, 1980) is a massive effort to *teach* the skills of logic and critical thinking to children. The two books on *Critical Thinking* by Harnadek (1980) have been widely adopted in gifted programs in the United States, as have the four books, *Building Thinking Skills* by Black and Black (1984). MACOS (Bruner, 1970) has been revived as inquiry training in many gifted programs. Taba's (1962) inquiry teaching model has enjoyed considerable revival in gifted programs. The Bloom *Taxonomy* (1956) has also had profound impact as a guide to higher-level thinking skills in gifted programs.

All of these thinking skills approaches are buttressed by a revival of interest in tests to measure thinking skills: the *Watson-Glaser Test of Critical Thinking* (1980); the *Ennis-Weir Critical Thinking Essay Test* (1985); the *Developing Cognitive Abilities Test* (1980), which measures skills at the higher levels of the Bloom *Taxonomy*; the *Ross Test of Higher Cognitive Processes* (1976); the *Structure of Intellect Learning Abilities Test* (Meeker, 1985); the *Cornell Critical Thinking Test* (Ennis & Millman, 1985); and the *Torrance Tests of Creative Thinking* (1974). When we have tests to measure thinking skills, we feel more confident that the constructs being measured really exist.

More explicit guidance linked to sound theory and research on how to teach thinking skills came in two volumes, *Thinking and learning Skills* (Chipman, Segal, & Glaser, 1985), reporting the results of a conference held at the University of Pittsburgh Learning Research and Development Center. These volumes are notable for their blend of researchers' and practitioners' (teachers') points of view. In *Thought and Knowledge: An Introduction to Critical Thinking,* Diane Halpern (1984) also provides a comprehensive overview of research and practice in the teaching of thinking skills, even though her title seems to indicate that only critical thinking is covered. Thus, with clear recognition that all this emphasis on thinking skills may lead to neglect of the importance of other learning activities, we nevertheless assert that a goal of all gifted programs should be to develop thinking skills to the highest levels possible. In a comprehensive review, Glaser (1984) presented a strong case, however, for the fundamental role of a knowledge base in teaching thinking skills. Glaser suggested that the proper interaction between youth and knowledge or subject matter is dynamic, interactive inquiry, problem solving, analysis, or synthesis activity. Thus, the process of teaching thinking skills is coterminous with the teaching of concepts and principles, for both must go on simultaneously. There is no teaching of thinking skills in isolation from a knowledge base, nor is a knowledge base developed without a dynamic, thinking type of interaction with the content.

Lipman, Sharp, and Oscanyan (1980) argued for the infusion of thinking skills into the entire school curriculum:

> *The integration of thinking skills into every aspect of the curriculum would*
> *sharpen children's capacity to make connections and draw distinctions, to define*

*and to classify, to assess factual information objectively and critically, to deal reflectively with the relationship between facts and values, and to differentiate their beliefs and what is true from their understanding of what is logically possible. These specific skills help children listen better, study better, learn better, and express themselves better. They, therefore, carry over into all academic areas. A thinking skills program must help children think both more logically and more meaningfully. (p. 15)*

The purpose of this chapter, then, is to review the fundamental rubric for teaching thinking skills as a part of the general process of developing a knowledge base. The knowledge base is conceived of as the ultimate source of creative production when gifted students have achieved the cognitive processing skills of insight as described by Sternberg (1985) in his triarchic theory of intelligence.

## The Bloom *Taxonomy*

The Bloom *Taxonomy* (1956) has been widely adopted as a model for conceptualizing higher-level thinking skills for gifted learners. Although originally developed for a quite different purpose (to classify instructional objectives and test items in a hierarchical fashion), it was a natural extension of the *Taxonomy* to its use as a hierarchical model of thinking processes or skills. Indeed, the authors of the *Taxonomy,* the College Board Committee of Examiners, had spelled out quite thoroughly the psychological and cognitive aspects of each level of the *Taxonomy*. Thus, they clearly viewed it as representing a cognitive explanation of learning and/or thinking processes. However, a host of other practitioners began to relate the levels of the *Taxonomy* to the teaching of thinking skills for gifted and talented youth or for children in general.

At this point, a review of the levels of the Bloom *Taxonomy* is appropriate. We begin at level one, which is called the *knowledge level*. This level represents all cognitions that simply represent remembering information or processes. The teaching method may involve lectures, drill and recitation, or having students read. The curriculum goals at this level may be stated as follows:

- *Name the major terrestial configurations.*
- *Detail the phases in the operation of a battery.*
- *List the characteristics of political essays.*

It is important to recognize that the knowledge level of the *Taxonomy* covers a wide range of types of information to be remembered:

- *Specific bits of information*
- *Terminology*
- *Facts such as dates, events, places*
- *Conventions*
- *Trends and sequences*
- *Criteria*
- *Methodology*
- *Principles*
- *Generalizations*
- *Theories*

Level two of the *Taxonomy* and all higher levels are referred to as representing intellectual abilities and skills. Level two is called the *comprehension level*. Here, higher forms of cognitive activity than memory are expected, such as interpretation, extrapolation, and translation. These might include:

- *Paraphrasing events*
- *Understanding the concept of peace*

Level three is called the *application level*. It refers to those intellectual activities in which students use principles, concepts, theories, generalizations, or other abstractions in solving problems or apply them in new situations. For example, goals might be stated as:

- *Able to use principles of economics in solving current financial problems*
- *Able to use principles of learning in specifying the best procedures for teaching a new concept*

Level four is called the *analysis level*. This may involve:

- *Identifying major elements in a communication*
- *Analyzing relationships among the ideas in a document*
- *Recognizing form and pattern in an essay*
- *Breaking a compound down into its constituent elements*

Always there is the expectation that the students will be able to dissect, detect elements, or see relationships among the parts.

The next level upward is called the *synthesis level*. It refers to all those intellectual activities in which students combine or integrate ideas, concepts, principles, or information into unified wholes that represent a new pattern or structure. The newness, of course, represents a creative element in the process. Thus, students might do any of the following:

- *Write an essay combining elements of the styles of Swift and Lamb.*
- *Propose a plan for testing a hypothesis.*
- *Write a scenario depicting life in the year 2000 based on current trends.*
- *Draw a picture that incorporates the impressionists' views.*

The final level of the *Taxonomy* is called the *evaluation level*. At this level, students are expected to make judgments using standards or criteria. For example:

- *What are the flaws in the main character's arguments?*
- *Compare the artistic qualities of Rembrandt and Titian.*
- *Judge the scientific arguments for and against evolution.*

These levels of the Bloom *Taxonomy* provide a guide for teachers of gifted learners to engage them in intellectual activity appropriate to their levels of ability. The goals of the higher levels call for appropriate instructional activities in which students are actively engaged in practicing high-level cognitive activity. Thus, for the goal "Compare the images used by different writers," an appropriate activity for gifted students might be to have small groups compare the images used by Edgar Allen Poe in "The Raven" and in "The Cask of Amontillado." Similarly, an activity for another gifted class with the goal of synthesizing ideas about propaganda might be to discuss the role of political messages in the election of President Clinton.

The Bloom *Taxonomy* is presented as a curriculum and instruction planning model by Tiedt and colleagues (1989). They related the model to all areas of the school curriculum and presented demonstration lesson plans. Each lesson begins with explicitly stated objectives based on the *Taxonomy* hierarchical structure, such as the following example:

> *Students will*
> *1. identify the basic characteristics of a particular tribe's culture, food, shelter, clothing, family structure, government, geographic setting, weapons and tools, religion, leisure, and language.*
> *2. research one tribe using filmstrips, books, encyclopedias, and other resources.*
> *3. create a publication or booklet worthy as a library resource for other students. (p. 74)*

A brief description of the lesson follows:

> *This lesson begins with cooperative research, We-Search, to locate descriptions of ten basic elements of a community group. The research culminates in the writing, illustrating, and publishing of a booklet by each group. (p. 74)*

The stimuli needed or media-materials are planned and presented next:

> *Locate a copy of* Ashanti to Zulu: African Traditions *by Margaret Musgrove. Read the book aloud to the class, showing the beautiful illustrations as you go. This book provides in pictorial form the symbols, animals, artifacts, costumes, and food of one African tribe for each letter of the alphabet. In addition, the author includes an outline map showing the locations of each tribe. A book of this kind offers a wonderful starting place for a class embarking on a quest of information on African tribes. In addition, it demonstrates one way of organizing the unit, an easy way to let the groups of students choose a tribe for their special study. Make copies of the outline map from the book to distribute to each cooperative learning group of five students. This map shows each tribe and its location, so it will facilitate group selections of tribes to research. (p. 75)*

The next part of the curriculum instruction plan is a description of the activity to be carried out:

> *Once the cooperative learning groups have each chosen a tribe, they will We-Search and bring essential materials from the library into class. Or, each small group can be scheduled for a period in the library to check out resources.*
> *We-Search groups of five spend several class periods in a circle exploring the*

*various books from the library, taking notes. They are guided in their quest for information by a list of ten basic needs: food, clothing, shelter, family structure, government, geographic setting, weapons and tools, religion, leisure, and language. Each student in the five member group will be responsible for two of the basic needs, thereby assuring coverage of all ten needs. (p. 75)*

Follow-up activities or procedures are then planned and presented:

*Schedule each group for two period blocks of time at the computer. (This works especially well for a core class or in an elementary self-contained classroom.) Students often work in pairs at the keyboard so that one can edit as the other composes. Those not at the computer can still offer advice and work quietly on further research, illustrations, or graphic plans for the completed pages.*

*After all groups have had at least two double periods at the computer or ample time to type and print their text and to make graphic titles and cover sheets for their booklets, students can cut, paste, and lay out the pages of their projects. (pp. 75–76)*

Finally, evaluation procedures are presented:

*Evaluate each completed document on the following criteria: coverage of the ten basic needs, authenticity of the writing by the students, organization, and creativity of the layout design.*

Sample Rubric
*5: full coverage of the ten basic needs, authentic writing by students, well-organized, and creatively laid out*

*3: average coverage of the ten basic needs, some authentic writing by students, some evidence of organization, and creative layout design*

*1: poor coverage of the ten basic needs, little if any authentic writing by students, little or no evidence of organization or design (p. 76)*

Many examples of such curriculum instruction planning are presented for grades K–12 in this excellent text *Teaching Thinking in K–12 Classrooms: Ideas, Activities, and Resources,* (Tiedt et al., 1989). This book is also rich in its presentation of material and resources to use in developing curriculum for gifted and talented children. Higher levels of the taxonomy, accelerated levels of subject matter, a faster pace, and more extensive and complex projects and products can be incorporated to fit the characteristics and precocity of gifted and talented children.

Given that teachers seem to spend a lot of class time purveying factual information to students (Goodlad, 1984; Sizer, 1985), the Bloom *Taxonomy* can be a valuable guide to teachers of the gifted in planning discussion questions, in organizing learning tasks for small groups of students, in developing instructional assignments, and in writing curriculum units of instruction. Combined with other approaches or systems for teaching thinking skills, it offers a unique approach to assuring that dynamic, creative interaction occurs between gifted students and course content.

## Critical Thinking

The area of critical thinking was delineated by Ennis (1962) as a special domain of human thinking. He noted that psychologists and educators had addressed creative thinking, concept formation, problem solving, and associative thinking, but had not investigated critical thinking skills. Ennis reviewed the literature on thinking skills, attempted to identify basic dimensions of critical thinking, and proposed the following list of twelve aspects of critical thinking:

1. Grasping the meaning of a statement
2. Judging whether there is ambiguity in a line of reasoning
3. Judging whether certain statements contradict each other
4. Judging whether a conclusion follows necessarily
5. Judging whether a statement is specific enough
6. Judging whether a statement is actually the application of a certain principle
7. Judging whether an observation statement is reliable
8. Judging whether an inductive conclusion is warranted
9. Judging whether the problem has been identified
10. Judging whether something is an assumption
11. Judging whether a definition is adequate
12. Judging whether a statement made by an alleged authority is acceptable

Ennis has refined his model or taxonomy of critical thinking skills (1985) to include three types of thinking skills and 13 dispositions of critical thinkers. They are presented in Figures 13–1 and 13–2. (See Sternberg & Baron, 1985, p. 42, for this version of Ennis's theoretical conception as well as Ennis's own presentation of the conception in the 1985 reference.) Ennis defines critical thinking as follows: "Critical thinking is reflective and

### FIGURE 13–1 Ennis's Three Types of Thinking Skills

1. Define and clarify:
   - Identify central issues and problems.
   - Identify conclusions.
   - Identify reasons.
   - Identify appropriate questions to ask, given a situation.
   - Identify assumptions.

2. Judge information:
   - Determine credibility of sources and observations.
   - Determine relevance.
   - Recognize consistency.

3. Infer—solve problems and draw reasonable conclusions:
   - Infer and judge inductive conclusions.
   - Deduce and judge deductive validity.
   - Predict probable consequences.

*Source:* R. H. Ennis, "A Logical Basis for Measuring Critical Thinking Skills," *Educational Leadership, 43* (2), 1985, p. 42.

## FIGURE 13–2    Ennis's Thirteen Dispositions of Critical Thinkers

The ability to:
1. Be open-minded.
2. Take a position (and change a position) when the evidence and reasons are sufficient to do so.
3. Take into account the total situation.
4. Try to be well informed.
5. Seek as much precision as the subject permits.
6. Deal in an orderly manner with the parts of a complex whole.
7. Look for alternatives.
8. Seek reasons.
9. Seek a clear statement of the issue.
10. Keep in mind the original and/or basic concern.
11. Use credible sources and mention them.
12. Remain relevant to the main point.
13. Be sensitive to the feelings, level of knowledge, and degree of sophistication of others.

*Source:* R. H. Ennis, "A Logical Basis for Measuring Critical Thinking Skills," *Educational Leadership, 43* (2), 1985, p. 42.

reasonable thinking that is focused on deciding what to believe or do" (p. 45). Note that there are creative activities covered by this definition, including formulating hypotheses, questions, alternatives, and plans for experiments.

## *Illustrative Objectives and Activities*

Illustrative objectives and activities follow for some of the critical thinking skills in the Ennis hierarchy presented above. Teachers who are developing curriculum for the gifted should note that most of the illustrations are embedded in curriculum content and not presented as abstract experiences. Thinking skills are learned best in the context of subject matter. Such experiences will ensure that the skills will not become task specific but will transfer to a variety of real-life thinking experiences.

An objective and activity for the first aspect or component of critical thinking might be as follows:

Objective:    Gifted learners will be able to explicate the meaning of complex excerpts from their reading materials.

Instructional    Reread the following passage, which was a part of your assigned readings.
Activity:    Then, working in small groups, try to answer the questions that follow.

Grappling with such abstract and complex ideas and trying to derive meaning from them is a first and basic aspect of critical thinking.

The second aspect of critical thinking and all subsequent aspects call for judgment. Whereas judgment is presented as the sixth or highest level of thinking in the Bloom *Taxonomy,* it is likely that all of the thinking skills that involve judging also involve the subordinate cognitive skills of comprehending, analyzing, and synthesizing.

More specifically, the second aspect of critical thinking is judging whether there is ambiguity in a line of reasoning. As an illustration, the following objective and instructional activity are presented:

Objective:    Judge whether there is a lack of clarity in a document that discusses a controversial issue.

Instructional Activity:    Read the following statement and decide if there is ambiguity or a lack of clarity anywhere in the statement. Underline the ambiguous elements, if any, and explain the ambiguity below:

*We must strive to nurture our environment for future generations. This is the only place that they will have to enjoy. We must respect their right to health and productive lives.*

The third aspect of critical thinking has to do with judging if contradictions exist within a document. The following objective might be written into a curriculum plan:

Objective:    Judge whether there are contradictions among or between statements within an essay.

Instructional Activity:    Read this statement and decide if there are contradictions within it. If there are, be ready to explain them:

*The United States is committed to the democratic freedoms for all people. The citizens of all nations should have the right to self-determination. The United Nations should have the power to mandate democratic rights for all peoples of the world.*

This activity can be pursued in social studies, literature, composition, or science classes, depending on where the illustrations are found. If the class is composition, there might be a principal emphasis on analyzing the contradictions in writing.

The fourth aspect of critical thinking is judging whether a conclusion necessarily follows. This is essentially a skill in logical thinking. An objective in this area might be stated as follows:

Objective:    Judge whether the following conclusions follow logically from the data and results of the experiment.

Instructional Activity:    A sword blade is held in a flame. The sword blade curls downward as though it has melted. The blade is removed from the flame and laid on a table with the edge upward whereupon it straightens out quickly. Which conclusions seem warranted and why?

1. The original bending of the blade was not due to melting.
2. Gravity caused the blade to bend downward.
3. The blade was bimetallic, made of metals with different expansion ratios, and thus was bent due to the conflict of the two ratios.
4. The blade melted.
5. It straightened out when laid on the table because it was a single metal and it resumed its natural straight shape.

This activity in science is drawn from the inquiry activities developed by Suchman (1965) but adapted for our illustration. It would best be presented to a group of gifted learners first as a demonstration with a bimetallic blade and a flame, followed by an inquiry discussion and a careful review of the possible conclusions to select those that are tenable.

Problems in pure logic may also be used as instruction under this objective. Here are examples adapted from Halpern (1984, p. 58). Judge if the conclusion follows from the premises:

| | |
|---|---|
| Premise #1: | All boys are athletes. |
| Premise #2: | All athletes are muscular. |
| Conclusion: | All boys are muscular. |
| Conclusion: | All muscular people are boys. |
| Premise #1: | Some lawyers are honest. |
| Premise #2: | Some honest people go to church. |
| Conclusion: | Some lawyers go to church. |
| Conclusion: | Some churchgoers are lawyers. |
| Premise #1: | Professors are erudite. |
| Premise #2: | Erudite people are boring. |
| Conclusion: | Professors are boring. |
| Conclusion: | Boring people are professors. |

These problems in logic can be taught through discussion, which might begin with Venn diagrams illustrating the inclusiveness of major and minor premises and their relationship to conclusions.

All A are B
All B are C

All A are C
All C are A

All A are B
Some B are C

Some A are C
Some C are A

Lipman's program (Lipman, Sharp, & Oscanyan, 1980), *Philosophy for Children*, provides some excellent training in the area of logic and critical thinking. *Mind Benders* published by Midwest Publications (Harnadek, 1978), *Playing with Logic* (Schoenfield & Rosenblatt, 1985), and *Critical Thinking* books (Harnadek, 1980) all offer excellent experiences for children in the areas of logical and critical thinking.

The next aspect of critical thinking is judging whether a statement is specific enough. Here is an objective and an instructional activity:

Objective:     Judge whether a statement is specific enough to draw conclusions from it.

Instructional     Read the following statement. Then try to answer the questions which
Activity:       follow or indicate that the information is not specific enough to answer the
                questions.

*All of the soldiers were poised at the barricades ready to charge into battle. The captain paced up and down behind them, wringing his hands and sighing audibly.*

1. The captain seemed to be agitated or concerned about the battle.
2. The captain was afraid to make the decision to order the troops into battle.

A class discussion could grow out of these questions as to what could be inferred or deduced from the stated condition. Comparable material could be developed in most areas of the curriculum.

The sixth aspect of critical thinking is judging whether a statement is the application of a principle. This calls for students to learn how to assess the relationship between a general rule and a specific application of the rule. (For the remaining aspects, we shall not give an illustrative objective and instructional activity but shall merely give brief illustrations.) For example, it is now a widely held political principle that economic sanctions by one country against another are not effective in changing the political behavior of the target country. Students may be asked to judge whether the economic boycott organized by President Bush against Iraq in 1990 is truly an application of the principle, and was it or was it not effective? They may also be asked to judge and contrast the value of economic sanctions against South Africa and to try to explain why one might be effective whereas the other is not.

The seventh aspect is to judge whether a statement is reliable. In a discussion of *Hamlet* in an English class, we are asked to judge the reliability of the following assertions:

1. The major issue with which Hamlet is grappling is power and the loss of power to his uncle.
2. Hamlet is a homosexual.
3. Hamlet's mother is an opportunist.

The eighth aspect is judging whether an inductive conclusion is warranted. The following are inductive conclusions:

1. World weather patterns are changing.
2. Nuclear power is too dangerous to be used to generate electricity.
3. Politicians rarely keep their word.
4. Samuel Clemens was really a racist person.

Based on reading of text material and other primary and secondary sources, students can make the judgments as to whether these statements are warranted inductive conclusions.

The ninth aspect is judging whether a problem has been identified. This is a valuable critical thinking skill in all problem-solving activities. Often, tense people attempt to solve the wrong problem given the problem situation. For example, cars often have accidents on icy bridges. What is the problem?

1. How to get the bridges sanded early after a storm begins
2. How to prevent ice from forming on bridges
3. How to prevent accidents on icy bridges
4. How to get drivers to exercise more caution
5. How to get a truck to salt bridges

Knowing that the problem is really how to prevent accidents on icy bridges gives the students a broader and hopefully more comprehensive approach to solve this problem.

The next aspect is judging whether something is an assumption. As in several other aspects of critical thinking, Ennis noted that this ability is not unitary but is really a complex of perceptual and cognitive abilities. Ennis gave the following illustration: "When the demand for nucroscopies decreases, the price decreases." What is the assumption regarding this specific situation and the general principle to which it is related?

The next critical thinking skill is judging whether a definition is adequate. Ennis gave rules for definition and various forms of definitions. For example, in definitions that are intended to classify a concept or object, Ennis stated the following rules:

1. The defining part should contain (a) a general class, and (b) a feature or features that set this member off from members of the general class.
2. The defining part should be equivalent to the part being defined.
3. The defining part should not use the term to be defined.
4. The defining part should not give more than enough to provide a complete classification.

Science students may now be asked to judge the adequacy of this definition of an isotope:

Any of two or more species of atoms of a chemical element with the same atomic number and position in the periodic table and nearly identical chemical behavior.

The final aspect is judging whether a statement made by an alleged authority is acceptable. As an illustration, an English teacher cites a noted movie critic who asserts that modern interpretations of *Macbeth* are nearly all influenced by Freudian psychology. Is the authority correct? Students in an English class will read several, hopefully representative, interpretations of characters' motives in *Macbeth* and judge whether those interpretations are based on Freudian psychological or philosophical tenets.

These various aspects of critical thinking are now taught explicitly in such published material as Harnadek's two-volume series, *Critical Thinking* (1980), which is intended for average high school students according to the publisher. We would therefore conclude that gifted junior high school students could also learn the concepts. It should also be the case that gifted students are given abundant practice to develop these thinking skills in each of the disciplines. This means that math teachers, literature teachers, composition teachers, and science teachers all find ways to structure discussion, small group work, and individual writing assignments in which students get ample opportunity to learn how to use these different aspects of critical and logical thinking in dealing with that area.

## Problem Solving, Creativity, and Creative Problem Solving

The major areas of thinking skills promoted in programs for gifted learners are problem solving, creative thinking, and creative problem solving. The pioneering work of Torrance (1962, 1965), Parnes (1967, 1977), Treffinger (1980), and Feldhusen and associates (1969, 1977) paved the way for a proliferation of instructional materials designed to teach creative thinking and problem solving (Feldhusen & Treffinger, 1985). Most gifted programs, especially at the elementary level, place major emphasis on the teaching of creative thinking and problem solving. The general rationale is that gifted learners have very high potential for creative activity and production in adulthood and that they should begin developing that potential as early as possible. A closely related goal is for gifted learners to become effective as high-level researchers and creators. To develop competence in research, these students need underlying competence in creative thinking and problem solving, a knowledge base in the area or discipline in which they may carry out research, and some specific research competencies or skills.

### Problem Solving

Problem solving is a comprehensive and complex set of cognitive operations that probably embrace many aspects of thinking subsumed under other rubrics such as creative thinking, critical thinking, decision making, and so on. Rubenstein (1986) proposed that a problem situation involves an initial state in which negation or lack is perceived; a vision, solution, or goal for an end state is formulated; and processes or actions to get to the goal are delineated. This is close to the model of problem solving proposed by Newell and Simon (1972). The initial state has come to be viewed as the problem facing an individual's capacity to discern, delineate, and/or pose the problem situation as a prelude to trying to formulate a goal, identify appropriate actions to solve or achieve the goal, and carry out the actions. Problem recognition and delineation as a critical element of the process was identified by Getzels and Csikszentmihalyi (1976) in their pioneering study of artists' approaches to the problem of depicting some aspects of human experiences.

Long-standing tradition is to describe problem solving formally as a series of steps. Beyer (1987) set forth such a model in his broader taxonomy of thinking skills:

1. *Recognize a problem*
2. *Represent the problem*
3. *Devise/choose a solution plan*
4. *Execute the plan*
5. *Evaluate the solution (p. 27)*

These formal steps may or may not characterize students' cognitive activity in a real problem situation. In a sense, they represent an ideal. The steps also define a convergent conception in that a single solution is envisioned, although the language of the model is open to alternative solutions from different problem solvers.

Another excellent and general problem-solving model was developed by Bransford and Stein (1984). The model has been used for large-scale project activity with gifted students in summer programs at Purdue University. IDEAL is the acronym for the program:

I  =  Identify a problem or potential problems.
D  =  Define, delineate, or clarify the problem.
E  =  Explore options or approaches to solving the problem(s).
A  =  Act or carry out the planned solution activities.
L  =  Look at the effects and evaluate the solution.

This model encourages divergent or creative thinking at several of the stages and works well as a general guide to higher cognitive activity for gifted students.

Divergent activity, or creative thinking, is probably a capacity possessed by all normal human beings, but we persist in thinking that some people have it and others don't. "Creative people are those rare birds who are uninhibited enough to be child-like in their thinking . . . they can maintain a playful attitude about the most serious concerns of life," (p. 46) stated Dacey in his comprehensive examination of the subject, *Fundamentals of Creative Thinking* (1989). While he and many other researchers and theorists often define creativity in terms of cognitive abilities, Dacey also delineates personality traits characteristic of creative or highly creative people. He suggested first of all that tolerance of ambiguity is the sine qua non or vital element of the creative process. Then seven other elements of personality make significant contributions:

Stimulus freedom
Functional freedom
Flexibility
Risk taking
Preference for disorder
Delay of gratification
Androgyny

All contribute to the tolerance of ambiguity or operate in conjunction with it.

What are the specific skills of creative thinking? Torrance led the way in focusing researchers and developers on the basic divergent thinking abilities of fluency, flexibility, originality, and elaboration. *Fluency* is the ability to think of or to recall many ideas or problems for a given concept or task. For example:

1. What are all the ways we might rewrite this equation and maintain the equality?
2. What are all the possible reasons you can think of for Hamlet's strange behavior toward Ophelia?
3. What are all the ways that might be used to enhance this chemical reaction?
4. Think of all the reasons you can for the anarchist behavior of Sacco and Vanzetti.
5. What are all the types of stitches that would best accommodate the design for this blouse?

From these examples it should be clear that creative thinking can be developed or taught in all school subjects. *Fluency* is the skill of being able to recall or think of a number of ideas or problems for a specific stimulus situation. It is one of the essences of insight behavior described by Davidson and Sternberg (1984) called "selective comparison." In selective comparison, one is able to relate new information to information acquired in the past.

During the exercise of fluent thinking, students may also be taught to develop their capacities for flexible and original thinking. Originality implies that selective combination occurs. Davidson and Sternberg described this as a process of synthesizing or associating hitherto unconnected ideas into a new unique or original whole. Thus, the objectives or directions for some school tasks might read as follows:

1. Think of new and original ways of grafting plants.
2. Develop a whole new set of operational symbols to denote mathematic operations. Try to create signs that look like their function.
3. Combine several forms of essay to create some new genre of essays.
4. What are some new ways to help people better understand the complexities of different cultures?

*Flexibility* is the capacity to produce new ideas that deviate from normally expected ideas and to be able to produce new ideas that shift categorically during the process of idea production. As with originality, the essential condition for idea production is a fluency-like task demand, and as with originality, the major effort to induce and train the cognition called "flexibility" is through a metacognitive process of becoming aware and striving to use the capacity. The following objectives or tasks are especially designed to evoke flexible thinking:

1. What are all the ways you can devise for weighing very light objects other than a balance or spring scale?
2. Shakespeare's *MacBeth* is a tragedy. What are ways you could change it to become a comedy?
3. Write a short essay that has no active verbs in it.
4. Write alternative forms of a given equation in which there are square root operations on both sides of the equal signs.

All of these illustrations open the door to flexibility or an alternate way of viewing an otherwise familiar concept or process.

*Elaboration* is a process of filling in details, developing ideas, or bringing an abstract concept to life. Fluent, original, and flexible thinking may yield many ideas. An intermediate process calls for evaluation or judgment concerning the worth of ideas produced. Judgment, of course, always implies criteria. Could this idea be developed and yield some practical payoff? If developed, would it alleviate hunger? Would people find it humorous? Once the evaluation or judgment is made and an idea is selected for expansion or development, the elaboration process has begun. Like the fluency function, it involves filling in details, thinking of illustrations, deciding on color, determining quantities, and selecting a mode of communication. Here are some elaboration tasks:

1. Think of many ideas for a story emphasizing characterization. Select the best idea. Develop it as a short story.
2. Think of a number of possible experiments in genetic mutations. Select the most original. Design a complete experiment.
3. Identify major problems facing the homeless in U.S. cities. Select the most serious one. Design a solution to that problem.

Slightly elaborated and usually carried out in groups is the process of *brainstorming* (Osborn, 1963). It combines all of the basic divergent thinking skills described above. Through long experience, a common set of rules for brainstorming has emerged. Feldhusen and Treffinger (1985) proposed the following guidelines:

1. Do not criticize or evaluate any ideas produced. Ideas should be free flowing and unhampered at this stage.
2. Crazy or humorous ideas are acceptable. Wild imaginative ideas may become practical when forced into problem situations from a different viewpoint. The emergence of an unusual or bizarre idea may spark yet another idea.
3. Quantity of ideas is important. Quality of ideas is not considered at this point. The more ideas there are, the greater the base for evaluation and selecting viable ideas becomes.
4. Work with others in the combination of ideas. No one person's ideas belong to that person; all ideas at this stage are thrown into the communal pot. Ideas that sprout from other ideas that have been suggested are fair game.

Brainstorming is an excellent method of helping students learn how to think creatively in groups. It can be thought of also as a problem-solving method, but the emphasis is on creating conditions and developing skills for the production of new, unique, or original ideas and solutions.

## Creative Problem Solving

A more complex form of creative thinking, now widely taught to students in programs for the gifted, is *creative problem solving*. The major model for this skill was developed by Parnes (1967), later popularized by Parnes, Noller, and Biondi (1977), proposed for gifted programs by Treffinger (1980), and elaborated as an instructional program by Isaksen and Treffinger (1985). Six steps or processes characterize the model:

1. Mess finding
2. Data finding
3. Problem finding
4. Idea finding
5. Solution finding
6. Acceptance finding

The main purpose of "mess finding" is to sort through a problem situation and find direction toward a broad goal or solution. In "data finding," participants sort through all available information about the mess and clarify the steps or direction to a solution. In "problem finding," a specific problem statement is formulated. "Idea finding" is a processing of finding many ideas for solution to *the* problem or parts of the problem. "Solution finding" is an evaluation or judgmental process of sorting among the ideas produced in the last step and selecting those most likely to produce solutions. Finally, in "acceptance finding," a plan is devised for implementing the good solutions. An adaptation of the creative problem-solving model is called "Future Problem Solving." It involves the application of the creative problem-solving model to studies of the future and to problems that are now emerging as major concerns for the future (Whaley, 1984).

Feldhusen and Treffinger (1985) extended the creative problem-solving model by suggesting that stage one should include opportunities for participants to identify their own problem within a specified domain of interest or study following the research presented by Getzels and Csikszentmihalyi (1976), which highlighted the crucial role of problem recognition as a part of the creative process. Feldhusen and Treffinger (1985) also suggested that the solution-finding stage should involve more than selecting best ideas; it should often involve synthesizing the best ideas into a more complex and creative solution.

A number of other creative thinking techniques have been described by Feldhusen and Treffinger (1985) in *Creative Thinking and Problem Solving in Gifted Education.* These include synectics, attribute listing, morphological analysis, and forced relationships. Generally, creative techniques give students opportunities to think and develop thinking skills without the stress or anxiety that is often associated with logic and critical thinking. This is not to say that creative thinking skills are all-purpose alternatives to the rigorous forms of thinking required in logical analysis and critical thinking. Both forms of thinking should be developed in students, and both should be developed in ways that help students learn how to generalize, transfer, and apply them in real problem situations. New skills can profitably be practiced initially in abstracted and artificial forms to help students grasp the cognitive model. They may also profitably learn new models through problem solving or exploratory experiences. Once they understand the nature of the process (e.g., brainstorming), they should then have more and more experience in dealing with real problem situations in which they can apply the model. In school that may mean moving from brainstorming experiences of a contrived nature toward problems and inquiry in the disciplines of mathematics, science, social studies, English, business, agriculture, and home economics. Whereas the initial problem might involve using brainstorming to think of uses of old tin cans, later experiences would include writing as many forms as possible of an equation, identifying a variety of caustic compounds, listing all the major environmental problems facing the United States, or writing alternate titles for a story.

In a concluding statement to his very extensive review of creativity, Tannenbaum (1983) concluded that "[Creativity] consists of a not yet known combination of general and specific abilities and personality traits associated with high potential that can be realized in a stimulating environment with the help of good fortune" (p. 328). Our state of knowledge or understanding of creative thinking, of how to measure it and how to teach it, may be no better and no worse than our knowledge of any of the other thinking processes.

## Questioning and Inquiry Skills

Questioning skills and inquiry methods have long been a part of the repertoire of thinking skills. In their book *Creative Learning and Teaching,* Torrance and Myers (1970) dealt extensively with the topics of questioning skills for both teachers and students. They illustrated all of the techniques, showing how to question for information, how to question for thinking, how to use provocative questions, and how to teach children to become good questioners. They proposed that teachers use the following forms of questions to stimulate students' thinking:

1. *Interpretation.* What does the following statement mean? Conspicuous consumption by Americans living in Africa is a supreme paradox.
2. *Comparison-Analysis.* How are parenting practices and family value systems different now than they were 100 years ago?
3. *Synthesis questions.* How could you combine elements of the philosophies of the Sierra Club and the Audubon Society to forge a stronger force for environmental protection in the United States?
4. *Evaluation.* Did the United States reveal moral bankruptcy by its failure to intervene when the Pol Pot regime massacred three million Cambodians?
5. *Sensitivity to problems.* What are the major problems of the United Nations Organization?
6. *Clarifying problems.* Why don't teachers enjoy higher professional status?
7. *Provocative questions.* What would be the results if a law was passed banning *all* killings and physical violence on TV?
8. *Hypothetical questions.* If you were principal of the school, how would things change?
9. *Questions to encourage thoughtful reading.* Why was Mozart called the "Boy Wonder"?
10. *Questions to encourage thoughtful listening* (beyond the literal message). Why did it take Morse so long to perfect his telegraph?
11. *Questions to see new relationships.* How is flooding in Pakistan related to America's love of big cars?

Students can be taught to be good questioners and their questioning skills can be developed, but it appears that an appropriate classroom atmosphere is also desirable to foster this development. Some of the major characteristics of such a classroom are the following:

1. The teacher is patient and waits for students to formulate questions.
2. There is no ridiculing of students by teachers or peers for "dumb" questions or ideas.
3. Offbeat and unusual ideas or questions are accepted for discussion.
4. Humor is accepted and encouraged.
5. The classroom is orderly but relaxed.
6. The classroom is a rich, stimulating environment with a lot of material resources.
7. The teacher is "with it" and dynamic.

Good questioning skills can be used in a variety of ways:

1. Analyze and clarify ambiguous situations.
2. Secure information.

**3.** Clarify problems.
**4.** Test hypotheses.
**5.** Evaluate possible solutions.

Sanders developed an extensive program of questioning skills, as reported in his book, *Classroom Questions, What Kinds?* (1966). The program is based on the Bloom *Taxonomy* (1965) and uses the six levels of the *Taxonomy* as guides to the formulation of questions. It should also be noted that the models for questioning proposed by Torrance and Meyers (1970), as discussed earlier in this chapter, also include several types of questions that are identical to Bloom *Taxonomy* levels.

Two major programs for the development of inquiry skills were developed by Taba (1962) and Suchman (1965). The Taba model is presented very thoroughly in Maker's (1982) *Teaching Models in Education of the Gifted*. The major strategies used in the Taba model are (1) concept development, (2) interpretation of data, (3) application of generalization, and (4) resolution of conflicts. Maker noted that the major factors in developing students' inquiry skills are the teacher's questions and the sequencing of learning experiences.

In the first stage, *concept development,* information is listed and tested for relevancy. Then the information is grouped according to common attributes or characteristics. Next, it is labeled through abstracting or synthesizing the basic aspects of the information. In the next step, called "subsuming," students search for relationships among the information. Finally, in the fifth step, the whole process is recycled to search for new ways of understanding the information.

The second phase of the Taba model is called *interpretation of data.* Students are involved in gathering data and drawing conclusions or inferences from it. Taba stresses that teachers may guide, but students must do their own inquiring.

In the third phase, *generalization,* students use previously learned generalizations and try applying them to new situations. The process may be one of predicting consequences. This would be essentially like some synthesis level activities in the Bloom *Taxonomy*.

Finally, there is a phase called *resolution of conflict.* This activity involves students in taking viewpoints, examining alternate positions, analyzing attitudes and values, and making judgments. This phase obviously involves students in activities comparable to level six of the Bloom *Taxonomy* (judgment or evaluation), but it is clear that level four (analysis) is probably also involved.

The Taba model is notable for its comprehensive approach to the involvement of students in a carefully sequenced set of steps through the thinking process. The model is designed to teach a set of inquiry skills that can be used in a wide variety of situations in life.

The Suchman model (1965) might be described as a system to teach students how to become active seekers and questioners in science. A puzzling or ambiguous situation is presented to the students in a film. The most popular illustration depicts a bimetallic strip bending upward at the ends when placed in a flame. Students do not know that it is bimetallic. They can ask questions about the phenomenon, but may receive only yes or no for answers. Suchman proposed that students go through three stages of inquiry in finding the explanation for such a discrepant event. The first he calls *episode analysis;* this is simply clarifying the basic facts of the situation. The second is called *determinance of relevance;* this is a process of figuring out the relevant and necessary aspects or elements of the situation. The third stage is called *induction of relational constructs;* this is the phase of discovery or understanding the relationship.

The author has observed students involved in Suchman's inquiry tasks and has led groups of children who are carrying out the inquiry process. The stages described by Suchman do occur but sometimes out of order. In early stages of training there is little systematic movement through the stages; there is much wild guessing. Later, students begin to cooperate and build on the discoveries of one another. The excitement grows as they get close to the principle.

These inquiry-discovery oriented thinking programs illustrate well the need for very active roles of students in learning how to think. They also illustrate well the value of small group work in which students interact and stimulate one another. Finally, they clearly show the role of the teacher in structuring the experience and guiding students through it.

*Metacognition* is the term that subsumes the processes of developing awareness of one's own thinking and techniques for controlling and improving thinking activities. Beyer (1987) proposed three main areas of metacognitive activity:

1. Planning
     Starting a goal
     Selecting operations to perform
     Sequencing operations
     Identifying potential obstacles/errors
     Identifying ways to recover from obstacles/errors
     Predicting results desired and/or anticipated
2. Monitoring
     Keeping the goal in mind
     Keeping one's place in a sequence
     Knowing when a subgoal has been achieved
     Deciding when to go on to the next operation
     Selecting next appropriate operation
     Knowing how to recover from errors, overcome obstacles
3. Assessing
     Assessing goal achievement
     Judging accuracy and adequacy of the results
     Evaluating appropriateness of procedures used
     Assessing handling of obstacles/errors
     Judging efficiency of the plan and its execution

All of these metacognitive skills can be addressed directly in process curriculum for the gifted and talented several grade levels earlier than in curriculum for average ability learners. A framework like Beyer's can be presented by explicit lecture, reading, and discussion followed by practice in a variety of applications such as the following:

*Objectives*

1. Show understanding of the metacognitive planning skills by defining and giving examples of each.
2. Exhibit initial mastery of the planning skills in the context of planning and conducting a debate on the defensibility of slavery practices among native American tribes.
3. Exhibit monitoring skills while planning and conducting the debate.
4. Show capacity to assess one's cognitive operations by a formal review at the end of the activity using the five metacognitive assessment skills as criteria.

Many additional opportunities in the same and other disciplines would be necessary to assure mastery and habitual use of the skills. The ultimate goal of such instruction would be for students to become more reflective about the effectiveness of their own thinking processes.

## Noncognitive Aspects of Thinking

The quality of our thinking is influenced not only by the level of our cognitive and metacognitive skills but also by our attitudes, motivations, and dispositions. Raths and colleagues (1986) suggested that these noncognitive aspects of thinking are partly the result of such teacher behaviors as:

*Listening to students*
*Appreciating individuality and openness*
*Encouraging open discussion*
*Promoting active learning*
*Accepting student ideas*
*Allowing time to think*
*Nurturing confidence*
*Giving helpful feedback*
*Appreciating student ideas (pp. 164–167)*

The result of these teacher behaviors, parent expectations, and other forces in the child's life may be the 13 dispositions of critical thinking presented in Figure 13–2. These dispositions look very similar to Beyer's metacognitive thinking skills, particularly in the sense of calling for self-monitoring. Raths et al. (1986) have also suggested that there are some behavioral dispositions that have a negative impact on thinking, such as impulsiveness, overdependence on the teacher, inability to concentrate, missing the meaning, dogmatism, overassertiveness, rigidity or inflexibility, lack of confidence in one's own ability to think, or downright unwillingness to think. Teachers can provide opportunities in the curriculum for gifted youth to recognize these shortcomings in their own behavior and then emphasize the positive disposition delineated by Ennis (Figure 13–2). Dispositions 1 and 13, "be open-minded" and "be sensitive to . . . others," are certainly highly affective in nature, whereas most of the others, such as 7 and 9, "look for alternatives" and "seek a clear statement of the issue," are essentially metacognitive skills that can be addressed directly in curriculum planning and instruction.

## Conclusion

This chapter has reviewed a variety of approaches to the teaching of thinking skills. All are applicable and useful in all areas of the curriculum. They call for active involvement of students in thinking, analyzing, inquiring, probing, synthesizing, and evaluating, and they demand teachers who are effective in structuring and guiding the experience.

The California State Department of Education (1979) has developed and published an extensive set of curriculum guides covering art, literature, science, music, and social studies across all the grades. These guides incorporate many of the thinking skills and illustrate many of the methods presented in this chapter. (See, for example, the volume on *Literature and Story Writing* for elementary and middle schools, which can be ordered from the California State Department of Education, P.O. Box 271, Sacramento, CA 95802.)

Teaching thinking skills requires not only a well-developed curriculum plan but also teachers who have learned the prerequisite skills of questioning, leading inquiry, small group work, discussion techniques, and problem solving, which are essential in guiding youth through complex cognitive activity. There are great risks in trying to incorporate thinking skills in the curriculum. It is easier to prepare and teach didactic lessons by lecturing, but the payoffs in learning for gifted students are infinitely superior when the teacher can guide them through the intricate maze of ideas to a clear understanding of concepts and principles and to enhanced skills of thinking.

### Key Points Summary

- *Thinking skills should be major goals of programs for gifted and talented youth.*
- *The Bloom Taxonomy is one valuable guide in teaching higher-level thinking skills to the gifted.*
- *There is a set of critical thinking skills that should be mastered by the gifted.*
- *The teaching of all thinking skills should turn quickly to the application of those skills in knowledge bases, disciplines, or real-world problem contexts.*
- *Creative thinking and creative problem solving are vital skills that gifted students need as prerequisites to productive thinking.*
- *Questioning and inquiry skills give gifted students the background they need for analytical activities.*

# References

Beyer, B. K. (1987). *Practical strategies for the teaching of thinking*. Boston: Allyn and Bacon.

Black, H., & Black, S. (1984). *Book 1: Building thinking skills*. Pacific Grove, CA: Midwest Publications.

Bloom B. S. (1965). *Taxonomy of educational objectives, handbook I, cognitive domain*. New York: Longman.

Bransford, J. D., & Stein, B. S. (1984). *The IDEAL problem solver: A guide for improving thinking, learning, and creativity*. New York: W. H. Freeman.

Bruner, J. (1970). *Man: A course of study*. Cambridge, MA: Educational Development Center.

California State Department of Education. (1979). *Principles, objectives and curricula for programs in the education of gifted and talented pupils— Kindergarten through grade twelve*. Sacramento: California State Department of Education.

Chipman, S. F., Segal, J. W., & Glaser, R. (1985). *Thinking and learning skills*. Hillsdale, NJ: Lawrence Erlbaum.

Costa, A. L. (1985). The behaviors of intelligence. In A. L. Costa (Ed.), *Developing minds* (pp. 66–68). Alexandria, VA: Association for Supervision and Curriculum Development.

Dacey, J. S. (1989). *Fundamentals of creative thinking*. Lexington, MA: D. C. Heath.

Davidson, J. E., & Sternberg, R. J. (1984). The role of insight in intellectual giftedness. *Gifted Child Quarterly, 28*, 58–64.

Ennis, R. H. (1962). A concept of critical thinking. *Harvard Educational Review, 32*, 81–111.

Ennis, R. H. (1985). A logical basis for measuring critical thinking skills. *Educational Leadership, 43* (2), 44–48.

Ennis, R. H., & Millman, J. (1985). *Cornell critical thinking test*. Pacific Palisades, CA: Midwest Publications.

Ennis, R. H., & Weir, E. (1980). *Ennis-Weir critical thinking essay test*. Pacific Palisades, CA: Midwest Publications.

Feldhusen, J. F., Bahlke, S. J., & Treffinger, D. J. (1969). Teaching creative thinking. *Elementary School Journal, 70*, 48–53.

Feldhusen, J. F., & Clinkenbeard, P. R. (1986). Creativity instructional materials: a review of research. *Journal of Creative Behavior, 20*.

Feldhusen, J. F., & Treffinger, D. J. (1975). Teachers' attitudes and practices in teaching creativity and problem solving to economically disadvantaged and minority children. *Psychological Reports, 37*, 1161–1162.

Feldhusen, J. F., & Treffinger, D. J. (1975). *Teaching creative thinking and problem solving*. Dubuque, IA: Kendall-Hunt.

Feldhusen, J. F., & Treffinger, D. J. (1985). *Creative thinking and problem solving in gifted education*. Dubuque, IA: Kendall-Hunt.

Getzels, J., & Csikszentmihalyi, M. (1976). *The creative vision: A longitudinal study of problem finding in art*. New York: Wiley.

Glaser, R. (1984). Education and thinking: The role of knowledge. *American Psychology, 39* (2), 893–904.

Goodlad, J. I. (1984). *A place called school*. New York: McGraw-Hill.

Guilford, J. P., & Hoepfner, R. (1971). *The analysis of intelligence*. New York: McGraw-Hill.

Halpern, D. F. (1984). *Thought and knowledge: An introduction to critical thinking*. Hillsdale, NJ: Lawrence Erlbaum.

Harnadek, A. (1978). *Mind benders*. Pacific Grove, CA: Midwest Publications.

Harnadek, A. (1980). *Critical thinking, Book 1 and 2*. Pacific Grove, CA: Midwest Publications.

Isaksen, S., & Treffinger, D. J. (1985). *Creative problem solving: The basic course*. Buffalo, NY: Bearly Limited.

Lipman, M., Sharp, A. M., & Oscanyan, F. F. (1980). *Philosophy in the classroom*. Philadelphia: Temple University Press.

Maker, C. J. (1982). *Teaching models in education of the gifted*. Rockville, MD: Aspen.

Meeker, M. (1982). *Divergent production of semantic units*. El Segundo, CA: SOI Institute.

Meeker, M., Meeker, R., & Roid, G. H. (1985). *Structure of intellect learning abilities test (SOI-LA)*. Los Angeles: Western Psychological Services.

Newell, A., & Simon, H. (1972). *Human problem solving*. Englewood Cliffs, NJ: Prentice Hall.

Osborn, A. (1963). *Applied imagination*. New York: Scribners.

Parnes, S. J. (1967). *Creative behavior guidebook*. New York: Scribners.

Parnes, S. J. (1977). Guiding creative action. *Gifted Child Quarterly, 21,* 460–476.

Parnes, S. J., Noller, R. B., & Biondi, A. M. (1977). *Guide to creative action.* New York: Charles Scribner.

Pollert, L. H., Feldhusen, J. F., VanMondfrans, A. P., & Treffinger, D. J. (1969). Role of memory in divergent thinking. *Psychological Reports, 25,* 151–156.

Raths, L. G., Wasserman, S., Jones, A., & Rothstein, A. (1986). *Teaching for thinking.* New York: Teachers College Press.

Ross, J. D., & Ross, C. M. (1976). *Ross test of higher cognitive processes.* Los Angeles: Western Psychological Services.

Rubinstein, M. F. (1986). *Tools for thinking and problem solving.* Englewood Cliffs, NJ: Prentice Hall.

Sanders, N. M. (1966). *Classroom questions, what kinds.* New York: Harper & Row.

Schoenfield, M., & Rosenblatt, J. (1985). *Playing with logic.* Belmont, CA: David S. Lake Publishers.

Sizer, T. R. (1985). *Horace's compromise: The dilemma of the American high school.* Boston: Houghton Mifflin.

Sternberg, R. J. (1985). *Beyond IQ: A triarchic theory of intelligence.* New York: Cambridge University Press.

Sternberg, R. J., & Baron, J. B. (1985). A statewide approach to measuring critical thinking skills. *Educational Leadership, 43* (2), 40–43.

Suchman, R. (1965). Inquiry and education. In J. Gallagher (Ed.), *Teaching gifted students: A book of readings.* Boston: Allyn and Bacon.

Taba, H. (1962). *Curriculum development, theory and practice.* New York: Harcourt Brace and World.

Tannenbaum, A. J. (1983). *Gifted children, psychological and educational perspectives.* New York: Macmillan.

Tiedt, I. M., Carlson, J. E., Howard, B. D., & Watanabe, K. S. O. (1989). *Teaching thinking in K–12 classrooms: Ideas, activities, and resources.* Boston: Allyn and Bacon.

Torrance, E. P. (1962). *Guiding creative talent.* Englewood Cliffs, NJ: Prentice Hall.

Torrance, E. P. (1965). *Rewarding creative behavior.* Englewood Cliffs, NJ: Prentice Hall.

Torrance, E. P. (1974). *Torrance tests of creative thinking, norms-technical manual.* Lexington, MA: Ginn.

Torrance, E. P. (1987). Teaching for creativity. In S. G. Isaksen (Ed.), *Frontiers of creativity research* (pp. 189–215). Buffalo, NY: Bearly Limited.

Torrance, E. P., & Myers, R. E. (1970). *Creative learning and teaching.* New York: Dodd, Mead.

Treffinger, D. J. (1980). *Encouraging creative learning for the gifted and talented.* Ventura, CA: Ventura County Supt. of Schools, LTI Publications.

Watson, G., & Glaser, E. M. (1980). *Watson-Glaser critical thinking appraisal.* New York: Psychological Corporation.

Whaley, C. E. (1984). *Future studies.* New York: Trillium Press.

Wick, J. W., & Smith, J. K. (1980). *Developing cognitive abilities test.* Glenview, IL: Scott, Foresman.

Williams, F. (1972). *A total creativity kit.* Englewood Cliffs, NJ: Educational Technology Publications.

# Affective Curriculum for the Gifted

*LINDA KREGER SILVERMAN*

*Without self-knowledge in depth we can have dreams, but no art. We can have the neurotic raw materials of literature but not mature literature. We can have no adults, but only aging children who are armed with words and paint and clay and atomic weapons, none of which they understand. And the greater the role in the educational process which is played by unconscious components of symbolic thinking, the wider must be this ancient and dishonorable gap between erudition and wisdom. —LAWRENCE KUBIE*

Since its inception, the main focus of gifted education has been on academic achievement. By comparison, the affective development of the gifted has received much less attention. However, neglect of the emotional lives of children affects their intellectual lives and motivation. The affective realm is not separate from the cognitive realm; they interact in learning and development (Piaget, 1967). In the last several years, interest in the affective domain has awakened. We are beginning to understand the critical importance of emotions to the learning process, to the full development of the individual, and to the future of society.

Sommers's (1981) research with college students reveals that cognitive complexity gives rise to emotional responsiveness. Therefore, one would expect the gifted to have a greater emotional capacity, which is exactly what has been found (Piechowski, 1991; Silverman, 1983, 1993). This emotional energy is essential to the process of self-actualization (Brennan & Piechowski, 1991). If we wish to promote self-actualization instead of simply knowledge acquisition, and if we wish our gifted students to develop humanitarian values rather than using their knowledge for self-aggrandizement, then we must nurture their emotional resources. Without focusing attention to their affective development, we risk the advancement of intellect without ethics and foster a self-centered perspective of talent instead of encouraging students to use their gifts in the service of humanity.

Although several writers in gifted education have pleaded for the integration of cognitive and affective curriculum for the gifted, the subject matter of affective education remains unclear. The content of an affective program has been variously depicted as the development of:

- *Individualized value systems (Krathwohl, Bloom, & Masia, 1964)*
- *Attitudes, beliefs, and values (Sellin & Birch, 1980)*
- *Interests and appreciations (Carin & Sund, 1978)*
- *Persistence, independence, and self-concept (Franks & Dolan, 1982)*
- *Feelings, emotions, and awareness of self and others (Treffinger, Borgers, Render, & Hoffman, 1976)*
- *Interpersonal relations (Treffinger et al., 1976)*
- *Humanitarianism (Fantini, 1981)*
- *Curiosity, risk taking, complexity, and imagination (Williams, 1970)*

Indeed, the term *affective* appears to encompass everything that cannot be considered purely cognitive or intellectual in nature. In this text, affective development refers to all of the *personal, social,* and *emotional* aspects of learning.

Affective development plays a unique role in the curriculum. It is both a part of it and apart from it. It is important to design specific learning activities to promote self-awareness and awareness of others. This would seem to be particularly pertinent to gifted education, since educators and parents alike are more concerned with the social development of gifted children than with the academic achievement (Anderson & Tollefson, 1991). Special programs for the gifted, which often have a flexible curriculum, can provide an excellent context for focusing on affective concerns.

However, affective development is not a discipline like English or mathematics, so it may seem to some to be out of place in a book of this nature and out of place in the curriculum. After all, one cannot major in affect! And at the middle and high school levels, where education is organized in disciplines, there seems to be no room for emotional development. Yet, the need for emphasis in this area increases in adolescence, when the personal curriculum of the fledgling adult is more salient than the desire for mastery that characterized an earlier developmental period. At these levels, seminars, discussion groups, and preventive counseling groups can supplement traditional subject matter offerings.

Schools have been reluctant to respond to the affective needs of the gifted. Among the reasons for this neglect are:

- *The lack of acknowledgment that the gifted have specific affective needs (Delisle, 1992; VanTassel-Baska, 1991)*
- *The traditional lack of concern in education for the affective domain (Tannenbaum, 1982)*

- *Attitudes on the part of parents that emotions are to be dealt with in the home rather than in the school (Elgersma, 1981)*
- *Fear of indoctrination (Bloom, Hastings, & Madaus, 1971)*
- *Lack of agreement as to the nature of affective education*
- *The position that if the school meets the child's cognitive needs, affective development will automatically follow (Mehrens & Lehman, 1973)*
- *Lack of reliable and valid tools for assessing affective development (Franks & Dolan, 1982)*
- *Lack of clarity as to the optimal level of affective functioning to be attained (Franks & Dolan, 1982)*
- *A belief that healthy emotional development among the gifted is automatic (Blackburn & Erikson, 1986)*

More clarification is needed of the goals of affective education to dispel parental fears that the school system plans to engage in indoctrination or infringe on the belief systems of the family. Instruments for assessing affective development would certainly be useful, although the dearth of such materials should not be used as an excuse to ignore children's emotional needs. Programs that are only concerned with cognitive development often breed competition rather than cooperation, and do not automatically produce responsive citizens. The main obstacle to the incorporation of an affective strand in the curriculum has been the attitude that the school is not responsible for the child's emotional life. The increasing number of adolescent suicides with which school personnel have had to contend has led to marked changes in this belief (Delisle, 1990; Hayes & Sloat, 1990).

The emotional lives of the gifted are very intense. Topics discussed on an intellectual level in school can have a profound impact on them. For example, an eight-year-old highly gifted girl cried nightly for weeks about the possibility of nuclear war, asking endless questions of her parents. When education emphasizes only cognition, neglecting emotional experiences, gifted children can become anxious, depressed, alienated, socially inept, or emotionally blocked. Since it is emotion that fuels commitment to ethical principles (Dabrowski & Piechowski, 1977; Piechowski, 1991), there are great benefits to be gained for both the child and society by paying closer attention to the affective realm.

A more supportive climate toward affective education for gifted children does appear to be slowly emerging in the schools. Studies of affective characteristics of the gifted are increasing (Janos & Robinson, 1985; Robinson & Noble, 1991). Group dynamics, values clarification, and affective activities are popular components of gifted programs even at the secondary level (Betts & Knapp, 1981; Curry, 1981).

## Affective Education Versus Counseling

One reason teachers are often hesitant to initiate an affective program is their concern that they have not had enough training in counseling. They fear that they will not be prepared to deal with the issues that might surface when children begin to explore their emotional lives. They don't want to open Pandora's box. Many teachers of the gifted really would like more of an emphasis on counseling in their training programs (Hultgren, 1981), but the lack of such training need not be a deterrent in providing for the affective needs of the students. An affective education program can be conducted effectively by the classroom teacher, with support services of the school counselor or social worker available as needed.

It is important to distinguish between affective education and counseling, so that the classroom teacher does not become overwhelmed by the responsibility of attending to the children's emotional needs. When the children's needs extend beyond the teacher's training and competence, then the counselor must take over. Affective education and counseling are both concerned with emotions and personal development; however, they differ in several important ways. Affective activities are less personal than counseling and deal with emotional issues in less depth. Through these activities, students learn more about their own beliefs and philosophies, and develop greater self-awareness and understanding of others.

The underlying philosophy of affective education is respect for the uniqueness of each student's beliefs and experiences. No attempt is made to change anyone's values or attitudes. Sharing is optional and privacy is respected. Although some people fear that discussion of values invites imposition of the teacher's values on the students, such an imposition would be antithetical to the purpose of affective education. Unlike counseling, which serves to promote positive changes in an individual's ability to cope with life, affective education promotes awareness, not necessarily change. Integration of affective objectives into the curriculum can prevent the need for counseling in some cases by building self-esteem and better interpersonal relations.

The following list summarizes some of the main differences between affective education and counseling.

| *Affective Education* | *Counseling* |
|---|---|
| • Oriented toward groups | • Oriented toward individuals |
| • Usually directed by the teacher (no special training required) | • Directed by an individual trained in counseling |
| • Involves self-awareness and sharing of feelings with others | • Involves problem solving, making choices, conflict resolution, and deeper understanding of self |
| • Consists of planned exercises and activities | • Consists of relatively unstructured private sessions or group sessions in which content is determined by students |
| • Unrelated to therapy | • Closely related to therapy |
| • Students helped to clarify their own values or beliefs | • Students helped to change their perceptions or methods of coping |
| • Personalizes the curriculum, making it more relevant to the student | • Unrelated to curriculum |

It would be ideal if a counselor could be involved in the planning of an affective program, as a consultant to the teacher and as a resource if referrals appear necessary. At the very least, teachers should receive an in-service on the signs of depression, sexual or physical abuse, and suicidal ideation, and be instructed as to methods of referral. At the junior and senior high school levels, the school counselor should be more involved in conducting the affective program and providing special assistance on career counseling (Silverman, 1993).

## Affective Education and Curriculum

An affective program is usually conceived as a specified time period devoted to affective concerns. At the primary level, the curriculum often includes units on the development of self-concept. There have been kits, programs, and book series written on social development (e.g., Cartledge & Milburn, 1980; LeCroy, 1982). Affective curricula now exist for middle school and junior high school students. At the junior and senior high school level, small group discussions on shared concerns provide a type of preventive counseling that can counteract depression and isolation—two major factors in adolescent suicide (Strip, Swassing, & Kidder, 1991).

It is also possible to construct a less visible affective program that is simply a part of every subject area. Affective education can be interwoven with the curriculum by constructing activities in such a manner that they enhance learning in the cognitive and affective domains simultaneously. Dealing with real issues (Renzulli, 1977) or children's interests strongly affects motivation. Designing activities so that the progression of difficulty is within the children's grasp—not so easy that they are bored nor so difficult that they are overwhelmed—builds self-confidence. Allowing children to work in pairs, triads, or small groups expands social development and leadership. Raising ethical issues or creating cognitive dissonance supports moral development. Kaplan (1974) recommended that affective objectives be written along with cognitive objectives when designing learning experiences for the gifted.

Gifted children usually have positive self-concepts about their learning abilities, but they frequently lack confidence in their social skills (Ross & Parker, 1980; Silverman, Chitwood, & Waters, 1986). Social skills, like other skills, are learned through positive experiences. Gifted students may need specific guidance in making friends, building the self-esteem of others, and working cooperatively. The development of these skills can be curricular objectives. They can be addressed on a cognitive level through literature, social sciences, and evaluating the global impact of scientific advances. Learning experiences can be designed to increase students' awareness of the emotional needs of others, and provide opportunities for students to develop leadership and work cooperatively toward group goals.

Since research indicates that grouping gifted students together for instruction enhances their self-esteem and social relations (Feldhusen, Sayler, Nielsen, & Kolloff, 1990), it is recommended that cooperative learning groups be formed within the gifted classroom. If this is not feasible, gifted students should be allowed to create their own cooperative learning groups in the regular classroom.

A challenging curriculum taught at a pace commensurate with the students' learning rate has been found to have a positive impact on their motivation, self-esteem, values, and love of learning (Hollingworth, 1930). Further, longitudinal studies indicate that these effects may be lifelong (Harris, 1992). Curriculum for the gifted will naturally enhance affective development if it includes opportunities for community service, exposure to philosophical and psychological theories, opportunities to construct moral dilemmas and examine ethical principles, biographical study, analysis of world events and their implications, and the study of history with close attention to values, global education, and future studies (Silverman, 1993).

## *Developing the Self-Concept*

Affective development is rooted in an individual's self-concept. Social skills, leadership ability, and moral development are founded on self-esteem. One's self-esteem can be likened to tea in a teacup—when the teacup is filled beyond capacity, it spills over into the saucer, and when the teacup is half empty, there is no surplus to share with others. In his "self-theory," Carl Rogers (1951) provided a basis for understanding self-concept. Rogers maintained that the self is the central aspect of personality. He described self-concept as an organized configuration of perceptions of one's characteristics and abilities that develops out of interpersonal relationships. Since it is formed through interactions with the world, it is vulnerable to feedback from others. The self is a dynamic force, shaping the person's perceptions and behavior. Snygg and Combs (1949) asserted that the basic drive of the individual is the maintenance and enhancement of the self.

Reviewing the research on the self, Clark (1983) summarized as follows:

> . . . *Researchers found that the view of the self determines achievement and enhances or limits the development of a person's potential.*
>     . . . *The beliefs we have about ourselves literally determine our actions and our perceptions of the world and other people. We construct our own reality from these beliefs and often operate as if this is the only view possible. (Clark, 1983, p. 108)*

Some children are buoyant in the face of daily challenges; others seem to view each challenge as an onslaught against their self-esteem. Gifted children are particularly vulnerable because they react in an intensified manner to experience. A mistake may be experienced as humiliation—proof of the child's unworthiness. The unique characteristics of the gifted—supersensitivity, perceptiveness, perfectionism, and self-criticism—furnish ample opportunities for them to feel inadequate, despite the number of successful achievements to their credit (Sisk, 1982). This paradoxical lack of self-esteem in the face of much success has been labeled the "imposter phenomenon" (Clance, 1985; Harvey, 1985). Experience shows that most gifted children suffer from this syndrome to some degree. They believe that they are not as smart as others perceive them to be, and they live in continuous dread of being unmasked as frauds.

Reversing a child's negative self-concept is a difficult task, but it can be done. The first step is recognition of the child's feelings of inadequacy. With many children, negative self-attitudes are apparent, but the gifted often mask these feelings. They may act superior when they are actually feeling inferior; they may appear emotionless to cover up heightened sensitivity and vulnerability (Silverman, 1990). Group discussions with other gifted students are invaluable for helping the gifted recognize that they are not alone in these feelings and for teaching them ways of coping with such feelings.

## An Affective Curriculum

A comprehensive affective program for the gifted includes opportunities to discuss common concerns with other gifted students. It is important to stress that effective groups are comprised of gifted students rather than a cross-section of the student population. Gifted children have different issues from their age-mates, and they will not reveal their true concerns in a mixed-ability group. This is due to the fact that many of their issues are related to their feeling a lack of emotional safety in the heterogeneous group (Silverman, 1991). They have many devices for hiding their abilities, such as playing dumb or becoming the class clown, in order to avoid being teased by their classmates. This is a serious concern that leads to inauthenticity and inner conflict as well as the potential for underachievement. This issue would never be brought up in a heterogeneous group, but it is likely to be addressed in a group of students with similar abilities.

Researchers, teachers, and counselors have observed a rather consistent set of issues that beset the gifted. For example, Strop (1983) found that a group of seventh- and eighth-grade Talent Search students worried most about universal concerns, performance, and getting along with others. When these students were asked to rank order specific issues, the following 10 concerns emerged in order of priority:

1. Establishing and maintaining positive relationships with peers
2. Dealing with oversensitivity to what others say and do
3. Making appropriate career choices
4. Developing the ability to relax and relieve tension
5. Maintaining the motivation and desire to achieve
6. Developing positive leadership skills
7. Getting along with siblings
8. Developing tolerance
9. Dealing with the striving for perfectionism
10. Avoiding prolonged periods of boredom

Affective curricula have been developed for middle school students (Beville, 1983) that address these concerns. A similar program developed by Delisle (1980) revolves around four specific adjustment problems of the gifted:

*Problem #1:* Problems associated with realizing the nature and significance of intellectual differences and the accompanying feelings of inferiority and inadequacy

*Problem #2:* Problems associated with social alienation or discomfort due to dissatisfaction with the frequency and merit of interpersonal relationships

*Problem #3:* Problems associated with a dull and meager school curriculum that provides little academic sustenance

*Problem #4:* Problems associated with locating and pursuing occupational and educational choices commensurate withe the gifted's interests and abilities (pp. 22–23)

Delisle (1980) presented activities designed to increase awareness of each problem area: discussion questions, books, films, cartoons, brainstorming activities, and quotations. An example of the activities follows:

*Communicate a series of goals that you expect to achieve and a series of goals that others expect you to achieve:*

*—compare these expectations;*
*—rate the financial, societal, and emotional benefits of each expectation.*
*(Delisle, 1980, p. 24)*

Delisle's article also includes an instrument for evaluating the success of a preventive counseling program.

In addition to the generic concerns of gifted children, some students deal with specific problems related to their situations or personalities. Among these specific problems are:

- *Underachievement*
- *Depression (often masked as boredom)*
- *Hiding abilities*
- *Understanding their introversion*
- *Uneven development*
- *Excessive competitiveness*
- *Hostility of others toward their abilities*
- *Feeling overly responsible for others*
- *Being overshadowed in the family by the eldest sibling*
- *Hidden handicaps*
- *Lack of true peers*

Taking into account the dominant themes expressed by most gifted students and the specific problems encountered by a portion of the population, the following topics are recommended as ingredients in an affective program.

### Topics for Affective Development

| | |
|---|---|
| Understanding Giftedness | Social Skills |
| Self-Expectations | Dealing with Stress |
| Fear of Failure | Sensitivity |
| Expectations of Others | Tolerance |
| Feeling Different | Family Dynamics |
| Uneven Development | Responsibility for Others |
| Introversion | Developing Study Habits |
| Peer Pressure | Developing Leadership Ability |
| Competitiveness | Career Exploration |
| Guilt | |

The order of presentation of these topics and the amount of time spent exploring each one would depend on the needs of the group. In the affective domain, it is difficult to predetermine a scope and sequence but not impossible. A school district dedicated to incorporating affective objectives into the curriculum in a comprehensive manner could take clusters of these topics and determine which ones would be stressed at each grade level. Some might be recycled at each grade level and dealt with in a different manner. For example, Understanding Giftedness and Feeling Different could be introductory units in the first year of middle school and high school, whereas Self-Expectations and Expectations of Others might be central themes at all grade levels. Some topics, such as Developing Study Skills and Career Exploration, lend themselves more readily to the development of a scope and sequence through the grades than topics such as Sensitivity and Tolerance.

Flexibility is essential in an affective program, so that the curriculum remains responsive to the immediate needs of the group. For example, if a group of students happens to be facing severe peer pressure or is dealing with stress from some other source, the discussion group needs to be structured in such a way that these issues can be dealt with at the time they occur, rather than waiting until their scheduled time in the curriculum (Colangelo & Peterson, 1993). In other words, a curriculum can be designed with set activities, but it would be more effective if there were also unstructured times when immediate issues could surface and be discussed.

The presence of a trained counselor at the secondary level would enhance the effectiveness of the group process; however, all teachers of the gifted should be trained to lead group discussions and to respond to the emotional needs of the students. The school counselor or social worker can be asked to participate in at least some discussions, and guest speakers can be invited from the community to discuss their career patterns. If certain topics would be more comfortable for girls to discuss in all-female group, some group sessions should be designed to accommodate this need (Kerr, 1986).

When affective development is incorporated into the curriculum itself instead of isolated as a separate set of experiences, the most comprehensive framework for doing so comes from the Taxonomy of Affective Objectives (Krathwohl, Bloom, & Masia, 1964).

## The Taxonomy of Affective Objectives

Since concern for the "whole child" has been a philosophical underpinning of elementary education, it would be reasonable to assume that affective education evolved from the elementary level to the higher educational levels. However, one of the major influences in this area originated at the college level as early as 1948. A committee of college examiners that produced Bloom's *Taxonomy of Cognitive Objectives* also developed the *Taxonomy of Affective Objectives* (Krathwohl, Bloom, & Masia, 1964). The original plan was to create one complete taxonomy in three major parts: cognitive, affective, and psychomotor domains (Bloom, 1956). The taxonomy of the cognitive domain was completed first, in 1956, and that of the affective domain followed in 1964.

The committee found the creation of an affective taxonomy to be an extremely arduous task. Due to the imprecision with which affective objectives were usually stated, they defied classification. Teachers were unclear as to the learning experiences appropriate to the objectives. Testing procedures were primitive. Whereas the cognitive domain could be assessed through the observation of overt behaviors, the affective domain was less observable. "It is difficult to describe the behaviors appropriate to these objectives since the internal or covert feelings and emotions are as significant for this domain as are the overt behavioral manifestations" (Bloom, 1956, p. 7).

In spite of these difficulties, the task was completed, and resulted in a much needed framework for the development of affective goals. The taxonomy addresses interests, attitudes, values, the development of appreciations, and emotional sets or biases (Krathwohl, Bloom, & Masia, 1964). It is hierarchically ordered from passive to active manifestations. As is true for the cognitive domain, each level incorporates all of the skills involved in the previous levels.

---

**AFFECTIVE DOMAIN**

1.0 Receiving
    1.1 Awareness
    1.2 Willingness to receive
    1.3 Controlled or selected attention

2.0 Responding
    2.1 Acquiescence in responding
    2.2 Willingness to respond
    2.3 Satisfaction in response

3.0 Valuing
    3.1 Acceptance of a value
    3.2 Preference for a value
    3.3 Commitment

4.0 Organization
    4.1 Conceptualization of a value
    4.2 Organization of a value system

5.0 Characterization by a Value or Value Complex
    5.1 Generalized set
    5.2 Characterized (Krathwohl, Bloom, & Masia, 1964, p. 95)

---

The first level of the taxonomy, *Receiving,* is concerned with gaining the student's attention. Three levels of attention are outlined, progressing from passive reception to active selection of stimuli. At first, the learner is only vaguely aware of particular affective elements and is unable to verbally describe them. At the next stage, the student demonstrates a willingness to receive the affective information but has not yet formed any judgments about it. At the final stage, the student shows a preference for certain affective experiences even in the pressence of competing stimuli.

An example of this progression of attention is in the enjoyment of classical music. If the teacher played baroque music quietly in the background while the children worked, some children would enjoy it, some would dislike it, and some would not notice it. As the children became more familiar with it, those who disliked it might come to tolerate it, and those who had not noticed at all would probably begin to pay attention to it. They might notice when it wasn't playing or when the tempo of the movements changed. As their awareness increased, they might indicate that they work better with music in the background, and when given a choice of different types of music, perhaps they would select classical music.

The next level, *Responding,* is characterized by active participation of the learner. This is the level at which interests are born. In the three stages, the student moves from compliance to active initiation and eventually to marked enthusiasm. Continuing with the example of classical music, the student might listen initially simply to satisfy the teacher, then start to ask for particular pieces to be played, and then express enjoyment with the music of certain composers.

Another example is the way in which some students respond to biographical studies. When a student is asked to read about the life of an eminent individual, he might do so at first out of obligation. As he begins to identify with the person, he may decide to read more about the woman on his own. If his interest increases, he may attempt to read everything that was ever written about her. Teaching is often concerned with this level of the taxonomy. Teachers expose their classes to a variety of topics in hopes that some of them will become lasting interests for the students.

*Valuing,* the third level, is at the heart of affective education. In the process of valuing, students examine their own beliefs and the beliefs of others, ascribe worth to certain of these values, and then commit themselves to living in accordance with the ones they have chosen. In the first stage, the belief is embraced but not necessarily acted upon. In the second stage, the student actively seeks the value and becomes identified with it. In the third stage, the person displays a high degree of certainty about the value and acts to promote it. An example of valuing would be learning about all sides of the nuclear power issue, taking a firm stand, and then writing letters to legislators or attempting in some other way to promote his or her position.

Work in values clarification appears to be an elaboration of this part of the taxonomy (Carin & Sund, 1978). Raths, Harmin, and Simon (1978) described three phases of valuing—choosing, prizing, and acting—which approximate the three stages of this level. They further subdivide the valuing process into seven steps.

---

**VALUING\***

| Acceptance of a value | Choosing | (1) freely |
| | | (2) from alternatives |
| | | (3) after thoughtful consideration of the consequences of each alternative |
| Preference for a value | Prizing | (4) cherishing, being happy with the choice |
| | | (5) enough to be willing to affirm the choice to others |
| Commitment | Acting | (6) or doing something with the choice |
| | | (7) repeatedly, in some pattern of life |

---

Adapted from L. E. Raths, M. Harmin, & S. B. Simon, *Values and Teaching: Working with Values in the Classroom,* 2nd ed. (Columbus, OH: Merrill, 1978).

In values clarification, the student chooses values freely, not on the basis of peer pressure or pressure from authority figures. Choice presupposes that the individual is aware of alternatives. The authors suggest that brainstorming many possible responses to a situation increases the likelihood that a value will emerge. Informed choice requires that the person understand the various consequences of all potential options. Prizing or cherishing means holding certain values dear. A value is affirmed when an individual lets others know that she or he holds it and wishes to be identified with it. Acting upon a value means that it shows up in some aspects of one's life. It also tends to be persistent—it shows up repeatedly in different situations and at different times (Raths, Harmin, & Simon, 1978).

In developing a set of values, the individual moves from weakly defined, conflicting values derived from external sources to a cohesive set of internally derived convictions (Dabrowski, 1964; Piechowski, 1991). Value construction is a lengthy process, requiring maturation, experience, and some degree of crisis. When values are adopted mindlessly in imitation of others, with no inner conflict, they are more susceptible to change. It is important for individuals to question the ready-made values in their world and then choose their own. Self-chosen values, which flow from a full comprehension of available alternatives, are highly resistant to change and more likely to become life-long commitments (Raths, Harmin, & Simon, 1978).

The last two ranks of the taxonomy, *Organization* and *Characterization,* are normally attained only by high school and college students, and adults. They require considerable depth and maturity, as well as a capacity for sophisticated thought processes. Organization involves analyzing the internal consistency of one's value structure, dealing with conflicting values, and prioritizing values to form a coherent system. The first step in this process is conceptualization, an analysis of each value in relation to others that are currently held and new ones that are emerging. The values to which one was previously committed are now reviewed, questioned, seen in relation to all others, and then expanded into abstract principles. The individual develops personal goals and ideals that serve as the basis for conscious choices.

The second phase, the organization of a value system, is a process of synthesis. The individual brings together a complex set of values, attitudes, and beliefs into a hierarchial system. Ideally, the value system that emerges from this process would be harmonious and internally consistent. However, since we often tend to hold some values that are diametrically opposed to each other, their integration may be less than perfect. Those values that cannot be harmonized may become less polarized or at least may be held in dynamic equilibrium. Potentialities and limitations are accepted realistically. The person begins to build a philosophy of life.

*Characterization by a Value or Value Complex* is the highest level in the taxonomy. At this level, the individual acts consistently in accordance with internalized principles. There are two stages to this level: generalized set and characterization. Generalized set is a persistent and predictable response pattern at a very high level of integration. The value structure serves as an inner core to guide behavior. Characterization implies a total way of life based on an internal hierarchy of values. The values exemplified are broader and more inclusive than those at earlier stages. Individuals who attain this level are conscious of their responsibility to all of life. Among the few who have achieved this level of humanitarianism are Lincoln, Gandhi, and Einstein (Carin & Sund, 1978).

*Realistically, formal education generally cannot reach this level. . . . The maturity and personal integration required at this level are not attained until at least some years after the individual has completed his formal education. Time and experience must interact with affective and cognitive learnings before the individual can answer the crucial questions, "Who am I?" and "What do I stand for?" (Krathwohl, Bloom, & Masia, 1964, p. 165)*

Since the affective domain and the cognitive domain are inextricably connected (Perrone & Pulvino, 1977; Maker, 1982; Piaget, 1967; Sommers, 1981), the cognitive and affective taxonomies developed by Bloom, Krathwohl, and their associates can be used in conjunction with each other for curricular planning. Most affective responses are predicated on knowledge, and all learning requires, at the very least, attention of the learner.

Vare (1979) recommended that the two domains be addressed simultaneously. She asserted that values and attitudes are transmitted not only by the curriculum but by the educational process itself: "How we learn is what we learn" (p. 488). Examples of the planned integration of cognitive and affective behaviors are Suchman's (1975) model for inquiry training and Williams's (1979) model for encouraging creativity in the classroom.

Integration of the two sets of objectives is implicit in their construction. The cognitive and affective taxonomies are related in the following manner:

| Affective | Cognitive |
| --- | --- |
| Receiving | Knowledge |
| Responding | Comprehension |
| Valuing | Application |
| Organization | Analysis |
| Characterization | Synthesis |
| | Evaluation |

*Source*: Krathwohl, Bloom, & Masia, 1964, pp. 49–50.

In their book, Eberle and Hall (1979) indicated how the combined affective and cognitive processes can be applied to aesthetic sensitivity, interpersonal relations, moral and ethical development and self-knowledge. Carin and Sund (1978) gave specific examples of teaching activities related to each level and subcategory of the affective taxonomy. L. Anderson (1981) described how affective characteristics can be assessed in the schools.

The materials available on affective education can provide a climate for affective development in the classroom. Following is a small sample of activities appropriate for classes for the gifted. Other sources of material for affective development are suggested later in this chapter.

## Affective Activities

The following affective activities can be used with groups of gifted students. The activities can be done orally in dyads, triads, or small groups. They may also be used as written exercises on an individual basis. If they are written, students may choose to share their responses with others, share them only with the teacher, or keep them private. The activities are appropriate for use with all children, not only the gifted; however, since gifted children are extremely perceptive, they are likely to take the activities to greater depths than would their peers.

1. Three Wishes (Self-Awareness)

    If you had three wishes, what would they be?

2. Ice Breakers (Sharing Feelings with Others; Feeling Different)

    a. What is your favorite TV program? Why?

    b. What is the best movie you ever saw? Why did you like it?

    c. What was the last book that you read? What did you like about it?

    d. What is your favorite sport?

    e. What is the most beautiful thing you have ever seen?

    f. What is the most unjust situation you know of?

    g. What would you like to be doing ten years from now?

    h. If you could meet anyone who ever lived, who would you want to meet?

    i. What do you love the most?

    j. What do you dislike the most?

    k. What do you look for most in a friend?

    l. What do you dream about?

    m. Who has had the most influence on your life?

    n. What are your three best qualities?

    o. If you could change one thing about yourself, what would you change?

    p. What talents do you wish you had?

    q. What is your biggest worry?

    r. What is the silliest thing you ever did?

    s. When do you feel the most lonely?

    t. When do you feel the most secure?

    u. If you could solve one of the world's problems, what problem would you want to solve?

3. Fantasy Friends (Feeling Different)

    a. Did you have an imaginary playmate when you were young?

    b. How old were you when you first created this friend?

    c. Describe as much about your friend (or friends) as you can remember.

    d. How long did you keep your friend?

    e. How old were you when you gave up this friend? Why did you do it?

    f. Do you miss your friend?

    g. What purpose do you think this friend served? (Davis, 1978)

4. Awards (Building Self-Esteem in Others; Social Skills)

    Pick someone's name out of a hat. Observe this person for a week. Write down everything you like about him or her. At the end of the week, create an award for this person and present it along with a speech in which you incorporate your observations. Each week choose a new individual to honor.

5. Collage Boxes (Introversion; Self-Awareness)

    Paste pictures from magazines on the outside of a shoebox. The magazine pictures should represent qualities that you feel others see in you. On the inside of the box paste magazine pictures that represent the "inside you." Portray the qualities you know about yourself and don't show to others. You may keep the inside of the box secret.

6. Mood Journal (Dealing with Stress)

   Keep a journal in which you write how you feel about things. Each day rate your mood on a scale from 1 to 10, with 10 being the happiest. Do you find that you are happy most of the time, unhappy most of the time, or mixed? Are there any cycles to your moods? Can you predict your next bad mood? Can you guess how long it will take before you feel better again?

7. Compliment Charts (Building Self-Esteem in Others; Social Skills)

   With masking tape, attach large sheets of butcher paper to the backs of everyone in the group. Distribute marking pens to the group. Write something you like about each person on his or her back. Be specific. Exchange pens often so that the writer cannot be identified by the color of the ink. Write in an unusual manner so that your writing cannot be identified.

8. Collections (Understanding Giftedness)

   Bring five favorite possessions to class. Describe what you like about each one. What does the collection say about you?

9. Put-Downs (Social Skills; Tolerance)

   Keep a list of all the put-downs you hear in a given day. On another day, list all of the compliments you hear. Which list is longer? Start a personal campaign to clean up put-down pollution. Make a pact with your friends to pay a penalty for each put-down. Call attention to self put-downs as well as put-downs of others. Raise consciousness within your group and see if the effect spreads to other groups. How do you feel when you receive and give fewer put-downs?

10. Pillow Talk (adapted from a Zen parable) (Conflict Resolution)

    When you are angry at someone, hold a pillow firmly in your hands and say aloud all of the reasons why you are right and the other person is wrong. Now turn the pillow upside down and say all of the reasons that the other person is right and you are wrong. Turn the pillow on its side and describe all the ways in which you both are right. Flip the pillow on its other side and describe all of the ways in which you both are wrong (Johnson, 1977).

11. Autobiography (Self-Awareness; Career Exploration)

    Write an autobiography of all the significant events in your life. Have those events helped to shape what you plan to do with your life? How?

12. Cocktail Party (Self-Expectations; Expectations of Others)

    What is the most important thing that you would like others to think about you? Think of a statement that conveys this quality. (For example, for the quality "understanding": "Tell me your problems.") Go around the room repeating your statement to everyone in the room while they do the same. Everyone talks and no one listens. When the facilitator says "Freeze!" everyone stops and then says an opposite statement (e.g., "Go away; don't bother me!"). How did you feel after this exercise? Which had more power: the first statement or its opposite? Which is the real you? (Johnson, 1977)

13. Saying No (Self-Expectations; Expectations of Others)

     Choose a partner. Ask your partner to do something completely unreasonable. Your partner should continue to refuse as long as you keep asking. After a few minutes, switch roles and have your partner ask you to do something unreasonable while you practice refusing. Then have your partner refuse while you ask something reasonable. After a few minutes, switch roles. How did each of you feel saying no? Was it easier to say no to an unreasonable request than to a reasonable one? (Wolf, 1977)

14. Family Sculpting (Family Dynamics)

     Assign one classmate to role play each of your family members. Tell them just a few things about the person each will pretend to be. Arrange the students in a manner that seems representative of your family. Who is closest to whom? Who is farthest away? Have each person tell how it feels to be that family member.

15. Setting Priorities (Self-Direction)

     Make a list of all the activities you typically engage in every week. Think of everything you do at home, at school, with friends, and so on. Now make another list of the activities that are most important to your present and future goals and values. Rank order this second list from most important to least important. Now go back to your first list and rank order how you spend your time from "most time consuming" to "least time consuming." Compare the two lists. Are you spending your time on the activities that matter the most to you? If not, how can you restructure your time so that your two lists are more closely aligned?

At the primary level, activities revolving around self-awareness, developing friendships, learning to say no to strangers, and self-protection are gradually becoming a part of the general curriculum. For the gifted, these can be supplemented with developing appreciations, as suggested in the Taxonomy of Affective Objectives (Krathwohl, Bloom & Masia, 1964).

At the intermediate grades, sensitivity to others, leadership skills, and values clarification appear to be pertinent themes. Several activity books developed for gifted students are geared to this age group (see page 342). They focus on understanding giftedness, feeling different, and getting along with others who are not as gifted. Special times can be set aside in a gifted program for students to engage in these activities.

Middle, junior, and senior high school concerns revolve around world issues, performance, and establishing positive relationships with peers. Sensitivity and perfectionism are common themes. Youngsters in these age groups need guidance in dealing with stress, both internal and external. Leadership and career exploration, two key affective areas, lend themselves well to a scope and sequence format, whereas other areas may be more situational and seem to be best dealt with in discussion groups. Specific activities can be designed or the groups can be kept more open-ended to respond to immediate concerns. Some combination of structured and unstructured activities is also effective (Colangelo & Peterson, 1993).

In addition to having a set time and place in the curriculum, affective aims can be met through instructional strategies, grouping of students, and imbedding these objectives within cognitive objectives. Suggestions for doing so have been included.

The importance of affective development cannot be overstressed. If school is preparation for life, then students must learn skills for coping with stress, understanding themselves, and developing meaningful relationships with others. We can no longer rely on the family to produce these skills, nor can we assume that this is not our responsibility. Gifted students, because of the intensity of their inner lives, need guidance in these areas to an even greater extent than other children if they are to grow into healthy, happy, productive adults.

## Conclusion

Affective development, the personal and interpersonal aspects of learning, is a vital part of the curriculum that often has been overlooked. It can be dealt with as a separate strand of the curriculum, with its own scope and sequence. The design of such a scope and sequence would be a highly creative task. However, given the current emphasis on multiple intelligences, including Gardner's (1983) "interpersonal intelligence," it would be a worthwhile endeavor.

### Key Points Summary

- *Affective development encompasses all of the personal, social, and emotional aspects of learning. It is both a part of and apart from curriculum.*
- *Much of the affective curriculum for the gifted emphasizes the enhancement of self-concept, self-direction, and social relations.*
- *Affective needs can be met through the curriculum, instructional strategies, or in preventive counseling groups.*
- *Affective education differs from counseling in that the former consists of a set of planned exercises for increasing self-awareness of groups of students and requires no special training of the group leader, whereas the latter focuses on helping individuals develop new coping strategies and is directed by a trained professional.*
- *At the elementary level, affective objectives can be interwoven with cognitive objectives, so that both needs are met simultaneously.*
- *The* Taxonomy of Affective Objectives, *developed by Krathwohl, Bloom, and Masia (1964) can be used in conjunction with Bloom's* Taxonomy *as a framework for the development of affective curricula through the grades.*
- *At the middle school, junior, and senior high-school levels, seminars are recommended to help gifted students deal effectively with specific issues.*
- *The recommended topics for an affective curriculum include: (1) understanding giftedness, (2) self-expectations, (3) fear of failure, (4) expectations of others, (5) feeling different, (6) uneven development, (7) introversion, (8) peer pressure, (9) competitiveness, (10) guilt, (11) social skills, (12) dealing with stress, (13) sensitivity, (14) tolerance, (15) family dynamics, (16) responsibility for others, (17) developing study habits, (18) developing leadership ability, and (19) career exploration.*

## *Selected Resources*

There are some excellent books available for gifted students to help them better understand themselves. There are also novels that feature gifted students and serve as a form of bibliotherapy. Some of these books are featured below:

*Giftedness: Living with It and Liking it.* (1984). S. M. Perry. Greeley, CO: ALPS.

> *A workbook for elementary students enrolled in gifted programs, this book is best suited for fourth-, fifth-, and sixth-graders. It contains eight units on understanding giftedness and dealing with it effectively. In the field testing, gifted children found the book informative and enjoyable.*

*On Being Gifted.* (1978). American Association for Gifted Children. New York: Walker.

> *This book is excellent for high school students, parents, and teachers. A symposium of gifted high school students describe their sensitivities, aspirations, attitudes toward their parents and teachers, and programs they felt were effective.*

*Gifted Kids Speak Out.* (1987). J. Delisle. Minneapolis, MN: Free Spirit.

> *Interviews were conducted with gifted students about their feelings and experiences. This is a moving book for elementary, middle school, and high school students—it is also revealing to their parents and teachers.*

*The Gifted Kids' Survival Guides.* (1984). J. Galbraith. Minneapolis, MN: Free Spirit. (1987). J. Galbraith and J. Delisle. Minneapolis, MN: Free Spirit.

> *This popular series includes information and activities for elementary-aged gifted students to understand better their abilities and learn how to get along with others.*

*Very Far Away from Anywhere Else.* (1976). V. LeGuin. New York: Bantam.

> *An excellent novel for junior and senior high school students to read, as well as gifted adults, this tiny book focuses on two different types of gifted individuals—one who lives for music and another who has diverse interests. One is supported by her family and the other is not understood at all. The novel provides important insights into the inner world of the gifted.*

*The Kid's Guide to Social Action.* (1991). B. A. Lewis. Minneapolis, MN: Free Spirit.

> *This book assists students in developing action plans to implement goals they set to "change the world." Real-life problems, ecological, and global concerns can be dealt with effectively by children with the help of this wonderful book. Replete with examples of heroic tasks initiated by children, the activities can be engaged in by entire classes, small groups, or individuals of all ages.*

*(George).* (1972). E. L. Konigsburg. New York: Atheneum.

> *This is a story of a highly gifted boy with an inner self who communicates to him. Misunderstood, the boy is taken for psychiatric help. Through some exciting adventures, he learns to trust his inner voice and integrate it.*

*A Time to Fly Free.* (1983). S. Tolan. New York: Scribner's.

> *A highly sensitive fifth-grade boy drops out of school after becoming alienated from his true self. His stepfather helps him to rediscover and appreciate himself.*

Other recommended novelists who feature gifted children in their books include Helen Cresswell, Paula Danziger, Louise Fitzhugh, Constance Greene, Maria Gripe, Virginia Hamilton, Mollie Hunter, Joseph Krumgold, Madeliene L'Engle, Sonia Leviten,

Lois Lowry, Zibby O'Neal, Katherine Paterson, K. M. Peyton, Mary Rodgers, and Cynthia Voigt.

Further resources on affective activities include *Meeting the Social and Emotional Needs of the Gifted* (Schmitz & Galbraith, 1985); *Teaching Social Skills to Children* (Cartledge & Milburn, 1980); "Eight Effective Activities to Enhance the Emotional and Social Development of the Gifted and Talented" (Betts & Neihart, 1985); *Self-Esteem in the Classroom* (Canfield, 1986); *Enhancing Self-Esteem* (2nd ed.) (Frey & Carlock, 1989); *Self Esteem Passport* (Krawetz, 1984); *Social Skills in the Classroom* (Stephens, 1978); *Social Skills Training for Children and Youth* (LeCroy, 1982); *Project Self Esteem* (McDaniel & Bielen, 1986); *Thinking, Changing, Rearranging* (J. Anderson, 1981); and *Self-Esteem, Communication and High Level Thinking Skills* (Greenlee, 1992).

# References

American Association for Gifted Children. (1978). *On being gifted*. New York: Walker.

Anderson, J. (1981). *Thinking, changing, rearranging: Improving self-esteem in young people*. Eugene, OR: Timberline Press.

Anderson, L. (1981). *Assessing affective characteristics in the schools*. Boston: Allyn and Bacon.

Anderson, R. W., & Tollefson, N. (1991). Do parents of gifted students emphasize sex role orientations for their sons and daughters? *Roeper Review, 13,* 154–157.

Betts, G. T., & Knapp. J. K. (1981). Autonomous learning and the gifted. In A. Arnold et al. (Eds.), *Secondary programs for the gifted/talented*. Ventura, CA: Office at Ventura County Superintendent of Schools.

Betts, G., & Neihart, M. (1985). Eight effective activities to enhance the emotional and social development of gifted and talented adolescents. *Roeper Review, 8,* 18–23.

Beville, K. (1983). The affective development curriculum. In S. M. Perry (Ed.), *The Aurora gifted and talented handbook for middle schools*. Aurora, CO: Aurora Public Schools.

Blackburn, A. C., & Erickson, D. B. (1986). Predictable crises of the gifted student. *Journal of Counseling and Development, 9,* 552–555.

Bloom, B. S. (Ed.). (1956). *Taxonomy of educational objectives. Handbook I: Cognitive domain*. New York: David McKay.

Bloom, B. S., Hastings, J. T., & Madaus, G. F.

(1971). *Handbook on formative and summative evaluation of student learning*. New York: McGraw-Hill.

Brennan, T. P., & Piechowski, M. M. (1991). The developmental framework for self-actualization: Evidence from case studies. *Journal of Humanistic Psychology, 31* (3), 43–64.

Canfield, J. (1986). *Self-esteem in the classroom*. Pacific Palisades, CA: Self Esteem Seminars.

Carin, A., & Sund, R. B. (1978). *Creative questioning and sensitive listening techniques: A self-concept approach* (2nd ed.). Columbus, OH: Charles E. Merrill.

Cartledge, G., & Milburn, J. F. (Eds.). (1980). *Teaching social skills to children*. New York: Pergamon.

Clance, P. R. (1985). *The imposter phenomenon: Overcoming the fear that haunts your success*. Atlanta, GA: Peachtree.

Clark, B. (1983). *Growing up gifted: Developing the potential of children at home and at school* (2nd ed.). Columbus, OH: Charles E. Merrill.

Combs, A. W., & Snygg, D. (1959). *Individual behavior* (2nd ed.). New York: Harper and Row.

Colangelo, N., & Peterson, J. (1993). Group counseling with gifted students. In L. K. Silverman (Ed.), *Counseling the gifted and talented*. Denver: Love.

Curry, J. (1981). Description of a junior high school program for the gifted/talented." In A. Arnold et al. (Eds.), *Secondary programs for the gifted/*

*talented*. Ventura, CA: Ventura County Superintendent of Schools Office.

Dabrowski, K. (1964). *Positive disintegration*. Boston: Little, Brown.

Dabrowski, K., & Piechowski, M. M. (1977). *Theory of levels of emotional development* (2 vols.). Oceanside, NY: Dabor Science.

Davis, C. (1978, December). Fantasy friends (classroom activity for junior high school students). Casper, WY.

Delisle, J. (1980). Preventive counseling for the gifted adolescent: From words to action. *Roeper Review, 3* (2), 21–25.

Delisle, J. R. (1987). *Gifted kids speak out*. Minneapolis, MN: Free Spirit.

Delisle, J. R. (1990). The gifted adolescent at risk: Strategies and resources for suicide prevention among gifted youth. *Journal for the Education of the Gifted, 13,* 212–228.

Delisle, J. R. (1992). *Guiding the social and emotional development of gifted youth: A practical guide for educators and counselors*. New York: Longman.

Delisle, J., & Galbraith, J. (1987). *The gifted kids survival guide II*. Minneapolis, MN: Free Spirit.

Eberle, B., & Hall, R. (1979). *Affective directions: Planning and teaching for thinking and feeling*. Buffalo, NY: D.O.K. Publishers.

Elgersma, R. (1981). Providing for affective growth in gifted education. *Roeper Review, 3* (4), 6–7.

Fantini, M. D. (1981). A caring curriculum for gifted children. *Roeper Review, 3* (4), 3–4.

Feldhusen, J. F., Sayler, M. F., Nielsen, M. E., & Kolloff, P. B. (1990). Self-concepts of gifted children in enrichment programs. *Journal for the Education of the Gifted, 13,* 380–387.

Franks, B., & Dolan, L. (1982). Affective characteristics of children: Educational implications. *Gifted Child Quarterly, 26,* 172–178.

Frey, D., & Carlock, J. (1989). *Enhancing self-esteem* (2nd ed.). Muncie, IN: Accelerated Development.

Galbraith, J. (1983). *The gifted kids survival guide*. Minneapolis, MN: Free Spirit.

Galbraith, J. (1984). *The gifted kids survival guide for ages 10 and under*. Minneapolis, MN: Free Spirt.

Gardner, H. (1983). *Frames of mind: The theory of multiple intelligences*. New York: Basic Books.

Greenlee, S. (1992). *Self-esteem, communication and high level thinking skills: A facilitator's handbook*. Boston: Allyn and Bacon.

Harris, C. R. (1992). The fruits of early intervention: The Hollingworth group today. *Advanced Development, 4,* 91–104.

Harvey, J. C., with Katz, C. (1985). *If I'm so successful, why do I feel like a fake: The imposter phenomenon*. New York: Random House.

Hayes, M. L., & Sloat, R. S. (1990). Suicide and the gifted adolescent. *Journal for the Education of the Gifted, 13,* 229–244.

Hollingworth, L. S. (1930). Personality development of special class children. *University of Pennsylvania Bulletin. Seventeenth Annual Schoolmen's Week Proceedings, 30,* 442–446.

Hultgren, H. (1981). *Competencies for teachers of the gifted*. Denver: University of Denver, unpublished dissertation.

Janos, P. M., & Robinson, N. M. (1985). Psychosocial development in intellectually gifted children. In F. D. Horowitz, & Marion O'Brien (Eds.), *The gifted and talented: Development perspectives* (pp. 149–195). Washington, DC: American Psychological Association.

Johnson, L. (1977, July). Bioenergetics Workshop. First Rocky Mountain Healing Festival, Ward, CO.

Kaplan, S. N. (1974). *Providing programs for the gifted and talented: A handbook*. Ventura, CA: Office of the Ventura County Superintendent of Schools, 1974.

Kerr, B. A. (1986). Career counseling for the gifted: Assessments and interventions. *Journal of Counseling and Development, 64,* 602–603.

Kerr, B. A. (1991). *A handbook for counseling the gifted and talented*. Alexandria, VA: American Association for Counseling and Development.

Konigsburg, E. L. (1972). *(George)*. New York: Atheneum.

Krathwohl, D. R., Bloom, B. S., & Masia, B. B. (1964). *Taxonomy of educational objectives. Handbook II: Affective domain*. New York: David McKay.

Krawetz, M. (1984). *Self esteem passport*. (2nd ed.). New York: Holt, Rinehart and Winston.

LeCroy, C. (Ed.). (1982). *Social skills training for children and youth*. New York: Haworth.

LeGuin, U. (1976). *Very far away from anywhere else*. New York: Bantam.

Lewis, B. A. (1991). *The kid's guide to social action:*

*How to solve the social problems you choose—and turn creative thinking into positive action.* Minneapolis, MN: Free Spirit.

Maker, C. J. (1982). *Teaching models in education of the gifted*. Rockville, MD: Aspen.

May R. (1967). *Psychology and the human dilemma*. Princeton, NJ: Van Nostrand.

McDaniel, S., & Bielen, P. (1986). *Project self esteem*. Rolling Hills Estates, CA: B. L. Winch.

Mehrens, W. A., & Lehman, I. J. (1973). *Measurement and evaluation in education and psychology*. New York: Holt, Rinehart and Winston.

Perrone, P. A., & Pulvino, C. J. (1977). New directions in the guidance of the gifted and talented. *The Gifted Child Quartely, 21,* 326–335.

Perry, S. M. (1985). *Giftedness: Living with it and liking it*. Greeley, CO: ALPS (Autonomous Learner Publications).

Piaget, J. (1967). *Six psychological studies*. New York: Random House.

Piechowski, M. M. (1991). Emotional development and emotional giftedness. In N. Colangelo & G. Davis (Eds.), *A handbook of gifted education* (pp. 285–306). Boston: Allyn and Bacon.

Raths, L. E., Harmin, M., & Simons, S. B. (1978). *Values and teaching: Working with values in the classroom* (2nd ed.). Columbus, OH: Charles E. Merrill.

Renzulli, J. S. (1977). *The enrichment triad model: A guide for developing defensible programs for the gifted and talented*. Wethersfield, CN: Creative Learning Press.

Robinson, N. M., & Noble, K. D. (1991). Social-emotional development and adjustment of gifted children. In M. C. Wang, M. C. Reynolds, & H. J. Walberg (Eds.), *Handbook of special education: Research and practice. Volume 4: Emerging programs* (pp. 57–76). New York: Pergamon.

Rogers, C. R. (1951). *Client-centered therapy*. Chicago: Houghton Mifflin.

Rogers, C. R. (1961). *On becoming a person*. Boston: Houghton Mifflin.

Ross, A., & Parker, M. (1980). Academic and social self concepts of the academically gifted. *Exceptional Children, 47,* 6–10.

Schmitz, C., & Galbraith, J. (1985). *Managing the social and emotional needs of the gifted*. Minneapolis, MN: Free Spirit.

Sellin, D. F., & Birch, J. W. (1980). *Educating gifted and talented learners*. Rockville, MD: Aspen.

Silverman, L. K. (1983). Personality development: The pursuit of excellence. *Journal for the Education of the Gifted, 6* (1), 5–19.

Silverman, L. K. (1990). Issues in affective development of the gifted. In J. VanTassel-Baska (Ed.), *A practical guide to counseling the gifted in a school setting* (2nd ed., pp. 15–30). Reston, VA: Council for Exceptional Children.

Silverman, L. K. (1991). Preventive counseling for the gifted. *Understanding Our Gifted, 3* (4), 1, 11–13.

Silverman, L. K. (Ed.). (1993). *Counseling the gifted and talented*. Denver: Love.

Silverman, L. K., Chitwood, D. G., & Waters, J. L. (1986). Young gifted children: Can parents identify giftedness? *Topics in Early Childhood Special Education, 6* (1), 23–38.

Sisk, D. A. (1982). Caring and sharing: Moral development of gifted students. *The Elementary School Journal, 82,* 221–229.

Snygg, D., & Combs, A. W. (1949). *Individual behavior*. New York: Harper and Row.

Sommers, S. (1981). Emotionality reconsidered: The role of cognition in emotional responsiveness. *Journal of Personality and Social Psychology, 41,* 553–561.

Stephens, T. (1978). *Social skills in the classroom*. Columbus, OH: Cedar Press.

Strip, C., Swassing, R., & Kidder, R. (1991). Female adolescents counseling female adolescents: A first step in emotional crisis intervention. *Roeper Review, 13,* 124–128.

Strop, J. (1983). *Counseling needs of the gifted*. Unpublished research. University of Denver.

Suchman, J. R. (1975). A model for the analysis of inquiry. In W. B. Barbe & J. S. Renzulli (Eds.), *Psychology and education of the gifted*. New York: Irvington.

Tannenbaum, A. J. (1982, July). Course notes from "The nature of intelligence." Denver: University of Denver.

Tolan, Stephanie. (1983). *A time to fly free*. New York: Scribner's.

Treffinger, D. J., Borgers, S. B., Render, G. F., & Hoffman, R. M. (1976). Encouraging affective development: A compendium of techniques and resources. *The Gifted Child Quarterly, 20,* 47–65.

VanTassel-Baska, J. (1991). Teachers as counselors for gifted students. In R. M. Milgram (Ed.),

*Counseling gifted and talented children: A guide for teachers, counselors, and parents* (pp. 37–52). Norwood, NJ: Ablex.

Vare, J. V. (1979). Moral education for the gifted: A confluent model. *The Gifted Child Quarterly, 23,* 487–499.

Williams, F. E. (1970). *Classroom ideas for encouraging thinking and feeling.* Buffalo, NY: D.O.K. Publishers.

Williams, F. E. (1979). Models for encouraging creativity in the classroom. In J. C. Gowan, J. Khatena, & E. P. Torrance (Eds.), *Educating the ablest: A book of readings on the education of gifted children* (2nd ed.). Itasca, IL: F.E. Peacock.

Wolf, M. H. (1977, March). Workshop on theater games. Jefferson County Public Schools, Golden, CO.

# Leadership Curriculum

*JOHN F. FELDHUSEN*

> *No scientific principle can tell us how to make the choice, which may sometimes be forced upon us by the insecticide problem, between the shade of the elm tree and the song of the robin. —BARRY COMMONER*

Leaders are people who influence the lives of others in positive or negative ways. That influence may come through inspirational pronouncements ("Ask not what your country can do for you . . ." or "I have a dream"), a widely promulgated philosophy ("Reaganomics"), political and governmental activity (Edward Kennedy's initiatives for liberal causes), guiding a business to financial success (Thomas Watson for IBM), developing and modeling new techniques in the arts (Picasso, O'Keefe, Robards, Mozart), marching a nation to conquest (Hitler), changing religious philosophy (Martin Luther), or expanding world horizons (Columbus, Magellan, Cortez).

Some of these examples of leadership are viewed as negative by nearly all observers (e.g., Hitler) and some others are viewed positively by some and negatively by others (Edward Kennedy's liberalism or "Reaganomics"), but there is little dispute that all have had substantial impact on the lives of people. Leaders influence and have an impact on the lives of others. They bring about change, hopefully of a type we can call progress.

Some leaders have social skills that enable them to act directly on others through command, order, appeal, guidance, counseling, or cajoling to get them to follow their wishes. Still others simply have powerful or good ideas that are seen as valuable and to be emulated or accepted. Darwin's theory of evolution has had a powerful impact on world thinking in science, religion, and philosophy, but Darwin himself was in no sense a social leader. His ideas were sent forth in print and speeches and accepted widely throughout the world. A social leader may combine a base of powerful ideas, a philosophy, with great social leadership skills, as was the case of Martin Luther King. King marched in front of thousands of people in the quest for civil rights for African Americans, and they followed him. Martin Luther developed and wrote his conceptions of reformed Catholicism and stood before the Diet at Worms to defend his theses.

In all cases, leaders are people who influence the lives, thoughts, and destinies of others. We recognize clearly that some people have developed the talents or gifts of mind to create new theories, paradigms, art forms, political concepts, inventions, or commercial products, and that others have developed their own talents or skills in working with people. The latter are able to help individuals, small groups, and large assemblies articulate and pursue common goals or solve common problems. Their skill in social leadership situations is a combination of pervasive talent or intelligences (Gardner, 1983) for understanding and working with people and acquired skills or understandings of the process of leadership.

In this chapter, we will examine the processes of leadership, the underlying talents and skills, the attitudes and work styles associated with leadership, methods of assessment of leadership talents and skills, and techniques and instruments for teaching-developing-nurturing leadership. Out of this examination, we will derive guidelines for leadership curriculum development and give illustrations of such a curriculum.

## *The Leader as One Who Has Valuable Ideas*

Leadership of an intellectual nature depends on the qualities of the leader's ideas and the zeitgeist or times in which they emerge. The discovery of the DNA molecule came at an appropriate time when the world of science was ready for this explanation of genetic determination. Feldman (1986) argued that prodigies can become geniuses only if they are born and grow in eras and locales that value their special talents. Nevertheless, beneath all is the need for the intellectual leader to possess (1) a powerful knowledge base, (2) skill in thinking, and (3) motivations, attitudes, and styles to facilitate intellectual thought.

Powerful ideas flow from people who have developed large knowledge bases (Sternberg, 1985), who are good thinkers (Dacey, 1989), and who have developed a disposition or style for creative production (Csikszentmihalyi, 1990b). Thus, we can expect leadership in the production of new ideas, conceptions, models, theories, art forms, inventories, and paradigms from people who have developed themselves to advanced cutting-edge levels in these three domains. The message, then, is quite clear for the initial assessment of talent potential and for the development of a leadership curriculum. Youth who show great intellectual precocity, whose fund of knowledge is large, who are motivated to understand the world of ideas, and who deal well with abstract conceptions and systems are primary candidates for selection into advanced education in the disciplines characteristically taught in school—science, mathematics literature, writing, social studies, political theory, history, and foreign languages. Pinpointing their strengths and guiding them into challenging, rich experiences and advanced courses will best provide the intellectual challenges they need. From a curricular point of view, what is needed is high-powered subject-matter options taught by knowledgeable and dynamic teachers focused on the ideational content and systems in given domains of knowledge.

Good leaders are good thinkers (Feldhusen & Kennedy, 1988), and there is evidence that thinking skills can be taught (Beyer, 1987). Thinking skills such as creative problem solving (Isaksen & Treffinger, 1985) can be taught initially as a metacognitive system in artificial contexts, but to facilitate transfer or application of the metacognitive thinking skills, there must be much practice in the real context of the discipline or subject matter.

For the curriculum, this means a heavy, planned infusion of the major thinking skill systems (critical thinking, logic, creative thinking, problem solving, decision making, and metacognition) into the daily interaction among students, teacher, and subject matter. Glaser (1984) concluded that effective learning of subject matter with the goal of developing expertise called for a dynamic interaction with the subject matter. This dynamic interaction is enhanced through the use of thinking skills. Perhaps the best guides to handling that interaction are found in Raths, Wasserman, Jonas, and Rothstein's (1986) *Teaching for Thinking* and Beyer's (1987) *Practical Strategies for The Teaching of Thinking*.

Finally, there is a set of motivations, attitudes, and styles that accompany the thinking and learning that lead to intellectual leadership in developing ideas, conceptions, paradigms, theories, art forms, and inventions. These have been well delineated by Amabile (1990). She has described the intrinsic motivation, the total absorption of the "flow" experience (Csikszentmihalyi, 1990a) that leads creative products, as contrasted with the extrinsic motivation of competition and rewards that operate negatively and block creativity.

For leadership curriculum there is a need to help students develop "habits of mind" and to assess the nature of students' motivations and cognitive styles within the context of learning particular subject matters. Through self-understanding, students can gain better control of the underlying motivations, dispositions, and styles that characterize their own work in the disciplines. The model set by the teacher and by historical figures in a discipline can also be sources of educational influence on students. Thus, the teacher and the historical leaders in a field can and should become a part of the curriculum in which persona are exhibited, analyzed, and emulated for their motivational, dispositional, and stylistic qualities.

Excellent curriculum can be built on this conception. Appendix A gives a curriculum plan for the hero in Greek and Roman tragedies. In this unit there is provision for the input of the knowledge base through reading, incorporation of thinking skills in classroom discussions and project activities, and modeling of motivation by examining the lives of heroes who contributed significantly to their societies.

## *The Social and Personal Skills of Leadership*

Leadership as a set of social skills in working with people has long been the dominant conception in the field of study devoted to leadership. From the Marland Report (1972) came a conception of giftedness as manifesting itself in six domains of human activity (intellectual, academic talents, creativity, art, psychomotor, and leadership). An earlier conception of giftedness (DeHaan & Kough, 1956) also included leadership among 10 types of giftedness. With the publication of the *Scales for Rating the Behavioral Characteristics of Superior Students* (Renzulli, Smith, White, Callahan, & Hartman, 1976), leadership was recognized as one of the set of traits that constitute giftedness. Gardner's

(1983) seven intelligences also identifies interpersonal intelligence as one of the seven basic human intelligences. In calling interpersonal skill or ability an intelligence, Gardner has quite clearly pointed to it as a set of traits that emerge through nurture and interaction with a surrounding world. The set of social skills that lead to effective leadership behavior may be viewed as talents or gifts that grow out of predetermined behavioral dispositions and interactions of those dispositions with the world and people around an individual. Thus, social leadership may be seen as a set of abilities that constitute a gift or talent.

Social leadership constitutes complex clusters of abilities. Feldhusen and Kennedy (1988) proposed that leadership talent involves or includes intellectual ability, motivational dimensions, moral sensibilities, thinking skills, and social-personal behaviors. Several of these elements—including motivational dimensions, moral sensibilities, and social-personal behavior—are related to personal-social interactions or dealings with people. Karnes and Chauvin (1985) listed 19 group dynamics skills, 21 personal skills, 12 written communication skills, and 14 speech communication skills in their Leadership Skills Inventory. The latter two, written communication skills and speech communication, clearly relate to interaction with people but are often viewed as essentially cognitive in nature.

In another study, Karnes and D'Ilio (1990) reported on a study of personal and social correlates of leadership. Among their sample of students with high leadership potential, they found the following personal and social factors: emotional maturity, conscientiousness, persistence, orientation to moral values, social responsibility, friendliness, low levels of inhibition, venturesomeness, low anxiety, ability to maintain a leadership role in group situations, and ability to control their own behavior. A general picture of extraversion in both personal and social behavior and a sound system of social and moral values emerges from this study as key facts of social leadership.

Myers, Slavin, and Southern (1990) studied a group of youth who were admitted to a special summer residential program on the basis of leadership potential. During the program, students were engaged in group problem-solving activities in which leadership could emerge naturally. Assessments were made retrospectively of the nature, quality, and emergence of leadership by staff members, students, and product evaluation. Their results indicated that early emerging leaders were students who were verbally fluent and aggressive. However, those who became more stable, long-range leaders were strong in personality, able to hold group attention, less domineering, positive in their attitudes, open to the ideas of others, effective in communication skills, and able to get group members to participate actively.

Bennis, a lifelong researcher of leadership, recently discussed what he called "basic truisms about leadership" (1991). He argued that leaders are conceptualists. They are able to engage people in formulating effective goals and a vision of what is to be accomplished. He proposed four fundamental leadership skills: management of attention, management of meaning, management of trust, and management of self. *Management of attention* means the leader can engage followers in the formulation and pursuit of goals and a vision of what is to be accomplished. *Management of meaning* means that the leader can articulate, communicate, and engage followers in ways that are cognitively comprehensible. *Management of trust* means that followers believe in and have faith in the leader. *Management of self,* like Gardner's (1983) intrapersonal intelligence, means that the leader has a good understanding of self, good self-control, and good self-esteem.

If the four leadership competencies function successfully, four outcomes are evident: (1) people feel significant in the group or organization, (2) learning and competence are valued and sought by followers (3) a sense of community develops among the followers, and (4) work becomes exciting and fulfilling.

These studies and views of the personal and social aspects of leadership have obvious curricular implications. Gifted learners who aspire to leadership and who have leadership talent need curriculum that provides the following opportunities:

1. To learn about basic personality dimensions that undergird leadership and to engage in self analysis of those dimensions to identify strengths and weakesses
2. To learn about the basic social skills that are parts of leadership behavior
3. To become aware of the moral, ethical, and philosophical concerns that are integrally involved in leadership
4. To observe gifted leaders through print and direct experience and see the personal, social, and ethical elements at work in diverse leadership situations
5. To discuss and clarify the observations toward the end of developing (writing) a personal statement of goals and philosophy for their own leadership development

## *Assessment of Leadership Talent and Potential*

Programs for leadership talent development should serve students who have a need for appropriate educational services, who want the services, and who will profit from them. Although some authors have argued that the services should be open to, or directed to, all youth, the reality in schools is that the services are limited—not widely available to those who need and could profit from them the most. Thus, we propose to search for youth with leadership talent and select them for educational programs. At the same time, we hope that there would be no need to turn away youth, who, while not scoring high enough in the screening procedures, still express a strong desire to enter the program. Our major effort, then, is a leadership talent search. The assessment should also yield information about leadership talent that can be used in developing leadership curriculum.

The search can begin with public announcements regarding the program, with a brief statement of criteria for admission, and a description of potential program activities. Prospective nominees should be expected to submit personal background information with their nominations (on a form supplied by the program directors), providing information about their past experiences in leadership situations, self-ratings of personal and social skills, descriptions or samples of products of their leadership activities, and ratings by adults who have observed their behavior in leadership situations.

The ratings by adults are probably best done with Karnes and Chauvin's (1985) Leadership Skills Inventory, an instrument with the best validity and reliability of any youth leadership scale available; it is more comprehensive than any other scale. The Leadership Skills Inventory has subscales for the assessment of (1) fundamentals of leadership, (2) written communication skills, (3) speech communication skills, (4) values clarification, (5) decision-making skills, (6) group dynamics skills, (7) problem-solving skills, (8) personal skills, and (9) planning skills. The Inventory can also be used for self-ratings by nominees.

Other leadership rating scales have been developed by Kough and DeHaan (1956), Renzulli and colleagues (1976), Richardson and Feldhusen (1986), and Roets (1986). However, all these scales are brief, lack the degree of standardization of the Leadership Skills Inventory, and offer little diagnostic information of the type yielded by the subscales of the Inventory.

Achievement test scores, grades in courses, and portfolios should all be accepted as evidence of a superior knowledge base. Achievement might be in any one or more of the major areas of the school curriculum: art, music, foreign language, home economics, business-economics, trade-industrial, agriculture, math, science, history, political science, government, and so on.

## Synthesizing Information

When all the information has been gathered for all nominees, it can be organized into three categories for final evaluation:

1. Ratings by adults of leadership potential
2. Self-ratings of leadership potential
3. Evidence concerning the level of achievement in given domains

Results from the rating scales can be combined and averaged to get an index score for each nominee, and these scores can be rank ordered. Evidence concerning the knowledge base from achievement tests and grades can also be numerically indexed and ranked. Evidence from portfolios must be judged and rated on some defensible numerical scale(s). If there is a sufficient number of such nominees, they too can be rank ordered. Ideally, there should be an equal number of portfolio cases as those based on achievement data. The ranks for each area of assessment can then be combined to get a composite rank order score. With final rankings in hand, youth are then selected, counting down from the top to a point representing the maximum number of youth the program can serve. Some places (e.g., 10 to 12) should be reserved for youth who fail to fall within the selection range but who (1) petition afterward for admission or (2) are judged by a selection committee to be qualified in spite of lower ranking.

The entire selection process should be supervised and guided by a committee and by one person who manages the process. The selection committee should be mindful of the need to assess reliability and validity of the selection process. Reliability of the Leadership Skills Inventory or rating scales can be judged from information provided in the manual that accompanies the Inventory. Reliability of the evaluation of portfolios is best determined by comparing judgments of two or more raters for a sample of portfolios. Validity of the selection process can be evaluated by correlating the selection subscores and total scores with measures of students' achievement or success in the program.

## Guidelines for Developing Leadership Curriculum

The assessment information derived from the identification of youth with leadership potential provides a rich source of information for general and individualized curriculum development. From the Leadership Skills Inventory (Karnes & Chauvin, 1985), for example, we may find strengths and weaknesses in the youth selected for the program that can be used for across-the-board determination of priority topics in the program. For example, one section of the Inventory assesses students' communication skills. When the selection process identifies youth who are strong enough on all or most of the other subscales but weak in communication skills, the program curriculum can be adapted to provide special instruction in this area. So, for all the scales, curriculum can be developed to address all of the areas at high levels where most students have strengths and at lower levels when weaknesses are noted in the assessment.

## The Leadership Development Program

Leadership development programs involve talented youth in reading, lectures, discussions, group projects, work with mentors, real leadership experiences, and self-assessment of skills, values, and attitudes related to leadership. There is (are) another knowledge base (bases) within subject matter or a discipline in which the talented youth is developing expertise. Ideally, the two domains of knowledge—leadership and subject matter—are pursued simultaneously. The latter can also be learned from reading, lectures, library study, and discussion. Through active participation in discussion of ideas from the subject matter and discussion of concepts and skills of leadership, talented youth can organize new ideas into existing cognitive structures or schema, expand and reorganize existing schema, and construct their own understandings regarding the subject matter and leadership.

Through mentoring experiences, youth talented in leadership can observe and learn from adult models of discipline, expertise, and leadership performance (Ellingson, Haeger, & Feldhusen, 1986; Haeger & Feldhusen, 1989; Nash & Treffinger, 1986; Torrance, 1984). The ideal mentor exhibits skill as a leader and expertise in a discipline or field. Mentorship is a valuable curriculum experience if the student can learn from the mentor.

Realistic experiences in leadership behavior offer talented youth opportunities to try out leadership behaviors learned from formal study, relate the experiences to self, and incorporate them into their repertoires of leadership skills.

Values clarification activities involve learning about major value systems from reading and lectures. Biographies and autobiographies are ideal sources for such learnings. The biographies of John F. Kennedy, Dr. Martin Luther King, Marie Curie, Eleanor Roosevelt, Mahatma Gandhi, and Thomas Jefferson offer splendid opportunities to learn about greatly contrasting value systems and to move students along the pathway to the development of their own value system. They can study Kohlberg's (1975) levels of moral development and engage in discussion of moral conflict situations as presented by Raths, Harmin, and Simon (1966), Simon, Howe, and Kirschenbaum (1972), and Simon, Kirschenbaum, and Fuhrmann (1972). These experiences involve both learning about alternative value systems and structuring their own values. It is essential that students with leadership talent develop knowledge about values, ethics, and philosophical systems as a prelude to meaningful discussions.

The curriculum for a leadership development program should also incorporate objectives related to thinking skills since leaders in all fields must be good thinkers. They must be able to use logic, critical and creative thinking, metacognitive control, and decision making in leadership situations. Thus, the fundamentals of thinking, as known theoretically in the areas just listed above, can be learned about, clarified and articulated in discussions, and tried out in real leadership activities. In another chapter in this book, the major subsets of thinking skills are delineated and illustrated (see Chapter 13).

Thinking skills can be taught in isolation from subject matter initially so that students can master the basic framework of steps and procedures, but they should then be practiced in the contexts of discussion, problem solving, and project activities so that general transfer or usefulness in other contexts will occur.

## *Formal Programs and Resource Materials for Teaching Leadership*

As noted earlier, Feldhusen and Kennedy (1988) offered what is probably the most comprehensive delineation of curriculum essentials for leadership development programs for the gifted. Other excellent resources include Roets's (1986) *Leadership, A Skills Training Program*. This book covers the following topics:

- *People of achievement*
- *The language of leadership*
- *Project planning*
- *Debate and discussion*
- *Teacher resources for leadership education*

*Leadership: Making Things Happen* by Sisk and Shallcross (1986) also offers excellent leadership development information and activities. Topics covered include:

- *Definitions of leadership*
- *Self-understanding*
- *Intuitive powers*
- *Communication*
- *Motivation*
- *Creative problem solving*
- *Future visions*
- *Learning styles*
- *Women in leadership*

This book also offers many student activities related to leadership behavior.

Richardson and Feldhusen's (1986) *Leadership Education: Developing Skills for Youth* was prepared after an extensive review of the leadership literature. The general design of the chapters, all addressed to secondary students, is to introduce a leadership concept with readings, go on to a group activity done in class under teacher guidance to illustrate the concept, and finally suggest out-of-class activities to generalize the concept to a still broader context. The major topics or concepts presented in this book include:

- *Leadership fundamentals*
- *Outcomes of leadership education*
- *Personal characteristics of effective leaders*
- *Skills of a group leader*
- *Communication skills of leaders*
- *Leadership skills for group members*
- *Developing group goals*
- *Planning group activities*
- *Committee organization*
- *Parliamentary procedures skills for leaders*
- *Leadership and special abilities.*

Leadership development guidelines for curriculum development have been researched and presented by a number of other authors. Hensel (1991) focused on social aspects of leadership and offered the following set of strategies for teachers:

- *Focus on different viewpoints in everyday interactions. Teachers can label their own feelings and ask children how they feel or think about interactions, events, or activities.*
- *Model caring behaviors toward adults, other children, and pets in the classroom (Doescher & Sugawara, 1989).*
- *Discuss situations that may occur in the classroom as well as other real-life problems and alternative ways of handling these problems (Passow, 1988).*
- *Help children learn to make decisions by having choices in the classroom about activities, play materials, and other appropriate areas for decisions.*
- *Help children develop interactive skills through collaborative work with other children (Kim & Stevens, 1987).*
- *Help children learn to talk about their feelings and ideas.*

Smith, Smith, and Barnette (1991) described a leadership development program with cognitive, affective, and physical challenge components. Their research evaluation showed the program to be most effective in developing teamwork skills, listening to alternative views, and taking risks. Also effective were solving problems, public speaking, setting goals, and dealing with people.

Fertman and Long (1990) described a leadership development program focused on leadership knowledge, attitudes, and skills. Topics taught include leadership awareness, communication, decision making, stress control, and assertiveness. Evaluation data showed the program to be effective in teaching leadership knowledge and attitudes.

Feldhusen, Hynes, and Richardson (1977) described their developmental work on leadership education and evaluated the effort. They too found their program most effective in imparting knowledge about leadership and improving attitudes toward leadership activities.

Karnes, Meriweather, and D'Illio (1987) reported on the effectiveness of their leadership studies program. Karnes has led the field of research on leadership assessment and education. She and her colleagues concluded that their programs were effective for youth in grades 6 through 11 in the following areas: enhancing knowledge and skills in the fundamentals of leadership, written and speech communication, values clarification, decision making, group dynamics, problem solving, personal development, and planning.

An example of a leadership program curriculum is presented at the end of this chapter (Example 15.A). It illustrates many of the concepts presented here. It has been used as the guide to leadership development in a public school setting and found to be effective in enhancing leadership skills among secondary gifted youth.

## Conclusion

There is much agreement among leadership education researchers and developers about the components of good programs, and the curriculum guidelines presented in this chapter can be used to develop excellent leadership education programs. All such programs involve teaching fundamentals of leadership behavior, developing the social or interpersonal and intrapersonal skills of leadership, and helping youth become "experts" or knowledgeable persons in one or more of the major subject matters or disciplines. The United States and the world need leaders to guide us and help us realize human potential for the twenty-first century. Leadership education programs can help us meet that need.

### Key Points Summary

- *Successful leadership development requires the teaching of fundamental leadership behaviors (i.e., thinking skills, verbal skills, and group process skills).*
- *The development of interpersonal and intrapersonal skills is central to the communication requisites for leadership.*
- *Becoming an "expert" or knowledgable person in a specific field is probably the best way of developing the competence and self-esteem to be capable of leadership.*
- *Leadership talent may be identified in a variety of fields through special instruments such as the Leadership Skills Inventory.*

## References

Amabile, T. M. (1990). Within you, without you: The social psychology of creativity, and beyond. In M. A. Runco & R. S. Albert (Eds.), *Theories of creativity* (pp. 61–91). Newbury Park, CA: Sage.

Bennis, W. (1991). Learning some basic truisms about leadership. *National Forum: The Phi Kappa Phi Journal, 71* (1), 12–15.

Beyer, B. K. (1987). *Practical strategies for the teaching of thinking.* Boston: Allyn and Bacon.

Csikszentmihalyi, M. (1990a). *Flow, the psychology of optimal experience.* New York: Harper and Row.

Csikszentmihalyi, M. (1990b). The domain of creativ-

ity. In M. A. Runco & R. S. Albert (Eds.), *Theories of creativity* (pp. 190–212). Newbury Park, CA: Sage.

Dacey, J. S. (1989). *Fundamentals of creative thinking.* Lexington, MA: D. C. Heath.

DeHaan, R. F., & Kough, J. (1956). *Identifying students with special needs.* Chicago: Science Research Associates.

Doescher, S. M., & Sugawara, A. I. (1989). Encouraging prosocial behavior in young children. *Childhood Education, 65* (4), 213–215.

Ellingson, M. K., Haeger, W. W., & Feldhusen, J. F. (1986). The Purdue mentor program: A university based mentorship experience for gifted children. *The Gifted Child Today, 9* (2), 2–5.

Feldhusen, J. F., Hynes, K. P., & Richardson, W. D. (1977). Curriculum materials for vocational organizations: An innovative approach. *Clearing House, 50,* 224–226.

Feldhusen, J. F., & Kennedy, D. M. (1988). Preparing gifted youth for leadership roles in a rapidly changing society. *Roeper Review, 10* (4), 226–230.

Feldman, D. H. (1986). *Nature's gambit: Child prodigies and the development of human potential.* New York: Basic Books.

Fertman, C. I., & Long, J. A. (1990). All students are leaders. *The School Counselor, 37* (5), 390–397.

Gardner, H. (1983). *Frames of mind: The theory of multiple intelligences.* New York: Basic Books.

Glaser, R. (1984). Education and thinking, the role of knowledge. *American Psychologist, 39* (2), 93–104.

Haeger, W. W., & Feldhusen, J. F. (1989). *Developing a mentor program.* East Aurora, NY: DOK Publishers.

Hensel, N. H. (1991). Social leadership in young children. *Roeper Review, 14* (1), 4–6.

Isaksen, S., & Treffinger, D. J. (1985). *Creative problem solving: The basic course.* Buffalo, NY: Bearly Limited.

Karnes, F. A., & Chauvin, J. C. (1985). *Leadership skills inventory, Administration manual.* East Aurora, NY: DOK Publishers.

Karnes, F. A., & D'Ilio, V. R. (1990). Correlations between personality and leadership concepts and skills as measured by the High School Personality Questionnaire and the Leadership Skills Inventory. *Psychological Reports, 66,* 851–856.

Karnes, F. A., Meriweather, S., & D'Illio, V. (1987). The effectiveness of the leadership studies program. *Roeper Review, 9* (4), 238–240.

Kim, Y. O., & Stevens, J. H. (1987). The socialization of prosocial behavior of children. *Childhood Education, 63* (3), 200–206.

Kohlberg, L. (1975). Moral education for a society in moral transition. *Educational Leadership, 33* (1), 46–54.

Kough, J., & DeHaan, R. (1956). *Identifying students with special needs.* Chicago: Science Research Associates.

Marland, S. P. (1972). *Education of the gifted and talented: Report to the Congress.* Washington, DC: U.S. Government Printing Office (Document 72-5020).

Myers, M. R., Slavin, M. J., & Southern, W. T. (1990). Emergence and maintenance of leadership among gifted students in group problem solving. *Roeper Review, 12* (4), 256–261.

Nash, D., & Treffinger, D. (1986). *The mentor.* East Aurora, NY: DOK Publishers.

Passow, A. H. (1988). Educating gifted persons who are caring and concerned. *Roeper Review, 11* (1), 13–15.

Raths, L., Harmin, M., & Simon, S. (1966). *Values and teaching.* Columbus, OH: Charles E. Merrill.

Raths, L. E., Wasserman, S., Jonas, A., & Rothstein, A. (1986). *Teaching for thinking.* New York: Teachers College Press.

Renzulli, J. S., Smith, L. H., White, A. J., Callahan, C. M., & Hartman, R. K. (1976). *Scales for rating the behavioral characteristics of superior students.* Wethersfield, CT: Creative Learning Press.

Richardson, W. B., & Feldhusen, J. F. (1986). *Leadership education: Developing skills for youth* (2nd ed.). New York: Trillium Press.

Roets, L. S. (1986). *Leadership, A skills training program.* New Sharon, IA: Leadership Publishers.

Simon, S., Howe, L., & Kirschenbaum, H. (1972). *Values clarification.* New York: Hart Publishers.

Simon, S., Kirschenbaum, H., & Fuhrmann, B. (1972). *An introduction to values clarification.* New York: Penney.

Sisk, D. A., & Shallcross, D. J. (1986). *Leadership: Making things happen.* Buffalo, NY: Bearly Limited.

Smith, D. L., Smith, L., & Barnette, J. (1991). Exploring the development of leadership giftedness. *Roeper Review, 14* (1), 7–12.

Sternberg, R. J. (1985). *Beyond IQ: A triarchic theory of human intelligence.* New York: Cambridge University Press.

Torrance, E. P. (1984). *Mentor relationships.* Buffalo, NY: Bearly Limited.

**EXAMPLE 15.A Sample Leadership Curriculum***

*By Pam Burger and Susan Brash*

### Theme 1: Interaction of Student Leadership with the School Environment

#### Goal 1: Students Will Become More Effective Communicators in the Schools

*Objective:* Students will be able to state the basic fundamentals of public speaking.

| *Activities:* | *Student Assessment:* |
|---|---|
| 1. Discuss methods for effective communication in the following areas: giving directions, listening, interpreting nonverbal cues, understanding people, making conversation and introductions, writing letters, and giving speeches. | 1. Teacher observation of student contribution. |
| 2. Using a mirror, practice nonverbal communication. Select several attitudes or emotions and try to portray them nonverbally. Present one or two to the class to see how well your classmates can interpret them. | 2. Peer interpretation. |
| 3. Begin a conversation with someone that you do not know, write a business letter, and make an introduction. | 3. Be prepared to evaluate each situation and discuss in class. |

*Objective:* Students will incorporate the necessary fundamentals and make a school presentation.

| *Activities:* | *Student Assessment:* |
|---|---|
| 1. Prepare a short demonstration for the class, explaining how to do something. Try to have enough materials available for everyone in the class to participate in the activity. | 1. Evaluate how well the class follows directions that were given by the leader. (checklist) |
| 2. Review the steps involved in preparing a speech or report. Prepare a 5- to 7-minute informative speech for the class. | 2. Peers complete checklist on the speaker. |

*\*Source:* Susan K. Brash, Director of Gifted Education, and Pamela D. Burger, Home Economics Instructor, Eastern Pulaski Community School Corporation, Winamac, Indiana. Reprinted with permission.

*Objective:* Students will listen to an oral presentation and critique it.

*Activities:*

1. Tape record your next group meeting. Play back the tape and write a one-page description of the effectiveness of the communication that occurred. Answer the attached list of questions.

*Student Assessment:*

1. Turn in answers to the questions on the Group Meeting Evaluation Form.

## Goal 2: Students Will Become More Effective Leaders in Their Co-Curricular and Extra-Curricular Activities.

*Objective:* Students will become aware of various leadership styles.

*Activities:*

1. Students will identify who the leaders are in the classroom and in the extra-curricular activities.

2. *Leaders One and All* Students create a fictitious but realistic leader who will embody the combination of types selected.

*Student Assessment:*

1. Are the leaders in the classroom those who are getting good grades or those who get in trouble?
Are the leaders in the extracurricular activities the officers and committee chairpersons?

2. Evaluate *Leaders One and All* based on how closely the character reflected the traits of the type of leader chosen.

*Objective:* Students will compare and contrast leaders in co-curricular activities to leaders in extracurricular.

*Activities:*

1. Analyze the characteristics of the students in each list and chart which students are in one or both.

*Student Assessment:*

1. Chart of Analysis: Is there a pattern?
Are there certain leadership characteristics consistently evident in a classroom leader as compared or opposed to an extracurricular activity leader?

*Objective:* Students will be able to judge various leadership styles.

*Activities:*

1. Students will evaluate the various leadership styles of school leaders they want to emulate.

*Student Assessment:*

1. Which type of leader are you? Which type of leader would you choose?

### Goal 3: Students Will Understand the Role of Leadership in School Government.

*Objective:* Students will demonstrate specific principles of parliamentary procedure in conducting a meeting.

| *Activities:* | *Student Assessment:* |
| --- | --- |
| 1. Students will be given a list of general guidelines for conducting a meeting and an information sheet on parliamentary motions. | 1. Outside judges, proficient in parliamentary procedure, will observe each group and complete a checklist using the guidelines and information that was provided to the students. |
| 2. Small groups of 8 to 12 students will plan a meeting in which all motions and parliamentary procedure will be staged. | |

*Objective:* Students will learn the basics of group interaction and use this information to form committees.

| *Activities:* | *Student Assessment:* |
| --- | --- |
| 1. Choose a committee and assume that you are the chairperson. Prepare an agenda for your first committee meeting and list your ideas for possible projects. Also describe how you would accomplish the project you propose. | 1. Evaluation of committee effectiveness after a prescribed time. (checklist) |
| 2. You are the president of a new club at your high school. The club has been organized for students who are interested in computers. What standing committees should be established this year? What type of person would you look for to serve as the chairperson of each committee? | 2. A paper that outlines the plan with rationale. |

*Objective:* Students will use leadership skills to produce a project for the school.

| *Activities:* | *Student Assessment:* |
| --- | --- |
| 1. Students will plan and implement the 8th grade orientation. | 1. Short survey to 8th-graders. |
| 2. Students will implement homecoming activities. | 2. Survey to principal, coaches, and student council members. |
| 3. Students will choose a project to organize and implement an activity within the club to which they belong. | 3. Survey to club members. |

*Objective:* Students will appraise their own performances and evaluate the other members in the group or on the committee.

| *Activities:* | *Student Assessment:* |
|---|---|
| 1. Students will develop a checklist to evaluate members of a group or committee. | 1. Checklist (self and peer). |
| 2. Students will interview partici- pants. | 2. Log of responses from interviews. |
| 3. Students will complete a self appraisal. | 3. Self-appraisal. |

## Theme 2: Interaction of Students' Leadership Within the Community

### Goal 1: Students Will Become More Effective Communicators in the Community.

*Objective:* Students will be able to identify various types of communication evident in the community.

| *Activities:* | *Student Assessment:* |
|---|---|
| 1. List as many potential guest speakers from your community or county as you can think of. | 1. Written lists. |
| 2. Brainstorm a list of resources and forms of communication, other than people, that are available to your group. | 2. Written lists. |

*Objective:* Students will be able to differentiate between clear and unclear written and oral forms of communication in the community.

| *Activities:* | *Student Assessment:* |
|---|---|
| 1. Tape record a radio or news broadcast. Compare and contrast two or more of these in a written paper. | 1. Written paper. |
| 2. Prepare a notebook of written communication and compare and contrast their effectiveness. | 2. Notebook of the analysis. |

*Objective:* Students will be able to effectively communicate with the community.

| *Activities:* | *Student Assessment:* |
|---|---|
| 1. Students will give a speech or write a letter to a civic or church organization. | 1. School personnel attending the function will be interviewed by the sponsor and their comments on the speech will be evaluated. |

*Objective:* Students will judge the effectiveness of community persons' oral and/ or written communication.

| *Activities:* | *Student Assessment:* |
| --- | --- |
| 1. Students will visit a civic organization in the community and critique its speaker. | 1. Written critique. |

### Goal 2: Students Will Understand the Effective Leadership Training Has on Community Leaders.

*Objective:* Students will learn organization and planning skills.

| *Activities:* | *Student Assessment:* |
| --- | --- |
| 1. In a group, brainstorm possible questions to be included on a leadership survey. Evaluate which questions will be used and compile the survey. Present the survey to a selected community leader. | 1. Evaluate the results of the survey. |

*Objective:* Students will learn how to develop personal and group goals.

| *Activities:* | *Student Assessment:* |
| --- | --- |
| 1. Divide into small groups and list goals of leadership for the group. Categorize the list as personal, career, and citizenship. | 1. Chart goals by categories. |
| 2. Students will respond to items on a checklist which best describes how they would most like to act if they were the leader of a group. (Richardson and Feldhusen, 1984, pp. 28–29). | 2. Students role play characteristics of a good leader in front of their peers. |

*Objective:* Students will be able to evaluate their own citizenship responsibilities and privileges at various levels.

| *Activities:* | *Student Assessment:* |
| --- | --- |
| 1. Develop a philosophy of citizenship and the responsibilities to our country, state and community, family, friend and school. Prepare posters to display in the community showing how the students view citizenship. | 1. Evaluate posters. |

### Goal 3: Students Will Understand the Role of Leadership in City Goverment.

*Objective:* Students will be able to state characteristics of effective city government.

| *Activities:* | *Student Assessment:* |
|---|---|
| 1. Students will brainstorm and list characteristics of effective city government. | 1. Objective quiz. |
| 2. Students will learn about the specific functions of community leaders. | 2. Objective quiz. |

*Objective:* Students will be able to emulate characteristics of effective town leaders.

| *Activities:* | *Student Assessment:* |
|---|---|
| 1. Students will replace different town leaders and conduct business as usual. | 1. The leaders who are being replaced will complete a short evaluation of their substitute. |

*Objective:* Students will compare and contrast characteristics of various community governments.

| *Activities:* | *Student Assessment:* |
|---|---|
| 1. Students will chart the characteristics of three government bodies in the community and list their similarities and differences. | 1. Chart. |

### Theme 3: Interaction of Student Leadership in the World

### Goal 1: Students Will Become More Effective Communicators in the World.

*Objective:* Students will evaluate good world communicators.

| *Activities:* | *Student Assessment:* |
|---|---|
| 1. Students will choose three nationally known news reporters and critique their broadcasts. | 1. Written critique. |

### Goal 2: Students Will Learn How to Become Effective Leaders in Their Future Careers.

*Objective:* Students will analyze their own special talents and abilities.

*Activities:*

1. Students will complete a personality assessment and list their special talents and abilities, noting those that indicate leadership potential.

*Student Assessment:*

1. Students will turn in their completed survey and list.

*Objective:* Students will outline steps for obtaining their leadership goals in life.

*Activities:*

1. Student will be taught a goal planning model (Richardson and Feldhusen, 1984, pp. 66–70).
2. Students will work in small groups to develop values, goals, and objectives for specific assignments.
3. Students will clarify their leadership goals by completing LEAD: A program for Planning Ahead (Richardson and Feldhusen, 1984, p. 72).

*Student Assessment:*

1. Peer evaluation of LEAD.

2. Peer evaluation of LEAD.

3. Peer evaluation of LEAD.

### Goal 3: Students Will Understand the Role of Leadership in the Governments of the World.

*Objective:* The student will construct examples of influence and power.

*Activities:*

1. Write the definitions for power and influence on the board and give examples of each.
DEFINITION: POWER is the ability to control.
Example: A powerful person may be one who can lift great weights or one who can lead people and make them obey.
DEFINITION: INFLUENCE is the ability to affect what others do or think.
Example: An influential senator can help get a law passed by persuading other senators to vote for it. A newspaper may be influential enough to defeat or elect a candidate.

*Student Assessment:*

1. Make a poster using pictures of world leaders and categorize them as powerful or influential.

2. Next give each student two index cards. Direct the students to write on one card an example of a person exerting power over another person or group of people. On the other card have students write an example of a person influencing another person or group of people. Collect the cards and read them aloud to the class. Have students indicate if the situation is an example of power or influence.

*Objective:* Students will evaluate leadership qualities in world leaders.

*Activities:*

1. Students will read three to five biographies of recognized world leaders. They will choose two and analyze which leadership qualities made them great.

*Student Assessment:*

1. Analysis paper.

# Strategies for Teaching the Gifted

*JOHN F. FELDHUSEN*

*Learning without thought is labor lost; thought without learning is perilous.*
*—CONFUCIUS*

Gifted and talented youth have special needs that call for differentiated strategies or methods of teaching. The needs are derived from research on the characteristics of gifted and talented youth and are based on the assumption that they can or will become creative leaders in the arts, sciences, engineering, professions, and so on. To reach such leadership goals, these students need to develop the following skills during their schooling years:

1. Large, fluent knowledge bases and domain-specific knowledge
2. High-level thinking skills
3. Metacognitive skills
4. Ability to deal with abstract, complex, and conceptual material
5. Intellectual dispositions, motivations, and styles

A number of researchers have delineated the needs of the gifted and talented (VanTassel, 1979; Feldhusen, 1982; Clark, 1992) based on their educational and psychological characteristics. These needs then can be translated into educational goals. Clark (1992), for example, has listed such needs as access to challenging curriculum and peers, to share ideas verbally and in depth, and to be exposed to varied subjects and concerns. VanTassel (1979) advocated meeting their needs for research experiences and project activity. Feldhusen (1982) suggested the need for interaction with intellectual peers and independent study experiences. The preceding five leadership goals are derived from conceptions of the needs of gifted youth, and are also based on the qualities of mature gifted adults. They, in turn, provide guidance to school personnel in designing appropriate instruction to meet gifted students' needs.

In the broadest sense, educational goals for the gifted should include the attainment of creative excellence in a worthwhile area of human endeavor, self-fulfillment, autonomy-independence, and self-actualization. Although perhaps never fully attainable, such goals should characterize the odyssey of gifted and talented youth and adults.

## Administrative and Curricular Arrangements

Schools can provide the special educational services needed by gifted and talented youth in a number of different ways. These administrative arrangements interact with potential teaching strategies to enhance or limit instructional conditions for gifted and talented youth. One such enhanced arrangement is the full-time class for the gifted and talented; others include special schools, special classes, and schools within schools. All of these arrangements are characterized by a grouping model that places gifted and talented youth together for all or part of their school time. Such arrangements make it possible to provide appropriate services.

Feldhusen and Sayler (1990) and Feldhusen (1991a) have described full-time classes for the gifted at the elementary level. They have been organized and are operating successfully in many school districts. There are now nine residential schools (Stanley, 1991) for high-ability secondary youth where the students live together and attend special classes. Honors classes and special seminars have been organized and taught successfully (Feldhusen & Kennedy, 1989; Kolloff & Feldhusen, 1986) in many schools. Schools within schools are special arrangements at the secondary level that offer differentiated class sequences for selected, high-ability youth. While operated within regular school settings, these schools offer essentially full-time opportunity for highly able youth to experience appropriate instruction.

These programs contrast sharply with part-time instruction for the gifted and talented, such as pull-out enrichment (Feldhusen & Kolloff, 1986), resource rooms (Renzulli & Reis, 1985), after-school Saturday, and summer programs (Feldhusen, 1991b). All of these alternatives limit severely the potential delivery of services to gifted and talented youth.

Most severely limiting of all are the efforts to provide for gifted and talented youth in mixed, heterogeneous classrooms (Parke, 1989; H. Feldhusen, 1990). Individualized and small group instruction with cluster grouping are advocated for these classrooms, but the actual differentiated instructional time is likely to be very low.

Finally, the presence of a general curriculum plan and a differentiated curriculum plan for gifted and talented youth has a major impact on the delivery of educational services to gifted and talented youth. The regular curriculum can include specification of alternative content for gifted and talented youth or there can be an entirely separate curriculum plan for the gifted and talented, as often is the case in special classes, full-time elementary programs, residential schools, and schools within schools. Such specified curriculum plans provide important directions for the strategies teachers can use with gifted and talented youth. In addition, special curriculum materials, designed specifically for the gifted, provide opportunities for the teacher to enhance learning.

## Strategies for Teaching Gifted and Talented Students

### Assessment

The first strategy to guide teaching of gifted and talented youth is to assess their current achievement and skill levels. What do they know? What are their skill levels? The most widely known approach to assessment is the approach advanced by Stanley (1980, 1991; see also Fox & Washington, 1985): diagnostic-prescriptive instruction (DT-PI). Pretesting is used to establish students' readiness levels for new instruction. Gifted students begin at the advanced levels for which they are ready and then proceed at a fast pace. They typically cover much more of the curriculum in an allotted time period than the regular classroom offers. Clark (1992) advocated such pretesting as a base for planning instruction, but she also advocated assessment of student interests and needs.

### Individualization

Clark (1992) and Stanley (1980) both advocated individualized teaching of the gifted in which students bypass what they know, begin at their readiness level, and proceed with learning as rapidly as they wish and are able. H. Feldhusen (1981, 1990) presented a comprehensive plan for individualized strategies at the elementary level. Parke (1989) also presented a comprehensive plan for all grade levels. Both of these models were designed for implementation in regular, heterogeneous classrooms. The Stanley model, in contrast, was designed for use in teaching the gifted in special groups and often in summer or Saturday programs. Milgram (1989) extended the model of individualization by dealing with individualization in relation to each subject matter area. All these models or strategies can be carried out by using traditional text material and helping gifted students guide themselves through a textbook from their own individual starting points and at their own pace.

### High Expectations

A valuable strategy for instruction of the gifted is to strive for high-level, creative goals in teaching. Levin's (1987) Accelerated Schools project shows that increasing the level and pace of instruction increases achievement of less able youth. The same advantages can be gained for gifted and talented youth if instruction is of the level and pace to be truly challenging and motivating to them. Many U.S. teachers set very low expectation levels to accommodate slow learners, underachievers, and children with handicaps. These low-level expectations often lead to problems in learning for gifted and talented youth.

### Challenge

The strategy of accommodating slow learners, underachievers, and handicapped learners often leads to boredom in the classroom (Feldhusen & Kroll, 1991; Larson & Richards,

1991) for gifted and talented students. A steady regimen of low expectations and no challenge leads the gifted to be apathetic about school and to use their giftedness to get by easily. The opposite teaching strategy is to be alert to children's boredom in school, to take it seriously, and to seek alternative, higher-level, challenging learning activities. One teacher announced to his class that anyone who felt bored should let him know immediately. Another student in a gifted program reported that he was never bored because the program was always challenging. Teachers must be alert to signs of boredom, use those signs as a stimulus for reassessment of achievement levels, and realign instruction to fit children's readiness levels. Two gifted second-graders were bored at the beginning of the year with the regular math offering. The teacher checked their general math achievement levels and found both to be at the 99th percentile level. She secured some fourth-grade math material, set them to learning long division, and found that they mastered it quickly and got over their boredom!

## Conceptual Complexity

Gifted and talented youth are able to deal with conceptually complex and abstract material at much higher levels than less able children. Teachers of the gifted should use teaching strategies that stress ideation, thinking, analyzing ideas, and developing broad schemata of understanding. Snow (1989), a specialist in aptitude-treatment interaction (ATI) research, suggested that high-ability youth need conceptually complex instruction, whereas less able youth need well-structured and less complex material. Findlay and Lumsden (1988) and Glaser (1984) described the formation of ideational schemata as the ultimate outcomes of high-quality instruction. Schemata are coherent networks of information organized around a conceptual base. These schemata reveal deep understanding and represent the instructional strategies advocated by Taba (1962). These strategies involve a constant effort through discussions in the classroom to help gifted youth organize ideas into related, connected patterns. It is also a process of helping youth discover connections. The strategy represents a dynamic interaction in the classroom among teachers, gifted students, information, and emerging schemata.

## Homework and Reading

An information or knowledge base is essential before one can organize schemata and develop deep understanding. This means that gifted and talented youth must learn to be independent seekers of knowledge through reading and study. Teachers can guide the process with reading assignments and well-designed study activities. The latter are often questions, problems, or research topics. Walberg (1984) reported that the research on homework indicates that it is one of the best techniques available for increasing student achievement. Gifted students have to learn how to acquire information, retain it, retrieve it when the task calls for it, relate it to other information, and create new associations of information (Sternberg, 1985).

## Lectures and Discussions

Lectures and classroom discussions provide another strategy for imparting information to students. Although there is much complaint against lectures among educators of the gifted, learning from lectures becomes an inevitable reality at the secondary and college levels. It is very likely that knowledgeable teachers, scholars, and mentors can impart much valuable information and concepts to gifted learners through lectures. The lecture format also provides one useful way of bringing gifted students into contact with highly knowledgeable teachers and scholars.

Classroom discussions also provide an excellent vehicle for teaching thinking skills, inducing understanding of complex, conceptual material, and teaching metacognitive skills of planning, mentoring, and evaluation. Good discussions actively involve gifted and talented youth in analyzing, synthesizing, problem solving, creating, evaluating, and conceptualizing. Through such experience, they construct their own complex schematics of understanding (vonGlaserfield, 1987).

## *Peer Modeling*

Gifted and talented youth need peer models who are actively involved in intellectual activity and processing. One good strategy for work with these students is to give them time to work with other gifted youth in small groups or cooperative learning arrangements (Slavin, 1990; Johnson & Johnson, 1989). Schunk (1987) has shown through research that youth model their behavior on others of similar ability who are coping effectively with the learning situation. Thus, teachers should provide and work with other youth of high ability who are doing well in school. This can best be accomplished in subject matter study in special classes and schools for the gifted. Pull-out and resource room programs are often of such limited duration that there is not enough time for gifted youth to see full-blown behavior upon which they can model.

## *Mentors*

Mentors are usually adults who serve as models for gifted youth, who may impart information or engage the student in an internship or project of interest to the student, or who serve as career guides. Haeger and Feldhusen (1989) described an extensive program in mentorship for gifted youth. However, mentoring can be a role for all teachers of the gifted if they model behavior associated with high-level, creative production and provide information to students about the educational routes and career paths to higher-level occupations. Mentoring can be a strategy of teaching gifted and talented youth that launches them on the way to the fulfillment of their intellectual potential.

## *Generative Learning or Constructivism*

Ultimately, learning is a process that takes place in the minds of students when they are actively engaged in thinking, solving problems, conceptualizing, evaluating, synthesizing ideas, and constructing their own schemata. The constructivists argue that students must construct their own knowledge—their own schemata—through active intellectual processes (Wheatley, 1991; vonGlasersfeld, 1987). Thus, an appropriate strategy for the teacher of gifted students is to engage them, through intrinsic motivation (Nicholls, 1983, 1984), in the quest to grasp, solve, or understand. The teacher acts as problem poser, facilitator, and encourager. The students are actively and cognitively engaged. At the end of a learning sequence, the teacher may lead the students in a discussion in which they verbalize and conceptualize the understandings derived from the activity. Throughout the sequence, the ideal strategy for the teacher might be to act as a role-model participant in the intellectual activity without assuming a didactic role.

## Thinking Skills

In addition to the conceptual learning outcomes and the emerging schemata in students' minds, through the active intellectual activity advocated by constructivists, gifted students can and should be learning thinking skills. The specific skills to be learned have been delineated by a number of researchers. Treffinger, Feldhusen, and Isaksen (1990) proposed the comprehensive model shown in Figure 16–1. This model is based on a conception of foundation skills (knowledge base, motivations and dispositions, and metacognitive skills), tool skills (creative and critical thinking), and complex cognitive operations (problem solving and decision making). All levels and aspects of the model are teachable. Thus, the appropriate teaching strategy with gifted youth is to demonstrate or model the desired skill by introducing each component with a short introductory lecture or explanation, leading students in trying the method in a relatively artificial task that highlights the steps in the process, discussing the activity with students, trying another task in a discipline or subject matter, and again discussing the application. Continued use of the method in a variety of contexts is needed to assure mastery by students of the conceptual framework and the skill process.

Thinking skills should then be used or practiced in other classroom activities such as discussion, problem solving, and writing. Teachers can model the use of good thinking when they interact with their students in discussions, small group work, and individual interactions. They can point out instances of faulty thinking and suggest alternatives. They can also set the stage for good thinking with appropriate questions.

It is important for teachers and gifted students to recognize that good thinking calls for, and results from, clear understanding, analysis, and evaluation of the fundamental concepts and conceptual framework of the disciplines or fields of study. Good thinking should be learned in the context of studying the conceptual schema of different fields and developing the complex and abstract structure of a given discipline.

## Metacognition

Another valuable instructional strategy is to teach metacognition skills to gifted students and to evoke those same skills in further thinking activities with gifted students. One of the most teachable models of metacognitive skills is that of Beyer (1987):

1. *Planning*
   Stating a goal
   Selecting operations to perform
   Sequencing operations
   Identifying potential obstacles/errors
   Identifying ways to recover from obstacles/errors
   Predicting results desired and/or anticipated

**Figure 16–1   Organization and Structure of Productive Thinking**

**C. The Complex Methods**

| | |
|---|---|
| *Problem Solving*<br>• Understanding the problem<br>  Identifying broad goals or objectives<br>  Describing an opportunity, concern,<br>    or challenge<br>  Gathering and sorting relevant data<br>  Defining a specific problem<br>• Generating new ideas<br>• Planning for action<br>  Evaluating promising solutions<br>  Building acceptance and creating a plan | *Decision Making*<br>• Identify the objective<br>• Describe the setting, context, and obstacles<br>• Gather relevant information<br>• Specify and analyze alternative actions<br>• Delineate possible outcomes<br>• Estimate payoffs or satisfaction for each<br>  outcome<br>• Choose best action<br>• Develop implementation plan |

**B. The "Tool" Skills**

| | |
|---|---|
| *Creative Thinking*<br>• Fluency<br>• Flexibility<br>• Originality<br>• Elaboration<br>• Curiosity<br>• Tolerance of ambiguity<br>• Risk-taking<br>• Dealing with complexity<br>• Imagination and humor<br>• Intensity and commitment | *Critical Thinking*<br>• Delineate a cognitive task or problem<br>• Understand and interpret information<br>• Judge accuracy and relevance of information<br>• Identify assumptions and biases<br>• Detect fallacies and biases<br>• Derive and evaluate inductive conclusions<br>• Reason deductively and judge validity of<br>  conclusions<br>• Apply strategies to compare, contrast, refine,<br>  and/or strengthen ideas or arguments. |

**A. The Foundations**

| *Knowledge Base*<br>*(Expertise, not*<br>*just "mechanical")* | | *Motivation and*<br>*Dispositions*<br>• Characteristics<br>• Style<br>• Attitudes<br>• Self-confidence<br>• Self-esteem<br>• Goals, interests<br>• Freedom from blocks<br>• Supportive context | *Management or*<br>*Metacognitive*<br>*Systems*<br>• Goal-setting<br>• Possible strategies<br>• Choose/apply strategies<br>• Feedback<br>• Monitoring or "self-checking"<br>• Evaluations |
|---|---|---|---|
| Content | Strategies<br>and<br>Intellectual<br>Skills | | |

   **2.** *Monitoring*
       Keeping the goal in mind
       Keeping one's place in a sequence
       Knowing when a subgoal has been achieved
       Deciding when to go on to the next operation
       Selecting next appropriate operation
       Spotting errors or obstacles
       Knowing how to recover from errors, overcome obstacles

3. *Assessing*
    Assessing goal achievement
    Judging accuracy and adequacy of the results
    Evaluating appropriateness of procedures used
    Assessing handling of obstacles/errors
    Judging efficiency of the plan and its execution

All other strategies are enhanced when students are equipped with metacognitive processing skills. Appropriate strategies for teaching and practicing the metacognitive skills follow those proposed for thinking skills.

## Small-Group, Cooperative Learning

Gifted students profit a great deal in learning complex, conceptual material, in developing their thinking and metacognitive skills, when they can interact with peers of high ability. Peers of equal or higher ability and rich knowledge bases provide the ideational challenges and enhancement that gifted youth need for their own intellectual growth. Excellent models for small group instruction are set forth by Slavin (1990) and Johnson and Johnson (1989). However, these educators mistakenly advocate cooperative learning with mixed ability, heterogeneous groups. As Robinson (1990) and Robinson and Feldhusen (1991) have shown, small group learning is probably much more effective for gifted and talented students when conducted in groups of intellectual peers. The level of abstraction, complexity, and conceptualization that is appropriate for the gifted may indeed be discouraging for less able students. Thus, an appropriate strategy for teachers is to group students by ability and background knowledge of the topic and to differentiate the tasks to students' levels of ability.

## Autonomy, Self-Direction, Independence

A number of teaching strategies can be used to achieve the goals of autonomy, self-direction, and independence in learning. Betts (1986) developed a comprehensive plan, the Autonomous Learner Model, for teaching students to be self-directing and independent in learning. In essence, the strategy is to involve gifted students extensively in planning and making their own educational and personal decisions. H. Feldhusen (1981) also developed a classroom teaching strategy in which gifted students plan, on a daily and weekly basis, their learning activities, the sequence in which they will study different subjects, and the amount of time they will spend on different activities. Teachers monitor students' self-direction and offer planning mechanisms and guidance to help students develop appropriate self-regulating skills. Treffinger (1986) has also presented a comprehensive plan for helping teachers develop strategies for use with gifted students to obtain the goal of being independent learners.

## Peer Interactions

An appropriate teaching strategy for gifted students is to help them develop good peer relations in general and especially with peers of equal ability. Brown, Clasen, and Eicher

(1986), and Berndt, Laychak, and Park (1990) have conducted extensive research on peer interactions and relationships in school. Some of those interactions and relationships are negative and anti-intellectual. For gifted youth who are often dubbed "brains" or "nerds," the peer influence can be devastatingly negative and hostile.

Teachers need to be aware of these peer relations and to help all youth find ways to interact positively with peers. The classroom meeting pioneered by Glasser (1969) offers one method to handle peer relations. Individual counseling, care in grouping, and group discussions with human relations experts can all be used to deal with these problems. From the teacher's point of view, the task or strategy is to be alert to signs of adverse peer relations and to be ready to deal with the problems in the ways suggested.

## *Intrinsic Motivation*

A host of achievement motivation researchers have reported that competition and rewards often lead to ego-oriented motivation in learning situations while intrinsic motivation is encouraged by emphasizing student interests and inherent inclinations toward a learning task or situation. Dweck and Leggett (1988) reviewed the literature and concluded that in the ideal learning situation, students are mastery oriented. That is, they earnestly commit themselves, without fear or ego defensiveness, to learn the material. In performance-oriented learning, they are simply going through motions dictated by teachers and are likely to withdraw from the task if it appears very difficult.

Good teaching strategy calls for teachers to evoke student interest in the task to be learned, to help them persist when it is difficult, to deflect them from ego threats, and to help them enjoy the results of persistence and success in learning. Amabile (1990) has argued strongly for the desirability of strategies that induce intrinsic motivation and mastery orientation, but she has acknowledged that some youth (we assume the gifted and talented) can also be motivated productively by competition and rewards without losing their intrinsic motivation. For gifted students, the motivational strategies of intrinsic interest, rewards, and competition can all be effective inducements to learn.

## *Environment—Learning Climate*

As a strategy of instruction, teachers working with gifted and talented students can arrange classroom physical and psychological climates to enhance learning. Teachers' strategies can be modified to encourage an open, nonpunitive atmosphere in which differences of opinion can be expressed, intellectual activity valued, precise thinking encouraged, and creativity promoted. The classroom can be a rich source of books, pictures, art work, models, materials, and periodicals to augment the ideational and aesthetic content of textbooks and teacher lectures.

In *Optimizing Learning,* Clark (1986) has described how to create the ideal classroom climate for learning. The ideal is a responsive environment in which students are active in creating a cognitively dynamic climate by creative leadership and responsiveness to one another's ideas. Field trips and expeditions are planned by students. The physical environment encourages cognitive interaction; students do not sit in rows. Student interests are fostered to encourage intrinsic motivation. Students are engaged in individual and group projects. Respect for one another and the ideas of one another are major goals of teaching. Resource people come to the classroom from the community. There are excellent discussions in which ideas are clarified, thinking skills are exercised, conclusions are drawn from project activity, and the joy of learning is modeled.

The strategy of the teacher is to help bring about and sustain such a productive learning climate and to draw all children into the learning activities. Gifted and talented students can thrive in such a climate.

## Assessment

Periodically, teachers' strategies must involve student assessment, feedback, and reinforcement. Objective tests are useful in assessing children's mastery of skills and conceptual knowledge. Essay tests are ideal for the assessment of concepts and organizational skills. Real-world problems, especially in math and science, are ideal for assessing students' mastery of principles, concepts, and skills. Project reports provide valuable information about students' understanding of an application of theoretical ideas to real-world contexts. Teachers can observe children at work in the classroom, in discussions, and in small group activity and assess their operational skills, and make notes of their observations. Students can also be taught to evaluate the work of one another. All these forms of assessment can be assembled in student portfolios as evidence of authentic achievement.

Currently, there is much interest in "authentic assessment," which is evaluation of students' products, performances, and achievements that have meaning in real life outside of school and that are not simply classroom exercises. For gifted students, authentic assessment includes evidence of skill in solving real problems, writing essays on real-world issues and problems, carrying out research projects, giving prepared and extemporaneous speeches, and similar tasks that reflect operations they will later carry out in professional, research, and creative occupations.

Teachers can assist gifted students in evaluating their own progress by providing corrective feedback when errors are made and reinforcement for student successes. The ideal assessment-evaluation strategy is one in which student progress is highlighted and a sense of mastery of material is engendered in students. Kryspin and Feldhusen (1974) provided extensive guidance to classroom teachers on test development. Gronlund (1981) provided guidelines for the broader context of student evaluation in the classroom. Wiggins (1992) delineated the criteria for "authentic assessment" of student achievements; the task is not limited to testing and grading. The ideal teacher strategy uses a variety of approaches to the assessment of student progress, involves gifted students in the evaluation process, and uses evaluation as a tool to develop intrinsic motivation and a mastery orientation among gifted students.

## Conclusion

This chapter has emphasized the need to consider a variety of strategies in meeting the needs of the gifted. The more heterogeneous the classroom context, the more intensively and inclusively these strategies will need to be employed by sensitive teachers. Although both programs and curricular materials can respond partially to the needs of the gifted, it is only through the application of carefully planned strategies that specific interventions become meaningful and successful.

### Key Points Summary

- *Grouping arrangements, curriculum planning, and materials interact with appropriate strategies either to enhance or to limit learning for the gifted.*
- *Key strategies essential for use with gifted learners are diagnostic assessment followed by individualization.*
- *Setting high expectations and exercising challenge in the curriculum are other essential strategies.*
- *Teaching gifted students pattern making with complex material is a powerful strategy, especially when reinforced through homework and outside reading.*
- *Lecture and discussion are both valuable tools in instructing the gifted learner.*
- *Use of significant others can enhance learning for the gifted, whether through peer modeling, cooperative grouping, or mentors.*
- *Consistent instruction in thinking skills and metacognition promotes high-powered learning in the gifted, especially if the role of the teacher is that of facilitator or metacognitive coach.*
- *Establishing a classroom climate conducive to learning and assessing student progress are key classroom strategies to implement.*

## References

Amabile, T. M. (1990). Within you, without you: The social psychology of creativity, and beyond. In M. A. Runco & R. S. Albert (Eds.), *Theories of creativity* (pp. 61–91). Newbury Park, CA: Sage.

Berndt, T. J., Laychak, A. E., & Park, K. (1990). Friends' influence on adolescents' academic achievement motivation: An experimental study. *Journal of Educational Study, 82,* 664–670.

Betts, G. T. (1986). The autonomous learner model for the gifted and talented. In J. S. Renzulli (Ed.), *Systems and models for developing programs for the gifted and talented* (pp. 27–56). Mansfield Center, CT: Creative Learning Press.

Beyer, B. K. (1987). *Practical strategies for the teaching of thinking.* Boston: Allyn and Bacon.

Brown, B. B., Clasen, D. R., & Eicher, S. A. (1986). Perceptions of peer pressure, peer conformity dispositions, and self-reported behavior among adolescents. *Developmental Psychology, 22,* 521–530.

Clark, B. (1986). *Optimizing learning.* Columbus, OH: Merrill.

Clark, B. A. (1992). *Growing up gifted.* New York: Merrill.

Dweck, C. S., & Leggett, E. L. (1988). A social-cognitive approach to motivation and personality. *Psychological Review, 95* (2), 256–273.

Feldhusen, H. J. (1981). Teaching gifted, creative, and talented students in an individualized classroom. *Gifted Child Quarterly, 25* (3), 108–111.

Feldhusen, H. J. (1990). *Individualized teaching of gifted children in regular classrooms.* East Aurora, NY: DOK Publications.

Feldhusen, J. F. (1982). Meeting the needs of gifted students through differentiated programming. *Gifted Child Quarterly, 26,* 37–41.

Feldhusen, J. F. (1991a). Full-time classes for gifted youth. *Gifted Child today, 14* (5), 10–13.

Feldhusen, J. F. (1991b). Saturday and summer programs. In N. Colangelo & G. A. Davis (Eds.), *Handbook of gifted education* (pp. 197–208). Boston: Allyn and Bacon.

Feldhusen, J. F., & Kennedy, D. M. (1989). Effects of honors classes on secondary students. *Roeper Review, 11* (3), 153–156.

Feldhusen, J. F., & Kolloff, M. B. (1986). The Purdue three-stage model. In J. R. Renzulli (Ed.), *Systems and models for developing programs for the gifted and talented* (pp. 126–152). Mansfield Center, CT: Creative Learning Press.

Feldhusen, J. F., & Kroll, M. D. (1991). Boredom or challenge for the academically talented. *Gifted Education International, 7* (2), 80–81.

Feldhusen, J. F., & Sayler, M. F. (1990). Special classes for academically gifted youth. *Roeper Review, 12* (4), 244–249.

Findlay, C. S., & Lumsden, C. J. (1988). The creative mind: Toward an evolutionary theory of discovery and innovation. *Journal of Social and Biological Structures, 11,* 3–55.

Fox, C. H., & Washington, J. (1985). Programs for the gifted and talented: Past, present and future. In F. D. Horowitz & M. O'Brien (Eds.), *The gifted and talented, developmental perspectives* (pp. 197–221). Washington, DC: American Psychological Association.

Glaser, R. (1984). Education and thinking, the role of knowledge. *American Psychologist, 39* (2), 93–104.

Glasser, W. (1969). *Schools without failure.* New York: Harper and Row.

Gronlund, N. E. (1981). *Measurement and evaluation in teaching.* New York: Macmillan.

Haeger, W. W., & Feldhusen, J. F. (1989). *Developing a mentor program.* East Aurora, NY: DOK Publishers.

Johnson, D. W., & Johnson, R. T. (1989). *Cooperation and competition, theory and research.* Edina, MN: Interaction Books.

Kolloff, P. B., & Feldhusen, J. F. (1986). The seminar: An instructional approach for gifted students. *Gifted Children Today, 9* (5), 2–7.

Kryspin, W. J., & Feldhusen, J. F. (1974). *Developing classroom tests.* Minneapolis, MN: Burgess.

Larson, R. W., & Richards, M. H. (1991). Boredom in the middle school years: Blaming schools versus blaming students. *American Journal of Education, 99* (4), 418–443.

Levin, H. M. (1987). Accelerated schools for disadvantaged students. *Educational Leadership, 44* (6), 19–21.

Milgram, R. M. (Ed.). (1989). *Teaching gifted and talented learners in regular classrooms.* Springfield, IL: Charles C. Thomas.

Nicholls, J. (1983). Conceptions of ability and achievement motivation. In S. G. Paris, G. M. Olson, & H. W. Stevenson (Eds.), *Learning and motivation in the classroom* (pp. 211–237). Hillsdale, NJ: Erlbaum.

Nicholls, J. (1984). Development and its discontents: The differentiation of the concept of ability. In J. Nicholls (Ed.), *The development of achievement motivation* (pp. 185–218). Greenwich, CT: JAI Press.

Parke, B. N. (1989). *Gifted students in regular classrooms.* Boston: Allyn and Bacon.

Renzulli, J. S., & Reis, S. M. (1985). *The schoolwide enrichment model: A comprehensive plan for educational excellence.* Mansfield Center, CT: Creative Learning Press.

Robinson, A. (1990). Cooperation or exploitation? The argument against cooperative learning for talented students. *Journal for the Education of the Gifted, 14* (1), 9–27.

Robinson, A. M., & Feldhusen, J. F. (1991). *Cooperative learning and the academically talented student.* A paper presented in a symposium at the World Conference on Gifted and Talented Youth, The Hague, The Netherlands.

Schunk, D. H. (1987). Peer models and children's behavioral change. *Review of Educational Research, 57* (2), 149–174.

Slavin, R. E. (1990). *Cooperative learning: Theory, research, and practice.* Englewood Cliffs, NJ: Prentice Hall.

Snow, R. E. (1989). Aptitude-treatment interaction as a framework for research on individual differences in learning. In P. L. Ackerman, R. J. Sternberg, & R. Glaser (Eds.), *Learning and individual differences* (pp. 13–59). New York: W. H. Freeman.

Stanley, J. C. (1980). On educating the gifted. *Educational Researcher, 9,* 8–12.

Stanley, J. C. (1991). A better model for residential high schools for talented youth. *Phi Delta Kappan, 72* (6), 471–473.

Sternberg, R. J. (1985). *Beyond IQ, a triarchic theory of intelligence.* New York: Cambridge University Press.

Taba, H. (1962). *Curriculum development, theory and practice.* New York, Harcourt, Brace & World.

Treffinger, D. J. (1986). *Blending gifted education with the total school program.* East Aurora, NY: DOK Publishers.

Treffinger, D. J., Feldhusen, J. F., & Isaksen, S.

G. (1990). Organization and structure of productive thinking. *Creative Learning Today, 4* (2), 6–8.

VanTassel, J. (1979). A needs assessment for gifted education. *Journal for the Education of the Gifted, 2* (3), 141–148.

vonGlasersfeld, E. (1987). *Constructivism as a scientific method.* New York: Pergamon Press.

Walberg, H. C. (1984). Improving the productivity of America's Schools. *Educational Leadership, 41* (8), 19–27.

Wheatley, G. H. (1991). Constructivist perspectives on science and mathematics learning. *Science Education, 75* (1), 9–21.

Wiggins, G. (1992). Creating tests worth taking. *Educational Leadership, 49* (8), 26–33.

Chapter *17*

# Educational Leadership

*KENNETH SEELEY*

*There is nothing more difficult to take in hand, more perilous to conduct, or more uncertain in its success than to take the lead in introducing a new order of things. —NICCOLO MACHIAVELLI*

Curriculum leadership implies that there arc educators who assume the major responsibility for planning and developing the curriculum. This is an ongoing process, as indicated in Chapter 2. Instructional leadership is different in that it involves the implementation of the curriculum, including staff development, curriculum field testing, evaluation, and curriculum modification. In many cases, curriculum leadership and instructional leadership are performed by some of the same persons or teams of professionals. Building principals often have input into curriculum development but they rarely enjoy the unilateral influence they exercise as instructional leaders.

In its simplest form, curriculum leadership creates what would be taught in schools, and instructional leadership implements and monitors the curriculum. Curriculum leaders confer with the instructional leaders over time to decide what changes are needed in the curriculum (Pierce, 1983).

Instructional leadership has become the central focus of the school principalship in recent years. The literature in school administration, as well as programs designed to train principals, reflect this emphasis. In examining the past 20 years in school administration, one can see the evolution of emphasis from humanistic leadership to management systems leadership and now, again, to the roots of the principalship: instructional leadership. The term *principal* was originally *principal teacher*. The dropping of *teacher* is historically significant as an evolution of social and professional status, but even more significant, it signaled a greater distance of the principal from the instructional process. Although the occasion to act as instructional leader was always inherent in the principalship, few principals cared to act on the opportunity.

In this evolution, from "principal teacher" to the present role of the principal, new educational positions emerged, creating a whole middle management that had not previously existed. As a result, instructional leadership became a complex network of professional positions with multiple responsibilities.

In order to view instructional leadership through the lens of educating gifted children, it is necessary to examine the complex set of relationships that typically constitute instructional leadership in most contemporary school districts. Figure 17–1 presents a three-dimensional model of instructional leadership. The three dimensions are: administrative hierarchy, context, and curriculum. The administrative hierarchy represents

**Figure 17–1    A Model for Instructional Leadership**

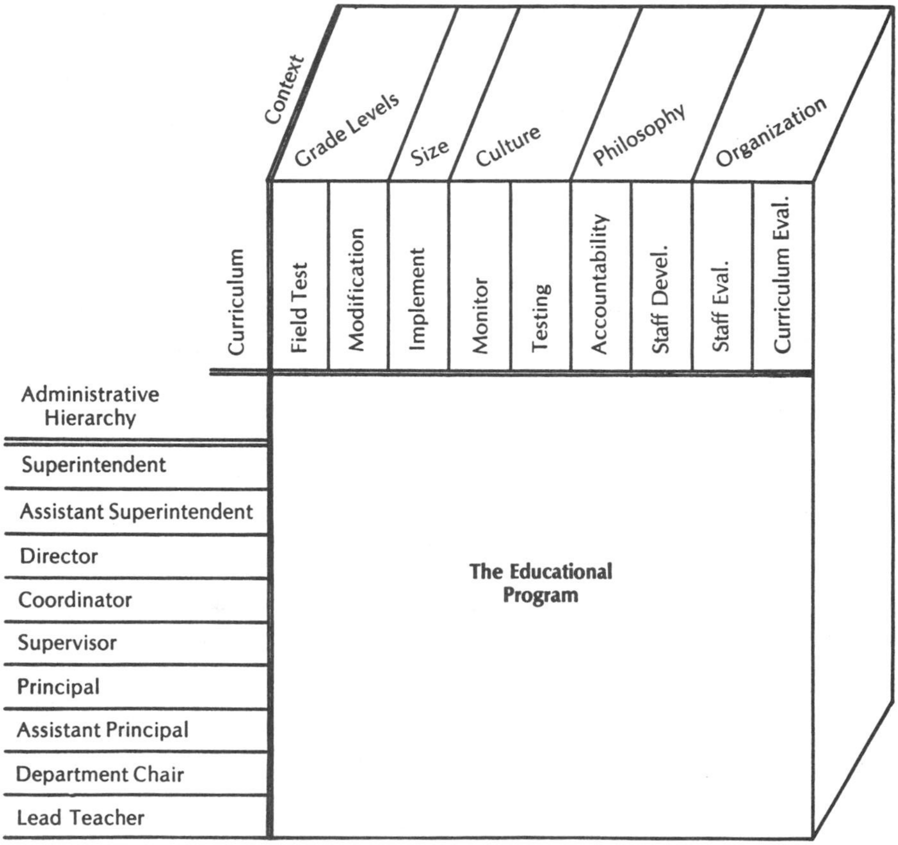

the personnel roles in leadership that vary from central administration to building-level administration. The context dimension deals with variables at the school building-level that affect leadership, such as grade levels, size of school, and culture of the school. The final dimension is the curriculum that constitutes the content of the instruction.

## Administrative Hierarchy

Implicit in the administrative hierarchy are various leadership roles that are typically found in schools. Sergiovanni (1984) described the leadership in school organizations as "a balance between delegation (differentiation) and coordination (integration)" (p. 95). To be effective, leadership personnel along the administrative hierarchy need to be constantly aware of differentiating roles by delegating tasks, and also to fulfill the coordination function in order to integrate the leadership of the organization. This balancing act interacts constantly with the other two dimensions of the model when we consider instructional leadership.

There is an old expression among school administrators that says, "Don't keep a dog and bark yourself." The joke speaks to the importance of delegating leadership responsibility, but it overlooks the coordination function of knowing what, how, and when the dog is barking. Merely delegating responsibility through different roles in the hierarchy does not qualify as effective leadership, unless the roles are also integrated in an interactive leadership model working toward the goals of the organization.

There are good delegators and good coordinators in schools, but it is the combination of these skills that is our best quality indicator. Those in the administrative hierarchy need to understand the differentiation of leadership roles and the coordination of those roles for the entire hierarchy, not just those above them or below them in the hierarchy.

No discussion of school administrative hierarchy would be complete without some attention to the military model upon which many schools operate that hierarchy. This notion is that the hierarchy is a series of ranks, moving from greater to lesser power that proceeds in lockstep fashion with communication only taking place between immediate superior and subordinate. Administrators are often chastised by superiors for "jumping the chain of command" because they shared ideas or information with someone in the hierarchy not immediately above or below them. Whereas the military organizational format maintains an orderliness to communication and decision making, it is not very successful in coordination and integration. Furthermore, it does not work well in nurturing effective instructional leadership in schools.

The military model falls apart in the middle management of public education. One could clearly state that the assistant superintendent for secondary education was the superior to the high school principal in the military model. However, is the secondary coordinator of mathematics superior to the high school principal? Is the director of elementary education superior to the elementary principals if those principals report directly to the superintendent in the organizational plan?

It is the middle management of public education that is charged with both instructional leadership and curriculum leadership. The greatest ambiguity of the line and staff relationships exists at this level. The application of the military chain of command fails in middle management, and the greatest loss is effective leadership in curriculum and instruction.

With the recent move to assign greater leadership of instruction to principals, there is question concerning whether the authority has gone with the responsibility. Many middle managers believe that the power for instructional leadership is elsewhere in the organizaion. Principals may feel that they are the pawns of the central office. Central office administrators believe that the principals must provide the leadership because they are closest to the instructional process, but these same administrators keep budgetary control, curriculum control, and control over staff development. In the worst case scenario, this leads to a cycle of helplessness where no one feels he or she can exert leadership.

Clearly, there is not one answer for all school organizations as to the most effective administrative hierarchy that will facilitate instructional leadership. As the model indicates, instructional leadership is a function of the interaction of the hierarchy with the curriculum and the context. To address the issue of leadership merely by delegating along the hierarchy overlooks the coordination with other key elements of the organization. Unfortunately, administrators make pronouncements like, "The principal is responsible for instructional leadership." It is an attempt to differentiate a role by delegating responsibility. However, it seems doomed to fail if the other side of the balancing act is not considered—coordination with others in the organization and the consumers.

## Impact of Educational Reform

Recent developments in reforming schools have led to a decentralization of power from school district offices to the buildings. Widely known as school-based or site-based management, this decentralization has affected middle management dramatically. Site-based management is the shift of authority, which assumes a sharing of power. When there is the assignment of responsibility to a school building, but not the power to manage locally, we see a chaotic middle management. This is the worst of both centralized and decentralized worlds because the decision making is muddled and budget and/or personnel authority do not follow program responsibility to the school-based leader. The assumption in site-based management is that there is a real power sharing at the local level.

A frequent companion of site-based management is collaborative decision making. The involvement of teachers, parents, and community leaders in decisions about education at the building level is another innovation emerging in school reform efforts. Both of these changes in the middle management of schools are grounded in the philosophy that those closest to the students are in the best position to respond to varied and changing needs. Together, site-based management and collaborative decision making create a responsiveness and flexibility that are essential in designing diverse programs that engage all students in high-level thinking, problem solving, and complex learning.

Implementing outcome-based education models also has become a major task of all administrators in schools under the mandates of educational reform. These models contain several key features, as outlined by Spady and Marshall (1991):

1. Clearly define outcomes, performance standards, and curriculum expectations for all programs of study.
2. Define and distribute rewards for learning that directly match those outcomes and standards and that encourage all students to reach those standards successfully.
3. Expand the opportunity conditions of the school to allow for and encourage more success by students.
4. Implement instructional delivery arrangements that enable staff to make better use of time, teacher talents, curriculum articulation, and student learning capabilities.

Although the reform movement may emphasize learning and achievement for all students, decision making at the level of implementation, and collaborative efforts, it also may prove problematic for those individuals who provide leadership to gifted programs.

In theory, site-based management results in greater reliance on the in-house staff for setting priorities for program and staff development. If gifted programming is not identified as a priority, the gifted coordinator's influence to provide districtwide services is greatly diminished. One strategy to prepare for this contingency is to create a multi-grade-level team in each building and focus support to them in the form of staff development, special materials, regular districtwide meetings, mentorship, and other supportive services. Where there is literally no support in a building, moving programs and consolidating them into designated schools can be a positive development.

The implications of the shift to site-based management and collaborative decision making for coordinators of gifted education would be dramatic. In the past, we have relied on district-level policies and parent advocacy to create and sustain programs. The power shift to buildings could mean a building-by-building program approach that would result in very uneven opportunities for gifted students within a school district. At first blush, it might appear that site-based management could mean the demise of gifted education; however, this power shift can also open some new opportunities for program development.

The movement toward outcome-based education (Spady & Marshall, 1991) could be helpful for gifted leaders depending on how it is applied. If attaining outcomes is tied to age-grade placement, then gifted learners could complete the mainstream education outcomes at a younger age. This might allow for early college admission or dual enrollment (high school and college). If, however, outcome-based education is limited to twelfth-grade school completion requirements, then it will work against gifted learners and the concept of differentiated levels of outcomes and the concept of mastery learning. Educational leaders need to be aware of the differentiated levels of outcomes structured by the National Assessment of Educational progress labeled as "basic," "proficient," and "advanced." These curriculum outcomes should accompany the broadly adopted outcomes of school districts and states to ensure advanced-level education for this country's gifted learners.

School reform, as it is currently playing out, does not generally bode well for gifted education. The tenor of school district initiatives calls for abandoning many of the individualization and grouping approaches used to deliver gifted programs in the past. There are also calls for dismantling many special classes or programs for the gifted in the name of using the same curriculum for all. These misguided efforts, however, are the legacy of a nascent field, viewed with suspicion by the educational establishment.

Coordinators of gifted programs have three central responsibilities during a period of retrenchment and limited resources. They must:

1. Preserve existing programs that have demonstrated effectiveness and let other "unproven" gifted programs go.
2. Support the efforts toward curriculum reform that emphasize higher-level thinking, interdisciplinary emphases, and active learning.
3. Encourage gifted staff specialists to cooperate with special education in collaborative teaching in the regular classroom.

Only through such a multifaceted approach can local programs expect to survive in a time of general educational reform. Moreover, gifted coordinators must work even harder now on establishing credibility within the administrative structure. Advocacy for programs and students in these changing times must continue while we also engage in self-examination to improve or reform what we do.

## The Role of Principals: Implications for Gifted Education

Traditionally, the building principal has enjoyed a large measure of autonomy in administering activities within her or his building. A coordinator of gifted education has not established much tradition as a public school administrator. For most school districts, the coordinator is a "new breed of cat" without an academic home in some content area of curriculum like other coordinators. The role and function of a reading coordinator, for example, is usually understood by most educators even though there is an overlap with the principal's role. The coordinator of gifted education enjoys no such general understanding, relates to all areas of curriculum, and is often viewed with suspicion by all in the administrative hierarchy. This lack of clarity in role often leads to conflict between the coordinator of gifted and the building principal in the following areas:

1. Planning and implementing districtwide programs for gifted students at the building level
2. Identification and placement of selected students for special programs
3. Selection and assignment of special personnel to work with gifted students
4. Developing and maintaining parent education programs for parents of gifted students
5. Allocation of categorical funds for personnel and materials for programs for gifted students
6. Basic attitudinal differences about who should be educated and in what manner in the public schools
7. Decision making among all middle managers in the hierarchy in curriculum modification at the building level
8. Implementation of effective data management systems for accountability requirements on gifted students and attendant personnel

Although principals have building-level autonomy, they are expected to carry out the district program. This program usually comes in the form of board policies, administrative procedures, and established curriculum. The coordinator of gifted education is often perceived as somewhat apart from the district program. This is a direct reflection of the whole issue of how gifted education relates to "regular education" as a temporary add-on to the regular education programs, so the coordinator of gifted education may be viewed as a temporary interloper impinging on the regular program.

It is therefore incumbent upon coordinators of gifted education to continually "sell" themselves as legitimate members of the middle-management team with a unique but complementary role to offer their colleagues. As tradition accumulates to the role, so with the level of credibility within the hierarchy. However, the most expedient way to build credibility is to demonstrate continually one's relatedness to the general education enterprise. As a trusted and valuable member of the administrative team, the coordinator of gifted programs can offer much to enhance curriculum and instruction in a school district.

## The Context for Leadership

The context for leadership is certainly as important a dynamic as either of the other two dimensions in that it imposes variability that is situationally based. Sensitivity to context necessitates that there is not just *one* approach to instructional leadership that can work in all situations. Some contexts require dictatorial leadership, whereas others might need very subtle nuances to be effective in impacting instruction.

Instruction takes place in a school building that has certain physical features that affect learning and teaching. The varible of school size, usually interpreted as pupil population, also includes the physical size and features of the building in relation to the people in it. Typically, the number of pupils dictates the number of staff for a building, and therefore the number of administrators is determined. Many schools have one principal as the only administrator, which allows for leadership to emerge from the teacher ranks in the form of team leaders or lead teachers. In larger schools, assistant principals can be assigned that instructional leadership or management role so that the principal can provide that kind of leadership.

Grade level is a major variable in determining the nature and extent of instructional leadership. Schools where individual teachers teach all or many different subject areas (elementary or middle schools) dictate a very different context for leadership than departmentalized approaches where teachers teach one subject area only. This subject-oriented approach of most secondary schools, coupled with larger pupil populations, often result in intricate building-level hierarchies with department chairs, curriculum committees, assistant principals, and various other professionals who might be called supervisors or coordinators. Secondary schools exemplify the extreme of middle management. The instructional leadership and curriculum leadership in secondary schools is the middle management of middle management. It is mind boggling to envision the complexity of attempting to implement any reform in curriculum or instruction at the secondary level. That probably explains why secondary schools have been the slowest and most resistant to change. It is an organizational nightmare.

Let us take an example of interest to educators of gifted students. Assume that a person in the administrative hierarchy wants to implement a small instructional change in the high school, such as allowing freshmen access to all Advanced Placement classes offered if they can document readiness either through previous courses or test performance. Such a plan would require review and approval by the following individuals: the principal, the assistant principal for instruction, the head of counseling services, the chairpersons of departments offering the Advanced Placement classes, the subject area curriculum coordinators from the central office, the Advanced Placement teachers, the high school curriculum committee, and perhaps even the assistant superintendent for secondary education. It is clearly middle management gone wild. With all the best intentions and commitment to participatory decision making, we have created a monster that almost defies effective instructional leadership at the secondary level.

All is not entirely bleak in secondary schools, however. New instructional leadership roles are emerging at the departmental levels from department chairpersons, supported by the principal and assistant principal. These departmental leaders are being encouraged to improve instruction and to experiment with new ideas. This is a small beginning toward improving instructional leadership by empowering those closest to the instructional process to assume responsibility that heretofore was the principal's duty, who was just too busy to do it well.

The context of grade level at the elementary school influences instructional leadership through a central building principal and how he or she delegates and coordinates the leadership functions. Too often there is a disproportionate amount of energy spent on curriculum leadership and too little attention paid to the instructional process. There is much to do about progress on curriculum objectives, and what reading series to purchase, rather than how well the teachers are teaching, how students might be grouped differently, and staff development needs. Most elementary schools offer a more manageable context for effective instructional leadership to occur. The size of the school and the staff usually permits easier delegation and coordination.

The culture of a school constitutes the complex network of relationships and values of all the people who enter therein. A classic quotation by Waller (1932) best describes the culture of a school:

> *There are, in the school, complex rituals of personal relationships, a set of folkways, mores, and irrational sanctions, a moral code based upon them. There are games which are sublimated wars, teams, and an elaborate set of ceremonies concerning them. There are traditions and traditionalists waging their world old battle against innovators. There are laws, and there is the problem of enforcing them. . . . There are specialized societies with a rigid structure and a limited membership. (p. 103)*

What the culture of a particular school might be results from the interaction of all those variables that Waller so well identifies. Anyone who wishes to exercise effective leadership needs to have a level of human sensitivity that can perceive the culture, develop a level of trust or respect from those in the culture, and build on the strengths of the culture.

Out of culture grows philosophy. The culture of the school building or of the school district largely determines what philosophy of education will prevail in the context for leadership. The values and traditions of the community and the educators who serve that community interact to produce a philosophical tone for education. It is rarely articulated, and yet those in the system feel its presence. It may be characterized as progressive or conservative, centralized or decentralized, and ultimately broken into subsets of characterizations by building. There is often wide variation among buildings as to the philosophy that is usually set by the administrative hierarchy in the building. The influence of a centralized philosophy in the school district on the building philosophy varies widely. Its greatest impact seems to be on the organizational patterns that a central administration imposes on the school building (e.g., personnel assignments, grade-level organization, curriculum accountability). Figure 17–2 illustrates the interaction of the variables that form the organization that creates the context for instructional leadership.

## The Curriculum

In its simplest form, curriculum is what is taught to students. This chapter attempts to separate curriculum from instruction as a means of differentiating leadership roles and responsibilities along school district hierarchies and context. In reality, curriculum is very complex and is inextricably tied to instruction. It is the successful collaboration of curriculum and instruction that promotes learning.

All curriculum is subject to adjustments of instruction which vary as to depth, breadth, and pace. Any instructor must decide these issues in order to teach any curriculum. These three dimensions of instruction are largely influenced by the nature and extent

**Figure 17–2   The Context for Leadership**

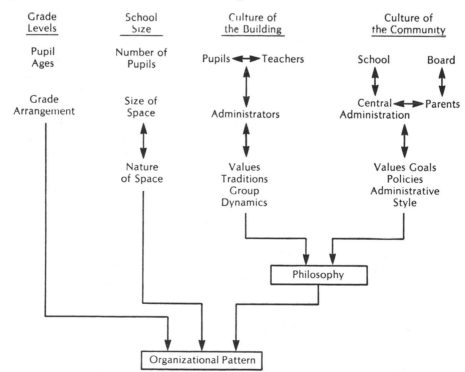

of curriculum material (usually texts), supervisory expectancies, and the instructor's experience. A wise curriculum professor once said, "The curriculum starts when the door closes." Schools spend enormous amounts of time and money producing curriculum guides in an often futile effort to create uniformity among grade levels and subject matter.

Curriculum for gifted learners implies modification of certain curriculum areas and instructional strategies (e.g., assessment of student's level of knowledge). Earlier, this book presented the idea that the content areas provide the base for appropriate curriculum for gifted learners. That curriculum base needs to be modified, extended, and integrated. This is done through instructional intervention requiring careful leadership.

The relationship between curriculum and instruction produces a three-part paradigm to which both curriculum leaders and instructional leaders must be sensitive. There is the curriculum that is published, the curriculum that is taught, and the curriculum that is learned. We know a good deal about the published curriculum. Months and years are spent on writing the published curriculum for each content area by grade level. One can refer to these curriculum guides to see what is to be taught and when. Some teachers try to stay within the published curriculum actually taught and the prescribed texts, but even here we find great differences among classrooms at the same grade level. Instructional leaders attempt to monitor the curriculum that is taught by observing the instruction and reviewing teachers' plans. However, there is limited time devoted to these activities. The curriculum about which we know least is the curriculum that is learned. Testing programs provide some indication about students' abilities to recall factual information. We also know something about reading, writing, and language skills of the students. However, rarely is this information used to adjust the curriculum for the student. Rather, it is a culminating accountability exercise.

Figure 17–3 presents the curriculum-instruction steps with associated leadership tasks. In order to provide instructional leadership to curriculum for gifted learners, it is important to reconfigure the three-curriculum paradigm, as shown in the lower portion of Figure 17–3. We must start with the learned curriculum and compare it to the published curriculum. Sufficient individual assessment information is needed to identify what the student knows and how he or she learns best. Instructional leaders must also ensure that there is sufficient mastery of basic skills and information required by the published curriculum. With these two curricula as a starting point, the taught curriculum for the gifted then requires modification, extension, and integration of the basic content areas. The leadership tasks here necessitate the support of teachers with staff development to perform the curriculum changes needed, and to provide formative evaluation data to adjust the curriculum to individual differences. The learner outcomes of the taught curriculum are different from the traditional learner curriculum in that they are quantitative and qualitative and must be reported by an individual learner as well as aggregated for the group of gifted learners. These outcome data cycle back to become the learned curriculum in another iteration of the steps, and are compared to the published curriculum to assure accountability requirements and mastery of basic skills.

## The Curriculum Process for Gifted Learners

As Figure 17–3 describes, the leadership tasks involve assessment and outcome reporting as important parts of planning and curriculum change. Front-end assessment of what a

**FIGURE 17–3   Leadership Tasks for Curriculum Development**

| Traditional Curriculum Process | | |
|---|---|---|
| **STEPS:** | The Published Curriculum → The Taught Curriculum | → The Learned Curriculum |
| **LEADERSHIP TASKS:** | Develop and Prescribe the Curriculum | Monitor and Evaluate the Teachers | Test, Evaluate, Report Quantitative Performance of Learners (Group Only) |

| Curriculum Process for Gifted Learners | | |
|---|---|---|
| **STEPS:** | The Learned Curriculum → The Taught Curriculum | → Learner Outcomes (Individual and Group) |
| | (Compared to the Published Curriculum) | | |
| **LEADERSHIP TASKS:** | Assure Individual Assessment | Support Teachers with Staff Development | Evaluate and Report both Quantitative and Qualitative Outcomes |
| | Assure Mastery of Basic Skills | Support Curriculum Changes | |
| | Report Differences Between Learned and Published Curriculum | Conduct Formative Evaluation | |

student knows at any point in the curriculum sequence is essential for gifted learners for two reasons: It assures mastery of basic skills and it gives individual planning information for accelerating the curriculum content. This instructional assessment is different from standardized accountability testing, which is intended for large-scale measurement of achievement trends.

Anrig (1992) listed the basic questions that this front-end instructional assessment should address:

- *What tasks will promote the desired learning?*
- *How are the standards for these activities shared with and understood by the students so that self-evaluation and improvement can occur?*
- *How do smaller learnings fit into larger learning goals?*
- *In what form can this information be organized for ready use by teachers to improve daily instruction? (p. 40)*

Anrig went on to recommend that assessment be integrated with curriculum so that there be no distinction. This would provide continuous performance feedback through mechanisms such as projects, portfolios, student-constructed responses, and computer-based learnings. A curriculum process that integrates performance assessment is an ideal framework for gifted learners. Although grades and test scores are important for periodic accountability, individual performance should be the gatekeeper for progress in the curriculum.

The outcomes of the curriculum process for gifted learners assumes that curriculum should move beyond the accumulation and mastery of facts as "knowledge" and should develop competence. Raven (1991) presented a forceful case for competence as a legitimate outcome of learning. He described competence as the intersection of skills and abilities; motivation; and situation or environment. This implies that curriculum that has typically been limited to skills should include attention to the interest ares of the learner and the situation in which the skills are performed. These components of competence help us understand the importance of a curriculum process that accommodates to interests, ability, and setting.

For example, we would expect a higher-level performance from a gifted student in a group of other gifted learners with similar interests in creative writing than if we put that same gifted student in a heterogeneously grouped language arts class with students of varying ability and interest in writing. If our curriculum outcomes include "competence" in writing, then we need to assure a high-level environment with motivated students to get the best performance.

## *Conclusion*

By examining the leadership tasks at the bottom of Figure 17–3, and the Model for Instructional Leadership (Figure 17–1), we have the basis for a job description for a curriculum/instruction leader in gifted education. The three dimensions from the Instructional Leadership Model form the basis for the job description, and the leadership tasks from the Curriculum Process for Gifted Learners provide more specific duties.

To summarize this chapter, the models and ideas are synthesized into the job description for the curriculum and instruction leader for gifted education. These are the key elements that can guide the selection of leadership personnel:

*General Qualifications*

1. Demonstrate an understanding of gifted and talented learners and their needs in the classroom context.
2. Be able to communicate effectively to an administrative hierarchy, from lead teachers to the superintendent, in articulating the program for gifted learners as an integral part of the educational program.
3. Be sensitive to the variations of educational settings in different school buildings and among different personnel where philosophy, values, size, level, organizational, and cultural conditions may affect the gifted program in different ways.
4. Demonstrate strong skills in curriculum development and implementation with special attention to modification and evaluation of curriculum for gifted learners.

*Specific Duties*

1. Design and implement an identification program that assures the individual assessment of potentially gifted students' knowledge and abilties.
2. Implement an appropriate curriculum for gifted learners that assures mastery of basic

skill requirements of the general curriculum and allows for modification, extention, and integration of this general curriculum into any specialized curriculum for the gifted.

3. Articulate to the administrative hierarchy the curriculum for the gifted program within the context of the general curriculum and what differences for a specialized curriculum are required.
4. Develop and implement a comprehensive staff development program for teachers of the gifted, as well as regular classroom teachers, that supports and improves the curriculum and instruction for gifted learners.
5. Design and conduct formative and summative evaluation of the gifted program that focuses on both quantitative and qualitative outcomes and leads to necessary revision of the curriculum and instructional approaches used in implementing that curriculum for gifted learners.

Instructional leadership for gifted education programs evolves from good leadership. It is not unique unto itself, but rather borrows from the best of systems intervention theory and learner-based program development. This chapter has presented a generic three-dimensional model for instructional leadership and discussed its application to middle management in education in general, and gifted education specifically. The concept of context for the leadership was presented with general guidelines that any instructional leader might find useful in approaching an individual school building. Finally, the chapter presented curriculum and its close ties to instruction. A model of traditional curriculum and instruction was contrasted with a model for gifted learners to demonstate some fundamental differences in approach with attendant leadership tasks.

The perceived quality of gifted education is largely determined by the quality of its leaders. That leadership must develop as a logical extension of the broader instructional endeavor of general education. There can be no room for "empire builders" or "saviors" who repudiate and denigrate the mainstream curriculum and instruction. Such leadership results in esoteric programs that are viewed as irrelevant and ultimately cast out as expensive frills. Effective instructional leadership that builds and extends the general education enterprise for gifted learners will result in enduring programs.

### *Key Points Summary*

- *Instructional leadership involves implementing curriculum in different contexts and within an administrative hierarchy.*
- *Instructional leadership is different from curriculum leadership in that it implies the implementation, monitoring, staff development, and evaluation of curriculum. Curriculum leadership is the planning and development of the content to be taught.*
- *Within the context of gifted education, instructional leadership is a middle-management function that requires coordinators of gifted programs to offer skills that are both unique and complementary to the general education enterprise.*
- *The context for instructional leadership involves the influence of grade level, school size, culture of the school building, and culture of the community on the school philosophy and organizational pattern that evolves.*
- *The curriculum process for gifted learners requires a comparison between the*

*published or prescribed school district curriculum and the curriculum that the student
has already learned.*

- *The notion of competence as the outcome of the curriculum process implies attention
  to abilities, interests, and environment.*
- *Assessment and curriculum must be integrated in order to improve performance.*
- *The curriculum that is taught to gifted learners evolves from the comparison of
  prescribed and learned curriculum and it is modified, extended, and integrated based
  on the learners' needs.*
- *Formative and sumative evaluation of gifted programs must focus on both qualitative
  and quantitative outcomes of student learning.*
- *The ideal role of the coordinator of gifted programs involves both instructional
  leadership and curriculum leadership.*

## *References*

Anrig, B. (1992, April 1). *Education Week,* Commentary, p. 40.

Gall, M. D., Gall, J., Jacobsen, D. R., & Bulluck, T. L. (1990). *Tools for learning* pp. 17–86), Alexandria, VA: ASCD.

Information—A key ingredient to successful leadership. (1986, April). Unauthored article in *NASSP Bulletin,* pp. 41–51.

Pharis, W. L., & Zachariya, S. B. (1979). *The elementary principal in 1978: A research study.* National Association of Elementary School Principals.

Pierce, R. (1983). In D. C. Baltzell & R. A. Dentler (Eds.), *Selecting American school principles: A*

*source book for educators.* National Institute for Education.

Raven, J. L. (1991). *The tragic illusion: Educational testing* (pp. 55–75). Oxford, U.K.: Oxford Psychologists Press.

Sergiovanni, T. (1984). *Handbook for effective department leadership: Concepts and practices in today's secondary schools,* 2nd ed. Boston: Allyn and Bacon.

Spady, W. J., & Marshall, K. J. (1991). Beyond traditional outcome-based education. *Educational Leadership, 49* (2), 67–72.

Waller, W. (1932). *Sociology of teaching* (p. 103). New York: Wiley & Sons.

# Chapter 18

# Toward Synthesis: A Vision of Comprehensive Articulated Curriculum for Gifted Learners

*JOYCE VanTASSEL-BASKA*

Alice: *"Would you please tell me which way I ought to go from here?"*
Cheshire Cat: *"That depends on where you want to get to."*
—*LEWIS CARROLL*

While each of the chapters has addressed various aspects of curriculum for the gifted, no one piece has attempted to integrate all of the various components that constitute an appropriate curriculum experience for gifted learners as they move through the continuum of K–12 schooling. That task lies ahead in the content of this final chapter. For it is ultimately in the understanding of important changes and adaptation of that *total* curriculum that the gifted are best served.

Part I of this book dealt with issues related to the curriculum development process itself. A philosophical framework for thinking about curriculum was provided; then the process of development that school districts need to consider was presented. Also integral to Part I was a discussion of central design elements that ought to be present in any written curriculum. These fundamental chapters are further supported by a close look at scope and sequence work and unit development.

What is central to our thinking about the processes involved in curriculum making for the gifted is the interrelationship of them, one to the other. Too frequently educators become entranced with one model or design as if it constituted the universe of consideration regarding a topic. What we have presented has relevance only to the extent that it is viewed comprehensively. To proceed into curriculum without a philosophy about curriculum, a way of "seeing" it, is as foolish as creating a design with no way to feed it into a relevant system of people who can critique, alter, and hopefully use it.

Part I was also sensitive to the need to respond at the level of the classroom and at the level of the school and district in respect to curriculum documents. For many practitioners, particularly teachers, the level of their work with curriculum will be limited to adapting existing subject matter areas and to the development of units. Thus, these processes are highlighted as the most important arenas for curriculum development. Since units come the closest to our ideas about the "delivered" curriculum, it is very important that those curriculum pieces are thoughtful and well designed. For other practitioners, like gifted program coordinators or curriculum directors, the focus on scope and sequence is crucial to their understanding of how to map out the larger picture of curriculum. Scope and sequence work provides the framework for curriculum articulation throughout the grades in key areas of learning, and it is necessary for planning the continuity of experiences for gifted learners. Obviously, at some point in the curriculum development process, these two strands of work must merge in a meaningful way so that the unit efforts are integrated appropriately into the total process.

In Part II of the book, traditional content areas were explored through ways to modify and adapt them to the needs of gifted learners and to use the curriculum ideas to serve as many students as might benefit from the adaptation. Since the verbal arts, mathematics, science, and the social sciences constitute the fundamental domains of study in schools, it seems reasonable to make them more appropriate for the gifted learner. Thus, these chapters provided direction and focus for the adaptation of these subjects through differential goal setting, an exploration of the application of the fundamental curriculum model delineated in Chapter 1, examples of successful curriculum that has been adapted, and strategies and resources to consider in undertaking the task.

The chapter on the humanities provided a detailed look at interdisciplinary approaches to curriculum making for the gifted and wove together the core domains of study in schools with other areas of value to gifted students. In that sense, the humanities chapter is the capstone for Part II of the book in that it reflects a more abstract level of conceptualizing curriculum in which all of the domains of study have a place. As with the content chapters that precede it, the humanities chapter provides rich examples of curriculum that have been organized for such programs. Whereas all of the core domains of study relate to more than one learning realm, it is only in the humanities that students come to apply cognitive, affective, social, aesthetic, and psychomotoric capacities in an integrated way.

Part III of the book explored important areas of a curriculum for gifted learners not generally considered by schools. Yet for gifted students, work in the areas of thinking skills, affective curriculum, leadership, and the arts all constitute important components of their total curriculum experience. Because these areas are so important in a curriculum for the gifted, the chapters demonstrate two fundamental approaches to including them. One approach taken is to view these areas as separate domains of study in and of themselves. Thus, the chapters provided examples of curriculum that constitute this view.

By the same token, a second approach treats these areas as part of all the core domains of study cited earlier. Thus, critical thinking, for example, could be a separate course of study for the gifted at fifth-grade level, but it could also be integral to the teaching of reading at that same level. This dual perspective on these vital areas of curriculum represents an important way of ensuring their inclusion in a program for the gifted as both content and process.

These chapters also provided another important service to the book. They distilled the essence of powerful learning realms and provided us with the keys to unlock them. Thus, they allowed us to access directly a side of learning not frequently utilized through the route of traditional subject matter teaching and learning. These areas need to be systematically tapped in programs for the gifted so that students have a balanced insight into (1) how they think and learn in the cognitive realm, (2) feelings of self-worth and identity in the affective realm, (3) understanding human relationships and the concepts underlying them in the social realm, and (4) various forms of human artistic expression in the aesthetic realm.

Part IV of the book, addressed important issues of support for implementing the curriculum. At the classroom level, we stressed the importance of the interaction between teacher and learner, and suggested facilitative modes for enhancing that relationship. At the school and district level, we illustrated the key role that effective educational leadership plays in facilitating the implementation of curriculum. Ideas were shared about how gifted program coordinators, in particular, might assume this role and move the curriculum development process along. We presented a model in this chapter that illustrated the interlocking aspects of our ideas about curriculum and instruction for the gifted student with the structure and organization of schools, including new reform measures that impact on the delivery system for curriculum to gifted students. Thus, in the final chapter, we reconcile the total curriculum effort with the real world of schools.

Finally, we have evolved to an integrated systems view of curriculum experiences for the gifted. Instead of seeing the curriculum effort as separate pieces or models to be merely added together, curriculum work for the gifted can be envisioned as a negotiated set of interlocking systems, each contributing in significant ways to the realization of appropriate, comprehensive, and articulated opportunities for gifted learners. Figure 18–1 illustrates this systems perspective.

## *Recommendations and Guidelines for Practitioners in Curriculum Development*

To provide final insights for practitioners regarding these systems, a set of practical recommendations and guidelines are offered for consideration. These recommendations represent a synthesis of key issues from each of the chapters.

**1.** *Practitioners in gifted programs need to understand the basic strands of thought in general curriculum and how they are translated into appropriate curriculum models for the gifted.* As noted in the opening chapter, these models are derived from the characteristics of gifted learners, research, and informed practice. Thus, they provide a common core

**FIGURE 18–1   The Chain of Curriculum Systems**

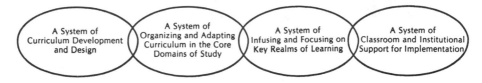

of understanding about fundamental curriculum and instructional dimensions in gifted programs.

**2.** *Practitioners need to recognize the importance of the curriculum development process as an ongoing cycle and the school district leadership tasks needed to energize it.* We have outlined the stages of curriculum development and provided practical guidelines for proceeding through each stage of the process. It is important that practitioners view this process as a blueprint for action over a three- to five-year period.

**3.** *Practitioners need to understand the curriculum design process and its fundamental importance in curriculum planning.* Important aspects of differentiation are encompassed at this crucial design level. Questions such as Where is our curriculum going? How do we get there? and How will we know when we have arrived? are answered by using a formalized design process. We have provided a translation of the design elements to salient issues in structuring curriculum for the gifted.

**4.** *Practitioners need to develop a scope and sequence in curriculum areas that provides a broad framework for curriculum work from kindergarten through grade 12.* Organization of such scope and sequence work should occur in several areas, based on the focus of the curriculum. Thus, content, process, product, and concept issues need to be considered. We have provided guidelines to consider in developing scope and sequence and also have given examples of several such efforts.

**5.** *Practitioners need to develop instructional units for use in gifted programs.* Manipulation of all the curriculum models at this level is important: content-based curriculum, process-oriented curriculum, and concept curriculum. We have described the process by which such units can be developed and provided illustrative examples of completed units.

**6.** *Practitioners need to facilitate the development of curriculum for the gifted in the core content areas that schools currently address.* Since the study in the areas of language arts, mathematics, science, and the social sciences comprise the majority of instructional time gifted students are in school, it is crucial that modifications of these areas be made at all levels of schooling. We have suggested several ways to modify these core areas for the gifted through both acceleration and enrichment strategies.

**7.** *Practitioners need to incorporate the humanities as an integrating force into curriculum for the gifted.* A broad-based humanities program can underscore and enhance concept learning within subject matter disciplines as well as provide a strong interdisciplinary focus. Using a creative process/product paradigm for teaching the humanities can also foster student growth in understanding "how man creates."

**8.** *Practitioners need to implement strategies for the inclusion and infusion of particular learning realms within a curriculum for the gifted.* These areas include thinking skills in the cognitive realm, affective curriculum in the affective realm, leadership in the social realm, and the arts in the aesthetic realm. Treatment of these areas might be considered as a separate part of the curriculum experience as well as embedded in the core subject matter areas. We have noted key models for use under both sets of conditions in Chapter 12. We have demonstrated that affective curriculum experiences can be treated as content in and of itself in addition to being an integral part of the teaching-learning process. We have cited leadership programs that are intact yet note leadership experiences that can occur in any classroom context. We have treated the arts as interrelated domains of study for the artistically gifted and as strands of experience for the intellectually gifted.

**9.** *Practitioners need to consider carefully both the dynamic interaction of curriculum with instruction and the effects of the instructional pattern on the learning of the gifted learner.* We have explored the realm of instructional practice to introduce those approaches that are most facilitative for gifted students' learning. Clearly, the more of these strategies that can be applied, the better the instructional climate will be for gifted learners and for other learners in the regular classroom.

**10.** *Practitioners need to select appropriate new technology to enhance the instructional process.* It is important to recognize the power of technological tools in the instructional process and to find powerful ways to harness them to the complex task of learning. Ideas for using technology effectively with gifted students may be found in each of the subject matter chapters.

**11.** *Practitioners need to recognize the importance of educational leadership in the context of gifted program administration.* We have provided a realistic view of how schools function and the problems that coordinators of gifted programs face in that context. Central to engaging in curriculum development is a support structure within the school and district that values the effort.

**12.** *Practitioners need to build comprehensive articulated curricular experiences for the gifted over the span of years they are in school.* Gifted education is not a frill; it is not an extra in the school-budgeting process. It is an essential and complete set of experiences for a targeted group of learners in our schools. Understanding and meeting the needs of the gifted means addressing all of those needs that can reasonably be undertaken in a school context and doing so over time. By building such a set of experiences, all students in our schools will benefit through enhanced classroom teaching and learning.

**13.** *Practitioners need to negotiate carefully the path of educational reform and its implications for a quality curriculum for gifted learners.* As the tide of educational reform initiatives rolls across local school districts, it is essential that educators of the gifted find the commonalities in the work of reformers with the goals of gifted education. It is equally important, however, that we not dismiss too quickly the positive curriculum experiences already in place. Special programs for the gifted based on valid curriculum experiences need to be used as models for what curriculum level is attainable at a particular stage of student development. Good gifted curriculum, where it exists, should set the standards for learning at world-class levels.

## Conclusion

These pages have provided multiple views of the comprehensive house of curriculum for the gifted and marked the direction toward a higher synthesis in understanding it. It remains for the educational community to value the enterprise of deliberate curriculum development for these learners sufficiently to engage in the process. The United States wants world-class education and students who can compete well internationally. Only through the development of challenging standards and a rigorous curriculum delivered on a K–12 continuum can such desire become reality. As educators, we owe such a quality education to our students and to our society.

# *Useful Paradigms and Models*

## *Useful Paradigms in Conceptualizing Curriculum for the Gifted*

*Phenix's (1986) Realms of Meaning*
- *Symbolics*
- *Empirics*
- *Esthetics*
- *Synoptic*
- *Ethics*
- *Synnoetics*

*Gardner's (1983) Frames of Mind*
- *Linguistic*
- *Musical*
- *Logical-mathematical*
- *Spatial*
- *Bodily-Kinesthetic*
- *Personal (interpersonal and intrapersonal)*

*Eisner's (1982) Ways of Knowing*
- *Aesthetic*
- *Formal*
- *Epistemological*

*Perry's (1970) Epistemological Positions in Learning*
- *Basic dualism*
- *Multiplicity*
- *Relativism subordinate*
- *Relativism*

*Child Development (Horowitz & O'Brien, 1985)*
- *Cognitive development*
- *Psychosocial development*
- *Moral development*
- *Environmental influences*
- *Creativity*

# Useful Models for Teaching Thinking Skills

## Ennis's (1962) Model for Critical Thinking

*Twelve Aspects of Critical Thinking*

1. Grasp the meaning of a statement.
2. Judge whether ambiguity exists.
3. Judge if contradictions exist.
4. Judge if a conclusion necessarily follows.
5. Judge the specificity of a statement.
6. Judge if a statement relates to a certain principle.
7. Judge the reliability of an observation.
8. Judge if an inductive conclusion is warranted.
9. Judge if a problem has been identified.
10. Judge if a definition is adequate.
11. Judge if a statement is credible.
12. Judge if something is an assumption.

## Parnes's (1967) Creative Problem-Solving Model

### Creative Problem-Solving Steps

Fact-finding (brainstorming)
Problem-finding and defining
Idea-generation and Alternative Solution-finding
Evaluating among solutions
Developing a plan of action (acceptance-finding)

## Sternberg's (1985) Metacomponents (Executive Processes)

1. Recognizing a problem
2. Defining the problem
3. Steps for solving the problem
4. Ordering
5. Deciding on a form for information
6. Allocating resources
7. Monitoring
8. Using feedback

## *Useful Paradigms for Implementing Curriculum*

### *Williams's (1977) Model for Implementing Cognitive-Affective Behaviors in the Classroom for the Gifted*

| *Desired Student Behaviors* | *Teacher Behaviors* |
|---|---|
| Fluent Thinking | Parodoxes |
| Flexible Thinking | Attributes |
| Original Thinking | Analogies |
| Elaborative Thinking | Discrepancies |
| Curiosity (willingness) | Provocative Questions |
| Risk Taking (courage) | Examples of Change |
| Complexity (challenge) | Examples of Habit |
| Imagination (intuition) | Organized Random Search |
| | Skills of Search |
| | Tolerance for Ambiguity |
| | Intuitive Expression |
| | Adjustment to Development |
| | Study Creative People and Process |
| | Evaluative Situations |
| | Creative Reading Skill |
| | Creative Listening Skill |
| | Creative Writing Skill |
| | Visualization Skill |

## *Useful Paradigms for Organizing Curriculum and Instruction for the Gifted*

*Bloom's (1956) Taxonomy*

- *Knowledge*
- *Comprehension*
- *Application*
- *Analysis*
- *Synthesis*
- *Evaluation*

*Krathwohl's Taxonomy (Krathwohl, Bloom, & Masia, 1964)*

- *Recurring*
- *Responding*
- *Valuing*
- *Organization*
- *Characterization by a value or value concept*

# References

Bloom, B. S. (1956). *Taxonomy of educational objectives, Handbook I: Cognitive domain*. New York: David McKay.

Eisner, E. W. (1982). Aesthetic education. In H. E. Mitzel (Ed.), *Encyclopedia of education* (Vol. I) (pp. 87–94). New York: Free Press.

Ennis, R. H. (1962). A concept of critical thinking. *Harvard Educational Review, 32,* 81–111.

Gardner, H. (1983). *Frames of mind*. New York: Basic Books.

Horowitz, F. D., & O'Brien, M. (1985). *The gifted and talented: Developmental perspectives*. Washington, DC: American Psychological Association.

Krathwohl, D. R., Bloom, B. S., & Masia, B. B. (1964). *Taxonomy of educational objectives, Handbook II: Affective domain*. New York: David McKay.

Parnes, S. J. (1967). *Creative behavior guide book*. New York: Scribners.

Perry, W. G. (1970). *Forms of intellectual and ethical development in the college years*. New York: Holt, Rinehart and Winston.

Phenix, P. H. (1986). *Realms of meaning*. Ventura, CA: Ventura County Superintendent of Schools.

Sternberg, R. J. (1985). *Beyond IQ*. New York: Cambridge University Press.

Williams, F. E. (1977). *Classroom ideas for encouraging thinking and feeling*. Buffalo, NY: DOK Publishers.

# Publishers of Curriculum Materials for Gifted and Talented Students

Creative Publications
P.O. Box 10328
Palo Alto, CA 94303

Curriculum Associates
1211 Connecticut Ave., NW,
Suite 414
Washington, D.C. 20036

Dale Seymour Publications
P.O. Box 10888
Palo Alto, CA 94303

D.O.K. Publishers
P.O. Box 357
East Aurora, NY 14052

Educational Impressions
Resource Materials for the G/T
249 Goffle Road
Hawthorne, NJ 07507

Engine-uity, Ltd.
Box 9610
Phoenix, AZ 85068

G/C/T Publishing Co., Inc.
350 Weinacker Avenue
P.O. Box 6448
Mobile, AL 36601-0448

Good Apple
Box 299
Carthage, IL 62321-0299

The Great Books Foundation
40 East Huron St.
Chicago, IL 60611

The Keystone Consortium
P.O. Box 2367
West Lafayette, IN 47906

Midwest Publications
P.O. Box 448
Pacific Grove, CA 93950

National Association for Gifted
Children
1155 15th. St., NW #1002
Washington, DC 20005

National/State Leadership Training
Institute on the Gifted and
the Talented
316 West Second Street, Suit PHC
Los Angeles, CA 90012

A. W. Peller and Associates, Inc.
Bright Ideas for the Gifted and
Talented (K–12)
Educational Materials
294 Goffle Road
Hawthorne, NJ 07507

SOI Institute
343 Richmond St.
El Segundo, CA 90245

Sunburst Communications
Room WV4
39 Washington Avenue
Pleasantville, NY 10570

Synergetics
P.O. Box 84
East Windsor Hill, CT 06028

Trillium Press
Box 921
New York, NY 10159

Zephyr Press
430 South Esset Lane
Tucson, AZ 85711

# *Index*